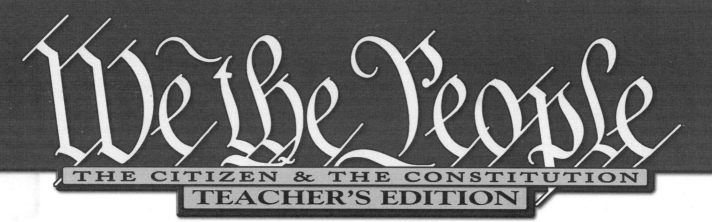

We the People

THE CITIZEN & THE CONSTITUTION
TEACHER'S EDITION

WE THE PEOPLE
THE CITIZEN & THE CONSTITUTION

LEVEL 2

CENTER FOR CIVIC EDUCATION
5145 Douglas Fir Road, Calabasas, CA 91302
818.591.9321   www.civiced.org

D1293792

DIRECTED BY THE
CENTER FOR CIVIC EDUCATION

AND FUNDED BY THE
U.S. DEPARTMENT OF EDUCATION

UNDER THE EDUCATION FOR DEMOCRACY ACT APPROVED BY THE
UNITED STATES CONGRESS

COVER

Frank Blackwell Mayer, *The Continentals*, Prints and Photographs Division, Library of Congress, PGA-Mayer-Continentals (C size)

COVER + INTERIOR DESIGN

Mark Stritzel

© 2007 CENTER FOR CIVIC EDUCATION

10 09 08   02 03 04

ISBN 13 978–089818174–6

ISBN 10 0–89818–174–7

ACKNOWLEDGMENTS

The following staff and consultants have contributed to the development of this text.

PRINCIPAL WRITERS
Dee Morgan
Andrea Mello

CONTRIBUTING WRITER
Charles F. Bahmueller

EDITORIAL DIRECTOR
Theresa M. Richard

EDITOR
David Hargrove

PRODUCTION EDITOR
Mark Gage

CREATIVE DIRECTOR
Mark Stritzel

ILLUSTRATOR
Richard Stein

PRODUCTION DESIGNER
Sean Fay

REVIEWERS
Charles F. Bahmuller
Margaret Stimmann Branson
Sally J. Broughton
Terri DuMont
Maria Gallo
Jackie Johnson
Dick Kean
Robert Leming
Clayton Lucas
Lori Mable
Robert McCoy
Donna Paoletti Phillips
Susan Roe
Darnell Tabron
Lynette Wallace

SPECIAL THANKS

We wish to express our thanks to the following individuals who also contributed to the text:

Kevin Fox, Suzanne Soule, and Sharareh Frouzesh Bennett for writing the student test; Rose Freeland for illustration retouching; Robert Meyers for prepress; Sally Mills, our print consultant; and Robert Sinclair at Sinclair Printing.

We the People: The Citizen & the Constitution

Dear Teacher:

We appreciate your participation in **We the People: The Citizen and the Constitution**. It is our hope that you and your students will find this program an effective means of developing a more profound understanding of and appreciation for the fundamental principles and values of our free society.

The enclosed materials have been carefully designed to help you conduct a successful educational program on the Constitution and Bill of Rights. Several thousand teachers throughout the nation have helped us develop and refine the program. Together, we have attempted to write the text and accompanying materials at a level useful for a wide range of student abilities while providing content challenging to the most academically able. Your experience in using the program with your students will undoubtedly result in the identification of ways it can be improved. We welcome your comments and suggestions regarding the strengths and weaknesses of the program so we can improve it for further use. We are particularly interested in receiving anecdotal information on the effects of the program on students' understanding, skills, attitudes, and behaviors.

We have provided you the best materials we have been able to develop. We realize, however, that the success of the program ultimately depends on you, the classroom teacher. We appreciate your interest in the program and your willingness to use it in your classroom. We want to provide whatever additional help you might need in its implementation.

Additional information, materials, or assistance may be obtained locally by contacting your congressional district coordinator. To contact your district coordinator or to provide feedback on the **We the People** program, go to the Center's website at www.civiced.org or contact our California office at 1-800-350-4223.

Sincerely,

Charles N. Quigley
EXECUTIVE DIRECTOR

Robert S. Leming
WE THE PEOPLE NATIONAL DIRECTOR

We the People: The Citizen & the Constitution

Teacher's Edition

WARREN E. BURGER
(1907–1995)

**CHAIRMAN, COMMISSION
ON THE BICENTENNIAL OF
THE UNITED STATES CONSTITUTION**

**CHIEF JUSTICE OF THE UNITED STATES
1969–1986**

Our Constitution has stood the tests and stresses of time, wars, and change. Although it was not perfect, as Benjamin Franklin and many others recognized, it has lasted because it was carefully crafted by men who understood the importance of a system of government sufficiently strong to meet the challenges of the day, yet sufficiently flexible to accommodate and adapt to new political, economic, and social conditions.

Many Americans have but a slight understanding of the Constitution, the Bill of Rights, and the later amendments to which we pledge our allegiance. The lessons in this book are designed to give you, the next generation of American citizens, an understanding of the background, creation, and subsequent history of the unique system of government brought into being by our Constitution. At the same time, it will help you understand the principles and ideals that underlie and give meaning to the Constitution, a system of government by those governed.

TABLE OF CONTENTS

TABLE OF CONTENTS

TABLE OF CONTENTS

TABLE OF CONTENTS

OVERVIEW OF WE THE PEOPLE PROGRAM

INTRODUCTION

We the People: The Citizen & the Constitution introduces middle school students to the study of constitutional government in the United States. It is not a conventional history text focusing on people and events. This book is a history of ideas. It is designed to help middle school students understand the most important ideas of our constitutional system and how they were developed. It is intended to provide students with knowledge about how the Constitution came into existence, why it took the form it did, and how it has functioned for the past two hundred years. By gaining such an understanding, students will be preparing themselves for the responsibilities of citizenship.

An effective class project for the program might be a bulletin board display, including a timeline and an illustrated map of the original thirteen colonies. The display can include articles, pictures, stories, poems, artwork, and newspaper headlines that illustrate the key ideas and events in each lesson. In Units Three, Four, Five, and Six, the display could demonstrate the relevance of the lessons to current political activities.

The display can include a timeline to show events that are being studied. Students may wish to add dates and events not mentioned in the text. Another method of displaying a timeline would be to hang the dates on a rope or clothesline.

The class may also illustrate an outline map of the original thirteen states. One method to do such a map would be to divide the class into thirteen groups. Each group would be responsible for one of the thirteen states. Each group would then explain to the class their reasons for selecting the facts, persons, or events they chose to illustrate.

TEACHING METHODS

The *We the People: The Citizen & the Constitution* text for middle school grades employs a conceptually oriented approach that stresses the development of analytic and evaluative skills. Because many of the concepts introduced in the program may be unfamiliar to students, the methodology draws heavily on strategies that research and field-testing have shown to be successful in developing conceptual understanding. Students will learn how to apply their understanding and knowledge to a wide variety of political questions and issues. They will develop the skills to relate their everyday experiences to basic issues of constitutional government and civic responsibility.

Teaching strategies are varied, including directed discussions, simulations, debates, role-playing, timeline construction, and small-group problem solving. The program allows for and depends on a wide use of interdisciplinary skills. Art, spelling, vocabulary, mathematics, writing, research, and social studies skills are incorporated in the structure of these lessons.

ASSESSMENT AND CULMINATING ACTIVITY

After students complete the lessons in the text, they take a fifty-question multiple-choice test. If they receive an acceptable score (usually 70% or above), they receive a certificate of achievement. Teachers may have certificates signed by their member of Congress or another prominent public official.

As a culminating activity of the program, teachers are encouraged to involve their classes in a simulated congressional hearing. The hearing provides an opportunity for students to demonstrate their knowledge and understanding of constitutional principles. The entire class, working in cooperative groups, prepares and presents statements and answers questions before a panel of community representatives who act as congressional committee members. Teachers and their students may select an in-school simulated congressional hearing or contact other teachers through their district coordinator for an extramural hearing.

Both of the program's major assessment components may be modified as needed to fit the chosen instructional plan. For more information about all aspects of participating in the **We the People** program, please see Appendix C at the back of this book.

CURRICULUM GOALS

The *We the People: The Citizen & the Constitution* curriculum is designed to promote an increased understanding of the institutions of our constitutional democracy and the fundamental principles and values on which they were founded; develop the skills needed to become effective and responsible citizens; increase understanding and willingness to use democratic processes when making decisions; and manage conflict, both in public and private life.

In studying *We the People: The Citizen & the Constitution*, students develop the ability to identify issues that require political action. They are encouraged through informed inquiry to make a personal commitment to accept the responsibilities associated with the rights we enjoy as citizens— responsibilities essential to the continued existence of a society based on the ideals of freedom, justice, equality, and human rights.

CURRICULUM ORGANIZATION

We the People: The Citizen & the Constitution is about ideas, values, and principles fundamental to understanding our constitutional democracy. The curriculum is organized around ideas that form part of the common core of civic values and concepts that are fundamental to the theory and practice of democratic citizenship in the United States.

We the People: The Citizen & the Constitution may be taught in its entirety, or the teacher may select specific lessons as they relate to general curriculum goals and learning outcomes in a school or district. The lessons need not be taught in any particular order. If you select a single lesson, however, you are only addressing the objectives of that specific lesson and not the goals of a unit.

CURRICULUM RATIONALE

A fundamental hypothesis of the *We the People: The Citizen & the Constitution* curriculum is that education can increase a person's capacity and inclination to act knowledgeably, effectively, and responsibly. It follows that the role of educational institutions must be to help students increase their capacity to make intelligent choices for themselves— to learn how to think, rather than what to think. The alternative, indoctrination, is improper for educational institutions in a free society.

The Center for Civic Education was founded on the belief that the learning experiences provided by a curriculum based on this philosophy result in significant progress toward students' development of a reasoned commitment to those principles, processes, and values that are essential to the preservation and improvement of our free society.

Unit Format

In the teacher's edition, the Unit Overview provides a brief introduction to the forthcoming group of lessons and their objectives. In some units, an optional unit project is also suggested. These special projects are varied; some are individual activities and some meant for small-group work. They are designed to complement the class projects that students will be working on throughout their course of study.

Lesson Format

This teacher's edition is designed to complement and extend the student text. Each student lesson begins with a brief narrative passage designed to stimulate student interest and guide their reading.

The narrative for each lesson is divided into small segments to make it manageable for students. Strategies for presenting and discussing these materials are given in the Teaching Procedures segment of the lesson plans. Skill-building activities are presented within the student text. In some lessons, the key concepts are introduced and are then reinforced through an activity. In other lessons, the activity introduces the concepts and is followed by an explanation and discussion of the concepts.

The lessons include illustrations and photographs designed to complement and enhance comprehension of the narrative material. Most of the illustrations and photographs are accompanied by a question and require students to interpret information, apply facts, theorize, think creatively, use reasoning, and employ decision-making skills. The illustrations and photographs lend themselves to small group or interactive teaching strategies.

Vocabulary terms are highlighted in the student text and defined within the narrative. Definitions explain the usage of the word in its specific textual context. All terms are also defined in the glossary. A variety of vocabulary-building activities can be employed to reinforce understanding of new terms. Students can create their own dictionaries, which they might illustrate. They might write sentences that use each of the terms. A vocabulary test or a writing assignment might be used at the end of the unit as a check for understanding.

Another option would be a class spelling bee that requires students to use the term correctly in a sentence as well as spell it.

Each lesson in the student text ends with a list of questions entitled Lesson Review that can conclude the class discussions. Questions might also be assigned for individual or small-group homework assignments. Additional and alternative activities to reinforce, extend, and enrich the concepts of the lesson are included in the Activities section.

CURRICULUM CHARACTERISTICS

Effective civic education programs are distinguished by at least four characteristics:

Extensive interaction among students

Teaching strategies that foster interactive and cooperative learning among students are keys to development of civic participation skills and responsible citizenship. Examples of these teaching strategies are small-group work, simulations, role-play activities, and moot courts.

Realistic content that includes balanced treatment of issues

Realistic and fair treatment of issues is an essential component of effective civic education. So is critical thinking about all sides to controversies. If our legal and political systems are presented as flawless or infallible, students will doubt the credibility of the teacher and the practicality of the content. By contrast, if only cases in which the system has failed are presented, students will be less likely to view the system as a positive means for maintaining social order, liberty, and justice. A balance should be sought between respect for the legal and political system and constructive criticism about its application in specific cases.

Use of community resource persons in the classroom

Interaction with a variety of adult role models who work within our political and legal systems adds credibility and reality to the curriculum and is a powerful influence on development of positive attitudes toward the political and legal systems. Appropriate use of resource persons in the classroom (e.g., government officials from the legislative, executive, and judicial branches; community leaders; and representatives of various international groups) is strongly associated with increased student interest in issues related to effective citizenship and with positive responses to teachers and the school.

Strong support for civic education by the principal and other important school administrators

A key to successful implementation of civic education in the schools is strong support by administrators, especially the school principal. Supportive administrators can aid civic education by organizing opportunities for peer support, rewarding teachers for outstanding work, helping teachers explain and justify the program to people in the community outside the school, and providing opportunities for staff development in the knowledge and skills needed to carry out civic education programs. In addition, positive attitudes about civic education on the part of teachers and their colleagues are very important to successful implementation.

Successful citizenship programs actively involve students in the learning process in ways that reflect a high regard for each person. Reflection, deliberation, and discourse are valued and systematically practiced. The development of knowledge and character are pursued in concert as equally important elements of responsible citizenship in our constitutional democracy. Every attempt has been made to incorporate these essential characteristics in the *We the People: The Citizen & the Constitution* curriculum.

CONDUCTING CLASS DISCUSSIONS

The study of the history of ideas includes controversy, debate, evaluation, and reflection. So, too, does the study of *We the People: The Citizen & the Constitution*. Effective civic education presents and discusses controversial subject matter. This approach is what makes the curriculum exciting for both students and teachers. Through the discussion process, students develop knowledge, decision-making skills, conflict management experience, and a commitment to citizenship participation.

To ensure that the experience with this curriculum is stimulating and rewarding for both you and your students, consider the following suggestions for successful classroom discussion of controversial issues and contemporary topics.

Emphasize the legitimacy of controversy, compromise, and consensus. They are the lifeblood of a democratic society.

Try to present the central issues of controversy in tangible form. Make allusions to similar problems and dilemmas students face in their own lives.

Stress historical antecedents so students can see how similar conflicts have been managed in the past. Acknowledge those times when we have not lived up to the ideals and principles on which our nation was founded. Examining the interpretation and application of these concepts over time will help students appreciate the flexibility of our constitutional system and the role individual citizens play in helping our nation better realize its goals.

Emphasize the legitimacy of various viewpoints by encouraging students to examine and present conflicting views in an unbiased fashion. It is incumbent on the teacher to raise any opposing views students may have missed.

Keep students focused on discussing or dealing with ideas or positions, rather than people. Stress that on controversial issues, reasonable people might very well differ.

Encourage students to offer dissenting opinions when they do not agree with the majority—even if they are alone in their dissent.

Help students identify specific points of agreement or disagreement, places where compromise might be possible, and places where it is unlikely to occur. Emphasize that the outcome or the decision that they reach on an issue may not be as important as improving their ability to develop a reasoned decision and to express it in a civil manner, respecting the views of others.

Conclude, or debrief, a lesson or discussion by evaluating the arguments presented and exploring the likely consequences of the various alternatives suggested. An effective debriefing also involves both the teacher and the students in evaluating the process used for conducting a discussion, preparing group work, or presenting a class activity.

Class discussion and sharing of opinions are critical components to this program, therefore, you may wish to establish a few basic ground rules. For example:

* When expressing an opinion, always be prepared to justify it.
* Listen to the opinions of others politely and respectfully. You may be called on to say which opinion (other than your own) you liked best.
* Everyone will get a chance to speak, but only one person will speak at a time.
* Argue with reasons and ideas; do not argue against people.
* You may change your opinion at any time. Be prepared to share your reasons for doing so.

EFFECTIVE QUESTIONING STRATEGIES

Question and response sequences are an important feature of the curriculum. The effective use of questions is critical to the learning process and requires careful planning. While some questions may be useful to establish how much knowledge students have gained, the primary goal of your questioning strategies should be to help students increase their knowledge, understanding, and ability to reach effective, responsible decisions. Therefore, you will want to choose questioning strategies that help students develop the skills of analysis, synthesis, and evaluation.

There are generally six categories of questions you should consider when planning class discussions. The following is a brief description and example of each:

Knowledge These questions involve recall of specific facts or information.

Example: What are the powers of the legislative branch of government?

Comprehension This involves the ability to understand the meaning of the material. This may be shown by translating material from one form to another and by interpreting material.

Example: Create a drawing illustrating a person fulfilling a responsibility of citizenship. What is the central idea of this lesson?

Application This involves the ability to use learned material in new situations.

Example: What examples can you cite from your own experience where these ideas apply? How might you use this process to resolve a conflict in the future?

Analysis This involves the ability to break down material into its component parts. This includes identifying the parts and establishing the relationship among the parts.

Example: What are the consequences of the government's invasion of privacy in this situation? Which consequences are advantages and which are disadvantages?

Synthesis This is the ability to put parts together to form a new whole. The emphasis is on creating new patterns of thought.

Example: What argument can you make to support the idea of increasing the authority of the U.S. Supreme Court?

Evaluation This is the ability to judge the value of the material for a given purpose. This may be a process for choosing among competing values or deciding whether a principle still meets the criteria of effectiveness for the common good.

Example: How useful are the critical thinking strategies in helping you make a decision about who is responsible for a particular event? What are the likely consequences of the alternatives you have suggested?

It is possible to structure questions so that students listen to and respond to each other and not just to their teacher.

Encourage students' active participation in the following ways:

- Pose a question and ask students to discuss the answer with a partner.

- Ask students to clarify their responses. This will benefit themselves as well as others.

- Ask students to extend their own or other students' responses by providing additional facts, information, viewpoints, etc.

- Ask students to generate questions of their own on material just presented in class.

- Pause at least seven seconds after asking a question to allow students time to think.

- Ask students to expand on their responses if they provide short or fragmentary answers.

- Call on more than one student per question.

- Encourage students to react to other students' responses.

- Call on nonvolunteers as well as volunteers.

ENCOURAGING SMALL-GROUP LEARNING

The critical thinking exercises in the student text are generally designed as cooperative learning activities with a study partner or in small-group environments. Each individual's participation is essential for the successful completion of an exercise. Students are encouraged not only to contribute academically, but to develop and use appropriate interpersonal skills.

Important issues arise for the teacher in planning and implementing cooperative group learning. One such issue concerns the size of groups. Consideration of the research can help you determine the optimum number of students per group within your classroom. Some excellent suggestions can be found at http://edtech.kennesaw.edu/intech/cooperative learning.htm.

David A. Welton and John T. Mallan, in their book *Children and Their World: Teaching Social Studies,* Seventh Edition, Houghton-Mifflin, 2001, have identified some general behavioral characteristics of differently sized groups:

Groups of two High exchange of information and a tendency to avoid disagreement are two features of pairs. In case of disagreement, however, deadlock occurs because there is no support within the group for either participant.

Groups of three Triads tend to be characterized by the power of the majority over the minority of one. However, triads are the most stable group structure with some occasional shifting of coalitions.

Groups of even numbers More disagreement is prevalent in groups with even numbers of members. This is due to the formation of subgroups of equal size resulting in deadlock.

ENCOURAGING SMALL-GROUP LEARNING (CONT'D)

Groups of five The most satisfying learning group size seems to be five. There is ease of movement within the group. The 2:3 division provides minority members with support. The group is large enough for stimulation, yet small enough for participation and personal recognition.

Groups larger than five As group size increases, so does the range of ability, expertise, and skill. However, so do the difficulties in keeping all members on task, ensuring everyone the opportunity to speak, and coordinating group actions.

Another issue teachers face in planning and implementing cooperative group learning is whether to allow groups to self-select or to establish the groups by assignment. David W. Johnson, et al., in *Circles of Learning: Cooperation in the Classroom*, published by the Association for Supervision and Curriculum Development, 1984, describes the following characteristics of groups:

Student-selected groups are frequently homogeneous with high-achieving students selecting other high achievers, males selecting males, and members of different cultural groups selecting those from similar backgrounds.

There is often less on-task behavior in student-selected than in teacher-selected groups.

More creative thinking, more frequent giving and receiving of explanations, and greater perspective-taking in discussion seems to occur in heterogeneous groups.

A useful modification of the select-your-own-groups method is to have students list three peers with whom they would like to work. Place the students with one person they chose; select the other peers yourself. Careful consideration should be given to building a supportive environment for students no one selects.

You also may want to consider randomly assigning students to groups by having them count off. For example, to establish six groups of five students each in a class of thirty, have the students count off from one to six, repeating the sequence at the end of six. Then, place the "ones" together, the "twos" together, and so forth. Once groups have been assembled, you may want to have them work together over a period of time rather than forming new groups for each activity in the student text.

Below are some general recommendations you may want to consider in implementing small-group work in your classroom:

- Make sure the students have the skills necessary to do the work. If they do not, you will quickly know because they will not remain long on task.
- Give clear instructions for completing work and check for understanding of the process or procedures to be followed during an activity.
- Allow adequate time to complete the assigned task. Think creatively about ways to constructively occupy groups that finish ahead of the others.
- Be explicit in dealing with management issues. If someone must report to the class on the group's work, be sure there is a process for selecting a reporter.
- Think about how your evaluation strategies are affected by the use of small groups. Develop methods to reward group efforts.
- Monitor group work and act as a resource to guide your students' development.

COMMUNITY RESOURCE PEOPLE

Involvement of people from the community who possess appropriate experience or expertise can greatly enhance and extend student understanding of the concepts presented in *We the People: The Citizen & the Constitution*. Community resource people can contribute in the following ways:

- Make the lessons come alive by sharing real-life experiences and applications of the ideas under consideration.
- Help implement activities in the classroom such as role plays, moot courts, and simulated legislative hearings and debates.
- Enrich field experiences by serving as a guide and by responding to questions during visits to places such as courtrooms and legislative chambers.
- Establish an ongoing relationship with a class in which the resource person is available regularly by phone to respond to questions or issues that may arise during a particular lesson.

The range of individuals who can serve as resource people is as varied as the community itself. Commonly, this includes government officials from the legislative, executive, and judicial branches, community leaders, and representatives of various international groups.

Making the involvement of a community resource person as meaningful as possible requires careful planning. Attention should be given to the following considerations:

A resource person's involvement should be relevant to the lesson or concept under consideration.

The principal mode of involvement should be interaction and participation with students. A resource person should be asked to assist students in preparing a role-play or moot court arguments. The resource person can act as a judge, serve on a panel with students, or respond to questions about specific details of a lesson. Also, a resource person should participate in the concluding discussion of a lesson or activity.

A resource person should offer a balanced picture of the topic, including a variety of perspectives. When objectivity is not possible, you might consider inviting a second resource person to ensure a balanced experience. The guest should avoid professional jargon and speak as simply as possible.

Before a visit by a resource person, students should be well prepared to maximize their thoughtful participation when the visitor is present.

Most resource persons are not trained teachers and should not be responsible for classroom management. The teacher should be in attendance during the entire visit. Sometimes it might be necessary for the teacher to give direction to the guest by asking appropriate questions or offering clues that can help the resource person communicate effectively with students.

For a successful visit, the resource person should receive a copy of the lesson in advance. Usually, a previsit meeting or phone call is useful to help clarify what is expected of the guest.

Owing to busy schedules and the limited length of this program, it is advisable to extend invitations as soon as possible. A committee of students should be responsible for hosting the guests on the day of their visit and for the follow-up thank you letter.

INTERACTIVE TEACHING STRATEGIES

An essential feature of *We the People: The Citizen & the Constitution* is the use of instructional methods that actively involve students in developing and presenting positions on related issues. Students learn to apply their knowledge to contemporary issues as well as to a variety of sociopolitical questions. In addition, these learning strategies promote certain dispositions and participatory skills that increase students' capacity to act effectively as citizens in a constitutional democracy. For example, students learn to work cooperatively to reach common goals, to evaluate, take, and defend positions on controversial issues, and to deal with conflicting opinions and positions in a constructive manner. These learning strategies also teach students how government works.

The key learning strategies in this curriculum include, among others, legislative hearings, moot courts, and town meetings. The following material describes these instructional methods and offers specific suggestions for implementation in the classroom.

LEGISLATIVE HEARINGS

Legislative hearings are held by committees of the U.S. Congress and other legislative bodies to gather information on matters of public concern. These hearings are a basic function of legislative branches of government.

Role-playing a legislative hearing provides participants with an opportunity to gain increased understanding of the purpose and procedures of such hearings as well as the roles and responsibilities of committee members. Participants also gain experience in identifying and clarifying the information, interests, and values associated with the subject being discussed.

HOW TO PROCEED

1. Clarify topics Help students understand the topic of the legislative hearing. The topics are clearly identified in the lessons in the student text and in this edition. You also will want to ensure that students understand the role of committees in the legislative process.

2. Contact resource persons Invite a local legislator, representatives of local groups, or chapters of a national organization to serve as resource people on the topic of the hearing.

3. Assign roles Explain to participants the purpose of a legislative hearing and assign the appropriate roles:

LEGISLATIVE HEARINGS (CONT'D)

a. Legislators Six legislators is a practical number for a committee, but the number may vary according to class needs. Designate one legislator as the chairperson to preside over the hearing.

b. Witnesses The number and nature of the witnesses depend on the topic being discussed. The specific roles described in the lessons and in this edition are designed to present differing points of view on the topic.

c. Recorder This role is optional. The recorder keeps a record of the proceedings and presents a review or summary of any recommendations that may emerge during the discussions.

d. Newspaper reporters This role is optional, but is useful in helping students gain insights on the function of the press in the democratic process. Select students to represent newspapers with varying perspectives. Ask them to interview legislators and witnesses, to observe the proceedings, and to write brief articles or editorials about the topic. They should share and discuss their work with the class.

4. Prepare presentations Allow time for participants to prepare for the legislative hearing in accordance with their assigned roles.

a. Legislators should identify the key issue(s) and prepare questions to ask each witness.

b. Witnesses should define their position on the issue(s), prepare an opening statement, anticipate questions from the legislators, and formulate possible responses.

c. Witnesses may wish to discuss similarities in positions with other witnesses.

d. When appropriate, have a resource person work with the students or allow students to contact outside resources for assistance in preparing their position on an issue.

5. Arrange the classroom Set up the classroom to resemble a legislative chamber. Include a table for the legislators, a desk for the recorder, and a desk or table for the witnesses. Provide a gavel and nameplates with the students' names and their roles. You may want to arrange the use of a hearing or committee room of a local legislative body.

6. Conduct the hearing The following procedures should be used to conduct this activity:

a. The committee chairperson calls the hearing to order, announces the purpose of the hearing, and specifies the order in which the witnesses will be called to testify.

b. The chairperson calls each witness. The witness makes an opening statement, followed by questions from members of the committee. You may want to establish time limits, usually three to four minutes for

openings and five to six minutes for questions from the legislators. Appoint a timekeeper to enforce time limitations.

c. The chairperson is the first to question the witness, followed by the other members of the committee. A committee member may interrupt to ask a question or make a comment any time during the proceedings.

d. After the witnesses have been heard, the legislators review the testimony, discuss the issue(s), and make recommendations on what their next step(s) will be.

7. Debrief the activity Debriefing questions vary according to the topic. Begin by having the legislators announce their decision. Discuss the facts and arguments presented on the topic and evaluate the strengths and weaknesses of the positions taken. Ask students to evaluate their experience with the hearing process itself. Conclude the debriefing by having students discuss the effectiveness of this activity as a tool for learning, including how well they performed their role in it. If a resource person assisted with the activity, that person should be included in the concluding discussion.

LEGISLATIVE DEBATE

Legislative debate is often used productively in the formulation and development of laws. Role-playing a legislative debate provides participants with an opportunity to increase their understanding of the power of legislatures to make laws and to debate matters of public policy.

HOW TO PROCEED

1. Clarify topics Help students understand the topic of the legislative debate. The topics are clearly identified in the lessons in the student text and in this edition. You also will want to ensure that students understand the process whereby bills are enacted into law.

2. Contact resource persons Contact state and national legislators or their staff assistants to help serve as resource persons.

3. Assign roles Consider the entire class as the legislative body with a student or the teacher assuming the role of the presiding officer. Legislators may then be assigned to groups representing various positions on the issue. Groups are clearly identified in the student text and in this edition. You also may want to assign a recorder responsible for tracking key points of discussion during the debate.

4. Prepare presentations Allow time for participants to prepare for the legislative hearing in accordance with their assigned roles.

Each group should select a spokesperson and a recorder and then proceed to follow the directions given in the lesson. Students should analyze and evaluate the issue before developing their positions. In some cases, they will be asked to offer amendments to the bills already given in the lesson. In others, they may write a proposed bill designed to alleviate problems raised by the issue.

As each group completes its amendment or proposed bill, the spokesperson reports to the presiding officer asking that the bill be placed on the agenda. Bills should be placed on the agenda in the order in which they are received. Students may wish to discuss any similarities in their proposed amendments or bills with other groups to predetermine whether they can unite behind a common proposal.

5. Arrange the classroom Set up the classroom to resemble a legislative chamber. Include a table for the presiding officer, a desk for the recorder, and a podium if you want to have presentations made more formally. Provide a gavel and nameplates with the students' names and their roles. You may want to arrange for the use of a legislative chamber in your community.

6. Conduct the legislative debate Time limits for the various steps in legislative debates should be decided ahead of time. The presiding officer should be empowered to cut off speakers when the time limit has been reached. Conduct the legislative debate using the following procedures:

a. The presiding officer calls the legislature to order, indicates that all votes will be decided by a simple majority, announces the issue, and opens the debate.

b. The first bill on the agenda is introduced by the group's spokesperson. The spokesperson stands, addresses the presiding officer, and describes the bill the group has written. After presenting the bill, the spokesperson may recognize two other members of the group who may make additional comments on the bill.

c. The bill is discussed and debated by the legislature. Representatives from other groups may ask questions, offer criticisms, or suggest modifications.

d. The steps above are repeated for any additional bills that might be introduced during the session.

e. When the discussion and debate on all proposed bills is completed, legislators may move that one of the bills be voted on or that the session be recessed to enable the groups to consider the bills that have been

LEGISLATIVE DEBATE (CONT'D)

presented. If the session is recessed, each group meets to decide on a course of action. A group may decide to support one of the bills as presented, suggest amendments to one of the bills presented, or develop a compromise bill.

f. When the session is reconvened, the presiding officer asks for a motion to vote on one of the bills as presented, for a motion to amend one of the bills, or for the introduction of a compromise bill. If amendments or compromise bills are proposed, they are individually debated and voted on.

g. This process is repeated until a bill is passed or the time allotted for the session is up and the legislature is adjourned.

7. Debrief the activity Debriefing questions vary according to the topic. Discuss the facts and arguments presented on the topic and evaluate the strengths and weaknesses of the positions taken. Also ask students to evaluate their experience with the legislative process itself. Conclude the debriefing by having students discuss the effectiveness of this activity as a tool for learning, including how well they performed their role in it. If a resource person assisted with the activity, that person should be included in the concluding discussion.

PRO SE COURT

A pro se (do it yourself) court allows students to role-play a court case using a minimum of participants and simple rules of evidence. The court is organized as a triad consisting of a judge, who will hear the two sides and make the final decision; a plaintiff, who is the person bringing the action before the judge; and the defendant, who is accused of wrongdoing or causing injury.

Pro se courts provide students with a simplified look at judicial decision making, and an opportunity for all students in a class to be involved in the activity.

HOW TO PROCEED

1. Clarify topic Help students understand the facts and issues in the case. The cases are clearly identified in the lessons.

2. Contact resource person Invite an attorney or judge to act as a resource person.

3. Assign roles Divide the class into three equal groups—judges, plaintiffs, and defendants.

4. Prepare presentations Have the students meet in their respective groups to help each other prepare their presentations. Each student will be actively involved in the role play, so preparation at this stage is vital to effective participation in the activity.

Instruct the judges to review the case and the issues raised. Ask them to prepare questions that they would like to ask of the plaintiffs and defendants during the presentation phase of the activity. The questions should be designed to clarify positions on the issues that the judges will be called on to decide. Do take some time to review with the judge's group some simple rules of procedure, such as the following:

a. The plaintiff should present first, without interruptions from the defense. The defense presents their case second.

b. Allow brief rebuttals from each side in the case.

c. The judge may interrupt the presentations at any time to pose questions designed to clarify the arguments being made. Instruct the plaintiff and defendant groups to prepare an opening statement and arguments supporting their positions on the issues raised in the case.

5. Arrange the classroom You will have multiple courts in session simultaneously; therefore, arrange the desks in the classroom into groups of three, one for each of the roles in the activity.

6. Conduct the court hearing Before beginning the activity, match one student from the judges' group with one student from the plaintiff and one from the defendant groups. You may want to have the judges first take a desk in each of the groupings arranged around the room. Then ask one plaintiff and one defendant to join the group. Matching role-players may be more easily accomplished by providing role "tags" so students can quickly identify who is a judge, plaintiff, and defendant. Conduct the activity using the following procedures:

a. Instruct the judges that when each has a plaintiff and a defendant, he or she may begin the court session.

b. The judge should first hear opening statements by the participants—first the plaintiff and then the defendant. An appropriate time limit should be imposed on these statements.

c. The plaintiff makes arguments and is questioned by the judge.

d. The defendant presents his or her defense and is questioned by the judge.

e. The judge asks each side for brief rebuttal statements.

f. The judge makes a decision and explains the reasoning that supports it.

7. Debrief the activity Debriefing questions vary according to the topic. Begin by asking individual judges to share with the class their decision and the reasoning supporting it. Discuss the facts and arguments presented in the case and evaluate the strengths and weaknesses of the positions taken. Also ask students to evaluate the court process itself. Conclude the debriefing by having students discuss the effectiveness of this activity as a tool for learning, including how well they performed their role in it. If a resource person assisted with the activity, that person should be included in the concluding discussion.

MOOT COURT

A moot court is patterned on an appeals court or Supreme Court hearing. The court, composed of a panel of judges or justices, is asked to rule on a lower court's decision. No witnesses are called, nor are the basic facts in a case disputed. Arguments are prepared and presented on the application of a law, the constitutionality of a law, or the fairness of previous court procedures. In many ways the moot court is like a debate because each side presents arguments for the consideration of the justices.

Because moot courts are not concerned with the credibility of witness testimony, they are an effective strategy for focusing student attention on the underlying principles and concepts of due process.

HOW TO PROCEED

1. Clarify topic Help students understand the facts and the legal or constitutional issues in the case. The cases are clearly identified in the lessons in the student text and in this edition. You may also want to ensure that students understand the purpose and procedures observed in appellate court proceedings.

2. Contact resource person Invite an attorney or judge to act as a resource person.

3. Assign roles Assign students to play the roles of justices of the court (in intermediate appellate courts, members of the panel are called judges; in the federal or state supreme

MOOT COURT (CONT'D)

courts they are called justices). You may establish a court of five, seven, or nine justices. Divide the remaining students into two groups representing the litigants in the case. One group will represent the person or group bringing the challenge before the court, or the plaintiff. The other group will represent the person or group defending against the challenge, or the defendant. Sometimes, terms like petitioner or respondent, or appellant and appellee, are used to identify the litigants in an appellate case. For pedagogical purposes, it is best to keep it simple by using the terms plaintiff and defendant.

4. Prepare presentations Each group should meet to prepare arguments for its side of the case. The group should select one or two students to present the arguments.

The justices should meet to discuss the issues involved and any questions they feel need to be addressed for them to reach a decision. The justices should select one student to serve as chief justice. The chief justice will preside over the hearing. He or she will call on each side to present its case or (more realistically) justices (judges) should ask questions without needing to be recognized. The judges should feel free to interrupt lawyers' presentations whenever they want.

Participants should understand that the factual details presented in the summary of the case were established by a trial and are not subject to further dispute.

Arguments should not concentrate on legal technicalities. Any argument that is persuasive from a philosophical, theoretical, conceptual, or practical standpoint can be made. Groups should rely on principles found or implied in the U.S. Constitution.

5. Arrange the classroom Set up the classroom to resemble an appellate court. The justices should be seated at a table at the front of the room. The attorneys for each side should sit on opposite sides of the room facing the justices. Other group members should sit behind their respective attorneys. You may want to take the class to an appellate court-room or to a mock trial room at a law school.

6. Conduct the moot court The chief justice should preside over the proceedings and begin by calling the court to order. The chief justice should observe the following procedures:

a. Each side should be allotted five to ten minutes for the initial presentation and five minutes for rebuttal. The chief justice should call for presentations in the following order:

Plaintiff Initial presentation
Defendant Initial presentation
Plaintiff Rebuttal presentation
Defendant Rebuttal presentation

b. During and/or after each presentation, the justices can and should actively question the attorneys in an effort to clarify the arguments. Attorneys may request time to consult with other group members before answering questions. For clarity and continuity, it is suggested that during the initial presentations, lawyers be given three minutes to present their cases before being interrupted with questions.

c. After arguments have been presented, the justices should organize themselves in a circle. They should consider the arguments and make a decision by a majority vote. Each justice should give reasons for his or her position. The rest of the class may sit outside of the circle and listen, but they may not talk or interrupt the deliberations.

7. Debrief the activity Debriefing questions vary according to the case. Begin by asking the justices to share with the class their decision and the reasoning supporting it. Justices should present dissenting opinions. Discuss the arguments presented in the case and evaluate the strengths and weaknesses of the positions taken. Also ask students to evaluate their experience with the appellate process itself. Conclude the debriefing by having students discuss the effectiveness of this activity as a tool for learning, including how well they performed their role in it. If a resource person assisted with the activity, that person should be included in the concluding discussion.

In an actual case, you should share the court's decision with the class during the debriefing. To dispel the notion that there is one "right" answer, also share relevant parts of the dissenting opinion. Help students understand the reasoning that supports both the majority and dissenting opinions.

TOWN MEETING

A town meeting provides members of a community with an opportunity to participate in the decision-making process. A community forum usually considers matters of public policy. A town meeting can serve as a local governing and decision-making body by performing functions similar to those of a representative town or city council. It also can be advisory in nature, providing elected representatives with the views of citizens.

HOW TO PROCEED

1. Clarify topic Help students understand the topic of the town meeting. The topics are clearly identified in the lessons in the student text and in this edition. You also will want to ensure that students understand the nature and purpose of a town meeting.

2. Contact resource person Invite a member of the city council or a local interest group to serve as a resource person on the topic of the meeting.

3. Assign roles Organize the town meeting by assigning individuals the following roles:

   a. chairperson

   b. elected officials who represent the entire community in the town or city council

   c. representative groups in favor of the proposition

   d. representative groups in opposition to the proposition

   e. community members at large

   f. recorder

4. Prepare presentations Allow time for students to prepare for the town meeting in accordance with their assigned roles.

5. Arrange the classroom Include a table for the chairperson and for the elected officials, a desk for the recorder, and a podium from which members of interest groups and the community can speak. Provide a gavel and nameplates with the students' names and their roles. You may want to arrange for the use of a hearing or committee room of a local legislative body.

6. Conduct the town meeting The following procedures should be used to conduct this activity:

   a. The chairperson calls the meeting to order, announces the purpose of the meeting, and introduces the elected officials in attendance. Elected officials may make a brief opening statement about the importance of the issue being considered (not his or her personal views on the topic). The chairperson also

TOWN MEETING (CONT'D)

establishes any rules that are to be followed during the meeting, such as time limits for presentations.

b. The chairperson has the authority to cut off debate when time limits have been reached. A person may not speak unless recognized by the chair, and no one may interrupt while another person is speaking. If a speaker wanders from the point, abuses other people, or in any way defeats the purpose of the meeting, the chairperson may declare him or her out of order.

c. The chairperson calls on a representative of the group favoring the proposition to describe that group's position. After the representative has finished speaking, he or she may ask people brought in as witnesses to stand and speak. The chairperson announces that any person in favor of the proposition may stand and speak. They will be recognized in the order in which they stand. Alternatively, you may want to have students sign in and ask the chairperson to recognize speakers by the order in which they signed in.

d. The chairperson calls on a representative of the group opposed to the proposition to speak. After the representative has finished speaking, he or she may ask people brought in as witnesses to stand and speak. The chairperson announces that those people opposed to the proposition will be recognized in the order in which they stand.

e. After all people on both sides of the proposition have had an opportunity to speak, the chairperson opens the question for additional discussion or debate. During this time any person may stand, be recognized, and present his or her point of view, or argue against the point of view of someone else.

f. At the end of the discussion or debate, the chairperson calls for the class to vote on the proposition. The vote is decided by a majority.

7. Debrief the activity Debriefing questions vary according to the topic. Begin by discussing the results of the vote taken on the proposition. Discuss the facts and argument presented on the topic. Ask students to evaluate the strength of the positions taken and of the procedures used to develop and support a position. Also ask students to evaluate their experience with the town meeting itself. Conclude the debriefing by having students discuss the effectiveness of this activity as a tool for learning, including how well they performed their role in it. If a resource person assisted with the activity, that person should be included in the concluding discussion.

DEBATE

Debate begins with the assumption that the debater has already found a solution or approach to a specific issue. The intent of the debater is to persuade others that his or her solution or approach is the proper one.

Debate can be an effective device for encouraging students to clearly and logically formulate arguments based on evidence. Debate teaches a means to adequately support a position on an issue. It also develops a sense of efficacy and confidence in a person's ability to sway public opinion or to change public policy.

HOW TO PROCEED

1. Clarify topic Help students understand the topic of the debate. The topics are clearly identified in the lessons in the student text and in this edition. Formulate the topic into a resolution (resolutions always ask for a change from the status quo, e.g., Resolved: that capital punishment should be found unconstitutional by the U.S. Supreme Court).

2. Contact resource person Invite someone from the community or a local interest group to serve as a resource person on the topic of the debate.

3. Assign roles Select students to take part in the debate. Divide them into two teams, one in support of the resolution, the other opposing it. Make certain that those participating in the debate are familiar with the procedures to be followed during the debate. Select a moderator and a timekeeper.

4. Prepare presentations Allow sufficient time for students to prepare their "constructive arguments" (arguments based on three to five major points logically developed and substantiated by factual evidence in support of a particular position). Help students see the dimensions of the problem and develop clear, logical arguments supported by evidence on the position they defend in the debate. Also, ask them to anticipate the views of the other side in preparation for their "rebuttal arguments."

Help students gain an understanding of some of the implicit values in debate such as learning to make convincing arguments from another frame of reference, as might be the case if one is debating a position that does not correspond with one's own beliefs. This furthers development of students' abilities to understand and respect the right of individuals to hold opinions and beliefs that are different from their own.

5. Arrange the classroom The moderator and debaters are seated at the front of the audience, usually with the team in opposition to the resolution to the left of the moderator.

6. Conduct the debate The form of debate described here is widely used, but is rather formalized. You may wish to make the procedures less formal or use some other form of debate.

a. The moderator briefly introduces the subject and the resolution to be debated and establishes the time limits to be observed by the speakers.

b. The moderator introduces the first speaker from the affirmative team and asks the speaker to present his or her constructive argument. The order in which constructive arguments will be given by each member of the team should be determined in advance of the debate. The timekeeper will inform the speaker when the time limit has been reached.

c. The moderator introduces the first speaker from the team in opposition to the resolution and asks the speaker to present his or her constructive argument.

d. The moderator next introduces the second speaker from the affirmative team. This procedure is alternated until each debater on both affirmative and opposition teams has given a constructive argument.

e. Rebuttal arguments follow the constructive arguments. At this time each debater is given the opportunity to weaken the position of the opponents by attacking their position and by answering attacks that have been made on his or her position. No new issues may be introduced during rebuttal arguments. Rebuttal arguments always begin with the team in opposition to the resolution. Again, follow the same alternating procedures used during constructive arguments.

f. At the conclusion of the debate, the moderator makes a few concluding remarks and the debate is ended.

7. Debrief the activity You may wish to evaluate the success of the debating teams by informally polling the class to determine how many people agree with the team in support of the resolution and how many agree with the team in opposition to the resolution. You may then ask class members to explain whether their own positions were strengthened or changed as a result of hearing the debate and why. Also ask students to evaluate their experience with the debate process itself. Conclude the debriefing by having students discuss the effectiveness of this activity as a tool for learning, including how well they performed their role in it. If a resource person assisted with the activity, that person should be included in the concluding discussion.

CONTINUUM

The continuum is an exercise in which participants are presented with a range of possible attitudes or approaches on a controversial issue. Participants are asked to determine which element of the continuum (e.g., strongly agree or strongly disagree) most approximates their own attitude. Issues that are clearly controversial positions are suitable for using this method. The issues should have legitimate opposing view points, such as whether equal rights can best be achieved by an amendment or whether gun control is an effective way to stop crime. Issues that are above debate, such as the morality of ethnic cleansing or the sexual abuse of children, are obviously not legitimate topics for a continuum.

The continuum is a useful tool for introducing controversial issues. It can help students see the ranges of values or opinions which exist on a given topic and understand the reasoning which supports those positions. The continuum provides an orderly method for discussing controversy, especially at the early stages of a lesson when students may be expressing "gut-level" reactions rather than informed opinions.

HOW TO PROCEED

1. Identify an issue to be discussed. The issue should be one in which one can identify polar positions, such as the death penalty.

2. Before initiating the activity, it is important to cultivate a classroom atmosphere of trust where opinions can be expressed freely. Being receptive and nonjudgmental is critical to open discussion.

3. The teacher should initiate the activity by describing the issue(s) in enough detail so that the polar positions are clearly understood. These should be written on the board.

4. Students should be asked to write their position on the issue (e.g., strongly agree, agree, disagree, strongly disagree, can't decide) and to list the two most compelling reasons why they believe as they do.

5. While the students are writing their statements, the teacher can draw a continuum line across the chalkboard. When the students are finished writing, the teacher can print along the continuum brief versions of some possible polar positions on the issue. Ask a limited number of students to stand at the point on the continuum where they believe their position on the issue falls.

6. At this point, students should be asked to explain or clarify, but not to defend their positions. They should be encouraged to move their position along the continuum as they listen to others clarify their positions.

7. Students now can be asked to state their reasons for positioning themselves as they have. The teacher may wish to post on the board the different reasons expressed by the students. At this point, students can respond to questions concerning their reasoning, but argumentation should be discouraged.

8. To make sure that students listen to and consider opposing points of view, all students should be asked to present the arguments that, although contrary to their positions, give them pause, make them think twice, or are the most persuasive.

9. Finally, students should be asked to consider the consequences of alternative policy choices. This involves identifying the existing law or policy on the issue being considered, if one exists. The class can then discuss what impact the polar positions presented on the continuum would have on society as a whole and on individuals.

KEEPING JOURNALS

Journal writing provides a systematic way for students to maintain a personal record of summary statements, reflections, or questions about what is being learned in a particular instance. Journal writing encourages students to reflect on the "what," "why," and "how" of their own learning. Taking time to reflect is a good study habit to develop. Journals have the additional benefit of improving writing skills.

Because the content introduced in *We the People: The Citizen & the Constitution* contains many new concepts and experiences, opportunities for students to reflect on what they are learning are especially important. Some opportunities for journal writing are identified in the teacher's edition, but many more exist in this curriculum. You may want to allow a few minutes at the conclusion of a lesson or at the close of an activity for students to complete a journal entry. Encourage students to discuss some aspect of the content studied, to record a personal reaction to the lesson or the outcome of an activity, or to record questions the lesson or activity raised about an issue. Sometimes you may want to assign journal notations as homework.

Whether journals are graded is a personal choice. You should collect journals periodically, however, to offer students some feedback on the content. Writing comments and personal observations in the journals can be an effective tool in establishing a personal dialogue with students. Do encourage students to share their journals with other students and with their parents if they wish. By so doing, students demonstrate to themselves and others what they have learned.

The methods used to evaluate student achievement of the concepts, knowledge, and skills offered in this curriculum need to be both comprehensive and varied. The methods selected for measuring progress may range from the more traditional paper-and-pencil tests to performance-based assessments.

Traditional paper-and-pencil tests are valuable for checking knowledge and understanding of specific concepts, ideas, or procedures. For this purpose, the *We the People: The Citizen & the Constitution* program provides a multiple-choice test in the back of this book. When teachers ask students to apply their complex knowledge and skills in various contexts, teachers need to measure students' achievement in similar contexts. For example, students who participate in a simulated legislative hearing during instruction should be asked to demonstrate their knowledge and skills in a similar context during testing. Thus, *We the People: The Citizen & the Constitution* includes performance assessment activities to measure achievement of the curriculum's higher-level goals and objectives. The culminating performance assessment activity for the curriculum is the simulated congressional hearing, which is fully explained in the Reference section of this guide in Appendix C, "Conducting a Simulated Congressional Hearing – Guidelines and Handouts."

Performance assessment differs from traditional testing in that students are not asked to recognize and select correct answers to questions focused on discrete, isolated facts. During performance assessment, students demonstrate their knowledge and skills by addressing complex questions within a meaningful context (i.e., a legislative hearing) for which there is usually not just one correct answer.

Students, therefore, construct or create appropriate answers, or a product, as a means of demonstrating what they know and what they can do.

Performance assessment is particularly well-suited to the content, skills, and learning experiences emphasized in the program. Classroom activities such as group discussions, debates, and other creative projects provide prime opportunities for integrating performance assessment as part of the learning.

Below are some general guidelines for performance assessment you may want to consider in designing your evaluation of student achievement in this program:

- Assess desired behavior in the context in which the behavior is used. To assess students' ability to do X, have them do X.

- Assess how well students can apply what they learned in one situation by asking them to apply similar knowledge and skills in other, similar situations. Structure situations in which students can construct or create appropriate answers, rather than select from a menu of choices.

- Assess the process and the quality of a performance or product, not the ability to identify correct answers. Stress the thinking and reasoning that supports a quality performance or product.

- Assess how well students see the connections among a variety of related ideas and skills. For example, in preparing for a debate students should combine reading, research, writing, speaking, and critical thinking skills. Students also should see how knowledge and skills from other disciplines can help them deal with challenging topics.

- Provide the criteria for successful performance in advance and make sure that they are clearly understood. When possible, provide models of exemplary performance.

- Provide criteria for effective and successful group work. Teamwork and group interaction are important skills that are given legitimacy when students know they are being assessed.

- Structure opportunities for students to assess their own progress, to judge for themselves when they have or have not done well. This will help them internalize high standards and learn to judge for themselves when they measure up. Because most learning strategies in this text are used more than once, students will have successive opportunities to reflect on their progress.

- Offer plenty of opportunities for students to receive feedback from the teacher, their peers, and community resource people who participate in activities with the class.

REFLECTING ON THE LEARNING EXPERIENCE

At the conclusion of each unit, it is recommended that students evaluate the extent to which they achieved the objectives of that particular unit. This includes thinking about the content as well as the instructional methods used to learn about that content.

Distribute "Reflecting on Your Experience," Handout D 13, to each student. Handouts are in the Appendix at the back of this book. Ask students to answer the questions. Remind them that they should not only reflect on and evaluate their own learning experiences, but also those of the entire class. Conduct a class discussion in which students have an opportunity to share their reflections on the learning experiences offered in *We the People: The Citizen & the Constitution*.

Inform students that they are about to begin a study of the Constitution of the United States. Explain that the text will provide them with an understanding of how the Constitution came into existence, why it took the form it did, and how it has worked for the past two hundred years.

Have students locate the Table of Contents and read aloud the titles to each of the units. Point out that each unit title and each lesson title asks a question. Tell students that they will learn the answers to these questions as they study each lesson. Ask students to find the Reference section; discuss the contents of the section and explain how it can be used.

Next, have the students turn to the Introduction to the text. Read the Introduction with the class and answer any questions.

introduction

Most history books tell the story of people and events of the past. This book is a history of ideas. It explains the most important ideas of our Constitution and how they were developed. It also highlights the people and events that were important in the history of these ideas.

The Constitution of the United States was created as a plan for the new government of our country. It was written in Philadelphia in 1787, more than 215 years ago. We study the Constitution and its history to understand our government and how it is supposed to work. Knowing our past will help us understand the rights and responsibilities that we have today.

In this book, you will discover what the people who wrote our Constitution thought the purposes of government should be. They believed government should protect our lives, liberty, and property. They also believed government should promote the common good. You will also learn why they thought it was necessary to limit the powers of government.

You will learn about some of the things that have happened to the Constitution since it was written in 1787. You will study ways in which it has changed and how these changes came about. You will also learn about ways the Constitution has stayed the same.

This book will help you develop a good understanding of the Constitution and our system of government. It will also help you understand more about how our government affects your life, and how you can influence your government.

unit ONE

What were the Founders' basic ideas about government?

UNIT OVERVIEW

The lessons in this unit help students understand who the Founders were and what ideas and experiences shaped their thinking about government.

Lesson 1 introduces students to the people who lived in the British colonies of North America during the 1770s and explains how they lived, what their background differences were, and how their colonial experiences shaped what they thought about government and rights. The lesson also gives a brief introduction to the Founders.

Lesson 2 presents the ideas of John Locke and explains the influence he had on the thinking of the Founders. Students have the opportunity to consider and reflect on the concepts of state of nature, natural rights, consent of the governed, social contracts, and the purpose of government.

Lesson 3 explains what the Founders learned about government from the Romans, what they saw as the advantages and disadvantages of republican government, and how they adapted republican government to American life. It introduces the ideas of republican government, common good, and civic virtue.

Lesson 4 introduces constitutional government. Students learn the differences between a constitution, constitutional government, and higher law. Students learn the distinction between a constitutional government and unlimited governments, such as dictatorial or autocratic governments, through an activity based on Sophocles' *Antigone*.

Lesson 5 explains why the Founders feared abuse of power by government. Students learn how the Founders organized our government to prevent this kind of abuse through the separation of powers among branches of government and a system of checks and balances.

UNIT OBJECTIVES

At the conclusion of this unit, students should be able to

- describe characteristics of life in the American colonies during the 1770s
- explain the concepts of natural rights, consent of the governed, and social contracts
- explain the characteristics of republican government
- discuss the role of civic virtue and the concept of common good
- distinguish between constitutional government and autocratic or dictatorial governments
- explain separation of powers and checks and balances, and how they help prevent the abuse of power

UNIT INTRODUCTION

Read the introduction with the class. Introduce the Key Concepts, and tell students that these terms will be explained fully as they go through the lesson. The illustrations throughout the unit are excellent teaching tools for reviewing and reinforcing learning. Use them as you find appropriate.

UNIT PROJECT (OPTIONAL)

Ask your students to write the Key Concepts in their notebooks and write definitions based on their current knowledge. Students can change and add to these initial definitions as the unit progresses.

unit**One**

KEY CONCEPTS

checks and balances

civic virtue

common good

consent of the governed

constitution

constitutional government

natural rights

purpose of government

republican government

separation of powers

social contract

In the spring and summer of 1787, fifty-five men met in Philadelphia. These men knew a great deal about government. They wrote our Constitution. They and many other Americans gained their knowledge by reading and discussing books about history and political philosophy. Political philosophy is the study of basic ideas of government.

Americans also knew about government from their own experience. Many of the men who met in Philadelphia had been leaders in the American colonies when they were ruled by Great Britain. Many were leaders in the new state governments formed after the American Revolution.

The men who wrote the Constitution used their knowledge and experience to create the best kind of government they could. An understanding of their knowledge and experience will give you some insight into why they created the kind of government we have today. It will also help you discover and appreciate the most important ideas in our Constitution.

What were the British colonies in America like in the 1770s?

LESSON PURPOSE

People living in the American colonies in the 1770s were in many ways quite different from the people living in Europe. The colonists brought British laws and customs to America—but they were developing their own way of life as well.

When you finish this lesson, you should be able to explain how the average person in the American colonies lived in the 1770s. You should also be able to explain how life in the colonies influenced people's ideas about good government.

OVERVIEW

This lesson is designed to introduce students to the people living in the British colonies in North America during the 1770s. Students consider the ways in which the British colonists, ruled by King George III, differed from Europeans in how they lived and thought. Students examine colonial life and the social, political, and economic opportunities available to the colonists. The lesson concludes with a brief introduction to the Founders.

OBJECTIVES

At the conclusion of this lesson, students should be able to

- describe who the colonists were and how they lived in the British colonies in America
- describe who the original inhabitants of the American continent were and how they lived
- explain the colonists' ideas about government and how the way they lived influenced their ideas
- name some of the Founders and explain what they did

MATERIALS

- map of the United States
- globe or map of the world

TEACHING PROCEDURES

INTRODUCTORY ACTIVITY

Have students read the Lesson Purpose and consider the objectives of the lesson. Emphasize that the original inhabitants of America had lived there for thousands of years. Explain that there were colonies in America ruled by other countries.

Write the Terms to Understand on the board or use a vocabulary-building activity. One alternative exercise is to assign one of the terms to small groups of students or to students paired with partners. Ask students to think about each

(continued next page)

word and write a definition from their current knowledge. Have them share their definition with the class. Ask students if they can add any ideas to each definition as it is presented. After all the words have been defined, ask each group to look up their word in the Glossary at the back of the text and in the dictionary. Have them add additional ideas to their original definition. You may wish to use chart paper or strips of paper for the definitions.

Reading and discussion sections. Assign individual students to read each section aloud or have the whole class read a section. You may wish to follow a section with questions to stimulate discussion and comprehension. Provide students with an opportunity, individually or in small groups, to speculate using "what do you think?"-type questions. Accept reasonable responses to questions of this nature.

READING, DISCUSSION, AND MAP ACTIVITIES

Why study the British colonies in North America?

After reading the section, ask the class to look at a map of the world and locate Europe and North America. Identify Great Britain, France, Spain, and the Netherlands. Point out that the American colonies were more than 3,000 miles away across the Atlantic Ocean. Ask students to consider the following questions:

- What do you think it would be like to live in a colony ruled by another country?

  Some students may be from countries that were recent colonies of another national power. They may be willing to share anecdotes. Accept any reasonable answer.

- Would you like to live under the rule of a king or queen? Why or why not?

  Because the powers of a monarch have not been explained, allow students to speculate on the pluses and minuses of such a system.

- Can you give some examples of people and institutions that make up government?

  Examples include governors, the president, senators and representatives, judges, school districts, local and county officials, government agencies, etc.

TERMS TO UNDERSTAND

Founders
government
indentured servants
self-sufficient
subject

Why study the British colonies in North America?

We begin our study of the U.S. Constitution by looking back in history. The period is the 1770s. By that time, there had been European colonies established in North America for more than 150 years. Nations that had set up colonies in America included France, Great Britain, the Netherlands, and Spain.

Our study will focus on the British colonies. It was these thirteen colonies that became the United States of America.

By the 1770s, the British colonies along the eastern coast of North America were well established. The British colonists were subjects of Great Britain. Being a **subject** in this case means being under the rule of a monarch. In 1770, King George III was the ruler of Great Britain. Our nation did not yet exist.

Learning about how the people lived in the British colonies can help us to understand why they developed their ideas about government. When we talk about **government** we mean the people and institutions with authority to make and enforce the laws and manage

What did it mean to the colonists to be subjects of King George III?

disputes about laws. People living in the 1770s in the British colonies held certain beliefs about good government that still affect our lives today.

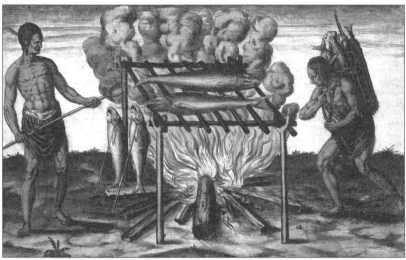

What was life like for American Indians along the eastern coast of North America?

How did American Indians live before the Europeans came?

The Europeans were newcomers to North America. Hundreds of different groups of Native American people had inhabited the continent for thousands of years. Along the eastern seacoast, where the British colonists settled, the native Indian people lived in well-organized tribes. They are known as the Eastern Woodland tribes. They lived by fishing, hunting, gathering wild plants, and tending small crops of corn.

The eastern tribes maintained loose political ties among themselves. In some cases, entire tribes formed leagues so that they could come together to discuss common problems. The best known league was the Iroquois League.

The Iroquois League was made up of five tribes that lived in what today is the state of New York.

Where did the British colonists settle?

The British colonies in America occupied a large area of land. The colonies stretched twelve hundred miles along the coast of the Atlantic Ocean and ran two hundred miles inland. Between the settled area and the Mississippi River lay a vast, forested country. Few Europeans had explored beyond the area of settlement. The nations of Europe were small in area compared to America. Great Britain was only slightly larger than the colony of New York.

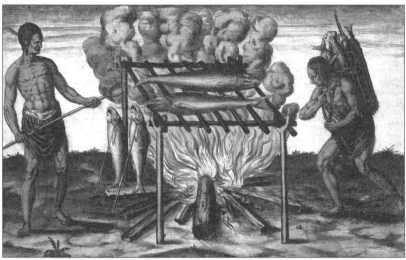

How did American Indians live before the Europeans came?

You may want to draw from students' previous studies of American Indians by asking them what they know about the American Indians in the East and how they interacted with the colonists. The illustration depicting Indians suggests the lifestyle of the tribe.

Some possible responses to the caption might include the following:

- *Some tribes were accepting and welcoming of the new colonists.*
- *They had important leaders who were respected and admired by members of the tribe.*
- *They had well-designed villages and towns and clearly established cultural and social norms.*

Ask students to do some research individually or in small groups in order to answer the following question. You may want to use a Venn diagram or a chart with columns labeled "similarities" and "differences."

- What were the differences between how the Indians lived and how the colonists lived?

  Indians lived in teepees or lodges and were organized into small tribes. They lived by fishing, hunting, gathering wild plants, and tending small crops of corn. Their customs, religions, and clothing were different from those of the colonists.

Where did the British colonists settle?

After reading this section use a map of the United States to have students identify the area occupied by the colonists. Then return to the map of the world and point out Europe again. Ask students to identify Great Britain, France, Spain, and the Netherlands and compare the sizes of these countries with the area the colonists inhabited. Finally, have them look at the area beyond the settlements and the Mississippi River. Help them grasp the difference in size between the population of four million people living in the colonies in 1790 and the population of more than 300 million people living in the United States today.

How did people in the colonies earn a living?

Have students read this section and discuss how their lives are different from the lives of the colonists during the 1770s. Students should not forget the contributions of indentured servants and enslaved people in the colonies. Have students complete one of the following activities:

- Divide the class into groups of four or five students. One group will pretend to be journalists working for a colonial newspaper. The remaining groups will create schedules describing a typical day on a farm in the New England colonies, on a plantation in the South, or of a person working in Boston, New York, or Philadelphia. The journalists will develop questions for the colonists and interview them in front of the entire class.

- Divide the class into groups of four or five students and ask each group to create a poster comparing a typical day in the life of a person today to a typical day in the life of a person in one of the following settings in colonial America: a small Northern farm, a Southern plantation, or a Northern city.

- Ask students to explain why they would or would not like to live in the colonies.

Although the land was expansive, there were few people living on it. In 1790, the population of the colonies was almost 4 million, compared with more than 300 million people living in the United States today.

How did people in the colonies earn a living?

Boston, New York, and Philadelphia were the largest cities in the colonies. Each had a population of more than 25,000 people. Most people in cities or towns earned their living by working in professions, trades, crafts, or small factories.

Most colonists did not live in cities. They lived in small communities or villages or on farms. Ninety percent of the colonists were farmers. A typical farm was between 90 and 160 acres. Farm size varied from the small 30-acre plot of the poorest New England farmers to giant Southern plantations with thousands of acres. Not all colonists were independent farmers. Some were hired laborers or craftspeople working on the larger farms.

Outside the cities and small communities, people in the colonies might live as far as ten miles from their nearest neighbor. As a result, they had to develop the knowledge and skills to provide for themselves in order to survive.

The people became self-sufficient. **Self-sufficient** means that people had to provide for their own needs. Not only did the colonists grow their own food,

How was life on a small, Northern farm different from life on a large, Southern plantation?

they also wove cloth to make their own clothing. They made their own medicines, built their own homes and barns, and made their furniture and tools. Colonists took the surplus produce from their farms and traded it for goods they could not make.

Although families worked independently, they traded among their neighbors and helped each other. Neighbors got together to build houses and barns. People rarely traveled more than fifty miles from their homes.

A farm family frequently included a hired laborer or an indentured servant. **Indentured servants** were men and women who sold their labor in exchange for the cost of the trip from Europe to the colonies. Farm families often relied on the labor of slaves, especially in the South.

The typical colonial family in the 1770s worked hard and had the highest standard of living in the world. The land was fertile and crops grew well. As a result, the colonists had diets rich in protein and tended to be healthier than people in Europe.

The colonists were also better educated than most Europeans. In fact, a greater percentage of people in the colonies were able to read and write than in any European nation. The most popular publications, other than the Bible, were newspapers. Four times as many newspapers were published in the colonies than in France.

While most colonists lived fairly well, this was not true of everyone. One-fifth of the population was held in slavery. The slaves were people who were brought as laborers to the colonies from different regions of Africa. Slavery was permitted in all the colonies, North and South. Slavery continued to be practiced until 1865.

How were the people living in the colonies different from one another?

Most colonists were descended from British or Irish settlers. Therefore, most people in the colonies spoke English. Some colonists did not come from English-speaking countries, however. Settlers came from France, Germany, the Netherlands, Spain, Sweden and other countries. All brought with them their own customs and ideas about government and rights.

The colonists also held different religious beliefs. There were many different groups of Protestants; there also were Catholics and Jews. Compared to most European nations of the time, the population of the colonies was diverse.

What contributions have people from other nations brought to the United States?

How were the people living in the colonies different from one another?

Have students read this section and discuss the ideas presented. They may break into small groups to answer the following questions:

- How does the diversity of people living in the colonies during the 1770s compare to the diversity of people living in the United States today?

  Emigrants to the colonies came mostly from Great Britain, Ireland, and other western European countries. Africans came as slaves. The native Indians already lived in America and had different customs, religions, and ways of life. Contemporary immigrants come from all over the world and bring with them a wide variety of languages and customs. People come to the United States today for many of the same reasons as the colonists— for better economic opportunities and freedom from tyranny.

- What contributions to American culture were made by enslaved people from Africa?

  Accept reasonable responses; some research may be helpful.

- Can you identify some of the groups living in America now that were not represented in the colonies in the 1770s and some of the ideas and customs they have brought with them?

  Accept reasonable responses; some research may be helpful.

IDEAS FOR DISCUSSION

**How did this colonial farmer compare
life in America with life in Great Britain?**

Assign this discussion section to the class. You may want students to read
different paragraphs aloud. Some students may need help with the vocabulary.
After students spend some time discussing the content of the narrative, have
them, individually or in small groups, respond to the questions at the end.

1. What was it that Crèvecoeur
   liked about life in the colonies?

   *There was no aristocracy that had extensive wealth at the expense
   of the majority of the population. It was possible to make a good living
   by working the land. Even the most modest home in the colonies was
   better than what many people had in Europe. There was much more
   freedom in America and government did not interfere extensively
   in everyday life.*

2. What rights did he enjoy?

   *Crèvecoeur was free to live without unreasonable interference
   from government because laws were fair and government did not
   abuse its authority. He had a right to make a living and increase
   his financial and social status.*

How did this colonial farmer compare life in America with life in Great Britain?

In the 1700s a French colonist who
settled in New York wrote a book that
contained a series of letters from a
fictional Pennsylvania farmer to his
friend in Great Britain. J. Hector
St. John was the pen name that Jean
de Crèvecoeur used for his book. The
letters describe Crèvecoeur's views
about life in America. Some sections
of these letters follow. Read them and
discuss the questions at the end.

*Behold, Sir, a humble American Planter…
addressing you from the farther side
of the Atlantic….*

*[The English traveler to America] is
arrived on a new continent; a modern
society… different from what he had
hitherto seen. It is not composed, as in
Europe, of great lords who possess everything and of a herd of people who have
nothing. Here are no aristocratical families,
no courts, no kings…. The rich and the poor
are not so far removed from each other as
they are in Europe. Some few towns
excepted, we are all tillers of the earth….
[Here we are] united by the silken bands
of mild government, all respecting the
laws, without dreading their power,
because they are equitable [fair].*

*[Here the traveler] views not the
hostile castle, and the haughty mansion,
contrasted with the clay-built hut and
miserable cabin, where cattle and men*

help to keep each other warm, and dwell in meanness [humility], smoke, and indigence [poverty].... The meanest [most humble] of our log-houses is a dry and comfortable habitation.

Lawyer or merchant are the fairest titles our towns afford.... We have no princes, for whom we toil, starve, and bleed: we are the most perfect society now existing in the world. Here man is free; as he ought to be....

Can a wretch...call England or any other kingdom his country? A country that had no bread for him, whose fields procured him no harvest, who met with nothing but the frowns of the rich, the severity of the laws, with jails and punishments; who owned not a single foot of the extensive surface of the planet? No! urged by a variety of motives here they came. Everything has tended to regenerate them; new laws, a new mode of living, a new social system....

Formerly they were not numbered in any civil lists of their country, except in those of the poor; here they rank as citizens.

❶ What was it that Crèvecoeur liked about life in the colonies?

❷ What rights did he enjoy?

❸ Given what you know of Crèvecoeur's experiences, explain why he would or would not favor laws that

- guarantee each individual the right to own property

- limit an individual's right to buy and sell goods to anyone he or she chooses

- give people certain rights because they are wealthy or from a certain family background or group

❹ How might people in Great Britain react to Crèvecoeur's comparisons of life in America and life in Europe? Explain.

3. Given what you know of Crèvecoeur's experiences, explain why he would or would not favor laws that

- guarantee each individual the right to own property

   He would favor this law because it would give more people opportunities to gain financial independence.

- limit an individual's right to buy and sell goods to anyone he or she chooses

   He would probably not favor this law since it would interfere with his sense of freedom and his ability to make his own decisions about buying and selling goods.

- give people certain rights because they are wealthy or from a certain family background or group

   He would not be in favor of this law. Crèvecoeur's narrative criticizes the social system of Europe and extols the virtues of the social system of the colonies. Giving a class of people special rights would eliminate the opportunity of the individual to make meaningful decisions about his or her own life. People would not be free under this arrangement.

4. How might people in Great Britain react to Crèvecoeur's comparisons of life in America and life in Europe? Explain.

   The British government and the aristocracy may not have liked the comparisons because Crèvecoeur clearly states that the social structure in Great Britain is unfair, abusive, and gives few rights to ordinary citizens. The poor may have felt envious of Americans and may have had a greater desire to emigrate to the colonies.

Reading and discussion

Why were class differences not important in the colonies? Whose opportunities were limited?

Divide the class into small groups or ask students to choose partners. Have students read these sections in their groups. After recalling how people in the colonies were different from each other, the role of class differences in the colonies, and limitations to opportunities, ask students to consider the following questions:

- Why do you think colonial men of little wealth were often able to become wealthy and were elected to government positions?

  There were more opportunities for men in the colonies than for men in Europe. There was an abundance of fertile land for growing crops. There was work for everyone. There was no titled nobility in America. Working hard was an important value for which one could be financially rewarded.

- Do you think this can still happen today?

  Accept any reasonable response.

- Identify groups that did not share these advantages.

  Native Americans, blacks, white men without property, and women.

Why were class differences not important in the colonies?

The colonies were not divided into a few rich people and a large mass of poor people as in most of Europe. In the colonies, there was no royalty and no titled nobility.

The difference between wealthy and poor people was less important in colonial society. A poor person could become wealthy by using knowledge, skills, and opportunities. In many cases, a man who was not part of the wealthy class could be elected to a government position.

Whose opportunities were limited?

Not all people shared the same opportunities to gain wealth or to become leaders. Usually, only adult white males who owned property could vote. In most colonies, a person had to own fifty acres of land to be qualified to vote. But land was easily available. Therefore, more people in the colonies had the right to vote than in any other country of that time.

Native Americans, blacks, white men without property, and women were typically not allowed to vote or hold office. Women usually were not allowed to own property. Under the law, married couples were considered one person and the husband controlled the property.

What does this picture tell you about the right to vote in colonial America?

What rights did the colonists value?

Since most colonists were self-sufficient, they valued their freedom highly. The people in the colonies thought that their society was superior to the corrupt societies of Europe. Colonists considered themselves to be virtuous, hardworking, simple people.

As subjects of Great Britain, the colonists enjoyed the rights included in the British constitution. You will learn about these rights in Lesson 6. Many colonial governments also protected the rights of the colonists. For example, the Massachusetts Body of Liberties of 1641 included the right to trial by jury, free elections, and the right of free men to own property. The state of Pennsylvania guaranteed freedom of belief or conscience.

In the years before the American Revolution, the colonists were very sensitive to any attempts by the British government to limit their rights. After the Revolution, Americans were concerned with protecting the rights they had just fought for.

John Adams, one of our nation's Founders, once said that "revolution was in the minds and hearts of the people before Lexington and Concord." What does this statement mean?

Who were the Founders?

Throughout this text, we refer to a group of people as the Founders. The **Founders** were the political leaders of the colonies. They had developed their own ideas about what might be the best kind of government. These ideas were formed from their own experiences and their studies of governments of the past. The Founders led the fight to free the American colonies from British rule. The Founders helped to create the state governments, and their ideas influenced the writing of the Constitution. Some of the Founders' names that you might recognize include John and Abigail Adams, Benjamin Franklin, Patrick Henry, Thomas Jefferson, Mercy Otis Warren, and George Washington.

What rights did the colonists value?
Who were the Founders?

Have students read these sections, ensuring that they understand what is meant by *freedom of belief or conscience*, which is defined in the glossary. Ask students why self-sufficient people would value freedom more than would people who are ruled by an autocratic government.

 see next student page

Lesson review

The questions in the student book are intended to assess learning and reinforce knowledge through discussion. The questions are directly related to the lesson objectives. You may wish to include additional questions developed by yourself or by students.

1. In what ways were people's lives in the British colonies of the 1770s different from those of people living in Europe?

   Ninety percent of colonists were farmers. Some owned farms and others worked as laborers or craftspeople. The colonists often lived long distances from their nearest neighbors. This required that they learn the skills necessary to provide for their own needs. However, colonists traded among neighbors and helped each other. Colonists worked hard and had the highest standard of living in the world. They were also better educated than most Europeans. Some colonists, especially slaves, white men who did not own property, and women, did not have the same opportunities or liberties as other colonists.

2. What diversity of people and ideas existed in the British colonies in the 1770s?

   Although most colonists were from Great Britain or Ireland, others came from France, Germany, the Netherlands, Spain, Sweden, and other countries. Some did not speak English. All brought with them customs from their cultures and their own religious beliefs. Some colonists were Catholics, some were Protestants, and some were Jews. Indian tribes lived in America long before the arrival of Europeans. They had well-established cultures and customs.

3. What difference did gender, race, and wealth make to people in colonial society?

The native Indian people and African slaves added to the diversity of the colonies. There was no European-style royalty and no titled nobility in the colonies. The differences between rich and poor people were less important because a poor person could change his financial status by using his knowledge and skills and by taking advantage of available opportunities. Women usually were not allowed to own property; couples were considered to be one person with the husband in control of the property. Only white male property owners were permitted to vote.

4. What rights did the colonists value?

The colonists valued the rights guaranteed by some colonial governments, such as the right to trial by jury, free elections, the right of free men to own property, and freedom of belief or conscience.

5. Who were the Founders?

The Founders were the political leaders of the colonies. They led the fight to free the American colonies from British rule. They helped create the state governments. Their ideas influenced the writing of the Constitution.

ACTIVITIES

The suggested activities are intended to extend and apply learning outside the classroom. You may wish to have students complete one or more of the activities. Have them share their results with the class.

LESSON REVIEW

❶ In what ways were people's lives in the British colonies of the 1770s different from those of people living in Europe?

❷ What diversity of people and ideas existed in the British colonies in the 1770s?

❸ What difference did gender, race, and wealth make to people in colonial society?

❹ What rights did the colonists value?

❺ Who were the Founders?

ACTIVITIES

❶ Go to your library or search the Internet. Find information about what life in the colonies was like for one of the following groups:

- children and adolescents
- indentured servants
- Native Americans
- people held in slavery
- women

❷ The British colonies in America are generally divided into three regions: the New England Colonies, the Middle Colonies, and the Southern Colonies. Learn more about what life was like in each region. Write a brief summary for your class.

❸ On an outline map of the United States, mark the British, French, and Spanish colonies with different colors. What states are these colonies now?

Why do we need government?

2

LESSON PURPOSE

Our form of government is based on a set of ideas. These ideas establish what the purpose of government should be and what kind of government is best. This lesson introduces you to some of the basic ideas that were of great importance to the Founders. In this lesson you will learn about the idea of natural rights.

When you finish this lesson, you should be able to explain what the Founders believed to be the natural rights of human beings. You should also be able to explain why the Founders believed that the people need a government, and how people create governments.

Overview

This lesson introduces the basic concepts of the natural rights philosophy. After being introduced to the concept of natural rights, students are asked to speculate on what might be the benefits and problems of living in a state of nature, a situation in which there are no laws or government. They compare their ideas about such a situation with those of the English philosopher John Locke. They learn Locke's ideas about social contracts, consent of the governed, and the idea that the purpose of government is to protect the natural rights of the individual.

Objectives

At the conclusion of the lesson, students should be able to

* explain the following terms from natural rights philosophy: natural rights, state of nature, consent, and social contract
* explain what the Founders believed to be the natural rights of human beings
* explain why people need a government
* explain how people create governments
* explain how government and laws can protect natural rights

TEACHING PROCEDURES

Introductory activity

Have students read the Lesson Purpose section and consider the objectives of the lesson. Write the Terms to Understand on the board or use a vocabulary-building activity of your choice. Students should look for these terms as they study the lesson. The definitions for these words are in the Glossary at the end of the student text.

READING AND DISCUSSION

How did the ideas of John Locke influence the Founders?

Have students read the section on pages 14 and 16, and discuss the questions John Locke pondered when considering the idea of a state of nature. Complete the discussion activity on page 15.

IDEAS FOR DISCUSSION

What might life be like in a state of nature?

Have students engage in this discussion activity before they read "What were Locke's ideas about natural rights?" on page 16. Encourage them to explore their own ideas first.

Read this section with the class and then organize students into small groups or ask students to choose partners. Each group member should write down her or his group's responses and be ready to share one of the ideas with the rest of the class. This will ensure that all members of the group will focus on the group discussion and will prepare to share at least one idea. After the groups share their ideas, have individual students share experiences about a problem arising because there were either no rules or there were no people to enforce the rules.

1. What might be some advantages and disadvantages of living in a state of nature?

    Advantages might include the following: you could do whatever you wanted to do—no one could tell you when to go to bed, when to go to school, or what to study; you could take whatever you wanted from someone else because there would be no rules to prevent you from doing so. Disadvantages might include the following: you would not feel secure because anyone could take things from you, beat you up, or even kill you; someone could take all the food and water for himself and leave you without enough to live on.

TERMS TO UNDERSTAND

consent
natural rights
purpose of government
social contract
state of nature

How did the ideas of John Locke influence the Founders?

The Founders were students of history and philosophy. They studied books, read newspapers, and listened to sermons in church. The Founders discussed and exchanged ideas with each other and with other people.

One philosopher whose writings influenced the thinking of the Founders was John Locke. John Locke was a well-known English philosopher. He lived from 1632 to 1704. Locke published a book called *Two Treatises of Government* in 1689. In that book Locke explained his ideas about natural rights. Locke's book was widely read and discussed in the American colonies. Many of the Founders' ideas about government were based on Locke's philosophy.

John Locke arrived at his ideas by imagining what life might be like if people were living in a **state of nature**. By this, Locke did not mean necessarily that people lived in the wilderness. Locke simply saw a state of nature as a condition in which no governments or laws existed at all.

What did John Locke mean by a state of nature?

14

IDEAS FOR DISCUSSION

What might life be like in a state of nature?

It is now your turn to be a philosopher like John Locke. First, imagine that you and all the students in your school are living in a state of nature. You have plenty of food and other resources to maintain life and to live well. But there is no government and there are no laws or rules that you have to follow. There is no one to tell you what to do and no one to protect you.

With your partner or group discuss the following questions about your rights in a state of nature. Be prepared to share your ideas with your class. Finally, compare your ideas with those of John Locke—after you read the section "What were Locke's ideas about natural rights?"

❶ What might be some advantages and disadvantages of living in a state of nature?

❷ What rights, if any, might you expect to have in a state of nature?

❸ What might people who are stronger or smarter than others try to do? Why?

❹ What might people who are weaker or less skilled than others try to do? Why?

❺ What might life be like for everyone living in a state of nature?

❻ Would anyone have the right to govern you? Would you have a right to govern anyone else? Why?

❼ What are some things the people could do to protect their lives, liberty, or property?

2. What rights, if any, might you expect to have in a state of nature?

    You would have the right to do whatever you wanted to do until someone stopped you from doing it. In reality, your rights would not be secure.

3. What might people who are stronger or smarter than others try to do? Why?

    People could take things from you or cause you bodily harm. There could be a shortage of food because stronger people could horde and hide it. Someone bigger and stronger or smarter might force you to do something you did not want to do. Smarter people might trick you into giving up your property or doing what they want you to do. On the other hand, smarter people might consider developing rules that would benefit the entire community.

4. What might people who are weaker or less skilled than others try to do? Why?

    Weaker or less skilled people might simply agree out of fear to do whatever others commanded. They might band together with others to form larger groups for mutual protection. This would allow them to negotiate and possibly retaliate against other groups and stronger people.

5. What might life be like for everyone living in a state of nature?

    Life might be good for the strong and bad for the weak if a few people controlled everyone else and were able to keep that control. However, life would be unpredictable because security and liberty could not be guaranteed.

6. Would anyone have the right to govern you? Would you have a right to govern anyone else? Why?

    No one would have the right to govern you unless you freely gave them that right through a social contract. Similarly, you would not have the right to govern anyone else unless you were freely given that right.

7. What are some things the people could do to protect their lives, liberty, or property?

    People could form a government to establish rules and laws designed to benefit the common good. These laws would protect life, liberty, and property.

READING, DISCUSSION, AND RESEARCH

What were Locke's ideas about natural rights?

Have students read the section on pages 16–17, and ask them to identify the ideas in the Declaration of Independence that correlate with the ideas of John Locke. The full text of the Declaration of Independence is in the Reference section on page 276.

Possible responses include "all Men are created equal," "endowed by their Creator with certain unalienable Rights," "Life, Liberty and the pursuit of Happiness," and "to secure these Rights, Governments are instituted among Men."

By imagining life in a state of nature, Locke was able to answer some important questions like these:

* What is human nature? For example, are all people mainly interested in their own welfare, or do they tend to care for the good of others?

* What should be the main purpose of government?

* How do people who run government get the right to govern?

* What kinds of government should people support and obey?

* What kinds of government should people resist?

The Founders discussed and debated John Locke's answers to these questions. The ideas of Locke were used in the Declaration of Independence to explain why Americans were opposed to British rule in the colonies. After winning the Revolutionary War, the Founders used most of the same ideas to write their state constitutions. The ideas of the natural rights philosophy also are important to the kind of government that we have today.

What were Locke's ideas about natural rights?

John Locke believed that through reasoning we can determine what rights people would have in a state of nature.

Locke reasoned that in a state of nature all people seek to have the following rights:

* **Life** People want to survive. People want to be as safe as possible from threats to their lives.

* **Liberty** People want to be as free as possible. People want to be able to make their own decisions and to live as they please.

* **Property** People want to own the things that are necessary to survive, such as food, houses, tools, or land. People want the freedom to work and to gain economic benefits.

Locke said that the rights to life, liberty, and property are **natural rights**. These rights are a part of the law of nature. This means that all people have the rights to life, liberty, and property just because they are human beings.

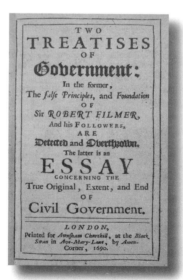

What were Locke's ideas about natural rights?

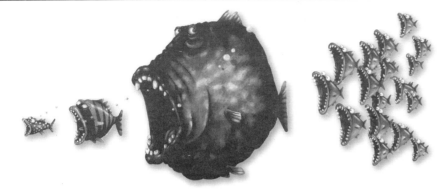

How does this illustration demonstrate what might happen in a state of nature?

What did John Locke say might happen in a state of nature?

Assign this reading to the class and allow time for discussion. Have students compare their responses from the Ideas for Discussion activity on page 15 with Locke's ideas. Locke believed that most people were reasonable and good and respected the rights of others. Yet people are also driven by self-interest. Some people even abuse others who are weaker or less skilled. Ask students to consider current events and identify situations where it appears that some people have abused others by taking away their rights of life, liberty, and property.

The Founders believed that such rights as those to life, liberty, and property are not man-made. Instead, our rights are based on the laws of nature, which were made by God. The Declaration of Independence, for example, speaks of "the Laws of Nature and of Nature's God." It says that people are "endowed by their Creator" with certain basic rights and that no one may take away these rights.

What did John Locke say might happen in a state of nature?

❶ Locke believed that most people are reasonable and good. Most people respect the rights of others because their conscience tells them that they have a duty to do so. But people are also driven by their self-interest. A few humans are not so reasonable and good. Sometimes people who are stronger or more skilled abuse those who are weaker or less skilled.

❷ Locke believed that in a state of nature, people protect their natural rights by using their own strength and skill. People who are weaker or less skilled would find it very hard to protect their rights. Instead, weaker people would try to protect their rights by joining together against the strong.

❸ Locke believed that in a state of nature, no one's life, liberty, or property would be safe. People would feel insecure. In a state of nature, there are no governments or laws to protect life, liberty, or property. This is why people agreed to form governments. According to Locke, governments do not exist until people create them.

❹ Locke believed that in a state of nature, no one would have the right to govern you, and you would not have the right to govern anyone else. According to Locke, there is only one way that people get the right to govern anyone else: the people to be governed must give their consent. **Consent** means to approve of something or allow something to take place. If the people have not given their consent to create a government, there is no legitimate government. In other words, the power of legitimate government comes from the consent of the people.

Why do people agree to form a social contract?

Have the class read this section and discuss the ideas about the purpose of government that influenced the Founders. Make sure that students grasp the significance of social contracts, the meaning of consent, and the relationship between the two ideas. Engage students in a discussion about how the concepts of social contracts and consent can be applied in the classroom and in their lives. Ask them to identify an example of a social contract in their own lives.

 see next student page

IDEAS FOR DISCUSSION

What rights do you think all people should have?

Finish the lesson with a discussion of rights.
Organize students into groups of three to five.

Ask each group to develop answers to the three questions in the activity and to write the answers on chart paper. Each group should select a recorder to do the writing and a reporter to report the group's responses to the rest of the class. Each group should post its chart on the wall.

As students report their ideas, you may wish to keep a tally of the rights put forth as "rights all people should have." After all groups have reported, compare the lists of the various groups. Ask students to state the similarities and differences among the groups' lists of rights—how many, if any, groups chose the same right as most important?

As a final activity, ask students to underline or highlight words and ideas from their lists that are similar to the ideas of Locke and the Founders.

1. List five rights that you think all people in our nation should have. Why do you think that it is important that all people should have these rights?
   Some things they might list are the following: to go where you want to go; to say, think, and do what you want; to choose your friends; to listen to

Why do people agree to form a social contract?

Although people agreed that certain natural rights existed, they worried about how those rights could be protected. In a state of nature, people might feel free to do anything they want to do. Their rights would not be protected, however, and that would make them feel insecure.

For John Locke and other natural rights philosophers, the great problem was to find a way to protect each person's natural rights so that everyone could enjoy them and live at peace with one another. Locke said that the best way to solve this problem is for each individual to agree with others to create and live under a government and give that government the power to make and enforce laws. Locke called this kind of agreement a **social contract**.

As in all contracts, to get something you must give up something. In a social contract everyone promises to give up the absolute right to do anything she or he wants to do. Absolute means without any limits. In return, everyone receives the security that can be provided by a government. Each person consents to obey the limits placed upon her or him by the laws created by the government. Everyone gains the security of knowing that their rights to life, liberty, and property are protected.

Government, then, is the better alternative to a state of nature, which would be imperfect because some people might not respect the rights of others. According to Locke, the main **purpose of government** is to protect those natural rights that the individual cannot effectively protect in a state of nature.

In a later lesson, you will study the Declaration of Independence. You will see how the Founders included all the ideas that you have studied in this lesson. You will also learn to examine questions about what kind of government the people should support and obey and what kind they should resist.

How might individuals protect their natural rights in a state of nature?

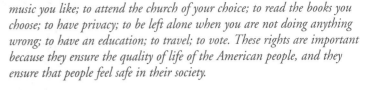

What rights do you think all people should have?

Most people would agree that there are certain rights all people should have. For example, you probably agree that everyone has the right to be protected from robbers and murderers. You probably also agree that a person's right to vote should be protected. Most people in the United States share the belief that everyone should have these rights.

Work with a partner or in a group of three students. Together answer the questions that follow. Be prepared to share your ideas with the class.

❶ List five rights that you think all people in our nation should have. Why do you think that it is important that all people should have these rights?

❷ Which of the rights on your list seem to be the most important? Arrange the rights you listed in the order of their importance. Explain why you ranked the rights on your list in this order.

❸ What might you do in order to ensure that these rights are protected?

In a state of nature, how might one's life, liberty, or property be protected?

music you like; to attend the church of your choice; to read the books you choose; to have privacy; to be left alone when you are not doing anything wrong; to have an education; to travel; to vote. These rights are important because they ensure the quality of life of the American people, and they ensure that people feel safe in their society.

2. Which of the rights on your list seem to be the most important? Arrange the rights you listed in the order of their importance. Explain why you ranked the rights on your list in this order.
   Accept reasonable responses.

3. What might you do in order to ensure that these rights are protected?
   Some responses might involve monitoring and requiring accountability of government, the police force, and the media; voting; becoming knowledgeable about their rights (studying the Constitution); serving on juries; serving in the military; etc. Accept reasonable responses.

 see next student page

LESSON REVIEW

The questions in the student book are intended to assess learning and to reinforce knowledge through discussion. The questions are directly related to the lesson objectives. You may wish to include additional questions developed by yourself or by your students.

1. What are natural rights? How do people get their natural rights?
   Natural rights are rights that all people have just by being human beings. These rights are a part of the laws of nature. Examples of natural rights are the right to life—the right to live without being injured or killed by others; the right to liberty—the right to think, believe, and read what you want and to speak freely; and the right to property—the right to own things.

2. What might life be like for people living in a state of nature? Explain.
   Life would unpredictable and insecure because there would be no laws to protect you or to ensure that you got your fair share of the available resources and opportunities.

(continued next page)

3. Where does government get its right to govern, according to the natural rights philosophy?

Government gets its right to govern from the people. Government is legitimate only when it is formed with the consent of the people.

4. What is a social contract?

A social contract is an agreement between the people and the government. With a social contract, the people agree to give up the absolute right to do whatever they want in order to gain the government's protection of their rights to life, liberty, and property.

5. What is the main purpose of government according to John Locke?

The purpose of government is to protect those natural rights that could not be protected in a state of nature.

ACTIVITIES

The suggested activities are intended to extend and apply learning outside the classroom. You may wish to have students complete one or more of the activities. Have them share their results with the class.

ENRICHMENT ACTIVITY

Have students keep a list of the times they see people's rights being violated during a one-week period. This might include situations they see at school, on television, in newspapers, or in the community. Ask your students to identify the rights involved and explain why they believe those rights were violated.

LESSON REVIEW

❶ What are natural rights? How do people get their natural rights?

❷ What might life be like for people living in a state of nature? Explain.

❸ Where does government get its right to govern, according to the natural rights philosophy?

❹ What is a social contract?

❺ What is the main purpose of government according to John Locke?

ACTIVITIES

❶ In this lesson you learned about the social contract. Most passengers aboard the *Mayflower* signed the Mayflower Compact in 1620, before the ship landed in Plymouth. Read the Mayflower Compact below. Write a brief essay explaining how the Mayflower Compact is an example of a social contract.

Having undertaken, for the glory of God, and advancement of the Christian Faith and Honour of our King and Country, a Voyage to plant the First Colony in the Northern Parts of Virginia, do by these presents solemnly and mutually in the presence of God and of one another, Covenant and Combine ourselves together into a Civil Body Politic, for our better ordering and preservation and further-ance of the ends aforesaid; and by virtue hereof, to enact, constitute, and frame such just and equal Laws, Ordinances, Acts, Constitutions, and Offices, from time to time, as shall be thought most meet and convenient for the general good of the Colony, unto which we promise all due submission and obedience.

❷ Draw a cartoon that illustrates what life might be like in a state of nature. Use your cartoon to illustrate why we need government.

❸ Read *Lord of the Flies* by William Golding. It is a novel about what happened when a group of young boys found themselves in a situation where there were no laws and no government. Share the story with your class. Does this story support Locke's ideas? If so, which ones?

❹ Write a short story that tells how the rights to life, liberty, and property apply to you and your family. Share your story with the class.

What is republican government?

LESSON PURPOSE

This lesson introduces the ideas of republican government, the common good, and civic virtue. These were ideas the Founders learned from studying the government of the ancient Roman Republic. You will learn how these ideas shaped the Founders' thinking about the kind of government they believed to be best.

When you finish this lesson you should be able to explain the ideas of republican government, the common good, and civic virtue.

OVERVIEW

Many of the ideas that influenced the Founders originated during the time of the Roman Republic. This lesson provides an opportunity for students to explore the meaning of republicanism, civic virtue, and the common good as historians have recorded their practice in ancient Rome, and to consider how these ideas influenced the Founders' thinking and behavior.

The lesson begins with a description of the form of government practiced by the Roman Republic and how republican ideas influenced the Founders. This is followed by a section that reveals what the Founders believed were the advantages and disadvantages of republican government. Students then learn how James Madison adapted the idea of republican government to American life and why civic virtue is necessary for a republican government to work. Students are introduced to the Roman citizen Cincinnatus in the Ideas for Discussion section and discover why he is considered a model of civic virtue. The lesson concludes with a description of how the American colonists were taught the value of civic virtue and other values of republican government. Students learn that the Founders' strong beliefs about the virtues of republican government increased their sense that Great Britain was violating these ideals. When the Founders were able to create their own government, they tried to make sure that this government did not violate the people's rights.

OBJECTIVES

At the conclusion of the lesson, students should be able to

- explain the ideas of republican government, the common good, and civic virtue
- state some advantages and disadvantages of republican government
- explain why the Founders thought republican government was the best type of government for the country
- describe how the ideas of republican government were promoted

TEACHING PROCEDURES

INTRODUCTORY ACTIVITY

Have students read the Lesson Purpose section and consider the objectives of the lesson. Write the Terms to Understand on the board or use a vocabulary activity of your own choice. Have students look up the words in the Glossary at the back of the text. Students should look for these words as they study the lesson. Have students, in groups or individually, draw a picture that would depict the meaning of each word or term.

READING AND DISCUSSION

What did the Founders learn about government from the Romans?

Direct students' attention to the illustrations depicting the Roman Senate and the U.S. House of Representatives. Tell students that they will be reading about life during the Roman Republic and explain that the Founders studied this period of history because they believed the government of the Roman Republic was one of the best governments that had ever existed. Draw on students' past learning and discuss what they remember about their studies of ancient Rome. Ask students the following questions:

- Who had the power to govern during the Roman Republic?

  Power was divided between the common people and the aristocrats. The people governed themselves and did not have a king.

- What are the three characteristics of a republican government?

  They are (1) citizens have the power to govern, (2) citizens delegate their power to leaders they elect to represent them and to serve their interests, and (3) citizens and their representatives work cooperatively to promote the common good rather than their own interests.

TERMS TO UNDERSTAND

aristocrats	representative democracy
civic virtue	republic
common good	republican government
delegate	
direct democracy	
factions	
representative	

What did the Founders learn about government from the Romans?

Two thousand years before our own nation began, there was a republic that greatly influenced the ideas of the Founders. A **republic** is a country that has a government in which power is held by the people who elect representatives. Those representatives manage the government for the people, for the sake of the common good.

The government that fascinated the Founders was the Roman Republic, which lasted nearly 500 years, from 509 BC to 27 BC. The capital of the Roman Republic was Rome, located in what today is Italy.

The Founders read what historians and the Romans themselves wrote about the people and government of the Roman Republic. The Founders learned that during the Republic, the Roman people governed themselves without a king. In the Roman Republic, both the common people and the **aristocrats**, or wealthy upper class, shared the power to govern.

The Founders called the government of Rome a republican government. **Republican government** is a type of government in which the

What did the Founders learn about government from the Roman Republic?

- citizens have the power to govern
- citizens **delegate** or entrust their power to leaders they elect to represent them and to serve their interests
- citizens and their representatives work cooperatively to promote the common good rather than their

What are the advantages of a republican government in a large and diverse society?

own interests. The term **common good**, or common welfare, means that which is good for the community as a whole.

What advantages did the Founders see in republican government?

The Founders thought a republican form of government was the best form of government they could create for themselves. They thought that they would have some of the same benefits that the ancient Romans had enjoyed. These are some of the benefits the Founders saw in republican government:

- **Representatives are elected to serve the common good**. A **representative** is a person elected to act and speak for others. The main purpose of republican government is to serve the common good. Representatives should not make laws to serve the interests of one person or one group. The representatives make laws that serve the entire community.

- **Having representatives make the laws is more efficient**. To make good and fair laws, you have to understand every problem well. But most people do not have the time to learn about every problem. Representatives can make laws faster and better because it becomes their responsibility to do so.

- **The people have a say in their government**. By delegating power to their representatives, the people do not give up their voice in government. The people still have to decide who will represent them. The people have to communicate their ideas and the actions they want taken to their representatives.

- **The representatives are responsible to the people**. The people hold their representatives responsible for making making good and fair laws. If the representatives do not make good and fair laws, the people can vote them out of office and select new leaders to represent them.

Reading, discussion, and activity

What advantages did the Founders see in republican government? What were the disadvantages of republican government?

Have students read these sections to themselves. Then have small groups or partners complete a table headed by three columns: "Benefits of a republican system of government," "Why is this a benefit?" and "What might interfere with this benefit?" On the next page, there is an example of what this table might look like and how it might be completed.

 see next student page

Sample

Benefits of a republican system of government	Why is this a benefit?	What might interfere with this benefit?
The people have a say in their government.	1. The people delegate power to their representatives but do not give up power. 2. The people, not someone else, decide who will represent them.	1. The people might fail to communicate their ideas to their representatives. 2. Their representatives might not take the appropriate actions if they do not know what the people want. 3. The community might be too large and the citizens might be too different for people to agree on what they want.

What were the disadvantages of republican government?

The Founders worried about whether republican government would work in the colonies. The Founders saw that republican government as practiced in the Roman Republic had a few disadvantages. These are some of the possible disadvantages:

- Republican government works best in small communities. In small communities, the people know and care for each other and the common good. The colonies, on the other hand, occupied a large territory.

- The people in a republic have to be very much alike. There cannot be a high degree of diversity. The people cannot be very different in their wealth, moral beliefs, or ways of life. In the colonies, however, the people had many different religious beliefs and ways of life.

- People in a large and diverse republic would naturally divide into **factions**, or interest groups. Such interest groups might work against other groups or the people as a whole, rather than work for the common good.

How can the common good be determined in a large and diverse society?

How did the Founders adapt the idea of republican government?

James Madison was one of the most important Founders. We often call him "the Father of the Constitution" because he played such an important role in creating our Constitution. Madison adapted the idea of republican government to the reality of American life.

Madison defined the difference between a direct democracy and republican government in the following ways:

* In a **direct democracy**, the people themselves control government. The people create the laws they need. Direct democracy works best in small communities. As communities grow larger, it becomes difficult for people to make the decisions that are needed for the good of all.

* In a republican government, the people's representatives make the laws and run government. This makes it possible for those in government to administer a much larger area.

Madison believed that America could and should have a republican form of government. Laws would be made and administered by representatives elected by the people. Madison said that members of government should be elected by a large number of the people rather than by a small number or a favored group. Such a government was a democracy in the sense that it received its right to govern from the people as a whole. This kind of government is now called

How did Madison adapt the ideas of republican government to the colonies?

a representative democracy. In a **representative democracy** the people choose leaders to make and administer laws for their country.

Madison also believed that you could organize government in a way that might help to avoid the abuse of power by any one person or faction. You will study these ideas in the next lesson.

How did the Founders adapt the idea of republican government?

Assign this section to the class to read. Draw a table with two column headings: "Direct Democracy" and "Republican Government/Representative Democracy." When students have finished reading this section, ask them to write the characteristics of each type of government in the table under the appropriate heading. Finally, ask students the following questions:

* Why do you think the Founders came to believe so strongly in republican government?

  The Founders had experience with other types of government and did not consider them to be good alternatives to a republican form of government. The colonists wanted and expected political freedom and the right to make decisions about their own lives.

* How do you think the Founders would feel about our government today?

  Accept any reasonable response.

Ideas for discussion

Why should citizens promote the common good?

Read the Ideas for Discussion section with the class. Divide the class into partners or groups of three and ask each group to prepare responses to the five questions that appear at the end of the section. Have each group report their responses to the class. Each group member should be responsible for answering at least one of the questions aloud to the class. Some possible responses to the questions:

1. What is the common good as represented in this story?
   What are the self-interests represented in the story?
   Do you agree with the actions taken by Cincinnatus?
   Why or why not?

   The common good was the need to protect Rome from invaders. Cincinnatus was pursuing his self-interest by working as a farmer when he was asked to become dictator and save Rome. The leaders of Rome pursued their own self-interest by asking Cincinnatus to assume power. Accept any reasonable responses for the questions that refer to the actions taken by Cincinnatus.

2. Describe a person you know or a leader in our nation who you think has civic virtue. Give reasons for your opinion based on the person's life.

   Accept any reasonable answer.

3. Explain some situations where you think you should put the common good above your own interests.

   Examples include following family, school, and classroom rules; obeying traffic signs; not interfering with other students' learning in the classroom; assisting in keeping the school campus clean; refraining from littering; getting vaccinated against communicable diseases; and not coming to school when sick.

Why should citizens promote the common good?

Examine the ideas of "common good" and "self-interest" in the story about Cincinnatus. Then respond to the questions that follow it.

You might want to work with a partner or in groups of three. A spokesperson for each group should explain its answers to the rest of the class.

CINCINNATUS: A MODEL OF CIVIC VIRTUE

In the year 460 BC, Rome was in great danger. An army from the east was burning and plundering the countryside. The enemy surrounded the defending Roman army on all sides. The leaders of the government of Rome decided to ask Cincinnatus, a skilled military leader, to help them during this crisis. The government leaders sent messengers asking Cincinnatus to serve as dictator of the country for as long as the crisis might last.

Cincinnatus was a hard-working farmer with only four acres of land. When the messengers found him, he was quietly plowing the fields. Because he loved his country, he left his plow to go to Rome to lead the army. In a battle that lasted two days, his army defeated the enemy and saved the country. In gratitude,

the people of Rome honored and praised Cincinnatus. But when the crisis was over, Cincinnatus did not try to remain as dictator of his country. He did not want continued power. Instead, he returned to his home and his life as a farmer and a citizen.

By returning to his home, Cincinnatus showed that he valued being a good citizen of Rome more than he valued fame and personal power. He respected the government of Rome. He did not want to use his popularity to take power away from the representatives elected by the citizens.

❶ What is the common good as represented in this story? What are the self-interests represented in the story? Do you agree with the actions taken by Cincinnatus? Why or why not?

❷ Describe a person you know or a leader in our nation who you think has civic virtue. Give reasons for your opinion based on the person's life.

❸ Explain some situations where you think you should put the common good above your own interests.

❹ Explain some situations in which you might not want to put the common good above your own interests.

❺ Explain some situations in which people might disagree about what is best for the common good. What should be done when there are such disagreements? Why?

4. Explain some situations in which you might not want to put the common good above your own interests.

Examples include objecting to the state's plans to destroy your house in order to build a freeway, the establishment of a landfill in your neighborhood, or the construction of a prison in your city. Although all these projects might serve the common good, a citizen might have legitimate reasons for opposing such plans.

5. Explain some situations in which people might disagree about what is best for the common good. What should be done when there are such disagreements? Why?

Examples include arguments about protecting society against terrorism, banning or allowing flag burning, and the extent to which firearms should be regulated. Accept any reasonable responses to the question about what to do when there are disagreements about the common good.

READING AND DISCUSSION

Why is civic virtue necessary for republican government to work well?

After students read this section, discuss with them the Founders' and Madison's ideas about civic virtue, human nature, and self-interest. Ask students the following questions:

- Do you agree with Madison that self-interest can promote the practice of civic virtue?
  Accept any reasonable response.

- Can you provide any examples of civic virtue in your own lives?
  Accept any reasonable response.

- Can you identify a person living today who consistently practices civic virtue?
  Accept any reasonable response.

How did the colonists teach the values of republican government?

Assign this section to the class and discuss the value the Founders put on civic virtue and how it was promoted among citizens.

- Do we teach civic virtue to our citizens today? Do you think it is important to teach civic virtue?
  Accept any reasonable answer.

- The Founders believed that the Roman Republic failed because the citizens lost their civic virtue. Do you think our citizens have lost their civic virtue?
  Accept any reasonable answer.

- Do you agree or disagree with the Founders that civic virtue is a critical component to the success of republican government?
  Accept any reasonable answer.

Why is civic virtue necessary for republican government to work well?

The Founders thought that republican government was possible in Rome only because of the high degree of civic virtue of the Roman citizens. **Civic virtue** meant that both citizens and their leaders were willing to set aside their private interests and personal concerns for the common good.

The Founders thought that civic virtue was important to make a government work well. Citizens need to participate in their government to promote the common good.

Do you think that a statesman's desire for fame and admiration can lead him or her to pursue the public or common good? Why or why not?

Madison understood the importance of civic virtue to good government. In this way, he was like the other Founders. Madison also accepted Locke's view of human nature. He believed that people are prompted to act by their self-interest. He thought that the pursuit of self-interest could in its own way further the common good. For example, a statesman's desire for fame and the admiration of others could lead him or her to practice civic virtue. The common good could be served by individuals pursuing their economic self-interest. Each would contribute to the general prosperity.

Madison also realized that as people pursue their own interests they sometimes act against the interests of the common good. He knew that civic virtue alone could not be relied upon. Madison wanted a government that would fit human nature as it is, not as one might wish it to be.

How did the colonists teach the values of republican government?

People living in the American colonies were taught the value of civic virtue and other values of republican government in many ways. Parents taught these values to their children. Teachers taught them in school. Clergy taught them in sermons and writings. Leading citizens of the country were expected to set good examples. The values of republican government were a part of the customs and traditions of the people.

The ideas and values of the Roman Republic were promoted throughout the

What ideals of republican government do you think our leaders should promote? Why?

American colonies in the stories that people read. Public buildings designed to resemble the buildings of ancient Rome also reminded people of the ideas and values of the Roman Republic.

The Founders thought it was important to teach and promote civic virtue among citizens. They believed that the Roman Republic had failed in the end because its citizens lost their civic virtue. They had promoted their own interests at the expense of the common good.

By the time of the American Revolution, the Founders had come to believe strongly in the ideals of republican government. They thought that Great Britain was violating these ideals. They claimed the British government was guilty of serving selfish interests at the expense of the common good. It had violated those rights that good government was supposed to protect.

After the Revolution, the Founders were able to establish their own government. They tried to make sure this government would not violate their rights. An essential step, they thought, was to create a constitutional government. You will learn what a constitution and constitutional government are in the next lesson.

 see next student page

LESSON REVIEW

The questions in the student book are intended to assess learning and to reinforce knowledge through discussion. The questions are directly related to the lesson objectives. You may wish to include additional questions developed by yourself or by your students.

1. What is republican government? What are the advantages and disadvantages of republican government?

   Advantages: *a republican government serves the common good; representatives make laws that serve the entire community; having representatives make the laws is more efficient; and people have a say in their government because they choose their representatives and hold them accountable for making good and fair laws.*

   Disadvantages: *republican government works best in small communities where there is little difference in the way the people think, believe, and live; and people in a republic could divide into factions that might work against the common good.*

2. What is the meaning of the term "common good"?

   The common good is that which is good for the community as a whole.

3. What is the difference between direct democracy and representative democracy?

   In a direct democracy, the people themselves make the laws and control the government. In a representative democracy, laws are made and administered by representatives elected by the people.

4. What is civic virtue? Why is it important that citizens and their representatives have civic virtue?

   Civic virtue is the willingness of both citizens and leaders to give up some of their own personal interests to serve the needs of the people. Civic virtue is important because government would not work well if citizens put their

(continued next page)

self-interests above the interests of the common good. If this were the case, the people might elect representatives who would not serve the interests of the people as a whole. Instead, the people might elect leaders who would serve only the interests of certain factions at the expense of the common good. Leaders who do not possess civic virtue might only serve their own interests at the expense of the people.

5. How were the values of republican government promoted in the colonies? Why were these values promoted?

    Parents taught republican values to their children, teachers taught them to their students, and the clergy taught them in sermons and writings. Leading citizens were expected to behave virtuously. Republican values became part of the customs and traditions of the people.

ACTIVITIES

The suggested activities are intended to extend and apply learning outside the classroom. You may wish to have students complete one or more of the activities. Have them share their results with the class.

LESSON REVIEW

❶ What is republican government? What are the advantages and disadvantages of republican government?

❷ What is the meaning of the term "common good"?

❸ What is the difference between direct democracy and representative democracy?

❹ What is civic virtue? Why is it important that citizens and their representatives have civic virtue?

❺ How were the values of republican government promoted in the colonies? Why were these values promoted?

ACTIVITIES

❶ His fellow Americans often referred to George Washington as "our Cincinnatus." Find stories and works of art that illustrate the life of George Washington as a model of civic virtue. Share what you learned with your class.

❷ Many government buildings in Washington, D.C., and many state capitols across the country look like Greek or Roman buildings. Find photographs of government buildings. Compare them with drawings or photographs of ancient Greek or Roman buildings. Explain how this architectural style in our country symbolizes the influences of ancient Greece and Rome on the Founders.

❸ In this lesson you learned about the values taught in colonial communities. The excerpts on the right are from the *Blue-Back Speller*, a popular school text of the late 1700s. What values do the lessons stress? Draw a poster or cartoon illustrating one of the lessons.

Lesson 6
I will not walk with bad men; that
I may not be cast off with them.
I will love the law, and keep it.
I will walk with the just, and do good.

Lesson 12
Be a good child; mind your book;
love your school and strive to learn.
Tell no tales; call no ill names;
you must not lie, nor swear,
nor cheat, nor steal.

Play not with bad boys; use no ill
words at play, spend your time well,
live in peace, and shun all strife.

This is the way to make good men of you,
and save your soul from pain and woe.

Lesson 15
As for those boys and girls that mind not
their books, and love not church and school,
but play with such as tell tales, tell lies,
curse, swear, and steal, they will come to
some bad end, and must be whipped till
they mend their ways.

❹ Look through different issues of your local newspaper. Find articles that concern the common good in your community. Share the articles with your class.

What is constitutional government?

LESSON PURPOSE

This lesson introduces the ideas of a constitution and constitutional government. It also introduces the idea that a constitution is a higher law.

When you finish this lesson, you should be able to explain the ideas of a constitution, constitutional government, and higher law. You should also be able to explain some of the important differences between constitutional governments and autocratic or dictatorial governments.

OVERVIEW

This lesson introduces students to key concepts the Founders had about government. Students learn the meanings of the terms "constitution," "constitutional government," "higher law," and "autocratic or dictatorial government." They also learn that even though all nations have either a written or unwritten constitution, this does not mean that they also have a constitutional government. Students examine the essential characteristics that differentiate constitutional government from autocratic or dictatorial government. The lesson concludes with an activity based on the Greek play *Antigone* by Sophocles, through which students learn the dangers of unlimited government.

OBJECTIVES

At the conclusion of this lesson, students should be able to

- explain the concepts of a constitution, constitutional government, and higher law
- explain the differences between constitutional government and autocratic or dictatorial governments

TEACHING PROCEDURES

INTRODUCTORY ACTIVITY

Have students read the Lesson Purpose and consider the objectives of the lesson. Write the Terms to Understand on the board or use a vocabulary-building activity of your choice. Have students look up the words in the Glossary at the back of the text. Ask them to look for these words as they read the lesson.

READING AND DISCUSSION

What is a constitution?

Read the section aloud or have students read it. Help students understand the two sets of questions about government and about citizens that all constitutions address. Be sure that they understand that all nations have a constitution outlining the laws of the land, regardless of whether the government is fair or unfair.

Ask them to compare the information in this section to the definition of "constitution" developed earlier.

TERMS TO UNDERSTAND

autocratic or dictatorial government

constitution

constitutional government

higher law

limits

monarchy

private domain

What is a constitution?

A **constitution** is a legal framework for government. A constitution tells how a government is organized and run. Every nation has a constitution. Both good and bad governments have constitutions.

Most constitutions are in writing. The United States and Russia are two examples of countries with written constitutions. Some constitutions contain both written and unwritten parts. The British constitution is the best-known example of this kind of constitution because it is based on both written laws and unwritten customs. It also is possible to have a constitution that is not in writing at all. Many societies in history had constitutions based on unwritten customs and traditions.

You can learn about a government and its citizens by studying a nation's constitution. Here are some of the questions a constitution usually answers:

What purpose of constitutional government does this painting illustrate?

QUESTIONS ABOUT GOVERNMENT

- What are the purposes of government?

- What is the organization of government? What parts does it have? What does each part do?

- How is government supposed to go about doing its business? For example, how does the government make its laws?

- How are people selected to serve in government?

32

QUESTIONS ABOUT CITIZENS

- Who is a citizen?

- Are citizens supposed to have control over their government? If so, how is this control supposed to work?

- What rights and responsibilities, if any, are the citizens supposed to have?

What is a constitutional government?

Having a constitution does not mean that a nation has a **constitutional government**. A constitutional government means that there are **limits** on the powers of the person or group running the government. The word "limits," as used here, means things that government may not do or actions that it may not take.

Our Constitution limits the power of government. The limits are written into the Constitution. For example, the courts cannot force a person to be a witness against himself. The courts cannot deny the accused the right to an attorney.

In some nations, the power of government is not limited. It is possible for the constitution of a nation to provide for the unlimited use of power. In other cases, the constitution of a nation might say that the power of government should be limited. But it might neglect to say how those limits are to be enforced.

Suppose the constitution of a nation does not limit the powers of its government. On the other hand, suppose it limits the power, but those limits are not enforced. In either case, the government is not a constitutional government. We call a government of unlimited power an **autocratic** or **dictatorial government**.

What are the advantages of constitutional government?

What is a constitutional government?

After students read this section, discuss and reinforce the idea that a constitutional government is one in which there are limits on the people running the government. In addition, in a constitutional government there must be ways to ensure that these limits are enforced. It is important that students understand that having a constitution is not the same thing as having a constitutional government.

Ask students to think about the previous lessons on natural rights and republican government. Then ask them to explain why the Founders believed a constitutional government was the best way to protect people's basic rights.

Direct students to the illustration and ask them to respond to the caption.

What is a higher law?

Assign this section to the class. You may wish to have it read aloud by different students. Ensure that students comprehend that in a constitutional government, the constitution is the higher law. Generate a discussion around the five characteristics of higher law, asking your students if they can think of any specific examples of these characteristics. Compare their original definition of higher law with the definition presented in this section. Make sure students understand the concept of private domain.

Assess student learning by examining the illustration and asking them the question in the caption.

What is a higher law?

In a constitutional government, the constitution must effectively limit the use of power. The constitution is a higher law. A **higher law** is a set of laws that establish and limit the power of government. All the people, including government leaders, must obey the higher law of the land. The people running the government must do what the constitution says. The constitution describes ways to ensure that people in government obey the limits on their power.

TEMPLE OF LIBERTY.

What role does a constitution play in a constitutional government?

In a constitutional government, the constitution has the following five important characteristics:

❶ It lists the basic rights of citizens to life, liberty, and property.

❷ It establishes the responsibility of government to protect those rights.

❸ It places limits on how the people in government may use their powers. Some examples of how our Constitution limits the powers of government are

* **Citizens' rights**. People in government cannot unfairly deprive a person of the right to freedom of speech.

* **How resources are distributed**. People in government cannot take a person's property without paying the person a fair price for it.

* **How conflicts are handled**. People in government must give all persons accused of a crime a fair trial.

❹ It establishes the principle of a **private domain**. A private domain is that part of a person's life that is not the business of government.

❺ It can only be changed with the widespread consent of citizens and according to certain set procedures.

How would you solve this issue of power?

Read "The Tragedy of Antigone." The story has been summarized and adapted from a Greek play written in 442 BC by Sophocles.

In the drama, Antigone disobeys her uncle, Creon, the ruler of Thebes. The government of Thebes was a monarchy. A **monarchy** is a form of government in which political power is held by a single ruler such as a king or queen. The king ruled the city; he made and enforced the laws, and he decided on punishments for people who violated his laws. The story raises questions about limits on the power of government.

THE TRAGEDY OF ANTIGONE

Thebes was an important city in ancient Greece. Antigone lived there with her sister, Ismene, her two brothers, Polyneices and Eteocles, and their uncle Creon.

The citizens of Thebes had chosen Eteocles, the younger brother, to be their king. Polyneices believed that since he was older it was his right to rule the land. The two brothers quarreled and Eteocles banished Polyneices from the city.

Polyneices left Thebes and gathered a large army to fight his brother for the throne. It was a long and bitter civil war; many people died and much property was destroyed. Finally, Polyneices and Eteocles killed each other.

The people of Thebes immediately elected Creon to be their next king. Creon decreed that Eteocles was to receive a

How would you solve this issue of power?

This activity will provide an opportunity for students to apply the concept of higher law in a realistic situation. Explain that in this adaptation of *Antigone*, Sophocles is illustrating the idea that it is not always easy to determine what is higher law in a government that has no limits.

Have students read "The Tragedy of Antigone." The following is a pronunciation guide to the names of the characters in the story:

Antigone—An·ti´·ga·ni
Ismene—Is·me´·ni
Polyneices—Po·ly·nee´·ces
Eteocles—E·te´·o·klees
Creon—Cre´·on

After students have read the text, elicit their opinions regarding the decision made by Antigone; have them explain the reasoning behind their opinions. Divide students into six groups; one group will be the Council of Advisors. Ask the other five groups to prepare the presentations they will make to the Council of Advisers. Remind them to be ready to respond to the council's questions. Before the council renders its decision, ask the class how Creon and Antigone used the concept of higher law to make the decisions that led to their actions.

Finally, after the Council of Advisers has explained its decision, have the entire class answer the questions posed in the Evaluating section.

hero's funeral for defending the city. But Polyneices was to rot on the battlefield. Any person who tried to bury Polyneices would be put to death. "These are my laws!" Creon declared. "Only by these laws can our city be safe and prosper. Only by obedience to these laws can we avoid civil war and ruin."

The citizens of Thebes debated the wisdom of Creon's law. On one side, many people were opposed to it. These people believed it was the duty of the living to bury the dead. According to this belief, unburied souls were doomed to wander alone throughout eternity. This group of people complained that Creon's law violated their rights without a good reason for doing so.

Other citizens supported Creon. They believed that Creon's law was justified because the city had suffered from rebels and lawbreakers. It was the king's duty to decide what to do with people who violated the law. They felt that the fate of Polyneices could serve as an example to those who did not respect the laws of the king.

Antigone believed that the laws of the gods were more important than the laws of any ruler. So Antigone decided to bury the body of her brother. "I will never be false to my brother," she said. Antigone attempted to convince Ismene to help her.

"Are you not going too far, exceeding the limits, when you do what the king has forbidden?" Ismene asked Antigone. "I do not wish to dishonor our brother, but I have no strength to defy the king. If we defy Creon's law, we will find ourselves alone against the powers of the king and we will perish! Since we

must obey Creon's law, we can ask the gods for forgiveness," Ismene said.

"Obey the law if you must, Ismene. I will not urge you further to join me," Antigone replied.

Later that day, a guard suddenly burst into the garden where Creon was resting. The guard brought the news that Polyneices had been buried. Creon angrily gave orders to find the guilty person. The guard returned with Antigone in custody.

"Tell me, did you not know that there is a law forbidding what you did? Why did you disobey it?" Creon asked. "You are my niece, how can this be?"

"I knew the law," Antigone answered. "If I had allowed my brother to lie unburied, that would have disturbed me deeply. Your law is not part of eternal justice. I disobeyed your law. I am not sorry for what I did," Antigone said to Creon.

"This brother of yours was attacking his own country," Creon replied. "The gods require no such loyalty to evildoers. It is my duty to produce order and peace in this land. If I do not act, the citizens of Thebes will think me weak. The public order, the state itself will be in jeopardy. It is the laws of the state that hold this city together. If those who break the law go unpunished, we will be a lawless city. Even the innocent will suffer. You have thrown away your future happiness, Antigone," Creon said. "You make it impossible for me to avoid putting you to death. Guards, take this woman and lock her away!"

As the guards escorted Antigone from the garden, she turned to Creon and said, "You further violate the rights of the people by passing sentence upon me without a fair and public hearing."

37

PREPARING

As you were able to observe in the story, there were no laws that set reasonable limits on the power of the king. But the king had a council of advisers, as in some other cities of ancient Greece. The role of the council was to investigate problems and to advise the king on what he might do to solve them.

Let us imagine that Antigone has asked the Council of Advisers to investigate the unlimited power of the king. Further, imagine that Creon agreed to permit the council to study the issue and to make recommendations. The Council of Advisers will conduct a hearing and then decide what recommendations, if any, to give the king.

Your class will work in six groups. Five of the groups should prepare to make a presentation that explains its ideas about limiting the power of the king. The sixth group is the Council of Advisers, who will listen to the presentations.

In preparing your presentations, use what you learned in the lesson as well as the ideas in the story. Each group also should prepare to answer questions from the council.

❶ Creon

Prepare arguments against any limits on the power of the king. Base your arguments on what you read about Creon in the story. During your presentation, be sure to explain the reasons why you believe the power of the king should remain as is.

❷ Citizens Who Support the King

Prepare arguments against limiting the power of the king. Present specific reasons why you support the actions of the king.

❸ Antigone

Prepare arguments in favor of limiting the power of the king. Base your arguments on what you read about Antigone in the story. During your presentation, propose specific limits on the king's power that you would like the council to recommend to Creon.

❹ Citizens Who Support Antigone

Prepare arguments that favor limiting the power of the king. Present specific reasons why you support Antigone's point of view.

❺ Ismene

Prepare arguments that represent Ismene's point of view. Present specific reasons why you hold this opinion.

❻ Council of Advisers

Reread the story and study the role of each group. Then prepare questions to ask each group during the hearing. Select a member of your group to be the president of the council.

PRESENTING

The president of the Council of Advisers will call the session to order and explain the purpose of the meeting.

Each group has four minutes to make a formal presentation to explain its position to the council.

After each presentation, council members may ask questions of the group. Every member of the group should help answer the council's questions.

After the hearing, the Council of Advisers will meet to decide what recommendations, if any, to make to the king. The council will then share its decision with the class.

EVALUATING

After the council has made its decision the class as a whole should evaluate the decision. Each student should answer the evaluation questions below and share their conclusions with the class.

- What were the strongest arguments made against limiting the power of the king? Which arguments were the weakest?

- What were the strongest arguments made in favor of limiting the power of the king? Which arguments were the weakest?

- What did you learn about the importance of constitutional government as a result of this activity?

 see next student page

LESSON REVIEW

The questions in the student book are intended to assess learning and to reinforce knowledge through discussion. The questions are directly related to the lesson objectives. You may wish to include additional questions developed by yourself or by your students.

1. What is a constitution? What can you learn about a nation's government by studying its constitution?

   A constitution is a set of rules and laws that tells how a government is organized and run. By studying a nation's constitution, you can see not only how its government is organized and run, but whether it limits the power of government. You can also determine the nation's values and ideals.

2. Explain the differences between a constitutional government and an autocratic or dictatorial government.

   A constitutional government specifically limits the powers of those who run the government and ensures that the limits of power are enforced. An autocratic or dictatorial government has no such limits or is limited by its constitution, but these limits are not enforced.

3. What are the characteristics that define a constitution as a "higher law"?

   A constitution must include the following:

   - *A list of citizens' basic rights to life, liberty, and property*
   - *Recognition that it is the responsibility of government to protect those rights*
   - *Limits on how people in government may use their powers*
   - *The establishment of the principle of private domain*
   - *Stipulation that the constitution can only be changed with the consent of citizens according to certain set procedures*

4. Identify two areas of private life in which you think government should not interfere. Explain why you think government should not intrude in these areas.

   Possible responses include a person's choice of friends, choice of television shows or movies watched, telephone conversations, religious practice, etc. Accept any reasonable response.

ACTIVITIES

The suggested activities are intended to extend and apply learning outside the classroom. You may wish to have students complete one or more of the activities. Have them share their results with the class.

ENRICHMENT

Instruct half of your students to write a constitution for the class that embodies the characteristics of a constitutional democracy and higher law. Instruct the other half to write a constitution for an autocratic or dictatorial form of government. Ask students to compare the two constitutions. Ask them to identify which constitution was the most difficult to write and explain their reasons for their opinions.

LESSON REVIEW

❶ What is a constitution? What can you learn about a nation's government by studying its constitution?

❷ Explain the differences between a constitutional government and an autocratic or dictatorial government.

❸ What are the characteristics that define a constitution as a "higher law"?

❹ Identify two areas of private life in which you think government should not interfere. Explain why you think government should not intrude in these areas.

ACTIVITIES

❶ In the history of the world, there have been governments that ignored the limits on their power. Conduct research on one of these governments and give examples of how it violated the natural rights of the people.

❷ Read the play *Antigone*. Research how the play was rewritten during World War II to inspire resistance to Nazi rule. Write a short report on your findings and share it with your class.

❸ Draw a cartoon for your class bulletin board that illustrates the difference between a constitutional government and a dictatorial government.

How can we organize government to prevent the abuse of power?

5

LESSON PURPOSE

Constitutional governments are designed to protect the people from abuses of government power. In this lesson you learn how people might organize government to make the abuse of power less likely.

When you finish this lesson, you should be able to explain the ideas of separation of powers and checks and balances, know the Founders' reasons for creating a system that limits governmental power, and list some powers of the three branches of government.

SVÆ·XLIX

OVERVIEW

In this lesson, students learn that constitutional governments are organized to prevent the misuse of government power. Students learn that the principles of separation of powers and checks and balances are applied to achieve this goal.

The lesson explains that the separation of powers and the system of checks and balances distribute power among the branches of government so that no one branch can exercise power without being checked by another branch. Students learn that the complexity of this system protects the people from abusive power. The system is sometimes cumbersome and it can take more time to get things done than in other forms of government. However, this inefficiency is an advantage because the system makes it more difficult for those in government to misuse power.

OBJECTIVES

At the conclusion of this lesson, students should be able to

- explain the ideas of separation of powers and checks and balances
- explain the Founders' reasons for creating a system that limits governmental power
- describe the three branches of government and list some of the powers of each

TEACHING PROCEDURES

INTRODUCTORY ACTIVITY

Have students read the Lesson Purpose section and consider the objectives of the lesson. Write the Terms to Understand on the board or use a vocabulary-building activity of your choice. Students should look for these terms as they study the lesson. Definitions are in the Glossary at the end of the student text.

After you introduce the lesson, engage students in the Ideas for Discussion activity on page 43: "Why did the Founders fear the abuse of power?" Refer to page 43 of this guide for possible responses to the questions posed in the Ideas for Discussion activity. Allow students to express their own ideas before they proceed with the readings.

READING AND DISCUSSION

How might people organize a government to prevent the abuse of power?

This lesson is designed so that the Ideas for Discussion activity on the next page should be done before this reading.

The lesson introduces the idea of limiting governmental power by use of the following methods:

- separating the powers of government among different branches
- creating a system of checks and balances

TERMS TO UNDERSTAND

bill
checks and balances
executive branch
judicial branch
legislative branch
separation of powers

How might people organize a government to prevent the abuse of power?

Constitutional governments are organized in such a way that one person or group cannot get enough power to dominate the government. Two common ways to do this are

- **Separate the powers of government.**

  Divide the powers of government among different branches, or parts. Doing so prevents any one person or group from having all the power.

- **Balance the powers among the branches of government.**

  Divide the powers of government in such a way that no one branch controls the other branches. Give each branch methods to check the use of power by the other branches.

Why did the Founders believe that all governments need limits on their power?

Why did the Founders fear the abuse of power?

The Founders knew that throughout history many governments had used their power unfairly. This is why they created the system of limits on power described in this lesson. To understand their thinking, read the quotations below. Then, with a partner, discuss the questions that follow.

❶ What does each quotation mean?

❷ What view of human nature did Alexander Hamilton, Benjamin Franklin, and George Mason share?

❸ Do you agree or disagree with these views of human nature? Why or why not?

❹ If you do agree with these views of human nature, how would you organize our government to protect your rights?

ALEXANDER HAMILTON

"Give all power to the many, they will oppress the few. Give all power to the few, they will oppress the many."

BENJAMIN FRANKLIN

"There are two passions which have a Powerful influence on the affairs of men. These are ambition and avarice [greed]; the love of power and the love of money."

GEORGE MASON

"From the nature of man, we may be sure that those who have power in their hands…will always, when they can…increase it."

IDEAS FOR DISCUSSION

Why did the Founders fear the abuse of power?

Have students read the three quotations and answer the four questions. They may work in small groups, in pairs, or as individuals. Groups and individuals should share their responses with the class.

1. What does each quotation mean?

   - *Alexander Hamilton says that if all power is given to only one group, no matter how large or small the group is, it will inevitably abuse its power.*
   - *Benjamin Franklin says that the desire for power and money can corrupt people.*
   - *George Mason says that it is the nature of human beings to always want more power.*

2. What view of human nature did Alexander Hamilton, Benjamin Franklin, and George Mason share?

   Unlike Locke, who believed that human nature is generally good and man is inclined to work for the best interests of all, these Founders believed that it was the nature of human beings to be selfish. They believed that people would need specific limits applied to them to become virtuous citizens.

3. Do you agree or disagree with these views of human nature? Why or why not?

   Accept any reasonable response.

4. If you do agree with these views of human nature, how would you organize our government to protect your rights?

   Accept any reasonable response. Ask students to compare and contrast their responses to the information in the "How does a system of checks and balances work?" section of the lesson.

Reading, discussion, and activity

How does separation of powers work?

Have students read these two sections aloud. Separation of powers works in our system by dividing the government into three distinct groups or branches with different powers, duties, and responsibilities delegated to each branch.

How does a system of checks and balances work?

Checks and balances work by ensuring that no one branch can dominate the others. For example:

- the executive branch can be checked by the legislative branch's power to override the president's veto with a two-thirds majority vote
- the legislative branch can be checked by the executive branch's power to veto bills passed by Congress
- the judicial branch can be checked by the executive branch's power to nominate people to serve as judges and the legislative branch's power to approve or reject the president's nominations
- in addition, the power of the legislative branch can be checked internally; this branch is divided into two houses, and each house can check the power of the other by refusing to pass a bill proposed by the other house

How does separation of powers work?

A study of constitutional governments shows that they are often divided into three different groups or branches. The power of government is not given to any one branch. Instead, some of the power is given to each branch. This is called **separation of powers**. For example, we divide our government into the following three branches:

- the **legislative branch** has the power to make laws
- the **executive branch** has the power to carry out and enforce laws
- the **judicial branch** has the power to manage conflicts about the meaning, application, and enforcement of laws.

How does a system of checks and balances work?

The phrase **checks and balances** means that the powers of the different branches of government are balanced. No one branch has so much power that it can completely dominate the others. Although each branch of government has its own special powers, the powers are checked because some powers are shared with the other branches.

Why are the powers of government separated and balanced?

Which branch of government has the final say about whether a law is constitutional?

According to our Constitution, Congress is the legislative branch. It has the power to make laws. The power of Congress is divided between two houses, the House of Representatives and the Senate. Each house can check the power of the other by refusing to pass a law proposed by the other house.

In addition, our Constitution gives the executive and judicial branches ways to check and control the power of Congress to make laws. For example:

- A **bill** is a proposed law. When Congress passes a bill, the president must sign it before it can become law. The president has the right to refuse to sign a bill. If this happens, the bill cannot become a law unless Congress votes again and passes the bill by a two-thirds majority of both houses.

- The U.S. Supreme Court can check the power of Congress. The Court can declare a law to be in violation of the Constitution and, therefore, invalid.

There are similar ways to check the powers of the president and U.S. Supreme Court. You will learn more about the system of checks and balances in a later lesson.

This system of separation of powers and checks and balances helps ensure that government power is limited. Because constitutional governments are organized in complicated ways, getting things done may take time. Although it might seem strange, this is often considered an advantage. Many people think that these complications make it more likely that when government does finally make a decision, it will be a well thought out one.

After reading the two sections aloud, have students create a chart that has four rows and three columns in the format shown. Fill in the chart as each concept is addressed throughout the text. Hang the chart where the whole class can see it for future reference and review.

Sample

Branch of government	Powers granted by the Constitution	How these powers are checked
legislative branch	makes laws	president can veto bills

 see next student page

LESSON REVIEW

The questions in the student book are intended to assess learning and to reinforce knowledge through discussion. The questions are directly related to the lesson objectives. You may wish to include additional questions developed by yourself or by your students.

1. How does a system of separation of powers work?
   Some power is given to each branch of government. It is not given to only one branch.

2. What are the three branches of our government and what power does each hold?
   The legislative branch has the power to make laws. The executive branch has the power to carry out and enforce laws. The judicial branch has the power to manage conflicts about the meaning, application, and enforcement of laws.

(continued next page)

3. How does a system of checks and balances work? Give some examples.

In a system that contains checks and balances, no one branch of government has enough power to dominate the other branches. Each branch has specific powers. These powers are checked because some powers are shared with the other branches. For example, the legislative branch has the power to make laws. Because this branch is divided into two parts—the Senate and the House of Representatives—each branch has the power to refuse to pass a law proposed by the other branch.

When Congress passes a bill, the president must sign it before it can become law. If the president refuses to sign a bill, it cannot become a law unless Congress votes again to pass the bill by a two-thirds majority of both houses.

The U.S. Supreme Court can declare a law to be in violation of the Constitution.

4. The separation and sharing of powers means that government cannot reach decisions quickly. Why might this be an advantage? Why might it be a disadvantage?

The separation and sharing of powers can be considered an advantage because they keep the executive and legislative branches from passing laws that may not be in the best interest of the country. The executive and legislative branches have the opportunity to examine bills, state their opinions, and prevent bills from becoming laws if they have concerns about them. The judicial branch manages conflicts about the meaning, application, and enforcement of laws.

A disadvantage is that with a system of separation and sharing of powers, it sometimes takes a long time to address issues that are important to the people.

ACTIVITIES

The suggested activities are intended to extend and apply learning outside the classroom. You may wish to have students complete one or more of the activities. Have them share their results with the class.

LESSON REVIEW

❶ How does a system of separation of powers work?

❷ What are the three branches of our government and what power does each hold?

❸ How does a system of checks and balances work? Give some examples.

❹ The separation and sharing of powers means that government cannot reach decisions quickly. Why might this be an advantage? Why might it be a disadvantage?

ACTIVITIES

❶ Read Articles I, II, and III of the U.S. Constitution. Then, examine the constitution of your state.

Create two charts that illustrate the process of checks and balances, one for your state government and one for the U.S. government. Share your charts with the class.

❷ Find newspaper or newsmagazine articles that illustrate our system of separation of powers and checks and balances. Use the articles to create a bulletin board for your classroom.

unit two

What shaped the Founders' thinking about government?

UNIT OVERVIEW

This unit helps students understand the Key Concepts and events that influenced the Founders' thinking about government and led to the Declaration of Independence and Articles of Confederation.

In **Lesson 6**, students study the development of constitutional government in England and learn the significance of the Magna Carta and the English Bill of Rights.

In **Lesson 7**, students explore how constitutional government was embodied in American colonial governments, why the colonists began to resist British control, and the particular events that led to armed resistance and ultimately to the writing of the Declaration of Independence.

Lesson 8 asks students to examine the Declaration of Independence and see how fundamental ideas on natural rights, social contract, consent of the governed, and the right to alter or abolish government are reflected in the document.

Lesson 9 gives historical background to the American fight for independence as well as descriptions of the military campaigns. It also explains how the fledgling government managed to win the war.

Lessons 10 and 11 are devoted to state governments and our first national government.

In **Lesson 10**, students learn the basic features of the new state constitutions, the significance of the Massachusetts constitution, and some inherent problems arising from how state constitutions were organized.

In **Lesson 11**, students direct their study to the first national government. Students learn about the Articles of Confederation and analyze the achievements and weaknesses of this document. Finally, students learn the significance of Shays' Rebellion and how that event and the problems with the Articles of Confederation led to the decision to write a new constitution.

UNIT OBJECTIVES

At the conclusion of the lesson, students should be able to

- describe constitutional development in England through the Magna Carta and the English Bill of Rights and the influence that development had on the colonial governments
- identify sections of the Declaration of Independence and the state constitutions that embody the natural rights philosophy, republicanism, and constitutionalism
- explain what significance the American Revolution had for the world
- describe some of the characteristics of the state constitutions and the problems that arose under them
- describe the Articles of Confederation, including the major accomplishments and weaknesses of the Articles
- explain the events that led to the writing of the Constitution and the Framers' reasons for writing it

UNIT INTRODUCTION

Read the introduction with the class. Introduce the Key Concepts and tell students that these ideas will be fully explained in the lessons of this unit. The illustrations throughout the unit are excellent teaching tools for reviewing and reinforcing the learning. Use them as you find appropriate.

UNIT PROJECT (OPTIONAL)

Ask your students to write the Key Concepts in their notebooks and write definitions based on their current knowledge. Students can change and add to these initial definitions as the unit progresses.

unit two

KEY CONCEPTS

Articles of Confederation

inalienable rights

popular sovereignty

rule of law

In the last unit, you learned some important ideas and questions concerning government. You studied natural rights philosophy, republicanism, and constitutionalism. These were the ideas that influenced the Founders of our nation and helped shape their views about government.

In this unit, you will learn more about the Founders. You will read about the experiences that shaped their thinking about government. You will study their values and the things they believed were important. You will also learn why they thought a new constitution was necessary.

How did constitutional government develop in Great Britain?

LESSON PURPOSE

Constitutional government developed in Great Britain over a period of many centuries. In this lesson you learn how the monarchy came to share power with the nobles. You will study some documents that limited the power of the British government. This study will help you to better understand our ideas about limited government.

When you finish this lesson, you should be able to describe the struggles for power between the English monarch and Parliament. You should be able to explain how these struggles led to a system of separated powers and representative government. You should also be able to describe some of the important constitutional documents in British history that influenced the writing of our constitution.

6

OVERVIEW

This lesson begins by explaining why American colonists had the same rights as English people. For example, colonists had the right to trial by jury and were protected from unlawful entry into their homes. Students learn that William the Conqueror invaded England and established the feudal system. In the feudal system, all people belonged to one of three social groups—the royalty, the nobility, or the common people. Power was shared among the royalty, nobility, and a group of common people, called vassals, through a series of agreements and contracts. The feudal system is an important step in the development of constitutional government because during this period, monarchs began to share power with the nobility.

Later in the lesson, students are introduced to the Magna Carta and the concept of the rule of law. The lesson concludes with an explanation of how all these events forced a shift in the balance of power from the monarchy to a representative government by the creation of Parliament and the establishment of the English Bill of Rights.

The illustrations throughout the lesson are teaching tools for reviewing and reinforcing the learning. Use them as you find appropriate.

OBJECTIVES

At the conclusion of this lesson, students should be able to

- describe the struggles between the English monarch and Parliament
- explain how the struggles between the English monarch and Parliament evolved into a system of separated powers and representative government
- describe the British constitutional documents, such as the Magna Carta and the English Bill of Rights, that influenced the writing of the U.S. Constitution

TEACHING PROCEDURES

INTRODUCTORY ACTIVITY

Have students read the Lesson Purpose and consider the objectives of the lesson. Make sure that students understand that most colonists of the 1700s were of English ancestry and had a common language, history, religion, and attitude toward government. Ask students what they know about the English government. Also review the definition of a constitutional government. Write the Terms to Understand on the board or use a vocabulary-building activity of your choice. Have students look up the words in the Glossary at the back of the text. Ask them to look for these words as they read the lesson.

READING AND DISCUSSION

Why did the American colonists have the rights of Englishmen?

Read this section aloud or have students read this section. Help students understand what the rights of Englishmen were and why the colonists were protected by them. Students should understand that the colonists' experiences with the British influenced what they thought about limited government.

TERMS TO UNDERSTAND

common law	rights of Englishmen
English Bill of Rights	rule of law
feudalism	
Magna Carta	
Parliament	
Petition of Right	

Why did the American colonists have the rights of Englishmen?

The **rights of Englishmen** were established during centuries of British history. These were certain basic rights that all subjects of the English king or queen were believed to have. They included

- the right to a trial by jury

- security from unlawful entry into one's home

- no taxation without consent

Before the American colonies became independent, the colonists were subjects of the British monarchy. As subjects of the king or queen, the colonists enjoyed the rights of Englishmen. All subjects of the king or queen had these rights. The colonists knew and understood their rights as Englishmen.

The colonists' experiences with British government greatly influenced what they thought about limited government. For our study, it is important to understand these rights and how they developed over time. It is also important to remember

What were some important rights of Englishmen?

that the constitution of Great Britain is not a single written document. Instead, it is made up of long-established practices known as common law and laws passed by Parliament. **Common law** is based on custom and the decisions of law courts. **Parliament** is the legislative body of British government.

What problems, if any, might arise from dividing society into social groups?

What was the feudal system?

Until 1066, each region of England had its own ruler. William the Conqueror from France invaded England in that year and became king of all the regions.

William the Conqueror brought a system for governing called feudalism. **Feudalism** was a system of social, economic, and political organization. The system was based on the control of land.

Under feudalism, the people in England belonged to one of three social groups.

❶ **Royalty**. This was the king and queen and their families. Government by a king or queen is a monarchy.

❷ **Nobility**. This group included the "lords" and "ladies" who held titles such as earl, duke, duchess, and baron. The noblemen worked for the monarchy and made it possible for the king or queen to control England.

❸ **Common people**. These were the rest of the people. This group included the knights, or soldiers of the king, merchants, and peasants. The peasants were also known as serfs. They farmed the land and were not free to leave the area in which they worked.

All public land in England belonged to the monarch, but it was too much land for one person to rule. So, the monarch gave some responsibility for governing the kingdom to the nobility. Under the feudal system, the nobles controlled parts of the land as well as the people who lived there. In exchange, the nobles pledged to be loyal to the king and to go to war for him.

The nobles further divided the land into smaller areas. A nobleman assigned control of the land and people living on it to men called vassals. The vassals in

What was the feudal system?

Assign this reading. To help develop students' understanding of the structure of feudalism, ask them to diagram the three social groups under the heading "Feudal System." Then ask them to describe the various components of the system under each group, such as the social, political, and economic aspects. Ask students to speculate on how the sharing of power between the king and his nobles eventually led to the growth of constitutional government. Use the illustration to augment the discussion and reinforce the concepts.

Why is the Magna Carta an important document?

After students read the section on pages 52 and 54, have them relate the content of this section to Unit One, referring to the ideas of (1) need for government, (2) republican government, and (3) constitutional government. Point out that the practice of sharing powers, which originally grew out of necessity, became a tradition that the nobles began to expect. Help students appreciate that the significance of the Magna Carta in the evolution of constitutional government was its contribution to the ideas of government by contract and limited government.

How did the Magna Carta limit the power of the king?

turn owed the nobleman loyalty and military service.

For the system to work, it depended on a series of agreements or contracts. There had to be contracts between the monarch and the nobles. There also had to be contracts between the nobles and vassals. Each contract included rights and responsibilities that the parties owed to one another. Thus, feudalism introduced the idea of government based on a contract. Those in power pledged to respect the rights of the people who gave them loyalty.

The feudal system was important to the development of constitutional government. It was during this period that the monarchs started to share power with the nobles.

Why is the Magna Carta an important document?

Under the feudal system, it became a custom or tradition for the royalty to share some of its power with the nobility. As a result, the nobles became used to having certain rights and powers. When King John tried to take back some of these rights, the nobles rebelled.

The nobles were powerful enough to force King John to sign an agreement with them in the year 1215. This agreement is the **Magna Carta**, or Great Charter. The Magna Carta was a major step in the growth of English constitutional government. The Magna Carta was perhaps the most important early example of a written statement of law limiting the power of a ruler. The Magna Carta contains two important ideas that influenced the Founders.

❶ Government is based on a contract between the ruler and people to be ruled. Government by contract also includes the idea that if either side breaks the contract, that contract is no longer valid.

❷ Both government and the governed must obey the law. This is called the **rule of law**. The law limits the powers of government. The king could not take away the property of a noble without following agreed-upon procedures and rules. The Magna Carta expresses the idea of limited government by requiring the king to govern according to established rules of law.

IDEAS FOR DISCUSSION

How do these rights limit the power of government?

Each of the rights listed below was a right of Englishmen listed in the Magna Carta. Work with a partner or in a group of three students. Read the statements below and respond to the four questions that follow them.

- *For a trivial* [minor] *offence, a free man shall be fined only in proportion to the degree of his offence, and for a serious offence correspondingly.*

- *No free man shall be taken, or imprisoned...exiled, or in any way harmed...save by the lawful judgment of his peers* [equals] *or by the law of the land.*

- *No constable* [officer] *or other bailiff* [sheriff] *of ours shall take the corn* [grain] *or other chattels* [personal property] *of any one except...he gives money for them.*

- *To none will we sell, to none deny or delay, right of justice.*

❶ What is the meaning of each statement?

❷ What right does the statement guarantee?

❸ Why is this right important?

❹ Explain how this right limits the power of government.

IDEAS FOR DISCUSSION

How do these rights limit the power of government?

Introduce the Ideas for Discussion. Break students into pairs or groups of three. Assign all the statements to each group or assign one to each group. Ask students to copy each question and write their answers below it. Share each group's ideas with the class.

Questions:

1. What is the meaning of each statement?
2. What right does the statement guarantee?
3. Why is this right important?
4. Explain how this right limits the power of government.

Suggested responses:

First Statement

1. *The punishment given for any offense should be related to the severity of the offense.*
2. *The statement guarantees that a person will be treated fairly under the law.*
3. *People guaranteed this right will not fear that they will be given an excessive sentence for a small offense.*
4. *This limits the power of government to impose an excessive consequence for a minor offense. The statement implies that there is either a written or traditional method of handling offenses.*

Second Statement

1. *This statement means that no one can be punished by government without a trial conducted by his or her equals that follows the law.*
2. *This statement guarantees the right of due process under the law.*
3. *This right is important because people want to feel secure in the knowledge that each person will have the right to be heard and that the decision will be reached through an understood and agreed-upon process.*
4. *This right forbids government to issue edicts unilaterally. It forces government to adhere to the legal process.*

(continued next page)

Third Statement

1. *Government may not take personal property from citizens unless it pays for that property.*
2. *The statement guarantees the right to own and possess personal property.*
3. *This right allows citizens to feel secure in the knowledge that their personal property cannot be confiscated by government.*
4. *Government is not allowed to take property from citizens for its own needs. Government must pay for anything it takes.*

Fourth Statement

1. *Each person accused of a crime will receive justice quickly and according to the law. The right to justice will not be sold or denied to anyone.*
2. *The statement guarantees the right to a fair and speedy trial.*
3. *This right is important because citizens must be tried and sentenced quickly and according to the facts of their cases rather than according to their ability to pay a bribe or according to the desires of people in government.*
4. *This right keeps government in check by prohibiting it from manipulating justice for its own gain.*

READING AND DISCUSSION

Why was the creation of Parliament important?

Have students read this section. Help them understand which social groups compose the two chambers of Parliament—the House of Lords and the House of Commons. Ask students to consider which groups of people were not represented in Parliament and whether they think these unrepresented groups received any benefit from its establishment. Throughout the discussion, help students understand that the importance of Parliament is that it embodies the idea of representative government. Students should understand that the establishment of Parliament shifted the balance of power from the monarch to Parliament.

What is the relationship between the Magna Carta and constitutional government?

The Magna Carta was a contract between the king and the nobility. Most of the people in England were not a part of this agreement. But the Magna Carta is an early step leading to the idea that government should be based on a contract that includes all the people.

Government by contract means that both sides of the agreement are responsible for fulfilling its terms. The Magna Carta states that the king cannot deprive the nobility of their rights. The nobility, in return, must support and obey the king and the laws.

Why was the creation of Parliament important?

Important changes in the English government caused the establishment of other basic principles of government. These principles are the separation of powers and representative government.

In 1258, the nobles forced the king to create an advisory council. This council was called Parliament. Parliament is the legislative branch of the English government. It was made up of two houses that represented the most powerful groups in the kingdom: the House of Lords and the House of Commons. The House of Lords represented the nobles. The House of Commons represented people who owned large amounts of land but were not nobles.

Gradually during the next centuries the role of Parliament grew. Its members were no longer simply advising the monarch, they were representing the interests of their regions. For hundreds of years after the creation of Parliament, the royalty, nobility, and commons had struggled for power. No one group was able to be completely in control for long.

Then in 1628, the king tried to pressure the people for money without the consent of Parliament. He also required the people to house soldiers in their homes. As a result, Parliament forced him to agree to the **Petition of Right** of 1628. The Petition stated that the king could only raise taxes with the consent of Parliament. It also no longer allowed the king to house soldiers in the homes of the people. The Petition of Right strengthened the idea that

English subjects had certain rights that government could not violate.

The struggle between the monarch and Parliament became so intense during the seventeenth century that a series of civil wars broke out. The nobles finally won and in 1649 Parliament ordered the execution of the king. By 1688 the balance of power had shifted in favor of Parliament.

What is the relationship of free speech in a legislative body to constitutional government?

What was the English Bill of Rights?

In 1689 Parliament passed the **English Bill of Rights**. This law gave certain rights to Parliament that further limited the powers of the monarch. It said among other things that elections to Parliament must be free and that the people have the right to petition the king. It also said that the monarchy was no longer allowed to

- collect taxes without the consent of Parliament
- interfere with the right to free speech and debate in Parliament
- maintain an army in peacetime
- prevent Protestants from having arms for their defense
- require excessive bail or administer cruel punishment for those accused or convicted of crimes
- declare that laws made by Parliament should not be obeyed

By the end of the 1600s, the British government was much more limited in what it could do. This was at the same time that the British were establishing colonies in North America. So, the colonists brought these ideas about good government with them to the new world.

What was the English Bill of Rights?

Ask your students to read this section and think about how the rights listed in the text compare with the rights we now enjoy. Emphasize that the English Bill of Rights was a clear sign of the shift of power away from the monarchy.

 see next student page

LESSON REVIEW

The questions in the student book are intended to assess learning and to reinforce knowledge through discussion. The questions are directly related to the lesson objectives. You may wish to include additional questions developed by yourself or by your students.

1. Explain how the feudal system promoted the idea that government is a contract between government and the governed.

   The success of the feudal system depended on a series of agreements and contracts between monarchs and nobles and between nobles and vassals (common people). The idea that government is a contract between the government and the governed was established through this tradition.

2. Explain the importance of each of these documents:
   - Magna Carta
   - Petition of Right
   - English Bill of Rights

   The Magna Carta formally established the concept that government is based on a contract between the ruler and the people to be ruled and that if either side breaks the contract, the contract is no longer valid. The Magna Carta also mandated that both the government and the governed must obey the law. This institutionalized the rule of law, which limited the power of government.

(continued next page)

The Petition of Right limited the king's ability to raise taxes without the consent of Parliament. The king was also prohibited from quartering soldiers in people's homes. The importance of the Petition of Right is that it strengthened the idea that English subjects had certain rights that government could not violate.

The English Bill of Rights further limited the powers of the king. The king was forbidden to collect taxes without the consent of Parliament, interfere with free speech and debate in Parliament, maintain an army in peacetime, prevent Protestants from having arms, require excessive bail or administer cruel punishments, and declare that Parliament's laws should not be obeyed. In addition, elections to Parliament were required to be free, and the people were granted the right to petition the king.

3. Explain how the struggles between the monarchy and the nobility led to limited government in Great Britain.

The struggles between the nobles and the king resulted in a mandate from the nobles that the king create an advisory council, called Parliament. It was composed of two houses. The House of Lords was reserved for the nobility, and the House of Commons was reserved for common people who owned land. Gradually, the role of Parliament changed from being an advisory body to the king to representing the interests of its constituents. By 1688, the balance of power had shifted to Parliament.

ACTIVITIES

The suggested activities are intended to extend and apply learning outside the classroom. You may wish to have students complete one or more of the activities. Have them share their results with the class.

LESSON REVIEW

❶ Explain how the feudal system promoted the idea that government is a contract between government and the governed.

❷ Explain the importance of each of these documents:

- Magna Carta
- Petition of Right
- English Bill of Rights

❸ Explain how the struggles between the monarchy and the nobility led to limited government in Great Britain.

ACTIVITIES

❶ Learn more about the social, economic, and political aspects of feudalism. Find information in your library or on the Internet. Create a diagram that illustrates how the system worked.

❷ Create a script for a talk show for an imaginary television station. The host of the program can interview some of the historical figures who lived during the time mentioned in this lesson such as William the Conqueror, King John, noblemen, vassals, and commoners.

❸ Imagine that you are a member of the nobility living in England in the 1200s. Write a letter to the editor or draw an editorial cartoon illustrating the importance of the rights listed in the Magna Carta.

What experiences led to the American Revolution?

7

LESSON PURPOSE

This lesson explains how British ideas about government were put to use in the colonies. The lesson also describes why the colonists came to feel that the British government threatened their rights.

When you finish the lesson, you should be able to explain how constitutional government developed in the colonies. You should also be able to explain why the colonists decided to fight for their independence.

OVERVIEW

In this lesson, students learn the basic ideas of constitutional government that the American colonists adopted to form their own colonial governments—ideas such as natural rights, representative government, the rule of law, separation of powers, and checks and balances. Students begin to understand that although the colonists considered themselves to be loyal subjects of England, they became accustomed to the relative freedom they had in creating their own form of colonial government because of the distance between America and England.

Students learn that the form of government chosen by the colonists protected them not only from the abuse of power by the British, but also from abuses by their own government. The colonists favored a representative form of government and over time began to ignore laws made by the British Parliament. The lesson describes the British view in the dispute with the colonists, the effect that British laws had on the colonies, and why the colonists resisted new British controls. Finally, students learn the particular events that led to the Revolutionary War.

OBJECTIVES

At the end of this lesson, students should be able to

- identify the basic ideas of constitutional government embodied in the American colonial governments
- describe British policies and why the colonists began to resist British control
- describe American actions that led to armed resistance and the writing of the Declaration of Independence
- explain why the colonists decided to fight for their independence

TEACHING PROCEDURES

INTRODUCTORY ACTIVITY

Read the Lesson Purpose to the class and ask them to consider the objectives of the lesson.

(continued next page)

Have students describe what kind of government exists in their school or in other schools they have attended. Ask them to identify any of the basic ideas about government they have learned from their student governments. Then have students identify ways in which the administration of their school reflects basic ideas of constitutional government.

Write the Terms to Understand on the board or use a vocabulary-building activity of your choice. Have students look up the words in the Glossary at the back of the text. Ask them to look for these words as they read the lesson.

READING AND DISCUSSION

Which ideas did the colonists in America use to create their governments?

Assign this reading to the class. Write the five characteristics of colonial governments mentioned in the text on the board or on chart paper. You may wish to have students write the characteristics down and write notes under each of them.

1. Natural rights
2. Representative government
3. Rule of law
4. Separation of powers
5. Checks and balances

TERMS TO UNDERSTAND

charter
committees of correspondence
Daughters of Liberty
First Continental Congress
Second Continental Congress
Sons of Liberty
writs of assistance

Which ideas did the colonists in America use to create their governments?

This is the royal charter for the state of Delaware. What is a charter? Why did the colonists need one?

To establish a British colony, one generally needed to have a charter from the king. A **charter** is a legal document. In colonial times, a charter granted land to a person or a company along with the right to start a colony on that land.

Most colonial charters said little about what kind of government a colony should have. As a result, the settlers had to develop their own form of government. Each of the thirteen colonies had a government of its own.

In creating their own governments, the colonists tried to do two things. They tried to protect themselves from abuse of power by the British government. They also tried to protect themselves from abuse of power by their colonial governments. To achieve these goals, the colonists used the basic ideas of constitutional government. All colonial governments were based on the following ideas:

❶ **Natural rights**. Colonial governments were based on the idea that the purpose of government is to protect the people's natural rights to life, liberty, and property.

❷ **Representative government**. The colonists elected representatives to their colonial legislatures. The first elected legislature was in Virginia in 1619.

58

Discuss with students how these ideas were used in the colonial government. Then ask them to speculate on the effect the colonists' experiences had on the development of self-government in the United States during the past two centuries. Ask them to consider what reaction the colonists might have had if the British government had attempted to reduce the rights that the colonists had become accustomed to.

At this time, you also may wish to review the reasons leading to the rebellion of the English nobility against their king and the subsequent creation of the Magna Carta.

This painting shows the founding of the colony of Maryland.
What basic ideas did colonists use when they created their governments?

❸ **Rule of law**. The colonists created a government of laws. The people who made and enforced the laws did not have unlimited power and they, too, had to obey the laws. The colonial governments recognized the idea of higher law. This meant that colonial governments could not pass laws that violated the British constitution.

❹ **Separation of powers**. The powers of the colonial governments were divided among three branches:

- A governor headed the executive branch. The governor carried out and enforced the law. In most colonies, the king or the owner of the colony appointed the governor.

- The legislative branch made the laws. Most colonies had legislatures with two houses.

- The judicial branch was made up of judges or magistrates. The governor usually appointed the judges. The judges were responsible for handling conflicts about the laws. The judges presided at the trials of people accused of a crime. The judges also made sure that colonial laws did not violate the British constitution.

❺ **Checks and balances**. In many colonies the branches of government shared power, but one branch could check the use of power by another branch. For example, the governors could not collect taxes without the consent of the legislature.

Why did the British government tighten control over the colonies?

This section explains why the British initially neglected the colonies but later began to tighten their control over the Americans. Assign the first part of this reading (up to the examples of British laws). Ensure that the students understand the reasons for the change in the British attitude toward the colonies.

Why did the British government tighten control over the colonies?

For much of the colonial period, Great Britain paid little attention to the colonies. Britain had become a world power and was often busy fighting wars in Europe. The government in Britain did not have much time to devote to the colonies. In addition, the colonies were a long distance away. Communication between the colonies and Britain was slow because news had to travel by ship. News of events in the colonies reached Britain months later. Orders from the government to the colonies took months to arrive.

During the years of British neglect, the colonists became used to ruling themselves. Further, the colonists had been able to ignore many of the laws made by Parliament.

By the mid-1700s, however, the British began to show a new interest in the colonies. In 1763, Britain won a long and costly war against France. The cost of the conflict left the British with a large national debt. Parliament saw the colonies as a source of much-needed money. They felt that the colonies should pay their portion of the cost of the war. To reduce the national debt, Parliament raised taxes in both Britain and the colonies. The British government also began to tighten trade regulations between the colonies and other nations.

These are some examples of British laws that affected the colonies.

- **Proclamation of 1763**. The law banned settlement in certain western lands. Its purpose was to reduce tensions between the colonists and Native Americans. The British army could then withdraw from the frontier and, thus, save the government money.

What does this picture illustrate about British control over the American colonies for most of the colonial period?

Have students read the second part of this section, which outlines the many laws that affected the colonists. Help students to understand the conflict between the British government and the Americans.

Ask students whether they believe that the British were correct in their dispute with the colonists. Ask them to explain the reasoning behind their opinions.

- **Sugar Act of 1764**. The purpose of the law was to stop the smuggling of goods into and out of the colonies. It gave the British navy greater power to search colonial ships. Naval officers used **writs of assistance**, or search warrants, that allowed them to board colonial ships. The law also required products such as tobacco, sugar, and timber to be shipped directly from the colonies to Britain. The law set taxes on cloth, sugar, coffee, and wine coming into the colonies.

- **Stamp Act, 1765**. The law imposed a tax on every legal document, newspaper, pamphlet, and deck of cards coming into the colonies.

- **Quartering Act, 1765**. The British government moved the army from the western lands into the cities. The law required colonists who were innkeepers or public officials to house and feed the British soldiers.

- **Declaratory Act, 1766**. The law stated that Parliament had the right to pass laws for the colonies in "all cases whatsoever." Its purpose was to remind the colonists that the authority of the king and Parliament was superior to colonial governments.

- **Tea Act, 1773**. The law gave the East India Company the sole right to sell tea to the colonies. The East India Company was a large and important corporation in Britain. The purpose of the law was to keep the company from going broke.

The colonists viewed the new laws differently than did the government in Great Britain. Many colonists came to believe that Parliament was threatening their rights. They believed that Britain was becoming oppressive.

The tax and trade laws meant that some colonists would lose money. More important, the laws went against the

What events led the British government to tighten its control over the colonies? Were the British justified? Why or why not?

READING AND DISCUSSION

How did the colonists resist British control?

This reading continues for two pages after the Ideas for Discussion section. Assign the reading. Direct a discussion about the sequence of events that led to the Revolutionary War. Ensure that students understand what the delegates to the Congress decided during the Second Continental Congress. Refer students to the illustrations and ask the questions posed in the captions.

colonists' belief in representative government. The colonies had no right to elect representatives to Parliament. Therefore, the colonists claimed, Parliament had no right to tax the colonies. The colonists felt that tax laws should be passed only by their colonial legislatures. "No taxation without representation" became a rallying cry of the colonists.

To the British, the laws seemed reasonable. King George felt that the colonists were acting like ungrateful children. The well-being and safety of the colonies were due to the help they got from the British government. It was only fair that the colonists pay their share of the cost of government. The issue of representation made little sense to most British people. Parliament did not represent individuals. Nor did it represent areas of the country. Instead, Parliament represented the interests of the whole nation, no matter where British subjects lived.

How did the colonists resist British control?

Between 1763 and 1775, tension was growing between the colonies and the British government. To protest against British actions the colonists organized town meetings and wrote angry letters to the newspapers. They also put together independent voluntary groups that organized other ways to resist the British.

The most significant of these groups were the **committees of correspondence**. Their mission was to make sure that each colony knew about events and opinions in the other colonies. Although the committees began as voluntary associations, their success led to their establishment by most of the colonial governments. The committees raised the spirits of the people and united them against the British. Eventually all the colonies were linked by committees of correspondence.

What was the result of colonial resistance?

IDEAS FOR DISCUSSION

Why are these rights important?

Divide the class into four groups, each representing one of the four colonists mentioned in the activity. Each group should discuss its particular case, list the rights the British government has violated, and explain why they think the rights are important. Have each group share their ideas with the whole class.

IDEAS FOR DISCUSSION

Why are these rights important?

Each of the following illustrates an event resulting from the enforcement of British laws in the colonies. Examine each situation. If you had been the colonist named in each case, what right or rights would you claim the British government had violated? Explain why you think having each right is important. Share your ideas with the class.

❶ Your name is Elsbeth Merrill. While you were baking bread and awaiting the return of your husband, an agent of the king arrived at your inn. The agent informed you that you must house and feed four British soldiers.

❷ Your name is Lemuel Adams and you have a warehouse full of goods near Boston Harbor. The king's magistrate issues a writ of assistance allowing British officials to search all homes, stores, and warehouses in Boston. The officials used the writ to search your business for evidence of smuggling.

❸ Your name is James Otis. You represent people who are in prison. The judge has denied the prisoners a trial by a jury in their own community. You argue that this is illegal because it violates the British constitution. The judge denies your request and sends the prisoners to England for trial.

❹ Your name is William Bradford. You printed an article in your newspaper criticizing the deputy governor of the colony. The king appointed the deputy governor. You wrote that the deputy governor was like a "large cocker spaniel about five foot five." You are under arrest. Your printing press in Philadelphia has been destroyed.

JAMES OTIS

WILLIAM BRADFORD

How did the Boston Massacre change the way some colonists thought about British rule?

Two other important groups were the **Sons of Liberty** and the **Daughters of Liberty**. The Sons began in 1765 and quickly spread throughout the country. The Sons of Liberty organized resistance to the Stamp Act. Mobs of people attacked the homes of tax collectors. The Sons of Liberty burned effigies, or straw dummies, made to look like royal officials. They marched in the streets and sometimes committed violent acts.

Women soon got together and formed the Daughters of Liberty. They helped to make the boycott of British trade effective. Instead of buying British goods, they began spinning their own yarn and making their own linen. After the British Parliament passed the Tea Act of 1773, many women gave up drinking tea.

Both the Sons and Daughters of Liberty continued with acts of resistance until the start of the Revolutionary War. There were two well-known events that resulted in violence.

- **The Boston Massacre, 1770**
  British troops opened fire on a crowd of protestors outside the customs house in Boston. Five people died as a result. The tragedy convinced many colonists that the British government would use military force to make them obey the laws.

- **The Boston Tea Party, 1773**
  The colonists attempted to prevent the unloading of a cargo of tea that had arrived in Boston Harbor. The protestors ripped open 342 chests and dumped the tea into the harbor. The British responded by closing the harbor to all trade.

By the fall of 1774, these events had led many colonists to decide that it was time to take united action. The committees of correspondence called for representatives from all the colonies to meet in a general congress once a year. They were to deliberate on the general interests of all the colonies.

This call laid the foundation for the Continental Congress. The **First Continental Congress** met in Philadelphia. Twelve of the thirteen colonies sent representatives. It was the start of a unified American government. The purpose of the Congress was to decide on the best response to the actions of the British government. The members of Congress agreed to impose their own ban on trade with Great Britain. Congress hoped that this move would force the British government to change its policies toward the colonies.

On April 19, 1775, fighting broke out between Great Britain and the American colonies. On that day, British troops marched to the towns of Lexington and Concord in Massachusetts. The army was supposed to capture hidden guns and supplies by surprise, but a system of signals warned the Americans. The Americans fired on the British and forced them back to Boston. That was the beginning of the Revolutionary War.

A few weeks later, representatives of the colonies met in Philadelphia for the **Second Continental Congress**. The delegates to the Congress decided to resist the British. Congress organized the Continental Army and called upon the colonies to send troops. The delegates selected George Washington to lead the army. A year later, Congress asked a committee to draft a document explaining why the colonists felt it was necessary to free themselves from British rule. This document is known as the Declaration of Independence.

What happened at the First Continental Congress?

 see next student page

LESSON REVIEW

The questions in the student book are intended to assess learning and to reinforce knowledge through discussion. The questions are directly related to the lesson objectives. You may wish to include additional questions developed by yourself or by your students.

1. Why was it necessary for the colonists to create their own colonial governments?

   Many of the charters granted by the British government said little about the kind of government a colony should have. Therefore, the colonists had to develop their own form of government.

2. What ideas of constitutional government did the colonists use in creating their governments?

   The colonists used basic ideas of constitutional government such as natural rights, representative government, the rule of law, separation of powers, and checks and balances.

3. Why did the British begin to tighten control over the colonies after 1763?

   Britain had just won an expensive war against France that left Britain with a very large debt. The British saw the colonies as a source of money that would help to pay off that debt. The British thought that the colonists should pay for their fair share of the cost of government.

(continued next page)

4. What tax and trade laws did Parliament pass? What was the purpose of these laws? What effects did the laws have on the colonists?

   Parliament passed the Proclamation of 1763, the Sugar Act of 1764, the Stamp Act of 1765, the Quartering Act of 1765, the Declaratory Act of 1766, and the Tea Act of 1773. These laws were intended to reduce the national debt of Britain. The laws caused the colonists to believe that Britain was becoming oppressive. Some of the colonists lost money because of the taxes.

5. Why did the colonists feel that the laws passed by Parliament violated their rights?

   The laws went against the colonists' belief in representative government. The colonists reasoned that because they had no representation in Parliament, Britain had no right to tax them.

6. Why did the British believe that the tax and trade laws were fair?

   The British believed that Parliament had the authority to tax the colonists because it represented the interests of the entire country, including the colonies. The British point of view was that the colonists owed their well-being and safety to the British government and that it was fair that the colonists pay for their share of the cost of government.

ACTIVITIES

The suggested activities are intended to extend and apply learning outside the classroom. You may wish to have students complete one or more of the activities. Have them share their results with the class.

LESSON REVIEW

❶ Why was it necessary for the colonists to create their own colonial governments?

❷ What ideas of constitutional government did the colonists use in creating their governments?

❸ Why did the British begin to tighten control over the colonies after 1763?

❹ What tax and trade laws did Parliament pass? What was the purpose of these laws? What effects did the laws have on the colonists?

❺ Why did the colonists feel that the laws passed by Parliament violated their rights?

❻ Why did the British believe that the tax and trade laws were fair?

ACTIVITIES

❶ Many people and groups played important roles in the Revolutionary War. Choose one of the organizations listed below to research. Share what you learn with your class.

- Committees of Correspondence
- Daughters of Liberty
- Sons of Liberty

❷ Research the life of Thomas Paine using the school library or the Internet. Write a review of his pamphlet, *Common Sense*. Explain the importance of Thomas Paine's writing to the Revolutionary War.

❸ Imagine that you were living in the colonies in the 1770s. Write a speech arguing why the laws passed by Parliament violated your rights. Then, imagine that you were a Member of Parliament. Write a speech arguing why these laws were necessary. Present your speeches to the class.

❹ Create a timeline of the important events discussed in this lesson. Illustrate your timeline with drawings.

❺ Draw two cartoons, one showing how the colonists felt about the Boston Tea Party and the other showing the same event from a British point of view.

What basic ideas about government are in the Declaration of Independence?

8

LESSON PURPOSE

One of the most important documents in American history is the Declaration of Independence. It summarizes the colonists' basic ideas about government. The Declaration lists the colonies' complaints against the British government. The Declaration also explains the reasons why the colonies decided to declare their independence from Great Britain.

When you finish this lesson, you should be able to explain the main ideas that are in the Declaration of Independence.

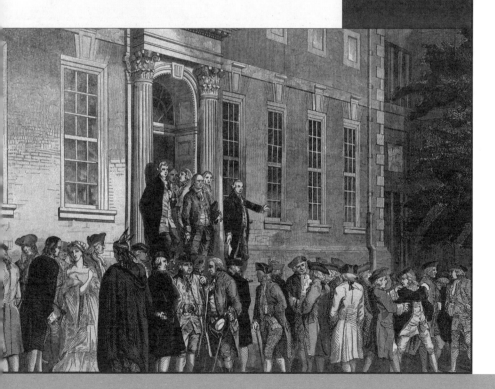

OVERVIEW

In this lesson, students closely examine the Declaration of Independence and see how the ideas of natural rights, the social contract, consent of the governed, and the right to alter or abolish government are reflected in the document. Students learn how these ideas were used to justify the American Revolution and what the conflicting views were among the colonists about the Revolution.

OBJECTIVES

At the conclusion of this lesson, students should be able to

- explain the basic ideas about government that are contained in the Declaration of Independence

- explain how the Declaration of Independence embodies the concept of natural rights philosophy, government in a republic, and constitutional government

- describe the arguments found in the Declaration of Independence that justify the separation of the colonies from Great Britain

- explain why some colonists did not want to separate from Great Britain

TEACHING PROCEDURES

INTRODUCTORY ACTIVITY

Have students write a short statement about a situation in which they feel the need to be independent. It might be personal independence from the authority of parents or school or some other situation. Have them describe why they believe this independence is justified. Ask them whether any of their arguments are based on ideas the Founders had about self-government. Have students write a statement declaring their independence and list the advantages and disadvantages of doing so. Invite volunteers to share their statements with the rest of the class. Have students compare their declarations to the Declaration of Independence.

(continued next page)

Have students read the Lesson Purpose and consider the objectives of the lesson. Write the Terms to Understand on the board or use a vocabulary-building activity of your choice. Have students look up the words in the Glossary at the back of the text. Ask them to look for these words as they read the lesson.

READING AND DISCUSSION

Why was the Declaration of Independence written?

Ask your students to read this section. Note that although Jefferson was an excellent writer, he was not an eloquent orator. Take the time to help students appreciate the task that the relatively young Jefferson was asked to do with the help of other members of the committee. Emphasize that writing is a powerful tool that allows people to explain complex ideas.

TERMS TO UNDERSTAND

abolish
Loyalists
natural law
Patriots
self-evident
Tories
unalienable rights

Why was the Declaration of Independence written?

On June 7, 1776, the Continental Congress called for the colonies to declare independence from Great Britain. The Congress had to inform the British and the world that the colonies were now free and independent states. The Congress wanted to be sure that the reasons for its actions were clear.

A committee to draft the Declaration of Independence was quickly appointed. Members of the committee were Benjamin Franklin, John Adams, Roger Sherman, Robert Livingston, and a young Virginian named Thomas Jefferson. Jefferson was a man of many talents. He was a statesman, diplomat, author, architect, and scientist. He was a member of the Continental Congress during the Revolutionary War. Jefferson was a quiet, shy man, not known as a great speaker. He worked well in small groups and was an excellent writer. The committee chose Jefferson to write the first draft of the Declaration of Independence.

Jefferson spent many days writing. He discussed the draft with other members of the committee. They suggested changes

Why do you think Congress appointed a committee to draft the Declaration of Independence?

and Jefferson made the revisions. When the committee finished its work, they sent the document to Congress.

On July 4, 1776, the members of Congress passed the Declaration of Independence.

How is the Declaration of Independence organized?

The Declaration is not a very long document. It is easy to understand when you see how it is organized. The Declaration has four important parts.

* **Ideals**. The Declaration sets forth the Founders' beliefs about the purposes of government. It explains how government is created. It is one of the best statements of the ideals of our nation.

* **Arguments**. The Declaration gives the reasons why the colonies thought they were justified in breaking away from Great Britain.

* **Complaints**. The Declaration includes a list of complaints against the British king. The items on the list are there to show how the British government violated the rights of the colonists.

Why do you think the Founders wanted a written Declaration of Independence?

* **Conclusion**. In the end, the Declaration states that the bond between Great Britain and the colonies is dissolved. It states "that these United Colonies are, and of Right ought to be, Free and Independent States."

What principles of government does the Declaration include?

The Declaration of Independence sets forth some of the most important ideals of our nation. The Declaration states that "all men are created equal" and that they all have certain basic rights. These are the rights to life, liberty, and the pursuit of happiness.

According to natural rights philosophy, what do the people have a right to do when the government breaks its contract with them?

How is the Declaration of Independence organized?

Ask the class to read this section. Write the four parts of the Declaration of Independence on the board: ideals, arguments, complaints, and conclusion. Have students offer words or phrases that would reflect the contents of each part. Save this to refer to when students read the Declaration of Independence later in the lesson. Another option is to have students divide into four groups. Each group would create a graphic illustrating one of the four sections of the Declaration. When completed, the graphics would then be presented to the whole class.

What principles of government does the Declaration include?

Have students read this section aloud. You may wish to divide the reading among several students. Discuss this section with students and allow time for questions. Then go back to the four parts from the previous section and have students add language from the Declaration to the section of the board labeled "ideals."

READING AND DISCUSSION

What reasons does the Declaration give for independence?

Assign this section to the class to read and review the arguments given for independence in the Declaration of Independence. Then refer back to the four parts of the Declaration and ask students to add specific arguments to the section of the board labeled "arguments."

What ideas from John Locke did Jefferson include in the Declaration of Independence?

Part of the Declaration is printed below.

*We hold these Truths to be **self-evident** [easy for anyone to see], that all Men are created equal, that they are endowed [given] by their Creator [God] with certain **unalienable Rights** [rights that cannot be taken away], that among these are Life, Liberty, and the Pursuit of Happiness—That to secure these Rights, Governments are instituted [established] among Men, deriving [receiving] their just Powers from the Consent [agreement] of the Governed, that whenever any Form of Government becomes destructive of these Ends [purposes], it is the Right of the People to alter or to abolish [overthrow or put an end to] it, and to institute new Government.*

What reasons does the Declaration give for independence?

The Declaration was a justification for the American Revolution. Jefferson used the ideas of the natural rights philosophy in this argument. The main points of the argument are listed below. See if you can identify its relationship to the natural rights philosophy.

❶ The rights of the people are based on **natural law**. This means that there is an unchanging set of laws that govern human relations. Natural law is a higher law than law made by man. The Founders believed that natural law came from God. No constitution or government may violate the natural law. The only purpose of government is to protect the people's natural rights.

❷ If a government violates the natural law, the people have the right to change or **abolish**—put an end to—that government and form a new one.

❸ An agreement existed between the colonists and the king. The colonists consented to be governed by the king so long as he protected their rights to life, liberty, and property.

❹ No agreement existed between the colonists and Parliament. Therefore, Parliament had no right to govern the colonies or to tax them. This was especially true, argued the colonists, since they did not have the right to send representatives to Parliament.

❺ The king violated his agreement with the colonists. The king acted, along with Parliament, to deprive the colonists of their rights. Therefore, the colonists had the right to withdraw their consent to be governed by the king. The colonists were free to establish their own government.

What complaints against the king does the Declaration include?

The Declaration contains a long list of complaints against the British king. For example, the Declaration accuses the king of

- refusing to approve laws necessary for the public good

- seeking to destroy the colonial legislatures

- obstructing justice by refusing to give certain powers to the colonial courts

- keeping standing armies in time of peace

- requiring the quartering or housing of British soldiers

- imposing taxes without the consent of the people to be taxed

- cutting off trade between the colonies and all parts of the world

- in some cases, denying the colonists the right to trial by jury

IDEAS FOR DISCUSSION

What ideas about government are in the Declaration of Independence?

Work with a partner or in groups of three. Each group should examine the text of the Declaration of Independence and select three complaints against the king. Groups should then complete the following steps and report their findings to the class.

- Rewrite the complaint in your own words.

- Explain the basis of the colonists' complaint.

- Explain what ideas about government are implied by each complaint.

What complaints against the king does the Declaration include?

Ask students to read this section and return to the four parts of the Declaration. Have students add specific complaints to the section of the board labeled "complaints."

IDEAS FOR DISCUSSION

What ideas about government are in the Declaration of Independence?

Assign students partners or divide them into groups of no more than three. Have students turn to page 276 of their books for the text of the Declaration of Independence. Ask them to read the Declaration and select three complaints against the king. As an alternative, you can assign specific complaints to the groups rather than asking them to select their own. Each group should rewrite the complaint in their own words, explain the basis of the complaint, and explain what ideas about government are implied by each complaint. Have students share their work with the class. Refer students to the photograph of the actual Declaration of Independence on pages 69 or 276.

READING AND DISCUSSION

Why did some colonists want to remain British subjects?

Ask individual students to read this section and discuss the situation that the Loyalists faced. You might ask them to explain why being a British subject was still important to so many of the colonists when they were living so far from England.

 see next student page

SOLVE THE PROBLEM

Would you favor or oppose independence?

Prepare the class for a debate. Divide the class into four groups. Two groups will represent the supporters of the Revolution, the Patriots, and two groups will represent the supporters of the British position, the Loyalists. Read the first two paragraphs of this section aloud and explain to students their roles and responsibilities. Groups one and three will read their letters supporting their positions aloud to the entire class. Groups two and four will draw editorial cartoons supporting their positions on posters. After all four groups have completed their assigned tasks, review the activity by asking all students to identify the most convincing arguments from each group.

Why did some colonists want to remain British subjects?

To rebel against the British government was a serious matter. After all, generations of colonists had been loyal to Great Britain. It is understandable, then, that some people did not support the Revolution.

The colonists were almost evenly divided into those who supported the Revolution, those who did not, and the undecided. The people who remained loyal to the king were called **Loyalists** or **Tories**. They held deep feelings of loyalty to the home country.

Many Loyalists were large landowners, wealthy merchants, or officials of the king. The Loyalists did not like British taxes or other limits on their freedom any more than the Patriots did. But they did not think that breaking away from Britain was the answer to these problems.

Some colonial families split apart when the Revolution began. Family members chose sides. Those who supported the Revolution were called **Patriots**. Those who remained loyal to Britain were known as Loyalists. For example, Benjamin Franklin was a Patriot. His son was a Loyalist.

Many Loyalists joined the British army and fought for the king. Some Loyalists moved back to Great Britain while others went to Canada or the West Indies. Those Loyalists who remained in the colonies had a hard time. Sometimes their property was taken from them. Sometimes they were humiliated or put in jail. Even so, the Loyalists as a group suffered less than dissenters in other revolutions.

This drawing illustrates Loyalists being received back into Great Britain. What rights of the Loyalists, if any, were violated by the Patriots?

see next student page

SOLVE THE PROBLEM

Would you favor or oppose independence?

Both the Patriots and the Loyalists held strong opinions about the Revolution. Patriots and Loyalists came from all sections of American life. Native Americans were forced to choose sides in the struggle. African Americans were Loyalists as well as Patriots.

Your class can debate both sides of the issue. Work in four groups. Two groups support the revolutionary cause and two groups oppose it.

Why do you think such bitter feelings arose during the debate between the Patriots and the Loyalists?

Supporters of the Revolution	Supporters of the British
PATRIOTS	**LOYALISTS**

Group one. You are members of the state legislature, writers, doctors, and their friends and families. Write letters to your family or the editor of a colonial newspaper defending the actions of the Second Continental Congress. Read your letters when it is your turn to speak in the debate.

Group two. You are backcountry farmers, trappers, and schoolteachers. Draw editorial cartoons defending the American position in the conflict with Great Britain. Display your posters on your side of the debate area.

Group three. You are landowners, shipbuilders, shopkeepers, and their friends and families. Write letters to the editor of a colonial newspaper explaining why the British actions were justified. Read your letters aloud when it is your turn to speak in the debate.

Group four. Your group is composed of colonial officials such as magistrates, sheriffs, soldiers, and their friends and families. Draw editorial cartoons supporting your ideas about loyalty to England. Display your posters in your side of the debate area.

LESSON REVIEW

The questions in the student book are intended to assess learning and to reinforce knowledge through discussion. The questions are directly related to the lesson objectives. You may wish to include additional questions developed by yourself or by your students.

1. What were the reasons for writing the Declaration of Independence?

   The Continental Congress had to inform the British and the world that the colonies were independent states free of British control. Congress also wanted to describe the reasons for its actions.

2. What are the four parts of the Declaration of Independence?

   The four parts of the Declaration of Independence are the ideals, arguments, complaints, and conclusion.

3. What arguments does the Declaration make in support of the colonies' independence?

   Jefferson used ideas from natural rights philosophy to justify the American Revolution. He stated that the rights of the people are based on natural law and that the purpose of government is to protect the people's natural rights. Jefferson argued that the king had violated his agreement with the colonists and deprived them of their rights. Therefore, the people had the right to abolish the government and form a new one.

4. What complaints did the colonists have against the king of Great Britain?

   The colonists complained that the king refused to approve laws needed for the public good. They thought that he was destroying the colonial legislatures and obstructing justice by refusing to give certain powers to colonial courts. They were unhappy with the practice of keeping a standing army in the colonies in times of peace and requiring the people to quarter soldiers. The colonists claimed that the king was imposing taxes without the consent of the people. They complained that the king had cut off trade between the colonies and the rest of the world. Finally, they accused the king of denying some colonists the right to trial by jury.

5. What is the purpose of government as described in the Declaration of Independence?

The purpose of government as described in the Declaration of Independence is to protect the natural rights of the people. The Declaration makes particular mention of the "unalienable" rights to "Life, Liberty and the pursuit of Happiness."

6. What does the Declaration say people have the right to do if a government does not protect their rights?

The Declaration states that the people have the right to alter or abolish the government and establish a new government if the existing government does not protect the rights of the people.

7. What do the following phrases from the Declaration mean?

- "all men are created equal"
  This phrase refers to the belief that everyone has the same rights. It is important to note that even though Jefferson wrote these words, certain rights, such as voting, had specific qualifications and that "men" did not necessarily refer to women, Native Americans, or African slaves.

- "consent of the governed"
  This phrase refers to the idea that the people agree to be governed and that an agreement exists between the governed (the people) and the government (those who govern).

- "self-evident"
  This phrase means that it is easy for everyone to see that a certain fact or idea exists.

- "unalienable rights"
  This phrase refers to the basic or natural rights of all people that cannot be taken away.

ACTIVITIES

The suggested activities are intended to extend and apply learning outside the classroom. You may wish to have students complete one or more of the activities. Have them share their results with the class.

LESSON REVIEW

❶ What were the reasons for writing the Declaration of Independence?

❷ What are the four parts of the Declaration of Independence?

❸ What arguments does the Declaration make in support of the colonies' independence?

❹ What complaints did the colonists have against the king of Great Britain?

❺ What is the purpose of government as described in the Declaration of Independence?

❻ What does the Declaration say people have the right to do if a government does not protect their rights?

❼ What do the following phrases from the Declaration mean?

- "all men are created equal"
- "consent of the governed"
- "self-evident"
- "unalienable rights"

ACTIVITIES

❶ Rewrite the first two paragraphs of the Declaration of Independence in contemporary language. Share your revision with the class.

❷ Read a novel about the Revolutionary War, such as *April Morning, Johnny Tremain, Cast Two Shadows,* or *My Brother Sam Is Dead.*

Select a character from the story. Explain his or her opinions about the Revolutionary War.

❸ Play the online game *"Liberty Or Loyalty"*

http://www.history.org/history/teaching/revolution/a1.html

or another online game about the American Revolution. The site is hosted by Colonial Williamsburg.

What happened during the American Revolution? How did the government function?

LESSON PURPOSE

In this lesson, you will learn what happened during the American Revolutionary War with Britain. You will also learn about the significance of the war for the rest of the world. You will learn about the difficulties of the colonists during the war and the role played by diplomacy.

When you have finished the lesson, you should be able to explain the course of the war and how the colonial armies overcame extreme difficulties. You should also be able to explain some problems of government that Congress had to deal with during the war.

OVERVIEW

This lesson introduces students to the American War for Independence. The Revolutionary War brought the former colonies their independence. Students learn how the war began and what course it took. They find that diplomacy, not just fighting by the American forces, was essential for victory. Students also learn about the problems of governing without a properly constituted national legislature during the Revolution. They learn how the former colonists tried to cope with the lack of central authority by writing the Articles of Confederation, which were not adopted until the war was nearly over. The lesson concludes with the British surrender at Yorktown, Virginia.

OBJECTIVES

At the conclusion of this lesson, students should be able to

- describe how the Revolutionary War began, what its course was, and explain the roles of courage and perseverance

- describe what problems the Second Continental Congress had with governing during the Revolutionary War and how they tried to cope with these problems

- explain why diplomacy was essential for gaining independence and describe the type of foreign aid the Americans received from abroad

- explain the significance that the American Revolution had for the world

TEACHING PROCEDURES

INTRODUCTORY ACTIVITY

Ask students to read the Lesson Purpose and to consider the lesson objectives. Ask students what they think the phrase "The shot heard 'round the world" means and ask them why they think it might be important. Let students know how difficult it was for the former colonies to fight and win a war against the world's best army—Britain's—without a centralized government with real authority over the states. Ask students what they know about the course of the war and if they know how close the Americans came to losing it.

Write the Terms to Understand on the board and ask students to look up the words in the Glossary at the back of the text.

READING, RESEARCH, AND LITERATURE ACTIVITY

How did the Revolutionary War begin, and what was its significance?

Have students read this section aloud. After doing so, read aloud or ask a student to read aloud the poems, "The Midnight Ride of Paul Revere," by Henry Wadsworth Longfellow, and "Concord Hymn," by Ralph Waldo Emerson. Both of these poems are easily available on the Internet. Ask students to explain what "the shot heard 'round the world" means. See if any students can name some more recent, twentieth-century attempts by colonies to rebel against their colonial rulers. The example of India, led by Mohandas K. Gandhi, which waged a struggle against British rule in the 1930s and 1940s, might be introduced to the class if no one mentions it. Other anticolonial twentieth-century movements include many in Africa, such as those against British rule in Kenya and Ghana, and against French rule in Algeria; and in Asia, in Vietnam against French rule, in Indonesia against Dutch rule, and in the Philippines against American rule.

Students should be told that the American example of national independence fomented anticolonial struggles soon after the end of the Revolutionary War in 1781. In the early nineteenth century, Spanish colonies in South America rebelled against their colonial status and won independence. In Haiti, a valiant struggle against French rule was waged during the same period.

These examples, among many others, should allow students to see the force and meaning of the term, "the shot heard 'round the world." Students should realize also that the Declaration of Independence was the key document that circulated throughout the world justifying revolution against colonial rule.

The French Revolution, which occurred later (1789), was very different from the American one. The French version was not a rebellion against colonial rule. Instead, as it progressed, it turned into a rebellion against the entire French social order, with its royal family, the hereditary aristocracy, and all the entrenched powers associated with these institutions. Students should know that it was the French Revolution that inspired the Russian Revolution, and, to a lesser extent, the Chinese Revolution of the twentieth

TERMS TO UNDERSTAND

Battle of Saratoga
diplomacy
Quebec Campaign
"The Shot Heard 'Round the World"
treason
Treaty of Paris
Yorktown Surrender

How did the Revolutionary War begin, and what was its significance?

The night before fighting broke out, Paul Revere made his famous midnight ride. He warned members of the citizen militia, called Minutemen, to get ready to fight. They gathered in Lexington and Concord. The role of the citizen militia reminds us that citizens are sometimes called upon to perform service to their nation. Calling upon the citizen militia as Revere did also gives us insight into why the Founders added the **Second Amendment** to the Constitution. The amendment says that "a well-regulated militia being necessary to the security of a free State, the right of the people to keep and bear Arms shall not be infringed."

The Revolutionary War, which lasted for six long years, ended in victory for the former American colonists. You learned in Lesson 7 that the first shots were fired on April 19, 1775. That morning, skirmishes between American colonists and British soldiers broke out. The gunfire that opened the fighting later became known as **"the shot heard 'round the world."** People said this because news of the

How did Paul Revere's ride affect the American Revolution?

American rebellion and its demand for independence spread all over the world. Many nations eventually made the same demand of their own colonial rulers. The American Revolution changed world history. Achieving independence, however, was far more difficult than declaring it. Success often seemed impossible, but the Americans did not give up.

What did the Second Continental Congress do to direct the Revolution?

On July 4, 1776, Congress issued its formal Declaration of Independence, making a complete break from Britain. There was no turning back. The Continental Congress endured great difficulties in trying to govern during the Revolution. There were many arguments among the delegates to Congress. Because it did not have a legal charter for its existence, Congress could not force the former colonies, now independent states, to pay the costs of fighting the British. So, soldiers often went unpaid, unfed, and without uniforms.

To finance military expenses, Congress decided to issue paper money. But the paper was not backed by any precious metal. Therefore, it could not hold a steady, reliable value. Paper money did not solve the problem of lack of funds, which remained for the whole war.

Congress tried to remedy the lack of a legal basis for its existence. In November 1777, Congress passed the Articles of Confederation. It was the country's first constitution. But the states took their time in agreeing to the new frame of government. It was not until March 1, 1781, when the fighting was nearly over, that the Articles took effect. Even then, the Articles did not solve the problems of the new national government. You will learn more about the Articles of Confederation in Lesson 11.

What problems were faced by the Continental Congress?

century. Both of these revolutions overturned the social order in its entirety and resulted in the deaths of tens of millions of people when totalitarian governments took power. All these considerations should help the class to realize the far-reaching influence of the American Revolution and the Declaration of Independence and how the Revolution was like and unlike other revolutions of the two centuries that followed.

READING AND DISCUSSION

What did the Second Continental Congress do to direct the Revolution?

Ask students to read this section aloud. Help them imagine what it would have been like to have been a member of the Second Continental Congress trying to direct the struggle against Britain. The Congress had no legal authority over the newly independent states, each of which was sovereign. Congress had no powers of taxation and the states gave little to the war effort—after all, the colonies' economies were badly injured by fighting and disruptions in trade. The result of these circumstances was that Congress could barely manage to keep armies in the field during some periods, as soldiers often were unpaid, unfed, ill-housed, and unequipped.

Guide the class through the measures that Congress took to deal with these grim circumstances. Ask them why they think the paper money issued by Congress lost its value because it was backed by no precious metals, whereas the paper money issued today retains its value, even though it, too, is not backed by precious metals. Finally, have the class take note of the fact that Congress did attempt to deal with its lack of legal authority by drawing up the Articles of Confederation that would serve as a basis to legitimize its position. The new states would have to ratify the Articles, however, before they went into effect, and this took a number of years.

READING AND DISCUSSION

How successful were the Americans at the beginning of the Revolutionary War?

Ask students to read this section. Make sure they understand that the early engagements of the Revolutionary War were seldom favorable to the American side. They should also see the imagination, courage, and daring of Washington's attacks on Trenton and Princeton. Although these were not militarily important, they were important for the morale both of troops and of civilians. It might be worthwhile to compare these attacks to the raid on Tokyo made by General James Doolittle in 1942, just months after the attack on Pearl Harbor. On both occasions, a militarily insignificant event raised American spirits.

Students should also learn how close the British came to strangling the American Revolution in its cradle with its plan to split the colonies in half by conquering the Hudson River Valley. The American victory at Saratoga—where material aid secretly financed by France was a factor—therefore looms large in the history of the war. Some historians call Saratoga the most decisive battle in the war.

How successful were the Americans at the beginning of the Revolutionary War?

At the beginning of the war, the Americans were not successful. They invaded Canada in the **Quebec Campaign** of 1775–76, but failed. Then in August 1776, in the Battle of Long Island, near New York City, the British defeated George Washington. But he managed to save most of his troops from capture. This occurred only two months after independence was declared.

The military situation was bleak. Washington understood how grave matters were. He tried to rally the former colonists, about a third of whom were against independence and another third were neutral, to the cause of fighting for independence by making daring raids on British positions. Near the end of December, he crossed the ice-choked Delaware River and won small battles at Trenton and Princeton, New Jersey. But prospects for the American cause were poor. The troops needed food, their pay, and equipment.

In 1777, Washington lost more encounters with the British in Pennsylvania at Germantown and Brandywine Creek. In the same year, the British tried to strangle the Revolution by cutting the colonies in two. They took control of the Hudson River, which ran through New York. But the British failed. Instead, the Americans scored a victory in the **Battle of Saratoga**. Arms and supplies secretly sent by the French government through a private arms merchant arrived in time to help the Americans. This may have been the Revolution's most important campaign. The British plan had been defeated.

What happened at Valley Forge, Pennsylvania, during the winter of 1777–78?

No one could see the importance of Saratoga until much later. In the meantime, conditions for the American army became desperate. Soldiers suffered terribly from lack of food and shelter during the winter of 1777–78 at their quarters in Valley Forge, Pennsylvania. But American spirits did not give out. Martha Washington joined her husband, sharing the hardships of a cold and bleak winter. She did what she could to assist the troops. She organized a campaign for supplies that the soldiers desperately

How did Martha Washington contribute to the success of the Revolutionary War?

needed. She was aided in her efforts by Benjamin Franklin's daughter, Sarah Franklin Bache. Together, they collected 2,200 shirts and 400 pairs of stockings for the freezing men.

During this winter in Valley Forge, Baron von Steuben, a German volunteer, gave important assistance by training the cold, ragged, half-starved soldiers. He raised their morale and helped make them into an effective fighting force. Some troops deserted, but others endured the terrible cold and hunger. The young French aristocrat and military commander, the Marquis de Lafayette, who was devoted to the American cause for independence, also spent the winter at Valley Forge. When spring arrived, the American forces, though in tatters, had endured.

What part did diplomacy play in the outcome of the war?

Events happening elsewhere, however, eventually turned the tide in the Americans' favor. Perhaps the most important event of 1778 occurred across the Atlantic in France. Congress had sent Silas Deane to France in 1776. He was successful in gaining arms and supplies as well as the services of competent military officers.

Later, however, Congress sent Benjamin Franklin to Paris, the capital of France, to seek aid. Franklin's fame as a writer and scientist preceded him. The French, who were sworn enemies of the British, admired him. For his part, Franklin showed great skill in diplomacy.

General George Washington with Lafayette at Valley Forge. What effect did the assistance of foreign nations have on the outcome of the war?

What happened at Valley Forge, Pennsylvania, during the winter of 1777–78?

Have the class read this section aloud. It deals with one of the most famous episodes in American history. Each year, many thousands of Americans travel to Valley Forge, Pennsylvania, to pay homage to the suffering of Washington's American army there and to recall the significance of the army's emergence from this close call with final disaster. The cause of American independence might have been dealt a deathblow were it not for the courage, perseverance, and assistance of American civilians, among them Martha Washington and Sarah Franklin Bache, daughter of Benjamin Franklin. Foreign military men, such as the Marquis de Lafayette and Baron von Steuben, also offered invaluable service.

Students should note the terrible conditions that existed for soldiers due to the lack of resources available to Congress throughout much of the war.

What part did diplomacy play in the outcome of the war?

Have the class read this section of the text. Impress on them how crucial diplomacy was for the eventual triumph of the American cause. Benjamin Franklin was not the only diplomat in Paris during the war, but he was by far the most important one—indeed the only important one. The French idolized Franklin for his numerous accomplishments as a writer, scientist, and inventor. Fellow American diplomats attempted to create trouble for Franklin in Congress by spreading gossip about his personal life. But the French made it clear that they wished to deal only with the famous Dr. Franklin. Franklin got all he wanted from the French and never lost his confidence. As a result of Franklin's successful diplomacy, France sent both soldiers and a fleet that allowed the Americans to win the Revolutionary War. Without France's help, including the help of the illustrious Lafayette, the Americans could not have prevailed.

Tell the class that when the United States came to the defense of the Allies in World War I, in 1917, on landing in France, General John J. Pershing, head of the American army, exclaimed, "Lafayette, we are here!"

What happened in the South during the war?

Have students read this section. Ask them if they knew there was fighting south of Virginia during the Revolutionary War. Point out that little fighting took place in the North after the American victory at Saratoga. Students should note that suffering and sacrifice were not limited to members of the army. The story of Eliza Lucas Pinckney presented in the text is only one among many famous, true stories of suffering endured by women and other civilians. Some others who contributed to the Revolutionary War effort are listed at the end of the lesson.

Diplomacy is the practice of carrying on formal relationships with governments of other countries. The official representatives of countries meet and discuss issues important to their governments. They work together in a peaceful manner to find solutions to common problems.

In 1778, aided by the American victory at Saratoga, Franklin secured formal treaties between France and the United States. The new alliance ensured the assistance of the French army and navy.

Making the most of his enormous popularity among the French, Franklin asked for loan after loan and was never refused. Franklin was not above hinting that the colonists might make peace with Britain, France's enemy, if the Americans did not receive what they needed. In the end, French loans, soldiers, and, especially, its navy were critical for the final victory in 1781.

What happened in the South during the war?

Little fighting took place in the Middle Atlantic region after Saratoga. In 1778–79, fighting shifted to the western frontier area, now Indiana, and to the South. Military campaigns took place in North and South Carolina and in Georgia, where Savannah fell to the British. In South Carolina, Charleston had resisted two British attacks. But in 1780 it, too, fell to the British.

Things were not going well with the American army in other parts of the former colonies. In 1780, the Americans had to endure the **treason**—the betrayal of one's country—of General Benedict Arnold when he defected to the British. Complaints about the inefficient government of Congress were voiced. Congress did not have the authority to raise money for the war from taxes. The government could only beg for funds from the states, but received little. Conditions regarding food, clothing, and pay were so poor that in January 1781, the soldiers could stand it no longer and they rebelled.

In the South, where most of the fighting was now taking place, there were great hardships. One example is that of Eliza Lucas Pinckney. She was a plantation owner famous for growing new crops to

Why was Benjamin Franklin successful in his diplomatic mission to France?

This scene depicts the surrender of Lord Cornwallis at Yorktown on October 17, 1781. What events led the British to surrender?

avoid dependence on cotton. When war broke out, Pinckney decided not to follow her economic interests. Believing in the ideas of political liberty, she supported the Revolution. But she paid dearly for her views. The British took over her mansion, burned her crops, and killed her farm animals. By the end of the war, she was economically ruined.

How did the Revolutionary War turn in the Americans' favor and come to an end?

By the early 1780s, military matters in the South turned for the better. In 1780, American forces had defeated the British at King's Mountain, South Carolina. In the following year, American commanders forced the British army under Lord Cornwallis to leave the Carolinas and

retreat to Virginia. Cornwallis soon found his armies trapped on the Yorktown Peninsula. With the French navy blocking the way, the British were unable to retreat by water.

Lafayette led American troops in containing the British on land. To the north, combined American–French forces marched south from New York to Virginia. On October 17–19, 1781, seeing that their position was hopeless, the British forces under Lord Cornwallis finally **surrendered at Yorktown**. The fighting was over. Two years later, in 1783, a formal peace treaty, known as the **Treaty of Paris**, was signed. A **treaty** is an official agreement between two or more countries. American independence was formally recognized.

READING, DISCUSSION, AND MAP ACTIVITY

How did the Revolutionary War turn in the Americans' favor and come to an end?

Have a map of Virginia or of the region ready for a discussion after the class reads this section. Ask members of the class to find the Yorktown Peninsula to show how the French fleet blocked the escape of the British army under Cornwallis. See how the American troops blocked the British escape by land. This impossible situation for the British led to their surrender in October 1781. Students should note that it took two more years for a treaty formally recognizing American independence to be signed.

 see next student page

LESSON REVIEW

1. What was the significance of the Revolutionary War for the world?

   It validated for other colonial peoples the right to self-government and the idea of revolution to fulfill this right. It also became a precedent for other peoples to overthrow their governments and set up new ones. The French Revolution was the first noncolonial revolution in modern Europe, but it entailed the overturning of social relations and institutions, not just government. South American colonies of Spain were the first to follow the American example. Countries in Asia, Africa, and the Caribbean continued these revolutions in the twentieth century.

2. How did the American army stay together during the worst times of the early part of the Revolutionary War?

   In the early part of the Revolution, the army had a difficult time. Despite Washington's daring raids, prospects for the Americans appeared poor. The winter at Valley Forge was especially grim. The army was aided by the leadership of Washington; the assistance of Baron von Steuben, who trained and disciplined the troops; and the support of the Marquis de Lafayette, who was devoted to the American cause. Martha Washington and Sarah Franklin Bache also did what they could to supply the troops with warm clothing and decent food.

3. What problems did the Second Continental Congress
have during the war, and how did Congress deal with them?

*Without good organization and resources, Congress was unable to prevent
severe suffering among the soldiers, even to the point of mutiny. Lacking
resources to pay and equip the troops, Congress issued its own paper money.
But, backed by no precious metals, money soon lost its value.*

4. How did the Congress attempt to
provide a legal basis for its authority?

*Problems for Congress began with its lack of a legal foundation.
To remedy this, it wrote the Articles of Confederation, which
were not ratified, however, until 1781.*

5. What role did diplomacy play in the war?

*The Revolutionary War was not won solely through military
campaigns. Diplomacy was all-important, because it was through
the diplomacy of Benjamin Franklin that France signed treaties
with the United States in 1778.*

6. How important was the assistance of France in the American victory?

*Without French assistance, the Revolution would not have succeeded.
The French provided an unfailing source of financial aid. They also
contributed the assistance of French troops and ships.*

7. What military campaigns led up to
the end of the Revolutionary War?

*By 1780, the military action in the Revolutionary War had moved
to the South, where the Americans began scoring successes. The pressure
brought to bear by the Americans on the British prompted the British
commander Lord Cornwallis to withdraw from the Carolinas to Virginia.
There, Cornwallis found himself cornered at the Yorktown Peninsula.
American and French forces blocked the British by land; the French fleet
blocked any exit by water. Cornwallis soon found his position hopeless
and surrendered.*

ACTIVITIES

The suggested activity is intended to extend and apply learning outside the
classroom. You may wish to have students complete the suggested activity.

LESSON REVIEW

❶ What was the significance of the
Revolutionary War for the world?

❷ How did the American army
stay together during the worst
times of the early part of the
Revolutionary War?

❸ What problems did the Second
Continental Congress have during
the war, and how did Congress
deal with them?

❹ How did the Congress attempt to
provide a legal basis for its authority?

❺ What role did diplomacy play in the war?

❻ How important was the assistance
of France in the American victory?

❼ What military campaigns led up
to the end of Revolutionary War?

ACTIVITIES

Listed below are examples of those who
played significant roles in the American
Revolution during the years leading to
the outbreak of fighting and during the
Revolutionary War. They did so through
political, diplomatic, or military leadership, or through other means. Look up at
least one person in each group and find out
who they were and why they are famous.

Foreign supporters who participated in
significant ways in the Revolutionary
War include:

John Paul Jones (English)
Marquis de Lafayette (French)
Thaddeus Kosciuszko (Polish)
Baron Friedrich von Steuben (German)

Abigail Adams	George Mason
John Adams	Robert Morris
Samuel Adams	Thomas Paine
Crispus Attucks	Eliza Lucas Pinckney
Benjamin Franklin	Molly Pitcher
Horatio Gates	Paul Revere
Nathaniel Greene	Deborah Simpson
John Hancock	Haym Solomon
Patrick Henry	Mercy Otis Warren
Agrippa Hull	George Washington
Thomas Jefferson	Martha Washington
Henry Knox	"Mad" Anthony Wayne

How did the states govern themselves after the Revolution?

LESSON PURPOSE

Shortly after the start of the Revolutionary War in 1775, many of the new states began to write their constitutions. In this lesson you will learn about these new state constitutions. You will explore the basic ideas on which the new governments were founded.

When you finish the lesson, you should be able to describe those basic ideas. You should also be able to explain the major differences between the Massachusetts constitution and the constitutions of the other states.

OVERVIEW

After the Revolutionary War, most colonies examined their constitutions and rewrote or revised them. In this lesson, students examine the main features of these state constitutions and are asked to trace the connections between state constitutions and political philosophy. Finally, students examine the Massachusetts constitution and are asked to contrast it with the constitutions of other states.

OBJECTIVES

At the conclusion of this lesson, students should be able to

- state the ideas learned from political philosophy and personal experience that the colonists included in their state constitutions
- describe the basic features of the new state constitutions and explain the concept of popular sovereignty
- explain the essential differences between the Massachusetts constitution and the other state constitutions
- list the arguments for and against legislative supremacy
- explain some of the problems that arose under the state constitutions

TEACHING PROCEDURES

INTRODUCTORY ACTIVITY

Use the illustrations to introduce the Lesson Purpose and to facilitate consideration of the lesson objectives.

Write the Terms to Understand on the board or use a vocabulary-building activity of your choice. Have students look up the words in the Glossary at the back of the text. Ask them to look for these words as they read the lesson.

Reading and activity

What were the basic ideas about government in the state constitutions?

Have students read this section. Then have them work with a partner to complete Handout D1; a master copy is in the Appendix of this guide. Ask students to write their responses in their own words in the second column. You may wish to have several students share their responses with the whole class. This activity will serve as a review and reinforcement of the basic ideas that the Founders included in the state constitutions.

TERMS TO UNDERSTAND

legislative supremacy
petition
popular sovereignty
veto

What were the basic ideas about government in the state constitutions?

After the Declaration of Independence, British government in the colonies came to an end. The colonies were free and independent states. Each state would have to create a new government.

The people wanted state governments that would protect their basic rights and promote the common good. When they began to write their state constitutions they used the ideas they had learned from political philosophy. They also used what they had learned from their own experience with colonial and British government.

The ideas they included in the state constitutions were not new. Most of the ideas had been used in the governments of the colonies. The Founders tried to design their new governments with the best ideas from the past. Their experiences with these state governments would help them design the Constitution in 1787.

These are the basic ideas that the Founders included in their state constitutions.

John Hancock was a governor of Massachusetts and a signer of the Declaration of Independence. In what ways did state constitutions limit the power of the governor?

❶ **Natural rights and higher law**. The purpose of government is to protect the rights of citizens to life, liberty, and property. Each state constitution was a higher law that everyone had to obey.

❷ **Social contract**. Each state made it clear that it believed that government is formed as a social contract. The people agreed to form a government to protect their natural rights.

❸ **Popular sovereignty**. The term sovereign means to have the highest authority or power. **Popular sovereignty** means that the people are the highest authority. All the states adopted the idea that the people are the source of the authority of government. The people delegate their authority to government. Government gets its right to govern from the people.

❹ **Representation**. Each state considered it very important that the legislature be made up of elected representatives of the people. In most states, the right to vote was limited to white men who owned

property. About seventy percent of the white men in America owned enough property to be able to vote. In contrast, only about ten percent were eligible to vote in Great Britain.

❺ **Separation of powers**. All the states used some form of separation of powers. They divided government into legislative, executive, and judicial branches.

❻ **Checks and balances**. Although the states favored a strong legislature, the constitutions did provide for some checks. Most of the checks were within the legislatures themselves. Most legislatures had two houses. Each house could check the power of the other. The people also could check the power of the legislatures. The voters could elect new representatives to both houses if they did not like the way the government was working.

Why do you think most states required people to own property in order to be eligible to vote?

Student Handout for Lesson 10

Sample

BASIC IDEAS ABOUT GOVERNMENT FOUND IN STATE CONSTITUTIONS	
Basic idea	**Meaning in your own words**
Natural rights and higher law	
Social contract	
Popular sovereignty	
Representation	
Separation of powers	
Checks and balances	
Legislative supremacy	

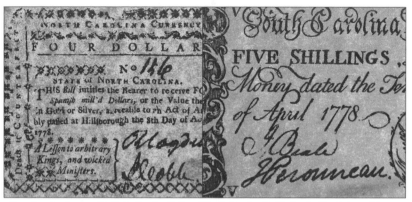

Examples of money used in North Carolina (left) and South Carolina (right) after the Revolutionary War. What problems might arise if each state could print its own paper money?

❼ **Legislative supremacy.** The majority of the states set up governments in which most of the power was given to the legislature. This system of government is known as **legislative supremacy**. The Founders believed that because the people elected the legislature, it was the most democratic branch of government. They were afraid of giving too much power to the executive branch. They remembered how the royal governors and the king had abused their power. So most of the state governors were given very limited power.

Despite checks on the power of the legislative branch the legislature had far greater power than the other two branches of government. Legislative supremacy led to some serious problems in most states.

- State governments did not protect the property rights of some citizens.

In these states, factions—groups of people who seek to promote their own interests—gained control of the legislature. The factions were accused of making laws that benefited themselves rather than the common good. They passed laws that canceled debts and they created paper money. These laws benefited the people who owed money and hurt those who had loaned it to them.

- The state legislatures passed laws that taxed and controlled their citizens far more than the British had done. The level of taxes during the 1780s was ten to twenty times what it had been before the Revolution.

- Many new state laws were passed which interfered with the private lives of the citizens. Laws were passed telling people what they should eat, drink, wear, and believe.

IDEAS FOR DISCUSSION

How was power distributed by the state constitutions?

Look at the two illustrations on this page and answer the questions that follow. Share the answers with the class.

❶ How was power distributed in most states?

❷ Compare the distribution of power in Massachusetts with the distribution of power in the other states. How is the distribution of power different in Massachusetts?

❸ What might be the advantages and disadvantages of giving most of the power of a government to the legislature?

❹ What might be the advantages and disadvantages of the system of government in Massachusetts?

IDEAS FOR DISCUSSION

How was power distributed by the state constitutions?

Have students work individually, with a partner, or in small groups, and ask them to examine the illustrations on this page and answer the four questions that follow. You may wish to have students make a chart for questions two through four so that they can compare the differences and list advantages and disadvantages. Invite students to share their answers with the class.

1. How was power distributed in most states?

   Although all state constitutions incorporated the ideas of separation of powers and checks and balances, most states believed in legislative supremacy and gave most of the power to the legislative branch.

2. Compare the distribution of power in Massachusetts with the distribution of power in the other states. How is the distribution of power different in Massachusetts?

   Massachusetts divided power more evenly among the branches of government. The governor received a fixed salary that could not be changed by the legislature. The governor could veto laws made by the legislature, but the legislature could overturn a veto with a two-thirds majority. The governor had the power to appoint officials in the executive branch and could appoint judges in the judicial branch.

3. What might be the advantages and disadvantages of giving most of the power of a government to the legislature?

   Advantages: *The legislative branch would be more democratic because the people would directly elect their representatives. This could prevent the abuse of power by the executive branch and could prevent the governor from having too much power.*

   Disadvantages: *Factions could gain control of the legislature and could pass laws that benefited themselves rather than the common good.*

(continued next page)

4. What might be the advantages and disadvantages of the system of government in Massachusetts?

Advantages: *Power was more evenly distributed among the branches of government. The governor had specific powers and was independent of the legislature. He could appoint officials in the executive branch and appoint judges in the judicial branch. The people were able to elect the governor directly.*

Disadvantages: *The governor had more power and was more independent of the legislature, which could result in the abuse of power. Because he could make appointments to both the executive and judicial branches, he might appoint his friends or people who did not represent all the people. Because only the wealthy could elect the governor, the governor might represent their interests over the interests of the common citizens. Not all qualified voters would be able to vote for all the elected officials, so these officials would not represent the interests of all the people.*

READING AND DISCUSSION

What was important about the Massachusetts constitution?

Assign this section to students to read. Ask students if they can identify the differences between the Massachusetts constitution and the constitutions of other states. Help them to understand that the essential difference is in the way the constitutions were designed to prevent the abuse of governmental power.

What was important about the Massachusetts constitution?

Massachusetts was the last state to write its constitution. The citizens adopted the state constitution in 1780. The people there had learned some important lessons from the experiences of the other states. They used this knowledge in creating their state government.

Most of the other states used the idea of legislative supremacy to protect people's rights. The Massachusetts constitution, however, distributed power more evenly among the branches of government. The governor had more power and was more independent of the legislature. This was possible because the people elected the governor directly. The people expected the governor to protect their interests.

Here is how some of the powers of the governor of Massachusetts were balanced in relation to the legislature.

- The governor received a fixed salary. His salary could not be changed by the legislature.

- The governor could **veto**—refuse to sign—proposed laws put forth by the legislature. A two-thirds

This is James Bowdoin II, who, along with John Adams and Samuel Adams, drafted the Massachusetts constitution. What were the strengths and weaknesses of the Massachusetts constitution?

vote of the legislature was needed to override his veto.

- The governor could appoint officials in the executive branch. He could also appoint judges in the judicial branch.

The Massachusetts constitution also divided the people into voting groups based on their wealth. They expected that government would then more accurately represent the interests of the groups that elected them.

- Only people with a large amount of property could vote for both the governor and the legislature.

- People with slightly less property could vote for both the upper and lower houses of the legislature.

- People with the minimum amount of property could only vote for the lower house of the legislature.

The experience of writing state constitutions was a useful one to the Founders. Americans were learning what type of government worked best. The differences between the Massachusetts constitution and those that were written earlier were a result of these experiences.

Did the Massachusetts constitution contradict the idea of popular sovereignty? Why or why not?

READING AND DISCUSSION

What were the state declarations of rights?

Read this section aloud with students. Emphasize that state constitutions began with a declaration of rights—those rights that existed before the creation of government. They varied from state to state but were based on the idea that people have basic rights that must be protected.

What were the state declarations of rights?

The states did not depend solely on a system of separation of powers to protect people's rights. The first part of most state constitutions was a declaration of rights, or bill of rights. This section of the constitution listed the basic rights of citizens.

Listing the rights of the people first showed that citizens had certain basic rights that existed before the creation of the government. No constitution or government could take away these rights. Although the declarations of rights were different from state to state, they were all based on the idea that people have certain basic rights that must be protected.

What important ideas are in the Virginia Declaration of Rights?

Virginia was the first state to adopt a bill of rights. George Mason wrote most of the Virginia Declaration of Rights. Mason later was opposed to the U.S. Constitution because it did not include a bill of rights. In writing Virginia's bill of rights, Mason relied on the writing of John Locke and the ideas of republican government.

The Virginia Declaration of Rights stated that

- all power comes from and is kept by the people

- all men are by nature equally free and independent; they have certain basic rights that no social contract can take away

Why do you think most states included protections against cruel and unusual punishments in their constitutions?

- government is created for the common good, protection, and safety of the people; if a government does not serve these purposes, the people have an inalienable right to alter or abolish it

The Virginia Declaration of Rights also listed many of the rights that we enjoy today. These include the right to

- trial by jury

- protection against forced self-incrimination

- protection against cruel and unusual punishment

- freedom of the press

- free exercise of religious beliefs

What rights were protected in the other states?

Most states adopted bills of rights like Virginia's. Some states' declarations also included the idea that civic virtue was essential to preserving freedom.

The states' bills of rights were different in the rights they chose to include or leave out. Most included such political guarantees as

- the right to vote by men who met certain property qualifications

- free and frequent elections

- freedom of speech and the press

- the right to **petition** (make a formal request of) government

- no taxation without representation

All the states' bills of rights included rights for people accused of a crime.

These included the right to have

- an attorney

- a jury trial

- protection from illegal searches and seizure

- protection against forced self-incrimination

- protection from excessive bail and fines

- protection against cruel and unusual punishment

Most of the states' bills of rights expressed a fear of standing armies. The bills of rights condemned standing armies in time of peace and the quartering of soldiers in civilian homes. Many bills of rights included the right of citizens to bear arms. The Vermont bill of rights was the first to outlaw the practice of slavery.

What is the importance of freedom of speech and the press?

READING AND DIAGRAM ACTIVITY

What important ideas are in the Virginia Declaration of Rights? What rights were protected in the other states?

Have students read these two sections, allowing time for discussion and questions. Using a Venn diagram, chart the rights listed in the Virginia Declaration of Rights and the rights protected in the other states, placing those rights that are similar to both Virginia and the other states in the overlapping area of the two circles. Ask students to reflect on the similarities and differences between the rights protected by the Virginia Declaration of Rights and those protected by the bills of rights of other states. Ask them to identify some rights specified in the Virginia Declaration of Rights that are enjoyed today. Use the illustrations as part of this reflection.

 see next student page

LESSON REVIEW

The questions in the student book are intended to assess learning and to reinforce knowledge through discussion. The questions are directly related to the lesson objectives. You may wish to include additional questions developed by yourself or by your students.

1. What basic ideas about good government were included in the state constitutions?

   The basic ideas of good government included in state constitutions can be separated into the following categories: natural rights and higher law, social contract, popular sovereignty, representation, separation of powers, checks and balances, and legislative supremacy.

2. Why did Americans believe that the legislature was the most democratic branch of government?

   Because the people elected the legislature, it was considered to be the most democratic branch of government. A powerful legislature was initially thought to be the best way to represent the interests of the people.

(continued next page)

3. Why did some Americans distrust the executive and judicial branches of government?

Americans distrusted the executive and judicial branches of government because they feared the abuse of power that they had experienced when they were subjects of the king and the royal governors.

4. How did the Massachusetts constitution differ from the constitutions of other states? Why was this important?

The Massachusetts constitution divided power more evenly among the three branches of government. Many of the other states adhered to the doctrine of legislative supremacy, delegating most of the power to the state legislature. The equal division of power provided by the Massachusetts constitution is important because it ensured more protection for the rights of the people by balancing power among three branches of government.

5. What was the Virginia Declaration of Rights? What rights of citizens did it include?

The Virginia Declaration of Rights was the first bill of rights adopted for a state constitution. The rights of the citizens protected by the Virginia Declaration of Rights include trial by jury, protection against self-incrimination, protection against cruel and unusual punishments, freedom of the press, and the free exercise of religious beliefs.

6. What rights did the state constitutions protect?

State constitutions protected political rights, such as the right to vote and hold free elections, guarantees of freedom of speech and the press, the right to petition the government, and protection against taxation without representation. States also protected the rights of people accused of crimes. These rights included the right to an attorney and a jury trial and protection from illegal search and seizure, forced self-incrimination, excessive bail and fines, and cruel and unusual punishments.

ACTIVITIES

The suggested activities are intended to extend and apply learning outside the classroom. You may wish to have students complete one or more of the activities. Have them share their results with the class.

LESSON REVIEW

❶ What basic ideas about good government were included in the state constitutions?

❷ Why did Americans believe that the legislature was the most democratic branch of government?

❸ Why did some Americans distrust the executive and judicial branches of government?

❹ How did the Massachusetts constitution differ from the constitutions of other states? Why was this important?

❺ What was the Virginia Declaration of Rights? What rights of citizens did it include?

❻ What rights did the state constitutions protect?

ACTIVITIES

❶ These are a few examples of the rights listed in the Maryland constitution of 1776. Examine each and write a brief explanation of what the right means and why it is important.

- That every man hath a right to petition the Legislature, for the redress of grievances, in a peaceable and orderly manner.

- That no...tax...ought to be set...without consent of the Legislature.

- That no freeman ought to be taken, or imprisoned...or deprived of his life, liberty, or property, but by the judgment of his peers, or by the law of the land.

- That the liberty of the press ought to be inviolably preserved.

❷ Create a news interview set in 1780. Interview your classmates acting as representatives of the states of Massachusetts and Virginia. During the interview, the representatives should discuss the differences between their state constitutions and why they are important.

❸ Find a copy of your state's constitution. What are some of the rights that your state constitution protects? How does your state constitution compare with the Virginia Declaration of Rights?

How did the Articles of Confederation organize the first national government?

11

LESSON PURPOSE

Our first government, the Continental Congress, drew up a constitution stating its powers. This constitution was called the Articles of Confederation. In this lesson you learn about some of the problems the Founders faced in creating our first national government. You will learn about the successes of the first national government. You also will learn about the weaknesses of government under the Articles and why some people believed that a new constitution was necessary.

When you finish this lesson, you should be able to explain how the Articles organized the national government. You should also be able to explain how the problems with the Articles caused the Founders to write a new constitution.

OVERVIEW

In this lesson, students learn about the need to organize a national government after the colonies declared their independence from Great Britain. Students learn that the colonists' fear of the abuse of power by a strong national government prompted them to create a weak national government under the Articles of Confederation. The lesson describes some accomplishments of the new government. It concludes with a description of how major weaknesses in the national government under the Articles and the fear produced by Shays' Rebellion eventually led to the decision to create a new constitution.

OBJECTIVES

At the conclusion of this lesson, students should be able to

- explain how the Articles of Confederation organized the national government
- explain how problems with the Articles of Confederation caused the Founders to write a new constitution
- explain the ideas and events that influenced the writing of the Articles of Confederation
- describe the achievements of the country under the Articles of Confederation
- describe the problems with the Articles of Confederation
- describe the causes of Shays' Rebellion

TEACHING PROCEDURES

INTRODUCTORY ACTIVITY

Have students read the Lesson Purpose and consider the objectives of the lesson. Write the Terms to Understand on the board or use a vocabulary-building activity of your choice. Have students look up the words in the Glossary at the back of the text. Ask them to look for these words as they read the lesson.

READING AND DISCUSSION

What are the Articles of Confederation?

Have students read this section and ask them why the Founders believed a national government was necessary.

TERMS TO UNDERSTAND

Articles of Confederation
national government
Northwest Ordinance
Shays' Rebellion

What are the Articles of Confederation?

Once the war against Great Britain had started, each state was like a separate nation. Each state had its own constitution and government. To the people, their state was their country.

The Founders believed that a **national government** was needed to unify the states and to conduct the war. A national government could also control trade and manage conflicts among the states. The states also needed to be united in how they related with the rest of the world.

On June 7, 1776, Richard Henry Lee introduced two proposals to the Second Continental Congress. In one, Lee proposed independence from Great Britain. In the other, Lee proposed a national government to unify the states. Both resolutions were adopted.

Our nation's first constitution was the **Articles of Confederation**. The Articles created our first national government. Congress adopted the Articles in 1777. Final approval by the states occurred in 1781, and then the Articles came into effect.

Why did the Founders believe that a national government was necessary?

What problems did the Founders face in writing the Articles of Confederation?

It was not easy to write and agree upon a constitution for the United States. The Founders had to deal with a number of difficult questions. What type of national government should they create? How much power should they give it?

The first problem the Founders faced was the people's fear of a strong national government. Americans believed that the British government had deprived people of their rights. They thought this was likely to happen with any national government that was both powerful and far away from the people. Citizens were convinced that government should be close to the people. That way the people could control their government and make certain that it did not violate their rights.

The second problem the Founders faced was the fear that some states would have more power in a national government than other states. The leaders in each state wanted to make sure that a national government would not threaten their state's interests. As a result, the most important issue was how states would vote in Congress. Would each state have one vote? Would states with greater population or wealth have more votes than the other states? Decisions in the Congress would be made by majority vote. Some leaders were afraid that the majority would use its power for its own interest at the expense of those who were in the minority.

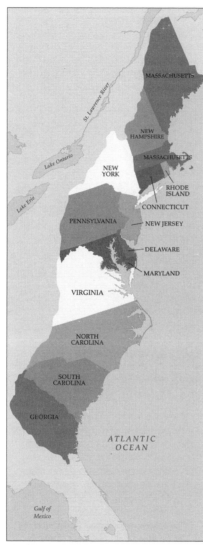

Looking at this map, why would some Founders fear that some states would have more power in a national government than others?

What problems did the Founders face in writing the Articles of Confederation?

Assign this section to students to read. Help them to understand why the Founders had the two major problems described in this section. Ask students to keep these two concerns in mind as they continue reading the lesson. Direct students' attention to the map and ask them the question in the caption.

How did the Articles of Confederation organize the national government?

Have students read this section. Ask them how the Articles of Confederation addressed the fears that were expressed in the previous section. Ask students whether they think the Articles addressed these fears. Ensure that students explain the reasoning behind their answers.

Why did the Founders keep the power of the national government weak?

How did the Articles of Confederation organize the national government?

The Founders did agree that the states needed a central government. Their solution to fears of a strong national government was to create a weak one. The national government under the Articles of Confederation was simply a legislature, Congress; there were no executive or judicial branches.

The states were afraid that Congress might be able to control them. So they made sure that Congress was weak and its powers limited. The Articles left most of the powers of government with the states. The national government had little power over the states and their citizens. Every action taken by Congress had to be with the consent, approval, and cooperation of the states.

To solve the problem of representation, the Articles gave each state one vote in Congress. The more populous states did not have more than one vote. The Articles also provided that on important matters, such as declaring war, nine states would have to agree. This way, the seven less populated states could not outvote the six larger states.

Why was it important that early settlers had the right to public education?

What did the national government achieve under the Articles of Confederation?

Despite a weak central government under the Articles of Confederation, the national government was responsible for a number of important achievements.

- It successfully waged the war for independence against Great Britain.
- It negotiated the peace treaty, known as the Treaty of Paris, to end the American Revolution.
- It provided that each state recognize the laws of the other states. For example, a marriage in one state would be valid in all other states. A citizen could travel freely from one state to another. Criminals who had crossed state borders could be sent back to the state in which they committed their crime.
- It passed the **Northwest Ordinance** of 1787. This was the most important law passed by Congress under the Articles. It gave people in the northwestern lands the right to organize their own governments. Once they had done this, they could ask to be admitted as new states with the same rights as the original thirteen states. The law also provided for public education and forbade slavery. The western settlers were guaranteed freedom of worship, the right to trial by jury, and due process of law.

What did the national government achieve under the Articles of Confederation?

Have students read this section. You may wish to have each student create a table that describes the advantages and disadvantages of the Articles of Confederation. Have students divide a piece of paper into two columns and write "Advantages" in the first column and "Disadvantages" in the second column. Then ask students the following question: "In what ways was the country better off as a result of the four achievements of the national government under the Articles of Confederation?"

Have students write down their responses in the "Advantages" column of the table they have created.

What problems did the country experience under the Articles of Confederation?

Have students read this section. Ask them the following question: "In what ways was it difficult to govern the country under the Articles of Confederation?"

Have students write down their responses in the "Disadvantages" column of the table they have created. Ask students to compare their answers in both columns. Ask them to speculate on whether the problems listed in the "Disadvantages" column were caused by the Articles of Confederation, the state constitutions, or both.

Remind students that a faction is what we would call an "interest group." Help students to understand why factions were thought to violate the basic idea of republicanism—that is, that factions were self-serving and not devoted to the common good. Point out the illustration as a review of student learning.

These were major accomplishments. There were serious problems with the national government, however, that led to the decision to develop a new constitution.

What problems did the country experience under the Articles of Confederation?

Governing the nation under the Articles of Confederation was difficult. Here is a list of some problems the nation experienced.

What problems did Congress face without the financial support of the states?

- **Congress did not have any money and it did not have the power to raise money**. Congress had no power to tax. All Congress could do was to ask the states to pay certain amounts to support the costs of the national government. The states argued about paying their fair shares of government expenses. Some states refused to pay. Congress could do nothing to force a state to pay its fair share.

- **Congress had no power over the state governments or their citizens**. State governments and individual citizens often ignored the laws passed by Congress. Congress had no way to make people obey its laws. For example, at the end of the Revolutionary War Congress signed a treaty with Great Britain. In the treaty, Congress promised to respect the rights of the Loyalists and ensure that they were treated fairly. Some state governments refused to respect the treaty. Those states refused to return property they had taken away from the Loyalists. These states also refused to force payment of money owed to the Loyalists before the start of the war. Thus, the national government was unable to live up to its promise to the British.

- **Congress could not make the states live up to trade agreements with other nations.** Sometimes citizens imported goods from other countries and then refused to pay for them. This made people in foreign countries unwilling to trade with the United States. Many Americans lost money because they could not sell their goods to people in other nations.

- **Congress had no power to regulate trade among the states.** Congress had no power to make laws regulating trade among the states. States taxed goods going from one state to another. Trading often became impossible. Business slowed down and people lost their jobs.

- **Citizens thought that their property rights were threatened.** Many people believed that the states were not protecting the property rights of their citizens. Some people in the states had formed factions to promote their own interests at the expense of the common good. These factions with special interests became the majority in some state legislatures. People accused the factions of making laws to benefit themselves while ignoring the property rights of the minority. For example, they passed laws that canceled debts for those who were members of the faction and other laws that confiscated the property of people who had been Loyalists. People who were hurt by such laws argued that the states were not protecting the property of all citizens. Many people thought that a strong national government was needed to protect property rights.

Why was Shays' Rebellion important?

By 1786, many Americans were in financial trouble. Businesses failed, trade suffered, and many people were in debt. Soldiers who had fought in the Revolution still had not been paid. Congress could not control the country and people worried about what would happen.

Farmers in Massachusetts had serious economic problems. Farm prices were low, and when farmers could not pay their debts, many lost their farms and homes. Some were even put in prison. Many people claimed that the new state taxes had put them in debt. As a result, they felt that the state was not protecting their interests.

Then a dramatic series of events that became known as **Shays' Rebellion** finally convinced many Americans that it was time for a change. In an attempt to keep the state from taking their farms, local farmers under the leadership of Daniel Shays began to close down the courts where their cases were heard. The action against the courts spread to other towns and into neighboring states.

In January 1787, Shays led 2,000 rebels to Springfield, Massachusetts, to raid the federal arsenal for weapons. Shays' Rebellion frightened many property owners. People feared that the actions of the farmers might become widespread. The national government had been unable to put down the rebellion. People were asking how the country could continue to exist if it could not maintain law and order.

Why was Shays' Rebellion important?

After students read this section, ask them what group of people was most affected by the problems described in the text. Then ask them why they think the country was having financial problems, why Shays' Rebellion could not be put down, and why the government was unable to resolve these issues. Accept any reasonable responses.

How did Shays' Rebellion force people to examine the weaknesses of the national government?

Read this section aloud to students. Help students understand that trade problems are what prompted the first meeting of state delegates; however, outbreaks of violence such as Shays' Rebellion drove the state delegates to write a report to Congress declaring the need for a convention of all the states. Emphasize that the instructions to the delegates from Congress were clear: "for the sole and express purpose of revising the Articles of Confederation." Point out the illustrations as a review of student learning.

How did Shays' Rebellion force people to examine the weaknesses of the national government?

In January of 1786, Virginia had invited all the states to send delegates to a meeting to be held in Annapolis the following September. The purpose of the meeting was to consider trade problems. Only five states sent representatives to the Annapolis meeting. Without the other states present, the delegates who did attend the meeting were not able to accomplish much.

Everyone who was there, however, agreed that the regulation of trade could not be discussed separately from the larger political issues. The general discontent was leading to outbreaks of violence such as those led by Daniel Shays. The delegates decided to write a report for Congress. In the report, they asked for a convention of all the states.

After much debate, Congress agreed and invited the states to send delegates to a convention in Philadelphia. This meeting would be "for the sole and express purpose of revising the Articles of Confederation."

What did Daniel Shays and his followers hope to gain by their rebellion?

100

Is a new constitution needed?

Imagine that your state is preparing to select delegates to send to the convention in Philadelphia. Your state has to decide what position its delegates will take regarding the Articles of Confederation. A heated debate is taking place. Some people argue that the Articles are fine as they are. Some people want to make changes to the Articles. Others want to throw away the Articles and write a new constitution.

Your class will work in three groups to debate this issue.

- **Group one**. Defend the Articles of Confederation as the best way to organize the national government. You should rely on the arguments in favor of a weak national government and strong state governments. Examine the successes of the national government under the Articles. Argue that the Articles should be kept, but revised to make up for their weaknesses. Propose possible revisions.

- **Group two**. Argue to throw away the Articles and write a new constitution. Examine the arguments against a weak national government and the problems with the Articles listed in this lesson. Examine the events of Shays' Rebellion as one example of problems that might arise when there is no strong national government. Explain why you believe that the nation needs a new constitution.

- **Group three**. Organize the class debate. While the other students are preparing their arguments, you should research debate procedures. During the debate, listen to the arguments presented by the other two groups. Then decide the position of your state's delegates based on the strongest evidence presented. You may want to review other lessons to help you make your choice.

SOLVE THE PROBLEM

Is a new constitution needed?

Divide the class into three groups. Have them complete the problem-solving activity as outlined in the text. End this activity by having all three groups discuss the outcome of the debate.

 see next student page

LESSON REVIEW

The questions in the student book are intended to assess learning and to reinforce knowledge through discussion. The questions are directly related to the lesson objectives. You may wish to include additional questions developed by yourself or by your students.

1. Why did the people in the newly independent states fear a strong national government?

   The people feared a strong national government because they believed that the British government had deprived the people of their rights. They thought the same thing might happen with any national government that was both powerful and far away from the people.

2. What were the Articles of Confederation? How did the Articles organize the national government to address the fears of the people and of the states?

   The Articles of Confederation were the first constitution of the nation. The Articles created our first national government. The Articles were organized to address the fears of the people and the states by creating only a legislative branch; they did not create an executive or judicial branch. Congress had little power over the states and their citizens, and every action of Congress had to have the consent, approval, and cooperation of the states. The problem of representation was resolved by giving each state one vote in Congress. The concerns of the more populous states were addressed by providing that nine states must agree on all important matters. This eliminated the possibility that the seven less populated states could outvote the six larger states.

(continued next page)

3. What parts of government were not
   included in the Articles of Confederation?

   *The Articles of Confederation created only one branch
   of government, the legislative branch. There were no executive
   or judicial branches under the Articles.*

4. What did the national government achieve
   under the Articles of Confederation?

   *The national government under the Articles of Confederation successfully
   waged war against Great Britain, negotiated a treaty to end the American
   Revolution, provided that each state recognize the laws of the other states,
   and passed the Northwest Ordinance of 1787.*

5. What were the weaknesses of the
   national government under the Articles?

   *The national government under the Articles of Confederation had many
   weaknesses. Congress had no power to tax and therefore could not raise
   money. Congress had no power over the state governments or their citizens.
   Congress could not make the states live up to the trade agreements it had
   with other nations. Congress did not have the power to regulate trade
   among the states. Finally, Congress could not protect property rights.*

6. Why was Shays' Rebellion an important event?

   *Shays' Rebellion illustrated the lack of power of the new national
   government. Because the national government was unable to put
   down the rebellion, people asked how the country could continue
   to exist if the government could not maintain law and order.
   Shays' Rebellion and the difficulties of governing under the Articles
   of Confederation ultimately led to the call for a new constitution.*

ACTIVITIES

The suggested activities are intended to extend and apply learning
outside the classroom. You may wish to have students complete one
or more of the activities. Have them share their results with the class.

LESSON REVIEW

❶ Why did the people in the newly
independent states fear a strong
national government?

❷ What were the Articles of Confederation? How did the Articles organize
the national government to address
the fears of the people and of
the states?

❸ What parts of government were
not included in the Articles of
Confederation?

❹ What did the national government
achieve under the Articles of
Confederation?

❺ What were the weaknesses of
the national government under
the Articles?

❻ Why was Shays' Rebellion
an important event?

ACTIVITIES

❶ Learn more about Shays' Rebellion.
Make posters illustrating the farmers'
point of view.

❷ Create a short play that shows one
of the problems of government under
the Articles of Confederation. Perform
the play for your class.

❸ Learn more about the Northwest
Ordinance of 1787. Explain how
the ordinance provided for public
education or the importance
of forbidding slavery in
the territories.

unit**three**

What happened at the Philadelphia Convention?

UNIT OVERVIEW

The unit begins by describing the Framers who attended the Philadelphia Convention and how the convention was organized. Students then explore some of the major conflicts the delegates had around the issues of representation in Congress, protective tariffs, slavery, and how much power to give to the national government. They will then learn how the Framers solved these disagreements through compromise.

UNIT OBJECTIVES

At the conclusion of this unit, students should be able to

- explain why Congress called for the Philadelphia Convention and what decisions were agreed to as the meeting began
- explain the reasons for the conflict over representation in Congress and how this conflict was resolved
- explain the conflicts about protective tariffs and slavery and how they were resolved
- describe the powers that the Constitution gave to Congress
- describe the powers of the executive and judicial branches of government
- describe the process for electing the president of the United States

UNIT INTRODUCTION

Read the introduction with the class. Introduce the Key Concepts and tell students that these terms will be fully explained in the lessons of this unit. The illustrations throughout the unit are excellent teaching tools for reviewing and reinforcing the learning. Use them as you find appropriate.

UNIT PROJECT (OPTIONAL)

Ask your students to write the Key Concepts in their notebooks and write definitions based on their current knowledge. Students can change and add to these initial definitions as the unit progresses.

unit three

KEY CONCEPTS

electoral college

enumerated powers

equal representation

ex post facto law

general welfare clause

Great Compromise

impeach

jurisdiction

necessary and proper clause

proportional representation

writ of habeas corpus

You now are familiar with the knowledge and experiences of the Founders of our government. This unit will help you understand why the Framers, the men who created the Constitution, wrote the Constitution as they did. You will study the major problems facing the Framers and how they solved them.

When you complete this unit, you will be able to explain how the Constitution was written. You will also be able to describe some disagreements that occurred during the Philadelphia Convention and how they were solved. Finally, you will be able to explain how the Framers allocated powers to the executive and judicial branches.

Who attended the Philadelphia Convention? How was it organized?

12

LESSON PURPOSE

In this lesson you will learn about the Philadelphia Convention in 1787. You will learn about some of the Framers who attended the convention. You will also learn about the decisions that the Framers made at the start of the meeting.

When you finish the lesson, you should be able to explain why Congress called for the Philadelphia Convention. You also should be able to explain the decisions that the delegates made at the start of the meeting.

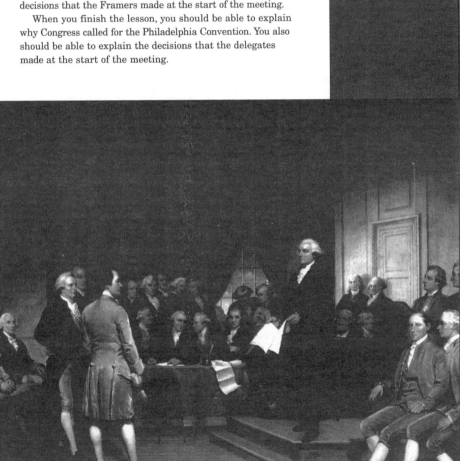

OVERVIEW

This lesson provides students with an understanding of the reasons for the Philadelphia Convention. Students learn about the men who attended the convention and read more detailed descriptions of four of the Framers—George Washington, James Madison, Benjamin Franklin, and Gouverneur Morris. Students examine why Thomas Jefferson, John Adams, and Patrick Henry did not attend the convention. Students learn the initial decisions made by the delegates and the reasons for those decisions.

The lesson begins by asking students to imagine that their principal has called for a constitutional convention to which one delegate from each class will be selected. Students consider what qualifications a delegate should have, what rules the delegates should be asked to follow, and whether they should keep the remainder of the school informed about what happens during the convention. When students have completed this activity, they should be able to relate their answers to what actually happened at the Philadelphia Convention.

OBJECTIVES

At the conclusion of this lesson, students should be able to

- explain why Congress called for the Philadelphia Convention
- explain the decisions that the delegates made at the start of the convention
- name some of the important Framers at the Philadelphia Convention and describe their characteristics
- name some Founders who did not attend the convention and explain why they did not attend
- name some segments of the population that were not represented at the Philadelphia Convention and suggest reasons for their exclusion

TEACHING PROCEDURES

INTRODUCTORY ACTIVITY

Have students read the Lesson Purpose and consider the objectives of the lesson.

You may wish to briefly review the Articles of Confederation and Shays' Rebellion with students to ensure that they have a solid understanding of why Congress called for the convention.

Write the Terms to Understand on the board or use a vocabulary-building activity of your choice. Have students look up the words in the Glossary in the back of the text. Ask them to look for these words as they read the lesson.

READING, DISCUSSION, AND ACTIVITY

Who attended the Philadelphia Convention?

The Ideas for Discussion section on page 108 is designed to stimulate students' critical thinking before they read and discuss this section and the following one, "Who did not attend the convention?" on page 109.

Discuss with students the purpose of the convention and the role of the delegates as outlined by Congress. Also help them to understand who some of the Framers were and why they were selected to represent their states.

TERMS TO UNDERSTAND

Framers
Philadelphia Convention

Who attended the Philadelphia Convention?

Congress called for a meeting to be held in Philadelphia in 1787. The members of Congress invited each state to send delegates. This important meeting is known as the **Philadelphia Convention**.

The purpose of the convention was to search for ways to improve the Articles of Confederation. At the end of the meeting, the delegates would submit a plan for Congress to approve. As far as members of Congress were concerned, the role of the delegates was advisory. But something very different was about to happen.

Fifty-five delegates attended the meeting. These delegates are called the **Framers** of the Constitution. All were men. Most were young. The average age was forty-two. Most had played important roles in the American Revolution. About three-fourths of the delegates had served in Congress. Most were leaders in their states. Some were rich; most were not, but nobody was poor.

The lives of all the Framers are worth learning about in detail. We will mention only a few.

Why is James Madison known as the "Father of the Constitution"?

James Madison. Madison of Virginia is known as the "Father of the Constitution." His influence during the convention was great. This was partly because Madison brought with him a plan for creating a stronger national government. Madison's ideas were the basis for discussing how to

106

An optional activity is to divide the class into groups of three or four students and assign each group a colonial state. Assign large, small, Northern, and Southern states so that students will begin to understand the issues that arose at the convention. Tell them that each group will create a "Delegates Wanted" poster for a particular state. They should consider the following aspects when developing their advertisements for delegates:

- gender, age, and status of applicants
- educational and religious backgrounds of applicants
- duties of the delegates while attending the convention
- experiences, skills, and beliefs necessary to be considered a potential delegate

Students should decide what qualities and characteristics they want their state's delegate to possess to best represent the needs and interests of their state. Note that it may be necessary to have them briefly research their assigned state to understand and anticipate the issues that would be most important to that state's representative at the convention. Have each group present its poster to the class.

George Washington refused to attend the convention at first. Why do you think his attendance at the convention was important?

structure a new government. Much of what we know about what happened at the convention is based on Madison's notes.

George Washington. Washington was probably the most respected and honored man in the country. He was convinced that a stronger national government was necessary, but he did not talk about it publicly. He did not want to become involved in politics. He preferred to return to Mount Vernon, Virginia, his home, to be a farmer. He thought that he had served enough. At first, Washington refused to attend the convention. He finally agreed. Washington was afraid that if he did not attend, people might think he had lost his faith in republican government.

Benjamin Franklin. Franklin was eighty-one years old and in poor health. He attended the convention as a delegate from the state of Pennsylvania. Franklin was one of the most respected men in America. He had a long and distinguished career as a printer, inventor, writer, revolutionary, peacemaker, and diplomat. Franklin's primary role during the convention was to encourage the delegates to cooperate with each other when they disagreed. He also supported the important compromises reached during the convention.

Gouverneur Morris. Morris was from New York. He had served in the state militia and in the New York legislature. Morris had also been a member of the Continental Congress. He was an exceptionally good speechmaker during the convention. He played an important role in writing the Constitution and prepared its final draft.

IDEAS FOR DISCUSSION

How would you organize a constitutional convention?

Divide the class into small groups or pair them with partners, and ask them to read the scenario provided. The groups should consider the three questions and write their responses on chart paper. Ask each group to share its responses with the rest of the class, and have each group put its chart on the wall. When all ideas have been presented, have students compare the charts for similarities and differences, underlining or highlighting similar ideas. Have students decide which ideas might provide the best solutions to the problems posed in the questions.

IDEAS FOR DISCUSSION

How would you organize a constitutional convention?

Imagine that the teachers and principal in your school have called for a constitutional convention for the school. They have asked each class to send delegates to the convention. A **delegate** is a person who represents other people at a meeting. In this case, the delegates represent the people of each class. The delegates are to recommend ways to improve the present school government under the school's code of conduct or constitution. Work with a partner to discuss the three questions below. Be prepared to share your ideas with the class.

❶ What qualifications should a delegate have to represent your class at a constitutional convention? How should these delegates be selected?

❷ What rules would you establish for the delegates to follow during the convention?

❸ Would you keep the rest of the school informed about what was happening at the convention? Why or why not?

What qualifications should a student have to represent your class as a delegate?

Who did not attend the convention?

Some important Americans did not attend the Philadelphia Convention. Thomas Jefferson was in France. John Adams was in England. Both men were in Europe representing the United States.

Patrick Henry refused to attend the convention. He is quoted as saying, "I smell a rat." He was against the idea of a strong national government. Henry thought that the delegates would not work on improving the Articles of Confederation. He suspected that the delegates would instead write a new constitution that would result in a strong national government. After the convention, Patrick Henry worked hard to get the people to reject the new Constitution.

Not all segments of the American population were represented at the Philadelphia Convention. There were no women among the delegates. There were no African Americans or American Indians. Poor farmers like those who took part in Shays' Rebellion were not present either.

The Rhode Island state legislature refused to send delegates to the convention. Citizens there were fiercely independent and hostile to the idea of a new constitution.

What rules did the Framers agree to follow during the convention?

By May 25, 1787, delegates from eleven states had arrived at the convention. We call the delegates **Framers** because they framed, or shaped, and wrote the U.S. Constitution. The Framers all agreed that George Washington should preside over the meetings.

At the start of the convention, the Framers agreed on three things. They agreed they would

- not try to find ways to improve the Articles of Confederation as Congress had asked them to do. The Framers thought the problems were too serious to try to correct them. Instead, the Framers decided to write a new constitution.

Patrick Henry said he did not attend the convention because he "smelled a rat." What do you think he meant by this?

Who did not attend the convention?

Have students read this section aloud. Ask them to consider why there were no women, African Americans, American Indians, or poor farmers at the convention. Ask them to speculate on how they think the outcome of the convention would have been different had these groups participated. Discuss why some prominent Americans did not attend the convention and why some other well-known Americans refused to attend.

What rules did the Framers agree to follow during the convention?

After reading this section, discuss the three agreements made by the delegates at the start of the convention and the reasons for these agreements. Ask students the following questions:

- Did the Framers have the authority to ignore the instructions of Congress to improve the Articles?
- Was the Framers' decision to ignore the instructions of Congress justified?
- Were the Framers correct in their decision to keep the convention proceedings secret for thirty years?
- Did the Framers have the authority to keep the convention proceedings secret?
- Would the Framers be able to keep the convention proceedings secret if the convention occurred today?

Ask students to explain the reasoning behind their answers. Accept any reasonable responses.

What ideas about government did the Framers agree to include in the new constitution?

Read this section aloud and help students to understand that the Framers shared basic beliefs about government. The Framers' common beliefs about government served as the framework from which our constitution was written.

- keep the record of what was said at the convention a secret for thirty years. The reason for secrecy was that the Framers wanted to develop the best constitution possible. Many feared that if their discussions were made public, the delegates would not express their opinions freely. Also, the Framers did not want people from the outside trying to influence what they were doing. Finally, the Framers wanted the new constitution to be accepted. A new constitution would have a greater chance of being approved if people did not know about the arguments that went on during the convention.

- give each state one vote in the convention proceedings, no matter the size of a state's population. The reason for this decision was to gain the cooperation of the small states. Delaware, for example, had threatened to withdraw from the convention if states with large populations were given more votes than states with small populations.

Why did the Framers keep the proceedings of the Philadelphia Convention secret?

What ideas about government did the Framers agree to include in the new constitution?

The Framers agreed that certain basic ideas about government should be included in the new constitution. These included the idea that

- the national government should be a constitutional government, that is, a government of limited powers

- the purpose of government should be to protect fundamental rights and promote the common good

- a strong national government was needed to protect fundamental rights

- a republican form of government of elected representatives was needed to make sure that government served the common good

- a system of separation of powers and checks and balances was needed to prevent the abuse of power

Because of their agreement on basic ideas about government, the Framers were able to write a new constitution. In less than four months they created a constitution that has lasted, with some revisions, for more than 200 years.

110

This is a reproduction of the first page of the original Constitution of the United States. Why do you think it was important to the Framers to make "We the People" so prominent on the top of the document?

 see next student page

LESSON REVIEW

The questions in the student book are intended to assess learning and to reinforce knowledge through discussion. The questions are directly related to the lesson objectives. You may wish to include additional questions developed by yourself or by your students.

1. What did Congress ask the delegates to do during the Philadelphia Convention? Did the delegates accomplish what Congress asked them to do? Explain your answer.

   Congress asked the delegates to improve the Articles of Confederation. They were to submit a plan to Congress for approval. Congress intended that the delegates would serve in an advisory capacity only, but the Framers agreed that they would scrap the Articles of Confederation and write a new constitution.

2. In what ways were the delegates at the Philadelphia Convention representative of the American people? In what ways were they not representative?

   The delegates were mostly young men who had participated in the American Revolution. Most had served in Congress. Most were not rich, but none of the delegates were poor. The delegates shared the basic ideas about government that were held by most Americans. Many Americans were not represented, including women, African Americans, poor farmers, and American Indians.

(continued next page)

3. What rules did the Framers establish for the convention? What was the purpose of these rules?

   After deciding that George Washington would preside over the meetings, the Framers agreed to keep the record of what was said at the convention a secret for thirty years and to give each state one vote in the convention proceedings.

   The Framers made these rules because they believed that the problems with the Articles were too serious to be corrected. They believed that secrecy was necessary to ensure that the delegates expressed their opinions freely. The Framers also believed that the Constitution would be more readily accepted if people were unaware of the many arguments that went on during the convention. The decision to give each state one vote, regardless of the state's population, ensured the cooperation of the small states.

4. What basic ideas about government did the Framers agree should be included in a new constitution?

   The Framers agreed that the national government should be a constitutional government; that the purpose of government should be to protect basic rights and promote the common good; that a strong national government was needed to protect the fundamental rights of the people; that the country needed a republican government composed of elected representatives; and that government should include a system of separation of powers and checks and balances to prevent the abuse of power.

ACTIVITIES

The suggested activities are intended to extend and apply learning outside the classroom. You may wish to have students complete one or more of the activities. Have them share their results with the class.

1. What did Congress ask the delegates to do during the Philadelphia Convention? Did the delegates accomplish what Congress asked them to do? Explain your answer.

2. In what ways were the delegates at the Philadelphia Convention representative of the American people? In what ways were they not representative?

3. What rules did the Framers establish for the convention? What was the purpose of these rules?

4. What basic ideas about government did the Framers agree should be included in a new constitution?

1. Find pictures of the people who attended the Philadelphia Convention. Use the pictures to create a gallery for your classroom. For each picture, write a brief biography of the Framer it represents.

2. George Washington did not want to attend the Philadelphia Convention. Conduct research to find out why Washington did not want to attend the convention, as well as why he finally changed his mind. Create a bibliography for the sources that you researched.

3. Create an editorial cartoon that expresses your opinion about whether the topics being discussed at the Philadelphia Convention should have been reported to the public during the time of the meeting.

How did the Framers resolve the conflict about representation in Congress?

13

LESSON PURPOSE

In this lesson you will learn about the disagreement the Framers had about how many representatives each state should be able to send to Congress. You will learn what compromises the Framers reached to resolve the conflict.

When you finish this lesson, you should be able to explain the reasons for the conflict and how it was resolved.

OVERVIEW

This lesson introduces students to the major conflict the Framers had over representation of the states in Congress. The conflict arose because of the different populations of the states. Students learn that the small states feared proportional representation—representation based on population—because they believed that the large states would control them. The large states thought that equal representation—each state having the same number of votes—was unfair.

Through an activity, students determine the total number of votes each of the thirteen states would have and begin to appreciate the reasons for the disagreement about representation. The lesson outlines two plans designed to offer solutions to the problem, the Virginia Plan and the New Jersey Plan. Students are asked to decide on the number of representatives each state should send to Congress. They are encouraged to write a new plan, if necessary. The lesson ends with a description of how the Framers ultimately resolved the representation problem with the Great Compromise.

OBJECTIVES

At the conclusion of this lesson, students should be able to

- explain why the states argued about representation in Congress
- explain how the conflict about representation was resolved
- explain the concepts of equal and proportional representation
- describe the key features of the Great Compromise

TEACHING PROCEDURES

INTRODUCTORY ACTIVITY

Read the Lesson Purpose and have students consider the objectives of the lesson.

Write the Terms to Understand on the board or use a vocabulary-building activity of your choice. Have students look up the words in the Glossary at the back of the text. Ask them to look for these words as they read the lesson.

READING AND DISCUSSION

What important conflict existed between the large and small states?

Assign this reading. Compare the reasons for the conflict described in this section with student responses in the Introductory Activity.

TERMS TO UNDERSTAND

equal representation
Great Compromise
New Jersey Plan
proportional representation
Virginia Plan

What important conflict existed between the large and small states?

One of the most important conflicts at the Philadelphia Convention was about representation. The Framers disagreed about how many representatives each state should be able to send to Congress. The conflict was between delegates from states with small populations and delegates from states with large populations.

Small states. The small states feared that the states with larger populations would control the national government. To avoid this problem, the small states wanted each state to have the same number of representatives in Congress. This is called **equal representation**.

Large states. The delegates from the states with larger populations thought that equal representation was unfair. A state with more people should have more votes. The large states wanted to base the number of representatives in Congress on the number of people living in a state. This is called **proportional representation**.

Why might people in states with smaller populations favor equal representation?

SOLVE THE PROBLEM

Which method of representation might better serve the states?

Work with a partner. Examine the population figures in the box below. Discuss the questions with your partner. After your discussion, explain your ideas to the class.

❶ Assume that in 1790 the small states were those with fewer than 250,000 people.

❷ Assume that the number of representatives from each state in Congress is the same and each state has one vote.

- How many total votes would the small states have?

- How many total votes would the large states have?

- Explain why the small states favored equal representation in Congress.

❸ Assume there is one representative in Congress for every 30,000 people and each representative has one vote.

- How many total votes would the large states have?

- How many total votes would the small states have?

- Explain why the large states favored proportional representation.

❹ Explain why the disagreement about representation in Congress was so important to the states.

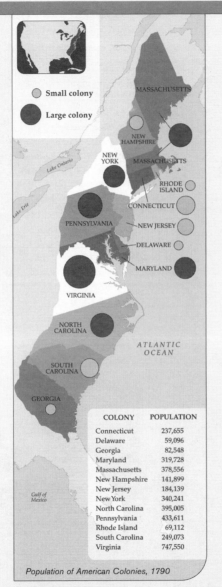

○ Small colony

● Large colony

COLONY	POPULATION
Connecticut	237,655
Delaware	59,096
Georgia	82,548
Maryland	319,728
Massachusetts	378,556
New Hampshire	141,899
New Jersey	184,139
New York	340,241
North Carolina	395,005
Pennsylvania	433,611
Rhode Island	69,112
South Carolina	249,073
Virginia	747,550

Population of American Colonies, 1790

SOLVE THE PROBLEM

Which method of representation might better serve the states?

Pair students with partners and ask them to imagine that they are delegates to the Philadelphia Convention and must decide how many representatives each state should be able to send to Congress. As they consider this task, ask them the following questions and accept any reasonable answers. As students share their responses, write them on chart paper for later reference.

- What problems might the delegates to the Philadelphia Convention have in deciding how many representatives each state should be able to send to Congress?

  Problems might arise as the delegates attempt to consider and accommodate the needs of both small and large states.

- What factors might the delegates consider when making their decision?

  The delegates might consider such factors as the population of each state and the various needs of the states.

- Why might the delegates be concerned about representation and how might the decision about representation affect the interests of the various states?

  Representation was a concern for the delegates because it was directly tied to the power each state would have in Congress. The small states might not have as much power as the large states if proportional representation was used, and the large states might not be fairly represented if equal representation was used.

Next, ask students to undertake the problem-solving exercise. The four questions posed in the activity will help them see the difficulties that the Framers had to address. The table on the next page is reproduced from Handout D2 of the Appendix. You may want to photocopy the handout, distribute it to students, and have them use it to complete this exercise.

Complete Handout D 2

How Many Representatives Should a State Have?			
Small States			
List the Small States	List the Population	List One Representative for Each State	List the Number of Representatives by Population (30,000 people = 1 representative; always round down)
1. Connecticut	237,655	1	7
2. Delaware	59,096	1	1
3. Georgia	82,548	1	2
4. New Hampshire	141,899	1	4
5. New Jersey	184,139	1	6
6. Rhode Island	69,112	1	2
7. South Carolina	249,073	1	8
Totals	1,023,522	7	30
Large States			
List the Large States	List the Population	List One Representative for Each State	List the Number of Representatives by Population (30,000 people = 1 representative; always round down)
1. Maryland	319,728	1	10
2. Massachusetts	378,556	1	12
3. New York	340,241	1	11
4. North Carolina	395,005	1	13
5. Pennsylvania	433,611	1	14
6. Virginia	747,550	1	24
Totals	2,614,691	6	84

Population numbers represent the total population of the states, excluding slaves. Population figures were taken from 1790 census data published by the Geospatial and Statistical Data Center at the University of Virginia Library (see http://fisher.lib.virginia.edu/collections/stats/histcensus). Students should round down when calculating the number of representatives per population, no matter how large the remaining fractional amount. For example, when calculating representation for Connecticut, dividing the population of 237,655 by 30,000 yields 7.92. This number is rounded down to 7, as indicated in the table. This reflects the "Jefferson Method," which was used to determine apportionment of the U.S. House of Representatives from 1790 to 1830 (see http://www.census.gov/population/www/censusdata/apportionment/history.html).

After completing the exercise, compare students' answers to question four with students' original responses to the question.

What was the Virginia Plan?

Before the convention started, James Madison had drafted a plan for a national government. He called it the **Virginia Plan**.

- The Virginia Plan proposed a strong national government.

- Under the Virginia Plan, two governments would govern the people. They would be individual state governments and the national government. Both state and national governments would get their power from the people. This is what we now call a federal system.

- The national government would have the power to make and enforce its own laws. It would have the power to collect its own taxes.

- The Virginia Plan divided the government into legislative, executive, and judicial branches.

- The national legislature was to have two houses: the House of Representatives and the Senate.

- The number of representatives in each house would be proportional.

There was considerable debate in the convention about the different parts of the Virginia Plan. The part that created the biggest problem was representation. The larger states favored proportional representation in both houses of Congress. The small states opposed the idea. The smaller states said that unless they had an equal voice in Congress, the larger states would dominate them.

By the middle of June, the debate about representation was no longer making progress. The delegates from the small states asked for time to come up with an alternative to the Virginia Plan.

Under the Virginia Plan, where would the federal and state governments get their power?

What was the New Jersey Plan?

William Paterson of New Jersey led the group of small states to develop a new plan for representation. Their plan was called the **New Jersey Plan**. The New Jersey Plan followed the framework of the Articles of Confederation.

- It favored a weak national government.

- It called for only one house of Congress.

- Each state would have equal representation.

- Congress would have the power to collect taxes on products and stamps, as well as to levy fines and collect money from the states if they refused to pay their taxes.

- Congress also would have the power to regulate trade among the states and with other nations.

- The New Jersey Plan also proposed executive and judicial branches of government. Congress would appoint several persons to serve in the executive branch. The executive branch would appoint the members of a U.S. Supreme Court.

The convention debated the New Jersey Plan. The Framers saw that neither the Virginia Plan nor the New Jersey Plan solved the problem of representation. The convention remained divided on this issue. Neither side was willing to accept the position of the other. Tension was growing. Some delegates threatened to quit and go home.

Finally, the convention decided to appoint a special committee to try to solve the conflict. One delegate from each state was asked to serve on the committee.

How did the New Jersey Plan differ from the Virginia Plan? How were they the same?

ACTIVITY AND DISCUSSION

What was the Virginia Plan?
What was the New Jersey Plan?

Divide students into small groups of three or four, or pair them with partners. Give each group a large piece of paper and have the group divide it into two columns. The first column should be labeled "Virginia Plan." The second column should be labeled "New Jersey Plan." Ask students to list the features of each plan and describe their advantages and disadvantages. Have them continue in this manner until they have examined all the features and their advantages and disadvantages. As an alternative, you can assign one plan to each group. Finish the exercise by having the class compare the similarities and differences between the two plans.

SOLVE THE PROBLEM

**How would you solve the problem
of representation in Congress?**

Conduct the activity according to the directions in the student text.
Help students understand that they are doing exactly what the Framers
did at the Philadelphia Convention.

When students have completed this activity, compare the ideas in their
newly formed plans with the three questions in the original problem-solving
exercise in order to determine similarities and differences.

SOLVE THE PROBLEM

How would you solve the problem of representation in Congress?

Work with a group of five students. Imagine that each group is a committee formed to solve the problem of representation in Congress. Each committee should have students who represent small states and students who represent large states. The task of each committee is as follows.

❶ Examine the descriptions of the Virginia Plan and the New Jersey Plan in this lesson. Decide whether Congress should have one or two houses. Then decide on the number of representatives each state should send to Congress. To resolve the problem, you may need to write a new plan.

❷ Select a spokesperson to present your plan to the entire class. All members of the committee may help to clarify the plan and defend it against criticisms by members of the other committees.

❸ Each committee may revise its plan if it wishes. Then, put the plan on the board or chart paper and display it in your class.

❹ Finally, the entire class should compare the plans developed by each committee. The class should try to reach an agreement on the question of representation. Compare the plan you have developed with the plan arrived at by the Framers.

Should Congress have one or two houses? What are the advantages and disadvantages of each approach?

How did the Great Compromise solve the problem of representation?

The committee appointed to solve the problem of representation came up with the Connecticut Compromise. It is now called the **Great Compromise**. The Great Compromise has three parts.

- Congress would have two houses, the Senate and the House of Representatives.

- Membership in the House would be based on proportional representation. The House would have the power to develop all bills dealing with taxes and government spending. As you learned from Lesson 5, a bill is a proposed law.

- Membership in the Senate would be based on equal representation. At first, the Senate only had power to accept or reject bills related to taxes and spending passed in the House. This power was later modified to let the Senate make changes to bills involving taxes and spending developed in the House.

As in most compromises, each side received a little and each gave up a little. The small states got equal representation in the Senate. The large states got proportional representation in the House. Also, the House would have important powers related to taxing and spending.

The compromise meant that the large states would have slightly more influence over issues of taxes and spending. In the Senate, the small states could check the large states by changing or rejecting taxes and spending bills passed in the House. The Great Compromise was hotly debated. It finally passed by one vote.

Can you name your representatives in the House and Senate? To find out the names of your representatives in Congress, go to www.senate.gov and www.house.gov.

READING AND DISCUSSION

How did the Great Compromise solve the problem of representation?

Ask students to read this section. Lead them in a discussion about the nature of compromise and how a compromise is reached. Ask them to identify compromises they have made in their own lives. You may wish to have them compare their solutions from the Solve the Problem exercise with those made by the Framers. Ask them if they agree that the Framers devised a reasonable solution to the conflict over representation. Ask them to explain their reasoning. Accept any reasonable answer.

 see next student page

LESSON REVIEW

The questions in the student book are intended to assess learning and to reinforce knowledge through discussion. The questions are directly related to the lesson objectives. You may wish to include additional questions developed by yourself or by your students.

1. What is the difference between equal representation and proportional representation? Why did the small states want equal representation? Why did the large states want proportional representation?

   A system of equal representation would give each state the same number of representatives in Congress, whereas in a system of proportional representation, the population of each state would determine the number of representatives to Congress. The small states supported equal representation because they were afraid that states with larger populations would be able to control the decisions made in Congress. The large states supported proportional representation because they had larger populations and believed that they should have more power to control decisions in Congress. Large states opposed equal representation because there were seven small states and six large states. A system of equal representation would tip the balance of power in Congress to the small states.

(continued next page)

2. What was the Virginia Plan?

The Virginia Plan was a plan for a national government drafted by James Madison. It called for a strong national government and state governments. All would derive their powers from the people. This is called a federal system. The Virginia Plan would give the national government the power to make and enforce its own laws and the power to collect its own taxes. The government would be divided into the legislative, executive, and judicial branches. The legislature would have two houses: the House of Representatives and the Senate. Each house would have representatives chosen on the basis of proportional representation.

3. What was the New Jersey Plan?

William Paterson led the smaller states in the development of the New Jersey Plan. This plan favored a weak national government. It provided for only one house of Congress where each state would have equal representation. Congress would have the power to collect taxes on products and stamps, levy fines, and collect money from the states if they refused to pay their taxes. Congress would have the power to regulate trade among the states and with other nations. Congress would have the power to appoint people to serve in the executive branch. The executive branch would appoint members to a U.S. Supreme Court.

4. How did the Great Compromise solve the conflict about representation? What did the small states and the large states gain as a result of the Great Compromise?

The Great Compromise provided two houses: the Senate, with equal representation, and the House, with proportional representation. Specific powers were given to each house, which served to check the power of the other. The small states gained equal representation in the Senate and the large states gained proportional representation in the House. The House was given important powers related to taxing and spending. This benefited the large states. However, small states could check the power of large states in the Senate by changing or rejecting taxation and spending bills passed in the House.

ACTIVITIES

The suggested activities are intended to extend and apply learning outside the classroom. You may wish to have students complete one or more of the activities. Have them share their results with the class.

LESSON REVIEW

❶ What is the difference between equal representation and proportional representation? Why did the small states want equal representation? Why did the large states want proportional representation?

❷ What was the Virginia Plan?

❸ What was the New Jersey Plan?

❹ How did the Great Compromise solve the conflict about representation? What did the small states and the large states gain as a result of the Great Compromise?

ACTIVITIES

❶ Find out who represents your state in the U.S. Senate. Visit their web pages on the Internet. Write a brief biography of your senators to share with your class.

❷ For purposes of representation in the House of Representatives, each state is divided into congressional districts. There is one representative for each district. Find the number of congressional districts in your state. Find the name of the person who represents your congressional district. Visit his or her website. Write a brief biography of your representative in the House to share with the class.

How did the Framers resolve the conflict between the Northern and Southern states?

LESSON PURPOSE

The states of the North and South had different economies and different economic interests. These differences led to another conflict at the Philadelphia Convention. The sources of this disagreement were protective tariffs and slavery.

When you finish the lesson, you should be able to explain the conflicts about protective tariffs and slavery and how they were resolved.

OVERVIEW

In this lesson, students learn about the conflict between the Northern and Southern states over the issues of tariffs and slavery. The lesson begins with a description of the economies in the Northern and Southern states. The differences between them led to conflicting points of view about the need for tariffs and the issue of slavery. Students are asked to resolve these two deeply divisive issues through a problem-solving activity and then compare their solutions with those the Framers wrote into the Constitution. Students will begin to understand why these compromises were made even though many Framers were opposed to slavery.

OBJECTIVES

At the conclusion of this lesson, students should be able to

- explain the differences between the economies of the North and South
- explain the conflicts about tariffs and slavery and how they were resolved

TEACHING PROCEDURES

INTRODUCTORY ACTIVITY

Have students read the Lesson Purpose and consider the objectives of the lesson. Write the Terms to Understand on the board or use a vocabulary-building activity of your choice. Have students look up the words in the Glossary at the back of the text. Ask them to look for these words as they read the lesson.

READING, DISCUSSION, AND ACTIVITY

How were the economies of the North and South different?

Ask students to read the section explaining the differences in the economies of the North and South. On the board or on chart paper, make two columns—one for the Northern states and one for the Southern states. When students have completed the reading, ask them to recall the differences between the two economies and write their responses under the appropriate columns in the chart.

TERMS TO UNDERSTAND

fugitive slave clause
tariff
three-fifths clause

How were the economies of the North and South different?

The economy of the South was almost completely agricultural. The Southern states grew products such as cotton, tobacco, and indigo.

The large farms in the Southern states used enslaved people to grow their crops. The farm owners depended on slave labor to make their goods more profitable. Slaves were treated as if they were property that could be bought or sold. People held in slavery were not citizens. They could not claim the rights of citizens.

Southern farmers shipped most of their products to Great Britain and other nations in Europe. They sold some in the Northern states. People in the South bought the manufactured goods they needed from Great Britain.

The economy of the North was more diverse than that of the South. Some people were farmers, fishers, merchants, or bankers. Other people manufactured goods or worked as laborers. The North's economy did not depend on slave labor.

Why was agriculture profitable in the South?

The North was also a center for ship-building and trade with other nations. The North had to compete for business with Great Britain's shipping and manufacturing industries.

Why did the states disagree
about the need for tariffs?

Have students read about the disagreement over tariffs and the positions
of the Northern and Southern states. Ask students to record their findings
in the appropriate columns. Keep the chart in view for the next section.

How did Northerners protect their businesses from foreign competition?

Why did the states disagree about the need for tariffs?

The economic differences between the North and South caused a conflict among the Framers at the Philadelphia Convention. One area of disagreement was the issue of tariffs. A **tariff** is a tax on goods and products imported from other nations. The purpose of a protective tariff is to raise the cost of the imports to protect local farmers and businesses against outside competition. The Northern and Southern delegates held different opinions about tariffs.

THE NORTHERN POSITION

The Northern states believed that tariffs were necessary for their businesses to prosper. Tariffs on British products would make those products cost more than similar ones made in America. As a result, Americans would be more likely to buy goods made in their own country instead of those made in other countries.

The Framers who came from the Northern states wanted to give the new national government the power to control trade between the states and trade with foreign nations. This included the power to pass tariffs.

123

Why was there a conflict about slavery?

After students finish reading this section, ask them to explain the views of the Northern and Southern states and write them in the chart mentioned in the previous section.

Why did the North believe tariffs were necessary?

How did economics affect the position of the South on slavery?

THE SOUTHERN POSITION

The South argued that tariffs would increase the cost of the manufactured goods that they bought from European nations. Southerners argued that tariffs unfairly favored the North. Southerners also feared that Great Britain might place its own tariffs on agricultural products grown in the South. This would make those products harder to sell in Europe.

The Southern states had fewer citizens than did Northern states. Southerners were afraid they would be a minority in Congress. They thought they might have less power in the new national government to decide issues of trade. So, the Framers who came from the Southern states opposed giving the national government power to regulate trade.

Why was there a conflict about slavery?

The conflict about slavery was more complicated than the issue of tariffs. Slavery began in the colonies soon after the first settlements were established, but most of the Northern states had put an end to the practice, at least officially. Most of the Framers from the Northern states were opposed to slavery, as were some Framers from Southern states.

Many Southern farmers, however, were still financially dependent on slavery and wanted it to continue. The Southerners believed that each state had a right to decide the issue for itself. The delegates from three Southern states said they refused to be part of a union of states that denied them the right to own and import slaves.

The Framers who opposed slavery faced a dilemma. They wanted all the states to be part of one country, but they did not want to allow slavery to continue.

124

SOLVE THE PROBLEM

How would you resolve the issues of tariffs and slavery?

Work with a group of six students. Divide the groups into two committees each. Each committee should have three students who represent the Northern states and three who represent the Southern states. The task of each committee is as follows.

❶ Develop a plan for dealing with the issues of tariffs and slavery. Your plan should be agreeable to the representatives of all the states.

❷ Select a spokesperson to present your committee's plan to the entire class. All members of the committee may help to clarify and defend the plan.

❸ Each committee may then revise its plan, if it wishes, and display it on the chalkboard or chart paper.

❹ The entire class should then compare the plans made by the committees and try to reach an agreement on one plan. After you have completed this exercise, compare the plan you have developed with the plan arrived at by the Framers.

What ideas did your class present to resolve the issues of slavery and tariffs?

SOLVE THE PROBLEM

How would you resolve the issues of tariffs and slavery?

Help students to understand that this problem-solving activity requires them to grapple with the conflicts in the same way that the Framers did by forming committees to develop a solution. Divide the class into groups of six and follow the directions in the student text. After students have presented their proposed solutions, ask them to reflect on the experience. Guide students by asking the following questions. Accept reasonable responses.

- What was the biggest difference of opinion in your group?
- How did you get the people holding different views to agree on a solution?
- What, if anything, did some members give up in order to get something they wanted?
- Did anyone get everything he or she wanted? How?

Continue with the activity and encourage students to reach an agreement on one plan. Ask them to compare their plan with the Framers' plan.

Reading and discussion

How did the Framers resolve the conflicts about tariffs and slavery?

Read this section with the class. You may wish to assign different sections to various students. As students read, allow time for discussion and questions about each section. Emphasize what the Northern and Southern states gave up and what they got in return through compromise. Help students understand the significance to the South of the three-fifths clause.

How did the Framers resolve the conflicts about tariffs and slavery?

After a long and sometimes bitter debate, the Framers reached a compromise over the issues of tariffs and slavery. Read the following parts of Article I, Sections 8 and 9 of the Constitution.

The Congress shall have the power:

SECTION 8

❶ To lay and collect Taxes, Duties, Imposts, and Excises.

❷ To regulate Commerce with foreign Nations, and among the several States, and with the Indian Tribes;

SECTION 9

❶ The Migration or Importation of such Persons as any of the States now existing shall think proper to admit, shall not be prohibited by the Congress prior to the Year one thousand eight hundred and eight.

As you can see, the Constitution gave Congress the power to place tariffs on imports. Congress also was given the power to control both interstate and foreign trade. To get this agreement from the Southern delegates, the Framers from the North agreed to Southern demands on the issue of slavery.

The Framers reached the following agreements about slavery.

* The national government would not end the slave trade before 1808.

* They included the three-fifths clause in Article I, Section 2, Clause 3.

This is a portrait of Paul Revere, a politically active Boston silversmith. How would tariffs have helped Northern craftsmen like Revere? How would they have hurt Southern farmers?

The **three-fifths clause** states that in deciding how many representatives a state could send to the House of Representatives, the numbers would be determined by counting free persons, indentured servants, and "three-fifths of all other persons" [slaves]. Congress was to use the same count for collecting direct taxes from the states. Indians were excluded.

- Finally, the Framers agreed to include the fugitive slave clause in Article IV, Section 2. The **fugitive slave clause** states that persons who escaped from slavery to a state where slavery was prohibited "shall be delivered up on Claim of the Party to whom such Service or Labour may be due."

The compromise on slavery was designed to satisfy the demands of some of the Southern states. It was accepted by a majority of the Framers to get the support of North Carolina, South Carolina, and Georgia. These states would not have supported the Constitution without this agreement. In spite of strong criticisms, the compromise was not as controversial in 1787 as it became in the 1800s and later.

Although the delegates agreed to the compromise, many people in both the North and the South were strongly opposed to slavery. For example, one Framer, Gouverneur Morris, denounced slavery as "the curse of Heaven on the states" where it existed. It is also interesting to note that nowhere in the Constitution did the writers use the words slave or slavery. Some people say that this is because the Framers were ashamed of slavery.

What compromise did the Framers reach on the issue of slavery? Why do you think the Framers left the words slave and slavery out of the Constitution?

 see next student page

LESSON REVIEW

The questions in the student book are intended to assess learning and to reinforce knowledge through discussion. The questions are directly related to the lesson objectives. You may wish to include additional questions developed by yourself or by your students.

1. In what ways were the economic interests of the Northern and Southern states different?

   The Southern states were almost exclusively agricultural and shipped most of their products to Great Britain and other European nations. Southerners bought most of their manufactured goods from Great Britain. Their economy depended on slave labor. The Northern states had a more diversified economy. Some people in the North worked as farmers, fishers, merchants, and bankers. Others manufactured goods or worked as laborers. The North was also a center for ship-building and trade with other nations. The North competed with Great Britain's shipping and manufacturing industries. The Northern economy did not depend on slave labor.

2. What was the position of the Northern states on the issue of tariffs? What was the position of the Southern states?

   Because the Northern states competed with Great Britain in manufacturing products, Northerners believed that placing tariffs on British products would raise the prices of British goods and encourage Americans to buy goods made in the North. Southerners argued that the tariffs would increase the cost of goods Southerners bought from European nations and that the tariffs unfairly favored the North. Southerners also feared that Great Britain might retaliate by placing tariffs on agricultural products grown in the South, thus making their products harder to sell in Europe.

(continued next page)

3. What was the position of the Northern states on the issue of slavery? What was the position of most of the Southern states?

Most of the Northern states had officially put an end to slavery by the time of the Philadelphia Convention, but its actual practice in the Northern states continued into the mid-1800s. The majority of Framers from the Northern states, however, were opposed to slavery.

Southern farmers were financially dependent on slavery and wanted it to continue. Southerners wanted each state to determine this issue for itself. Some delegates from the South stated that they would not be part of a union that denied the right to own and import slaves.

4. What compromise did the Framers reach on the issues of tariffs and slavery?

The Framers agreed that Congress would have the power to impose and collect taxes, duties, imposts, and excises, and would regulate commerce with foreign nations, among the states, and with Indian tribes. They agreed that the federal government would not end slavery before 1808. The Framers also agreed to count three-fifths of slaves when deciding how many representatives a state would send to the House of Representatives. They included the fugitive slave clause, which forced residents of states where slavery was illegal to hand over any slaves who had escaped from states where slavery was allowed.

5. What reason did the Framers have for compromising on the issue of slavery? Do you agree or disagree that the compromise violated fundamental principles that you have been studying in this text? Why?

The Framers compromised on the issue of slavery to satisfy the demands of some of the Southern states. These states would not have supported the Constitution without this compromise. The Framers believed that it was more important to bind the states together into one nation than to prohibit slavery. Allow students to share their opinions about the Framers' decision.

ACTIVITIES

The suggested activities are intended to extend and apply learning outside the classroom. You may wish to have students complete one or more of the activities. Have them share their results with the class.

LESSON REVIEW

❶ In what ways were the economic interests of the Northern and Southern states different?

❷ What was the position of the Northern states on the issue of tariffs? What was the position of the Southern states?

❸ What was the position of the Northern states on the issue of slavery? What was the position of most of the Southern states?

❹ What compromise did the Framers reach on the issues of tariffs and slavery?

❺ What reason did the Framers have for compromising on the issue of slavery? Do you agree or disagree that the compromise violated fundamental principles that you have been studying in this text? Why?

ACTIVITIES

❶ Go to your library or use the Internet to find some of the Framers' speeches about slavery. George Mason's is of particular interest. Share the speech with your class.

❷ Research the use of tariffs today. Create a drawing that illustrates how tariffs are employed. Write a paragraph explaining the point of view your drawing expresses on the issue.

How did the Framers resolve the conflict about the powers of the legislative branch?

15

LESSON PURPOSE

One problem facing the Framers at the Philadelphia Convention was how much power to give to the legislative branch. In this lesson you will learn about the debates that the Framers had concerning which powers to delegate to Congress.

When you finish the lesson, you should be able to explain the powers that the Constitution gives Congress.

OVERVIEW

The Framers agreed that a stronger national government was needed, although there was no consensus on the amount of power that government should hold. In this lesson, students examine the debate over the scope and limits of the powers of the new Congress. Students examine the difficult task of creating a national government that was strong enough to protect the rights of the people, yet not so strong that it would violate these rights. Students learn about the dispute over the use of specific and general language in the Constitution to define the powers given to Congress. They examine the specific limits of the powers of Congress. In the Solve the Problem activity, students have the opportunity to apply what they have learned about enumerated and general powers to a series of proposed bills. The lesson concludes with a description of how the executive and judicial branches check the power of Congress.

OBJECTIVES

At the conclusion of this lesson, students should be able to

- explain the powers that the Constitution gives to Congress
- explain the reasons why the Framers were uncertain about how much power to give the three branches of the national government
- describe the arguments in the debate over congressional power and describe how these arguments shaped the way the Constitution was written
- explain the enumerated powers of Congress, the necessary and proper and general welfare clauses, and the reasons for them
- describe the limits placed on the powers of Congress
- describe how other branches of government check the power of Congress

INTRODUCTORY ACTIVITY

Have students read the Lesson Purpose and consider the objectives of the lesson. Help students recall the reasons why the Founders had originally created a weak national government and why they feared a strong national government. As students read the lesson, ask them to watch for evidence of the fears of the Founders in the portions of the Constitution that are discussed in the text.

Write the Terms to Understand on the board or use a vocabulary-building activity of your choice. Have students look up the words in the Glossary at the back of the text. Ask them to look for these words as they read the lesson.

READING AND DISCUSSION

How much power should Congress have?

Assign this section to students to read. Help them to understand that the Articles of Confederation prevented Congress from dealing with trade and economic problems, enforcing its laws in the states, and raising taxes. Explain to them that although most of the Framers agreed that there was a need for a stronger national government, they disagreed about how much power Congress should have. Help students appreciate the difficulty of the task of creating a national government strong enough to protect the rights of the people, yet not so strong that it would endanger those rights.

TERMS TO UNDERSTAND

bill of attainder
enumerated powers
ex post facto law
general welfare clause
necessary and proper clause
unconstitutional
writ of habeas corpus

How much power should Congress have?

Under the Articles of Confederation, Congress was unable to deal with the trade and economic problems of the country. More importantly, Congress was not strong enough to control the actions of state governments. The Framers were convinced that the state legislatures were passing laws that violated the property rights of many citizens.

A basic problem with the Articles of Confederation was that Congress did not have the power to act directly on the people. When Congress passed laws, it had to depend on the states to enforce them. Congress could not raise taxes to support itself; it could only ask the states for money. Many states ignored congressional requests for funds.

Most of the Framers agreed that there was a need for a stronger national government. There were still some areas of disagreement, however. The American experience with the British government had caused many of the Framers to be suspicious of a central government and executive power.

Why did some Framers believe that the state governments had too much power under the Articles of Confederation? Why did some Framers believe that there should be a strong national government?

How did the Framers solve the problem of distributing power between the state governments and the national government?

The compromises about representation and slavery reduced resistance to increasing the power of the national government. The delegates, however, still disagreed about how much power to give to each of the three branches of the national government. The problem facing the Framers was how to create a national government that was strong enough to protect the rights of the people, and yet not so strong that it would endanger those rights.

How should the Constitution be written to give power to Congress?

James Madison argued that the new Congress should keep the powers that it had under the Articles of Confederation. He also wanted Congress to make the laws that the state legislatures were prevented from making. He thought that Congress should also be given the power to reject or turn down laws made by state legislatures.

Madison's recommendations would have given the national government great power over the states and the people. To give all this power to the national government meant that the new constitution would have to be written in very general language. For example, the constitution might say, "Congress shall have the power to make all laws that are necessary."

Many of the Framers disagreed with Madison. They saw a problem with general language in the new constitution. General language could be understood to mean that government was given the power to do almost anything it wanted to do. It does not provide a good way to limit the powers of government.

Many delegates also opposed giving Congress the power to veto laws made by state legislatures. Under British rule, royal governors and Parliament had vetoed acts of the colonial legislatures. The Framers did not want to give this power to Congress.

An alternative was to write the new constitution in very specific language.

How should the Constitution be written to give power to Congress?

Have students read this section and allow time for discussion and questions. It is important that students understand the benefits and potential problems of using general and specific language to both give and limit Congressional power. Discuss with students the Framers' justification for using general and specific language in the Constitution.

What are the enumerated powers of Congress?
What are the general powers of Congress?

Have students read the two sections, allowing time for discussion and questions. Ensure that students understand the meaning of the general welfare and necessary and proper clauses. Ask students to identify examples of how the two clauses might be used to act on one of the enumerated laws. Use the ability of Congress to require citizens to serve in the armed forces as an example.

Specific language meant writing down exactly what powers Congress would have. For example, "Congress shall have the power to collect taxes." The Framers wanted a government of enumerated powers. **Enumerated powers** are powers that are specifically listed in a constitution. The problem with enumerated powers was that a constitution might leave out important powers needed by Congress to deal with unforeseen situations.

The solution was to use both general and specific language. The new constitution would give specific powers to Congress and place limitations on these powers. It would also include two general clauses that would give Congress the power to deal with unexpected situations.

What are the enumerated powers of Congress?

Article I deals with the legislative branch. Article I alone makes up more than half of the Constitution. It shows just how important the legislative branch was to the Framers.

Article I, Section 8 includes seventeen enumerated powers. Some of these powers give Congress the right to

- impose and collect taxes and duties
- borrow money
- regulate commerce with foreign nations and among the states
- coin money
- establish post offices
- declare war
- raise and support an army and navy

Should the federal government regulate postal services? Why or why not?

What are the general powers of Congress?

Article I, Section 8 also includes two general statements of power given to Congress. These are the power of Congress to

- "provide for the common Defense and general Welfare [common good] of the United States." This is called the **general welfare clause**.

- "make all Laws which shall be necessary and proper" for carrying out the other powers that the Constitution grants to Congress. This is called the **necessary and proper clause**. For example, under the enumerated powers, Congress has the power to raise and support an army. To exercise this power, it might be necessary and proper that Congress pass a law requiring citizens to serve in the armed forces.

Neither of these general clauses caused any disagreements at the convention. They did cause strong disagreements in the states about whether to approve the Constitution. Both clauses were the source of conflicts in the early years of the new government. You will learn more about these conflicts in later lessons.

What limits are there on the powers of Congress?

The Constitution includes several limits on the powers of Congress. Article I, Section 9 prohibits Congress from

- banning the slave trade before 1808

- suspending the privilege of the **writ of habeas corpus** except in

Elvis Presley was drafted into the Army in 1958. What parts of the Constitution can be used to justify the power of Congress to draft people into the armed forces?

emergencies. In Latin, habeas corpus means to "have the body." A writ of habeas corpus orders government to deliver a person it has arrested to a court of law. Government must explain why that person has been arrested and held. If government cannot show that the person has broken the law, the person must be set free.

- passing **ex post facto laws**. This is a law that makes an act a crime even though the act was legal when it took place.

- passing **bills of attainder**. This is a legislative act that declared a person guilty of violating the law and set the punishment without a court trial.

133

What limits are there on the powers of Congress?

Read this section with students. You may wish to have them write descriptions of the limitations of the powers of Congress in their notebooks. Ask them if any of these limitations reflect the experiences the Framers had with the British monarchy, and if so, how?

How do the other branches check the power of Congress?

Have students read this section. Help them to understand that dividing the powers of government into separate branches is not sufficient to control the power of each branch. Ask students to list the checks that the executive and judicial branches have on the legislative branch. Ask them how this attention to checks on the powers of the branches of government reflects the Founders' distrust of a powerful national government.

 see next student page

SOLVE THE PROBLEM

Would these bills be allowed to become law under the Constitution?

Divide the class into groups and follow the directions in the student text. Have students present their arguments and their ideas about the two questions to the class. Point out similarities and differences in the opinions and ideas of students.

Students might suggest that using only enumerated powers to decide whether Congress should pass a law might be too restrictive and not allow it to respond to unforeseen situations. On the other hand, using only general powers might allow Congress to pass any law it finds necessary. There would not be any specific limitations to its power.

1. This is an example of a bill that could be authorized by the general welfare clause. It could protect children from seeing some websites intended only for adults, thus providing for their welfare.
2. This bill is authorized by the necessary and proper clause. It supports the enumerated power of Congress to raise an army.
3. This bill is also authorized by the necessary and proper clause because it supports the enumerated power of Congress to support an army.
4. Article I, Section 8 of the Constitution gives Congress the power to regulate how taxes are spent and the ability to provide for the general welfare. Students might notice that Article I, Section 8, Number 8 states that Congress has the power to promote the progress of science. Although this power refers to copyrights and patents, students could argue that space exploration is a form of scientific progress and is

- taxing anything exported from a state
- taking money from the treasury without first passing a law to do so
- granting titles of nobility

In this way, the Framers tried to balance the need for a strong government with the need to limit its powers. Those limits were included to make sure that government did not become a threat to the people's rights.

What part of Article I, Section 8 of the Constitution gives Congress the power to conduct a space exploration program?

How do the other branches check the power of Congress?

Remember that Congress is divided into two "houses." This arrangement is a check on the power of Congress to pass laws. For example, when the House of Representatives passes a bill, it must be sent to the Senate. The bill must also pass the Senate by a majority vote before it can become law.

The executive and judicial branches also have checks, or controls, on Congress. If a bill passes in both houses of Congress, the bill must be sent to the president for approval and signature. When the president signs the bill it becomes a law.

The president may refuse to sign a bill and send it back to Congress. This is the president's power to veto a bill passed in Congress. When the president vetoes a bill, the bill can only become law if approved by a two-thirds majority in both houses of Congress.

The U.S. Supreme Court has the power to declare a law made by Congress unconstitutional. **Unconstitutional** means that the law or action is not permitted by the Constitution. The Court may say that the Constitution does not give Congress the right to pass such a law. In this case, the law can no longer be carried out or enforced. You will learn more about this power of the U.S. Supreme Court in a future lesson.

SOLVE THE PROBLEM

Would these bills be allowed to become law under the Constitution?

A bill is a proposed law. Members of Congress create bills and try to get a majority of both houses to vote for them.

Your class should be divided into congressional committees of about five members each. Complete the following activity and report your findings to the entire class.

Your committee wants to introduce six bills in Congress. Review the general and enumerated powers granted to Congress. For each bill in the next column identify which of these two types of powers enables Congress to pass it. Support your opinion.

Answer these two questions as part of your discussion:

- If you used only the enumerated powers of Congress to decide whether to pass a law, what problems might arise?

- If you used only the general powers of Congress to decide whether to pass a law, what problems might arise?

Bills under consideration to become laws. A law to

❶ allow government to keep watch over websites on the Internet to protect children from potentially harmful material

❷ allow government to draft citizens to serve in the armed forces

❸ provide money to pay the expenses of the army and navy

❹ allow the executive branch to conduct a space exploration program

❺ allow government to impose fines as punishment for industries that pollute the air

❻ require government to use tax money to provide medical assistance

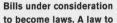

135

justified by Number 8. In this case, a bill supporting the conduct of space exploration programs would be authorized by the necessary and proper clause because the law proposed by this bill would be necessary to carry out the enumerated power.

5. This bill would be authorized by the general welfare clause because it would provide for the common good.

6. This bill would be authorized by the general welfare clause. The power to tax is an enumerated power.

see next student page

LESSON REVIEW

The questions in the student book are intended to assess learning and to reinforce knowledge through discussion. The questions are directly related to the lesson objectives. You may wish to include additional questions developed by yourself or by your students.

1. What disagreements about the powers of Congress did the Framers have? How did they resolve these disagreements?

   Although the Framers agreed that there was a need for a stronger national government, their experiences with the British government caused many of the Framers to be suspicious of a strong national government and of executive power. Many Framers disagreed with Madison's suggestion that the Constitution be written in general language that would give power to government to make all laws that it decided were necessary. Some Framers were concerned that this would not provide limits on the powers of government. They also opposed the idea that Congress would have the power to veto state laws. The Framers eventually agreed that the Constitution would include specific language that would enumerate the powers of Congress and place limits on these powers. They would also use general language in the Constitution to give Congress the power to deal with unexpected situations.

2. What enumerated powers does Article I, Section 8 grant to Congress?

   Some of the enumerated rights in Article I, Section 8 grant Congress the ability to impose and collect taxes and duties, borrow money, regulate commerce with foreign nations and among the states, coin money, establish post offices, declare war, and raise and support an army and navy.

3. What general powers does Article I, Section 8 grant to Congress? Why are these general powers necessary?

   The general powers granted to Congress under Article I, Section 8 include the power to "provide for the common Defense and general Welfare of the United States," called the general welfare clause, and the power to "make all Laws which shall be necessary and proper," called the necessary and proper clause. These powers are necessary so that Congress can respond to unexpected situations.

4. What limits does Article I place on the powers of Congress? Explain how these limitations protect the rights of citizens.

   Article I, Section 9 limits the power of Congress by prohibiting it from banning the slave trade before 1808, and from suspending the privilege of the writ of habeas corpus except in emergencies, passing ex post facto laws, passing bills of attainder, taxing anything exported from a state, taking money from the treasury without first passing a law to do so, and granting titles of nobility.

   These limits help to ensure that government does not become a threat to people's rights. It should be noted, however, that although allowing slavery to continue may have protected the economic welfare of those who owned slaves, it did not protect the rights of slaves to life, liberty, and the pursuit of happiness.

5. Explain some ways in which the executive and judicial branches can check the powers of Congress.

   The president's ability to veto a bill passed by Congress acts as a check by the executive branch on the powers of Congress. However, Congress can override the president's veto by approving a bill with a two-thirds majority of both houses. The U.S. Supreme Court checks the powers of Congress through its ability to declare laws made by Congress unconstitutional.

ACTIVITIES

The suggested activities are intended to extend and apply learning outside the classroom. You may wish to have students complete one or more of the activities. Have them share their results with the class.

LESSON REVIEW

❶ What disagreements about the powers of Congress did the Framers have? How did they resolve these disagreements?

❷ What enumerated powers does Article I, Section 8 grant to Congress?

❸ What general powers does Article I, Section 8 grant to Congress? Why are these general powers necessary?

❹ What limits does Article I place on the powers of Congress? Explain how these limitations protect the rights of citizens.

❺ Explain some ways in which the executive and judicial branches can check the powers of Congress.

ACTIVITIES

❶ Draw three illustrations. Each one should show how the limits on Congress protect the rights of citizens. Make one illustration focus on a writ of habeas corpus, one on ex post facto laws, and one on bills of attainder.

❷ Article IV gives Congress power to create new states from the territories. Find out how a territory can become a state.

❸ Sometimes it becomes necessary to make changes to the Constitution. This has happened twenty-seven times in the history of the United States. Read Article V in the Constitution. Explain the process for amending the Constitution.

❹ Research an attempt to amend the Constitution that failed. Why did it fail? Would it be more successful today? Has the issue that the amendment was meant to correct been addressed in other ways?

How much power should be given to the executive and judicial branches?

16

LESSON PURPOSE

In this lesson you will learn about the powers that the Constitution gives to the executive and judicial branches. You will learn how the legislative and judicial branches check the power of the executive branch. You also will learn about the system that the Constitution established for electing a president.

When you finish this lesson, you should be able to explain the powers of the executive and judicial branches of government. You should also be able to explain the process for electing the president of the United States.

OVERVIEW

This lesson introduces students to the executive and judicial branches of government. Students learn that the decisions regarding the scope and limits of power of these two branches were a result of the Framers' fear that the executive and judicial branches of government would have too much power. Students examine the specific powers and limits of the executive branch and learn how and why the electoral college was created as the body that elects the president. Students participate in an activity where they consider the qualifications necessary to be president. Finally, students learn the specific powers granted to the judicial branch. They examine how the supremacy clause of the Constitution gives the U.S. Supreme Court the power to overrule state laws that violate the Constitution or the laws made by Congress.

OBJECTIVES

At the conclusion of the lesson, students should be able to

- explain the powers of the executive branch
- explain how the powers of the president are limited
- describe the process for electing the president
- explain the powers of the judicial branch

TEACHING PROCEDURES

INTRODUCTORY ACTIVITY

Have students read the Lesson Purpose and consider the objectives of the lesson. Write the Terms to Understand on the board or use a vocabulary-building activity of your choice. Have students look up the words in the Glossary at the back of the text. Ask them to look for these words as they read the lesson.

READING AND DISCUSSION

What challenge did the Framers face in creating the executive branch?

As students read this section, help them to remember how the experiences of the Framers influenced their decisions about the amount of power that should be granted to the executive branch.

TERMS TO UNDERSTAND

advice and consent
appellate jurisdiction
electoral college
impeach
jurisdiction
original jurisdiction
Twenty-second Amendment

What challenge did the Framers face in creating the executive branch?

In 1787, Americans still remembered how much trouble they had experienced with the executive branch of the British government. Americans believed that the king and his royal governors and other officials had violated their rights.

With this experience in mind, the Framers faced the problem of creating an executive branch of government. They wanted an executive branch with enough power to carry out its responsibilities yet not strong enough to overwhelm the other branches. An executive branch with too much power could endanger the rights of the people.

What powers does the Constitution give to the executive branch?

Article II of the Constitution created the executive branch. The Framers wrote Article II in more general terms than they did Article I. As a result, Article II is shorter.

What powers does Article II of the Constitution grant to the president?

138

Egyptian President Anwar Sadat, U.S. President Jimmy Carter, and Israeli Prime Minister Menachem Begin at the White House on March 26, 1979, as they completed signing of the Treaty of Peace between Egypt and Israel. Why would the Constitution require the president and the Congress to share power when negotiating treaties with other nations?

The list of powers it gives to the president is brief. These include the powers to

- carry out and enforce laws made by Congress

- make treaties with foreign nations

- appoint certain important government officials

- act as commander-in-chief of the armed forces

- veto laws passed by Congress

The president also can send and receive ambassadors to and from other countries. The president has the power to pardon people convicted of crimes against the United States.

How does the Constitution limit the powers of the executive branch?

The Constitution limits the powers of the executive branch by making it share most of its powers with Congress. Here are some examples of how this works.

- **Appointments**. The president has the power to nominate people for important jobs in government with the advice and consent of the Senate. **Advice and consent** is the term used for this process. The president also nominates people to serve in the executive and judicial branches of the national government. The Senate has the power to approve or reject the president's nominations.

What powers does the Constitution give to the executive branch? How does the Constitution limit the powers of the executive branch?

Ask students to form groups of three or four, or pair them with partners. Have each group divide a piece of paper into two columns. One column should be labeled "Powers." The second column should be labeled "Limits." At the top of the page, have students write "Executive Branch." As students read these sections, have them write the powers of the executive branch and the limits of each power in the appropriate column. When students have completed the two columns, ask them to think of specific examples of the various powers and, if possible, specific instances where limits on these powers were applied.

READING AND DISCUSSION

How should the president be selected?

Assign this reading. Allow time for discussion and questions, placing particular emphasis on the electoral college, its process and purpose. You may wish to have students research how the electoral college in their state functions today and compare it to the way the electoral college originally functioned. Ask students whether they believe the electoral college is a valid way to elect the president today. Ask them to consider the presidential election of 2000 and to explain whether that election followed the process for electing a president established by the Framers in the Constitution. Information on the 2000 election can easily be found on the Internet. Students may find CNN's website (www.cnn.com/ELECTION/2000/) particularly useful.

- **Treaties**. The president has the power to negotiate treaties with another nation. The Senate has the power to approve or reject these treaties.

- **War**. Although the president can conduct a war as commander-in-chief, only Congress can declare war. In addition, only Congress has the power to provide money to conduct a war.

- **Veto**. The president may veto laws passed by Congress. Congress, however, may override the veto by a two-thirds vote of both houses.

The Constitution provides another important way to limit the power of the president and prevent the abuse of power. It gives the House of Representatives the power to impeach the president. To **impeach** means "to bring to trial." This means the House can accuse the president of serious crimes. The Senate then holds a trial. If the Senate finds the

Why did the Framers allow for the impeachment of presidents?

president guilty, he or she can be removed from office. While it is rarely used, impeachment is an important power that Congress has for checking the power of the executive branch.

How should the president be selected?

The Framers had given important powers to the president. It is not surprising that the Framers were concerned about how to select people to fill this position. The Framers took it for granted that George Washington would be the first president. Washington was patriotic, honest, devoted to the public good, and not interested in using power for his own advantage.

The Framers wanted a way of selecting future presidents who would be as qualified as Washington. The Framers discussed the problem for some time. They also discussed how long a president should be able to stay in office.

The Framers finally agreed that a president would serve for four years and

Why did the Framers allow presidents the power to veto laws passed by Congress?

Connecticut's electors cast their ballot during the 2004 presidential election. Do you agree with the reasoning of the Framers in their decision to establish an electoral college rather than have the people elect the president directly? Why or why not?

could be reelected any number of times. This was changed in 1951 by the **Twenty-second Amendment**. The president can now be reelected only once.

A few Framers wanted the people to elect the president directly. But James Madison thought that in such a large country the people would not know enough about the candidates to make good choices. Madison also believed that the people might not always have the wisdom to select the best person for president. Most Framers agreed with Madison.

In most states, the head of the executive branch was chosen by the state legislature. But the Framers thought that if Congress chose the executive, Congress would control the president. The result would be a weak executive branch. The Framers also thought that if the president were to be selected by the state governments, then the states would control the president. This too would result in a weak executive branch.

Either of these choices would not have helped the Framers create a stronger national government.

The method the Framers finally created for electing the president is complicated. They decided that an **electoral college** would be created once every four years to choose the president. Each state would have electors equal to the number of senators and representatives it had in Congress. Each state would decide how to select persons to serve as their electors in the college. The candidate who received a majority of votes in the electoral college would become president.

But what if no candidate got a majority of votes in the electoral college? In that case, the House of Representatives would select the president by majority vote. Each state would have one vote.

We still use the electoral college today. But it does not work the way the Framers originally planned.

IDEAS FOR DISCUSSION

What qualifications should a person have to be president?

Have students complete this section as outlined in the student text.
Suggested responses are as follows:

Duties, powers, limits	Qualifications
What are the duties of the president? 1. Act as commander-in-chief of the armed forces 2. Appoint certain important government officials 3. Inform Congress of the state of the union 4. Ensure that laws are faithfully executed	**What qualifications should a person have to carry out these duties?** 1. The president should have the wisdom to decide which conflicts to enter and which to avoid. 2. The president should have good judgment to be able to choose the most qualified candidates. 3. The president should have the ability to speak in public and inspire confidence in the nation. 4. The president should be conscientious in ensuring that the intent of the laws passed in Congress are being carried out.
What are the powers of the president? 1. Veto laws passed by Congress 2. Make treaties with foreign nations 3. Fill vacancies that occur during the Senate's recess 4. Convene and adjourn Congress on extraordinary occasions	**What qualifications should a person have to exercise these powers?** 1. The president should be intelligent enough to discern good legislation from bad legislation. 2. The president should have skill at diplomacy. 3. The president should be fair in his or her appointments, having the best interest of the country at heart. 4. The president should possess a sense of duty to help his or her nation during troubled times.
What are the limits on the powers of the president? 1. The Senate can approve or reject the president's nominations. 2. The Senate can approve or reject treaties signed by the president. 3. Congress has the power to provide money to conduct a war. 4. Congress can override a veto by a two-thirds vote of both houses.	**What qualifications should a person have to observe these limits to power?** 1. The president should be humble enough to compromise on occasion. 2. The president should be well-informed so that he or she can make good decisions about entering into treaties with foreign powers. 3. The president should be prudent in his or her dealings with other nations in order to avoid war. 4. The president should be patient enough to be able to work with others to find mutually agreeable solutions to problems.

IDEAS FOR DISCUSSION

What qualifications should a person have to be president?

Work with a group of three students. Examine Article II of the Constitution and review what you learned in this lesson to help you complete the chart.

PRESIDENT

duties, powers, limits   qualifications

What are the duties of the president?

1 _____
2 _____
3 _____
4 _____

What are the powers of the president?

1 _____
2 _____
3 _____
4 _____

What are the limits on the powers of the president?

1 _____
2 _____
3 _____
4 _____

What qualifications should a person have to carry out these duties?

1 _____
2 _____
3 _____
4 _____

What qualifications should a person have to exercise these powers?

1 _____
2 _____
3 _____
4 _____

What qualifications should a person have to observe these limits to power?

1 _____
2 _____
3 _____
4 _____

What powers does the Constitution give to the judicial branch?

To complete the system of separation of powers, the Framers planned for a judicial branch. A national judiciary was needed to decide disputes between state governments and between citizens of two or more states; it was also needed for disputes between the national government and a state or a citizen.

The Framers had few problems agreeing on the powers of the judicial branch. Article III of the Constitution establishes the judicial branch. Article III includes the following ideas about a national court system.

❶ Judges should be appointed, not elected. Thus, judges would be independent of politics. They could use their best judgment to decide cases and not worry about the influence of political pressures.

❷ Judges should keep their positions "during good Behavior." Judges cannot be removed from office unless they are impeached. Then the judge would have to be tried and convicted of "Treason, Bribery, or other high Crimes and Misdemeanors." This means that judges should be able to make decisions without fear of losing their jobs. It also means that judges can keep their jobs for life.

❸ There should be a single U.S. Supreme Court with two types of jurisdiction. **Jurisdiction** means the power or authority to hear cases and make decisions. The types of jurisdiction are original and appellate.

- The U.S. Supreme Court has original jurisdiction in cases involving a state government or an ambassador. **Original jurisdiction** means that these cases go directly to the U.S. Supreme Court. A lower court does not try these cases first.

- In all other cases, the U.S. Supreme Court has **appellate jurisdiction**. The case is tried first in a lower court. Then the decision of the lower court is appealed to the U.S. Supreme Court. The Supreme Court may decide whether to hear a case on appeal.

The Constitution clearly gave the U.S. Supreme Court the power to overrule state laws that violate the Constitution or the laws made by Congress. The power is based on the supremacy clause in Article VI. You will study the supremacy clause in Lesson 17.

The national government is supreme in those areas where the Constitution gives it the power to act. For example, suppose a state passes a law allowing factories to pollute the air. Then Congress passes a law controlling the pollution a factory can produce. The national government's laws would have to be obeyed over state laws.

Washington, Madison, and the other Framers who agreed with them got the strong national government they wanted. But the battle was not yet won. Many people in the United States were still afraid of a strong national government. They believed that it would be a threat to their rights and to their state governments.

What powers does the Constitution give to the judicial branch?

Because this section is somewhat complicated, you may wish to have students read each subsection separately and discuss its implications. Ask students to describe the advantages and disadvantages of the provisions for a national court system as outlined in Article III and Article VI of the Constitution. Share some examples of how these clauses have been employed (e.g., in *Plessy v. Ferguson* [1896], *Brown v. Board of Education of Topeka* [1954], *Bush v. Gore* [2000], *Hamdi v. Rumsfeld* [2004], etc.). The Legal Information Institute at Cornell University (www.law.cornell.edu) is a good source for U.S. Supreme Court decisions. Ask students whether they agree with the Framers that these three provisions work in the best interest of the people.

 see next student page

LESSON REVIEW

The questions in the student book are intended to assess learning and to reinforce knowledge through discussion. The questions are directly related to the lesson objectives. You may wish to include additional questions developed by yourself or by your students.

1. What challenges did the Framers face in creating the executive branch?

   The Framers believed their rights had been violated by the king and his royal governors and did not trust a powerful executive branch. Their challenge was how to create an executive branch that has enough power to carry out its designated responsibilities, yet is not so powerful as to dominate and control the other branches.

2. What powers does the Constitution grant to the president?

   The powers granted to the president by the Constitution include, among others, the power to carry out and enforce laws made by Congress, make treaties with foreign nations, appoint certain important government officials, act as commander in chief of the armed forces, and veto laws passed by Congress.

3. Explain how the system of checks and balances limits the powers of the president. Give specific examples.

   The president shares most of his or her powers with Congress. For example, when a president nominates a person for a position in the executive or

(continued next page)

judicial branches of government, the Senate has the power to approve or reject the nomination. The Senate has the power to approve or reject treaties signed by the president. The president can conduct war and serves as commander in chief of the armed forces, but only Congress has the power to declare war and provide the money needed to conduct a war. The president may veto laws passed by Congress, but Congress can override the president's veto by a two-thirds majority of both houses. The president's power is also limited because the House of Representatives can impeach the president. If the House impeaches the president, the Senate can hold a trial to decide whether to remove the president from office.

4. Explain the process for selecting a president.

   An electoral college is created once every four years to choose the president. Each state has electors equal to the number of senators and representatives it has in Congress. States determine the process for choosing electors. The candidate receiving a majority of votes in the electoral college becomes president. In the event of a tie, the House of Representatives selects the president by majority vote, with each state having one vote. This process has changed since the Framers devised the electoral college.

5. What are the powers of the judicial branch? Why is it important that judges are appointed to office rather than elected and that they cannot be removed from office unless impeached?

   The powers of the judicial branch are explained by its two types of jurisdiction: original jurisdiction and appellate jurisdiction. Original jurisdiction means that the U.S. Supreme Court has the sole power to hear cases involving a state government or ambassador. Appellate jurisdiction means that the U.S. Supreme Court hears appeals of decisions in cases that have been first tried by lower courts.

   Judges are appointed rather than elected so that they are free of the influence of political pressures and free to use their best judgment in deciding cases rather than worrying about such pressures. By serving for life unless impeached, judges can make decisions without fear of losing their jobs.

6. What branch of the federal government has the power to overrule state laws that violate the U.S. Constitution?

   The Constitution clearly gives the U.S. Supreme Court the power to overrule state laws that violate the Constitution or laws made by Congress. The power is based on the supremacy clause in Article VI.

LESSON REVIEW

❶ What challenges did the Framers face in creating the executive branch?

❷ What powers does the Constitution grant to the president?

❸ Explain how the system of checks and balances limits the powers of the president. Give specific examples.

❹ Explain the process for selecting a president.

❺ What are the powers of the judicial branch? Why is it important that judges are appointed to office rather than elected and that they cannot be removed from office unless impeached?

❻ What branch of the federal government has the power to overrule state laws that violate the U.S. Constitution?

ACTIVITIES

❶ Only two presidents have faced impeachment: Andrew Johnson and William Jefferson Clinton. Richard Nixon faced the threat of impeachment, but he resigned from office. Learn more about the impeachment process and what happened with each of the three presidents listed. Share what you learned with your class.

❷ Find out how electors to the electoral college are selected in your state. Share what you learned with your class.

❸ Examine the Twenty-fifth Amendment to the Constitution. Draw a chart that illustrates who is next in line to become the president if a president dies while in office or otherwise cannot carry out his or her duties.

❹ Learn more about John Jay and John Marshall, two justices of the U.S. Supreme Court. You can find information about these important men in your library or on the Internet.

unit four

How was the Constitution used to establish our government?

UNIT OVERVIEW

This unit describes how the Constitution set forth the basic organization of our system of government and some of the resulting developments under the new Constitution. Students first learn what a federal system is and how the Constitution established a federal system based on popular sovereignty. They study the arguments put forth by the Anti-Federalists—opponents of ratification—and the Federalists—proponents of ratification—and the process used by the Framers to ensure ratification. As students study the disagreements between the Federalists and the Anti-Federalists, they begin to appreciate that these disagreements were a result of differing views of the natural rights philosophy, republicanism, and constitutionalism.

They learn how the new government was organized under the Constitution, and how and why the Bill of Rights was added. Students examine the rise of political parties, a development the Framers had not anticipated, and how they have emerged as an integral part of our government today. Finally, students will learn about judicial review.

Unit objectives

At the conclusion of this unit, students should be able to

- explain the basic elements of our federal system, its basis in popular sovereignty, and some of the problems arising from our federal system
- explain why the ratification process was important
- describe the arguments for and against ratification made by the Federalists and Anti-Federalists
- describe how the executive and judicial branches were organized
- explain how and why the Bill of Rights was added to the Constitution
- describe why the development of political parties was important
- define judicial review, explain how it developed, and describe some of the disputes that arose around it

Unit introduction

Read the introduction with the class. Introduce the Key Concepts and tell students that these terms will be fully explained in the lessons of this unit. The illustrations throughout the unit are excellent teaching tools for reviewing and reinforcing the learning. Use them as you find appropriate.

Unit project (optional)

Ask your students to write the Key Concepts in their notebooks and write definitions based on their current knowledge. Students can change and add to these initial definitions as the unit progresses.

unit four

KEY CONCEPTS

Anti-Federalists

confederation

federal system

Federalists

judicial review

political parties

supremacy clause

Why is our nation's Constitution so short? The Framers wrote the Constitution as a general framework, or plan, for the new government. They left out many details because they knew that future presidents and members of Congress would add them.

In this unit, you will discover how government was organized under the Constitution. You will be able to explain the positions of the Founders who supported the Constitution and the positions of those who were against it. You will also learn about some unexpected developments that have influenced the way our nation is governed today.

How did the Constitution create a federal system of government?

17

LESSON PURPOSE

The Constitution organized government in a new way. It created a federal system of government. The Constitution gives certain powers only to the national government and certain powers only to the state governments. There are also certain powers that they share. All other powers are kept by the people.

When you finish this lesson, you should be able to explain what a federal system is. You should know how it differs from other forms of government. You should be able to explain what powers the Constitution gives to the federal government and what powers it gives to the state governments.

OVERVIEW

This lesson helps students understand the federal system of government created by the Framers. Students learn how this system differs from a unitary form of government, in which the central government controls the state and local governments, and how it differs from the confederate system, in which states are independent and have control over the laws that affect their citizens. Students learn that the Preamble to the Constitution makes it clear that under our system of government, sovereignty belongs to the people and that the people delegate power to both the national and state governments. Students examine the specific powers delegated to the state and federal governments, and learn which powers the Constitution denies to the state and federal governments. Students test their understanding of the federal system by deciding which level of government would decide some proposed actions. At the end of the lesson, students learn that the supremacy clause establishes the authority of the Constitution as the supreme law of the nation, and that states cannot make laws that conflict with the Constitution or with laws made by Congress.

OBJECTIVES

At the conclusion of this lesson, students should be able to

- describe our federal system of government
- explain the essential differences between unitary, confederate, and federal systems of government
- explain what powers the Constitution delegates to the federal government and what powers it delegates to the state governments
- explain how the Constitution gives the federal government supreme power over the state governments

TEACHING PROCEDURES

INTRODUCTORY ACTIVITY

Explain to students that they will be examining how power was to be distributed between the new federal government and the state governments. Remind students that although the Framers wanted to create a more powerful federal government, they were still suspicious of making the federal government too powerful at the expense of the state governments.

(continued next page)

Have students read the Lesson Purpose and consider the objectives of the lesson. Write the Terms to Understand on the board or use a vocabulary-building activity of your choice. Have students look up the words in the Glossary at the back of the text. Ask them to look for these words as they read the lesson.

READING, DISCUSSION, AND ACTIVITIES

How do some other nations organize their governments?

Create a two-column chart. Label the first column "Unitary Government." Label the second column "Confederation." As students read this section, have them write down ideas about these two forms of government and examples of each form of government. Discuss their charts and emphasize that our first form of government under the Articles of Confederation was a confederation.

TERMS TO UNDERSTAND

confederation
federal system
federalism
sovereign
supremacy clause
unitary government

How do some other nations organize their governments?

Not all nations organize government in the same way. Some nations have a unitary form of government. A **unitary government** is one in which a central government controls the state and local governments. The central government acts directly on the people. The power of state and local governments comes from the central government and it can be taken away at any time. As a result, the central government is much stronger and more powerful than the state and local governments. The United Kingdom, France, and Sweden are examples of unitary government.

Some nations have a form of government called a confederation. In a **confederation** the states are independent and have control of anything that affects their citizens and territory. In a confederation, the central government only handles those things that are of common concern. The states can withdraw from the confederation at any time. The central government acts on the states, not directly on the people. The United States under the Articles of Confederation had a confederate form of government.

This is the Swiss Bundeshaus, or Parliament. What form of government does Switzerland have? How does it differ from our form of government?

Switzerland is a modern example of a confederation.

Before the Framers created the Constitution, most nations had either a unitary or confederate form of government. The kind of government that the Framers created in our Constitution is a federal system of government.

What is a federal system of government?

After students read this section, divide them into pairs or small groups of three or four students. Ask each group to create a graphic illustrating the federal system of government. Emphasize that the graphic should clearly show where the powers come from, and where and to whom they are directed. Ask students to label the depiction of "sovereign" as it is shown in their graphic. Have the groups share their drawings with the class. You may wish to put them up on the wall for future reference.

How do these three types of government differ in their distribution of power?

What is a federal system of government?

According to the natural rights philosophy, the people have a right to create a government. The people delegate to government the right, or authority, to govern them. In return, government is responsible for protecting the people's rights to life, liberty, and property.

The Constitution begins with the words "We the People of the United States." The people have created a government and have given it the authority to govern them. Power flows upward from the people to their government. The people remain sovereign at all times. **Sovereign** means to have the highest rank of authority. The people have ultimate authority to control government.

At the time the Framers wrote the Constitution, the people in most other nations were not sovereign. Governments held authority over the people. In some countries the king was sovereign.

In a **federal system** of government, the sovereign people decide how to delegate their authority. When creating the Constitution the Framers decided to delegate the power of the people to more than one government. They delegated some powers only to the national government. They delegated other power to the state governments. Some powers, they decided, should be shared by the state and national governments. Finally, all other powers, or rights, are kept by the people.

A federal system of government may also be described as a government that is based on the principle of federalism. **Federalism** refers to the practice of dividing and sharing the powers of government between a central government and regional governments such as state governments.

What powers are delegated to the state and federal governments?

Create a chart with four columns. Label the columns "Powers of the Federal Government," "Powers of State Governments," "Powers Shared by Federal and State Governments," and "Powers or Rights of Citizens." As students read this section, have them write their findings under each heading. Discuss with students their opinions of the powers delegated to the different levels of government. Ask them to explain why they agree or disagree with the way the powers have been divided.

What powers are delegated to the state and federal governments?

As citizens of the United States, the people delegate certain powers to the federal, or national, government. These powers are in the Constitution. They include the power to

- create post offices
- regulate interstate and foreign trade
- declare and conduct war
- create a national currency

This is President Franklin Roosevelt signing the congressional declaration of war against Japan in December 1941. Why do you think that only the federal government has the authority to engage in war?

As citizens of the various states, the people delegate certain powers to their state governments. These powers are in each state's constitution. They include the power to

- regulate trade within the state
- establish public schools
- create traffic and motor vehicle laws
- regulate marriage and divorce practices

The state and federal governments share certain powers. These include the powers to

- make their own laws
- tax the people
- borrow money
- create their own court system
- provide for the health and welfare of the people

Finally, the people have kept certain rights or powers and have not delegated them to any government. These include the right to

- believe what we wish
- form or join organizations
- select our careers and live our lives as we choose
- choose our friends
- travel where we wish to go inside or outside the country
- raise a family

What powers does the Constitution deny to the federal and state governments?

A constitutional government means that the powers of government are limited. The U.S. Constitution limits the powers of both the federal and state governments.

LIMITS ON THE POWER OF THE FEDERAL GOVERNMENT

The federal government may not

- tax exports

- spend money in a way that is not approved by law

- enact laws that favor trade in one state over the others

- exercise powers that belong to the states

- suspend the right to a writ of habeas corpus, except in a national emergency

LIMITS ON THE POWER OF THE STATE GOVERNMENTS

The state governments may not

- coin or print money

- enter into treaties with other nations

- tax imports or exports

- keep an army or navy in time of peace

- engage in war unless invaded or in immediate danger of being invaded

What powers and rights do the people keep for themselves?

LIMITS ON BOTH THE FEDERAL AND STATE GOVERNMENTS

Neither the federal nor state governments may

- deny the right to trial by jury

- enact ex post facto laws or bills of attainder

- grant titles of nobility

The Bill of Rights places other limits on federal and state governments. You will examine these in the next unit.

151

What powers does the Constitution deny to the federal and state governments?

Assign this section to students to read. Draw a Venn diagram on the board or on chart paper. Label one circle "Limits on the Federal Government." Label the other circle "Limits on State Government." Ask students to list the way the Constitution limits the federal government and the state governments. Write the limits in the appropriate circle. The limits shared by the federal and state governments should be written within the intersecting area of the circles.

Ask students what they think about placing these limits on the federal and state governments and whether they think any further limits should be placed on either level of government. An optional activity is to have students locate examples of the limitations placed on the federal and state governments in newspapers or magazines. Ask students to describe how these limits affect our everyday lives.

Solve the Problem

Do state governments or the national government have the power to do what you propose?

Introduce the activity to students as directed in the student text. Have students use Handout D3 of the Appendix to designate whether the power to perform the action belongs to national government, state governments, both, or neither. Discuss students' responses before giving the answers below.

1. national government
2. state government
3. both
4. state government
5. national government
6. national government
7. neither
8. neither
9. national government
10. state government

 see next student page

Reading and Discussion

What is the supremacy clause?

Have students read this section. Ensure that they understand the meaning of the supremacy clause and that many U.S. Supreme Court cases are the result of laws made by the states that are in conflict with the Constitution or federal laws. Ask students if they can think of a time when a state has made a law that has been in conflict with either the Constitution or laws made by Congress.

SOLVE THE PROBLEM

Do state governments or the national government have the power to do what you propose?

Work with a partner. Imagine that you want to do each of the things listed below. First, you need to decide which level of government, state or national, has the power to do what you propose. Examine each item. Decide if the power belongs to the national government, the state governments, both, or neither.

❶ You want a law to help control what people can put on the Internet for children to see and read.

❷ You want to increase the age at which people may buy tobacco to twenty-five.

❸ You want a law that helps to control who may or may not buy and sell guns.

❹ You want a law to limit driving privileges for people over eighty-five years of age.

❺ You think that we no longer need a one-cent coin. You want a law to end the minting of pennies.

❻ You want a law to stop the sale of sport shoes made by children who work long hours for little pay in some other countries.

❼ You want a law to make it more difficult for parents of very young children to get a divorce.

❽ You think that the leader of another country is not able to run the government of that country. You want a law to punish anyone who supports this leader.

❾ You want a treaty that requires all nations to pass laws to clean up the air and water.

❿ You want a law to raise the minimum age requirement for children to remain in school.

What part of government would negotiate treaties among nations requiring them to pass laws to clean up the air and water?

What is the supremacy clause?

There were disagreements among the Framers over what powers the federal government should have. The Framers did agree that the powers of the federal government were to be greater than the powers of the state governments. As you learned in Lesson 16, this is clearly stated in the supremacy clause of Article VI. The **supremacy clause** says,

> This Constitution, and the Laws of the United States...shall be the supreme Law of the Land.

The states cannot make laws that conflict with the Constitution or laws made by Congress.

The supremacy clause gives the courts the power to decide disagreements between the states and the federal government. It does not change the fact, however, that the Constitution limits the powers of both the federal and state governments.

What might be the advantages and disadvantages of the supremacy clause?

How has the relation between federal and state governments changed?

The Framers created a new and very complicated form of government. They could not predict exactly what powers the state and federal governments would eventually have. Early in our history, the state governments were very powerful. Today, the federal government has far more power over the state governments than most of the Framers could have imagined.

In thinking about the relationship between the federal and state governments, it is important to understand the following things:

- In spite of the increase in the power of the federal government, most of the laws that affect us directly are state or local laws. These include laws regarding education, most property, contracts, families, and criminal behavior.

- Congress makes most of the decisions about how much power is left to the states. Congress decides whether the federal or state governments should carry out certain responsibilities.

This complicated system is sometimes not as efficient as a unitary system of government. But the Framers did not see this as a disadvantage. In fact, the Framers thought that the separation of powers between the federal and state governments was one way to protect the rights of the people.

153

How has the relation between federal and state governments changed?

Have students read this section. Emphasize that our government has evolved from very powerful state governments and a weak national government to less powerful state governments and a very strong national government.

Ask students to reflect on the idea that despite the increase in power of the federal government, most of the laws that affect us directly are state or local laws. Ask them if they agree with this statement.

 see next student page

LESSON REVIEW

The questions in the student book are intended to assess learning and to reinforce knowledge through discussion. The questions are directly related to the lesson objectives. You may wish to include additional questions developed by yourself or by students.

1. Explain the major differences between a unitary form of government and a confederation.

   A unitary form of government is one in which the central government controls the state and local governments. The central government acts directly on the people. Power can be delegated to state and local governments, and can be taken away at any time. In a confederation, independent states have authority over their own citizens and territory. The central government in a confederation can act only on the states, not directly on the people. States can withdraw from a confederation at any time.

2. What is a federal system?

   In a federal system of government, the people determine which powers are divided between the national and state governments, which powers the two forms of government share, and which powers are kept by the people.

3. What powers does the Constitution delegate to the federal government?

   The federal government has the power to create post offices, control interstate and foreign trade, declare and conduct war, and create a national currency.

(continued next page)

4. What powers belong to the states?

   State governments have been given the power to control trade within the state, establish public schools, create traffic and motor vehicle laws, and control marriage and divorce practices.

5. What powers do the state and federal governments share?

   The federal and state governments share the power to make their own laws, tax the people, borrow money, create their own court systems, and provide for the health and welfare of the people.

6. What powers did the people keep for themselves?

   The people have kept certain rights or powers—they did not delegate them to any level of government. These include the right to believe what we wish; form or join organizations; select careers and live our lives as we choose; choose our friends; travel where we wish, inside or outside the country; and raise a family.

7. What powers does the Constitution deny to the federal government?

   The federal government may not tax exports; spend money in a way that is not approved by law; enact laws that favor trade in one state over the others; exercise powers that belong to the states; and suspend the right to a writ of habeas corpus, except in a national emergency.

8. What powers does the Constitution deny to the state governments?

   State governments may not coin or print money, enter into treaties with other nations, tax imports or exports, keep an army or navy in time of peace, and engage in war unless invaded or in immediate danger of being invaded.

9. What is the supremacy clause? Why is it important?

   The supremacy clause establishes the Constitution as the supreme law of the land. States cannot make laws that conflict with the Constitution or with laws made by Congress. The supremacy clause is important because it provides a way to settle conflicts between the state and federal governments. The courts have been given the power to settle such disagreements.

ACTIVITIES

The suggested activities are intended to extend and apply learning outside the classroom. You may wish to have students complete one or more of the activities. Have them share their results with the class.

LESSON REVIEW

❶ Explain the major differences between a unitary form of government and a confederation.

❷ What is a federal system?

❸ What powers does the Constitution delegate to the federal government?

❹ What powers belong to the states?

❺ What powers do the state and federal governments share?

❻ What powers did the people keep for themselves?

❼ What powers does the Constitution deny to the federal government?

❽ What powers does the Constitution deny to the state governments?

❾ What is the supremacy clause? Why is it important?

ACTIVITIES

❶ Draw a diagram that shows how the federal system works in the United States. Your diagram should show the powers that belong to the states and powers that belong to the national government. Your diagram should also show the powers that both states and the national government share.

❷ Look in a newspaper to find articles that illustrate how the federal system works. You may find articles that illustrate federal powers, state powers, and powers that both levels of government share.

❸ Plan a short play. Suppose you and a few friends were in a situation like that of the Framers. You must organize a government. Explain to your classmates, the "people," what you think might be some advantages and disadvantages of a federal system of government.

- Which responsibilities and powers would you give to the national government?

- Which powers would you give to the state governments?

- Which powers would you keep for the people?

How did the people approve the new Constitution?

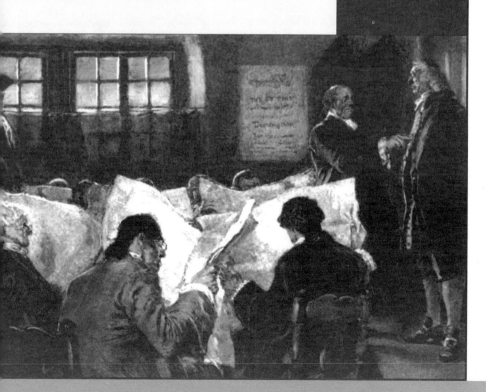

LESSON PURPOSE

In this lesson you will learn about the struggle to get the Constitution ratified. You will learn how the Framers planned to have the people decide whether or not to approve the Constitution. You will also examine the arguments made by the Anti-Federalists and the Federalists for and against the new Constitution.

When you finish the lesson, you should be able to explain why the ratification process was important. You should also be able to describe the arguments for and against approving the Constitution.

OVERVIEW

In this lesson, students learn about the challenges that faced the Framers as they attempted to get the Constitution ratified. Students study Madison's plan to have the people select delegates for ratification conventions to be held in each state rather than asking Congress or the state legislatures for approval of the Constitution. Students learn that the Framers used the concepts of a social contract and consent of the governed to get the Constitution approved. Students examine the arguments for and against ratification through a debate activity in which they take positions on whether a republican government will work in a large country, whether the Constitution gives the national government too much power, and whether a bill of rights is needed.

OBJECTIVES

At the conclusion of this lesson, students should be able to

- explain why the ratification process was important
- describe the arguments for and against approving the Constitution
- explain why the Federalists agreed to a bill of rights

TEACHING PROCEDURES

INTRODUCTORY ACTIVITY

Have students read the Lesson Purpose and consider the objectives of the lesson. Ask them to consider how they could generate support for an idea that would need the approval of a large group of people. The idea could be related to school or to something else. Write students' ideas on the board. As they read the lesson, students can compare their list of strategies with the plan used by the Framers.

Write the Terms to Understand on the board or use a vocabulary-building activity of your choice. Have students look up the words in the Glossary at the back of the text. Ask them to look for these words as they read the lesson.

READING AND DISCUSSION

Why did the Framers want the people to ratify the Constitution?

Assign this section to students to read. Ask them to identify the reasons for Madison's plan. You may wish to have students write these reasons on a piece of paper. Ask students to share their findings with the class. Compare students' ideas from the Introductory Activity with those of the Framers and ask them how they are similar and how they are different.

TERMS TO UNDERSTAND

Anti-Federalists
Federalists
ratify
The Federalist

Why did the Framers want the people to ratify the Constitution?

The Framers did not believe they had created a perfect plan of government. The four months they spent creating the Constitution had been filled with disagreements. A few delegates had walked out of the convention. Some delegates refused to sign the Constitution. The great majority of Framers, however, thought they had done a good job.

After creating the Constitution, the Framers knew that they had to get it approved. James Madison was afraid that the Constitution would be rejected if either the Congress or the state legislatures were asked to ratify it. To **ratify** means to approve. To avoid rejection, Madison developed a plan. His plan was to get the voters to ratify the Constitution at special conventions to be held in each state. The delegates to these conventions would be elected by popular vote of the people for the sole purpose of approving the Constitution.

Madison based his plan on the idea in the Preamble to the Constitution. The first words in the Preamble are "We the People...do ordain and establish this

How did Madison plan to get the people to approve the new Constitution?

Constitution." The people who were to be governed by the new national government would consent to its creation and agree to obey its decisions. This was the method for establishing a government set forth in the natural rights philosophy and in the Declaration of Independence. Thus, the Framers used the idea of a social

How were people in cities far from Washington, D.C., able to participate in government? How is it easier to participate in government now than it was in the late 1700s?

contract to get the Constitution approved. It was to be approved by an agreement among the people to create a national government.

The Framers approved Madison's plan. Article VII said that the Constitution would be in effect after it had been ratified by the conventions of nine of the thirteen states. The Framers required approval of the voters of nine states because they were afraid they would not get the approval of all thirteen.

Who were the Federalists and Anti-Federalists?

Once the Philadelphia Convention ended, the Federalists went to work. The **Federalists** were the people who supported ratifying the Constitution. The Federalists asked the states to organize their ratifying conventions as quickly as possible. They knew that their opponents had not had much time to prepare their arguments. By contrast, the supporters of the Constitution had worked on it for four months. They knew the arguments for and against it.

To explain the new Constitution to the people, Alexander Hamilton, James Madison, and John Jay wrote a series of articles for a New York newspaper supporting ratification. These collected articles are called **The Federalist**. *The Federalist* was read in other states as well. Today, *The Federalist* remains one of the most important explanations of constitutional government ever written.

The **Anti-Federalists** were the people who opposed ratifying the Constitution. Anti-Federalist leaders included George Mason, Edmund Randolph, and Elbridge Gerry. Each had attended the Philadelphia Convention but refused to sign the Constitution. Although John Hancock, Samuel Adams, and Richard Henry Lee had all signed the Declaration of Independence, they too were against ratification.

Who were the Federalists and Anti-Federalists?

After students read this section, help them to remember that many Americans were suspicious of a strong national government. Engage in a discussion that helps them to understand how this fear strongly influenced the Anti-Federalists' opposition to ratification.

Reading, discussion, and activity

What issues related to the new Constitution did the people debate?

This section provides the arguments for and against ratification of the Constitution. Divide the class into groups of six students. Subdivide each group into pairs of students. Assign each pair in each group one of the three topics of debate between the Federalists and Anti-Federalists.

The subgroups will read the Anti-Federalist and Federalist positions on pages 160 and 161 for their assigned sections and prepare to teach these positions to the other four students in their groups of six. When all subgroups have taught their sections, ask the students to share their opinions about the strength and validity of the arguments.

Patrick Henry had always opposed the idea of a strong national government. Henry became a leading Anti-Federalist. Mercy Otis Warren, a playwright, also was against ratification. She wrote pamphlets explaining why she did not support the Constitution.

Most Americans were very suspicious of government, but the Anti-Federalists were especially mistrustful of government in general and strong national government in particular. This mistrust was the basis of their opposition to the Constitution. They feared it had created a government the people could not control. The Anti-Federalists feared that flaws they saw in the Constitution would be a threat to their natural rights. During the ratification debates, the Anti-Federalists put up a strong fight.

Why were Anti-Federalists like Mercy Otis Warren opposed to ratification of the Constitution?

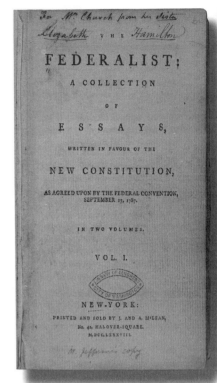

What is The Federalist? *Who wrote it? Why is it important?*

What issues related to the new Constitution did the people debate?

The debates in the states lasted ten months. It was an intense and sometimes bitter political struggle.

Both the Federalists and Anti-Federalists made many arguments for and against the Constitution. However,

The small republics of the ancient past eventually collapsed. How did the Federalists propose to prevent this from happening to the new nation?

the most intense arguments were about three basic issues:

- whether the Constitution would maintain republican government,

- whether the national government would have too much power, and

- whether a bill of rights was needed in the Constitution.

The chart on the next two pages will help you see both sides of the debate. The chart summarizes how the Federalists and Anti-Federalists responded to each of the three issues.

Do you think a bill of rights would cause intense debate today? Why or why not?

READING FOR FEDERALIST/ANTI-FEDERALIST ACTIVITY

The readings on these two pages address the positions of the Federalists and Anti-Federalists by sorting the issues into three sections:

1. Allocation of power:
   Does the national government have too much power?

2. Adherence to principles of representative democracy:
   Does the Constitution provide for republican government?

3. Protection of the rights of the people:
   Does the Constitution need to have a bill of rights?

Does the national government have too much power?

ANTI-FEDERALISTS	FEDERALISTS
The Constitution gives the national government too much power at the expense of the state governments. It gives government the power to tax citizens. It gives government the power to raise and keep an army during peacetime. This army could be used by government to suppress the people.	The national government will have greater power than it did under the Articles of Confederation. But its powers are limited to solving problems that face the entire nation, such as trade and defense. The recent history of the states shows that a stronger national government is needed to deal with such problems.
The supremacy clause means that all the national government's laws are superior to laws made by the states. It will only be a matter of time until the state governments are destroyed.	The Constitution provides protections for the state governments by specifically reserving certain powers for the states. This will prevent the states from being destroyed by the national government.
The necessary and proper clause is too general. It gives too much power to the national government. It is dangerous not to list all the powers of government in order to put clear limits on them.	The necessary and proper clause and general welfare clause are needed if the national government is to do the things it is responsible for doing.
The Constitution gives too much power to the executive branch of government. It will soon become a monarchy.	A strong executive branch is necessary. It is needed if the national government is to fulfill its responsibilities. Congress and the U.S. Supreme Court have checks on the use of power by the executive branch. The executive branch cannot become a monarchy.
	The powers of the national government are separated and balanced among the three branches. No one branch can dominate the others. This system makes it impossible for any person or group to take complete control of government.

Does the Constitution provide for republican government?

ANTI-FEDERALISTS	FEDERALISTS
Throughout history, the only places where republican governments worked had been in small communities. There, the people had similar wealth and the same values. People who are not too rich or too poor are more likely to have civic virtue. Such people are more likely to agree on what is best for their common good. The new nation would be too large and diverse. The people will not be able to agree on their common welfare.	History has proven that selfish groups destroyed all of the small republics of the past. The civic virtue of the citizens was not enough to keep people from seeking their own interests. People did not work for the common good. A large republic where power is divided between the national and state governments is a better solution. It is also better to organize government based on checks and balances. Under such a government, it will be more difficult for special interests to work against the common good.
Free government requires the active participation of the people. The national government will be located far from where most people live. People will be unable to participate in government. As a result, the only way government will be able to rule will be with military force. The result will be a tyranny.	The national government cannot become a tyranny. The limits placed on government by the system of separation of powers and checks and balances will prevent it. Government will be so good at protecting the rights of the people that it will soon gain their loyalty and support.

Is a Bill of Rights needed for the Constitution?

ANTI-FEDERALISTS	FEDERALISTS
The Constitution does not include a bill of rights. A bill of rights is necessary to protect people against the power of the national government. There is no mention of freedom of religion, speech, press, or assembly. Since these freedoms are not in the Constitution, government is free to violate them. Americans recently fought a war to secure their fundamental rights. They do not want a constitution that places those rights in jeopardy.	A bill of rights is not needed. The Constitution is the ultimate protection for people's rights and the people are the ultimate sovereigns. The Constitution does not give government the power to deprive people of their rights. It gives government only limited power to do certain things. A bill of rights will give the impression that the people can expect protection only for the rights that are actually listed. The Constitution protects a number of rights by requiring writs of habeas corpus, and prohibiting ex post facto laws and bills of attainder.

 see student pages 162 and 163

Why did the Federalists agree to add a bill of rights to the Constitution?

Read this section with students, emphasizing that the debate between the Federalists and Anti-Federalists led to the agreement to develop a bill of rights.

PARTICIPATING IN A CLASS ACTIVITY

Would your class ratify the new constitution?

Introduce the activity to the class as directed in the student text. You should allow about an hour for the debate—thirty minutes for preparation and thirty minutes for the debate itself. You may wish to divide the class as follows to prepare for the debate:

- Divide the class into two groups. One group represents the Anti-Federalists. The other group represents the Federalists.
- Select three people from each group to present two-minute statements in support of or in opposition to each of the three questions.
- Select three people from each group to present the rebuttal to the other group's positions on the three questions. These people should prepare for their rebuttal in advance, but will also listen carefully to the other group's positions during the debate, and take notes in order to effectively rebut their arguments.
- The remaining group members should split into two subgroups. The first subgroup will help each of the three people presenting two-minute statements to develop their arguments for the statements. The second subgroup will help students who are presenting rebuttals to anticipate the positions of the other group and prepare arguments to oppose those positions.

When the class is prepared to conduct the debate, you may wish to use the following procedure:

- The moderator will introduce both groups and read the three questions to be debated.
- The Federalists will present their statement of their position regarding question one.
- The Anti-Federalists will present a rebuttal.
- The Anti-Federalists will present a statement of their position regarding question one.
- The Federalists will present a two-minute rebuttal.
- The Federalists will present a two-minute statement of their position regarding question two.
- The Anti-Federalists will present a two-minute rebuttal.
- The Anti-Federalists will present a two-minute statement of their position regarding question two.
- The Federalists will present a two-minute rebuttal.
- The Federalists will present a two-minute statement of their position regarding question three.
- The Anti-Federalists will present a two-minute rebuttal.
- The Anti-Federalists will present a two-minute statement of their position regarding question three.
- The Federalists will present a two-minute rebuttal.
- A person from the Federalist group will give a short summary of their group's arguments.
- A person from the Anti-Federalist group will give a short summary of their group's arguments.
- The moderator will make a few closing comments.
- The instructor conducts a vote on whether to ratify the new constitution.
- The instructor will tally the votes and announce the results to the class.
- Students will evaluate the debate as suggested in the student text.

What compromise did the Federalists finally agree to make in order to get enough support for the Constitution to be ratified?

Why did the Federalists agree to add a bill of rights to the Constitution?

A compromise was reached on the issue of a bill of rights. The Federalists made this compromise to get enough support for the Constitution so that it would be ratified. They agreed that when the first Congress was held, it would draft a bill of rights.

The argument to add a bill of rights was a victory for the Anti-Federalists. It was an important addition to the Constitution and has been of great importance in the protection of the basic rights of the American people.

Would your class ratify the new constitution?

Imagine that your class is one of the original thirteen states. You are holding a ratifying convention to decide if your state will approve the new constitution. The students in the class are delegates to the state convention. Divide the class into two groups. One group represents the Anti-Federalists. The other group represents the Federalists.

GETTING READY FOR THE DEBATE

The debate questions are below:

- Will republican government work in such a large country?

- Does the Constitution give the national government too much power?

- Does the Constitution need to have a bill of rights?

Apply what you have learned from this text to help you prepare your arguments. You may want to divide your group into three smaller groups, so that each smaller group can prepare responses for one of the questions.

PARTICIPATING IN THE DEBATE

Before the debate begins, establish a few rules. Decide upon the amount of time each group gets to speak and how many turns each group should get.

Decide which group gets to speak first on each of the three questions.

Select one student from your group to moderate the debate. He or she should read the questions aloud to the class, call on groups to speak, and keep track of time limits.

At the end of the debate, each group should give a short summary of its arguments. Finally, everyone in the class should vote on whether or not to ratify the new constitution.

EVALUATING THE DECISION

Your class should discuss the results of the debate.

❶ What do you think were the best arguments for ratifying the Constitution?

❷ What were the best arguments against ratifying the Constitution?

❸ What might have happened to the country if the states had not ratified the Constitution?

LESSON REVIEW

The questions in the student book are intended to assess learning and to reinforce knowledge through discussion. The questions are directly related to the lesson objectives. You may wish to include additional questions developed by yourself or by your students.

1. Why did the Framers oppose submitting the Constitution to the existing Congress or state governments for ratification?

    During the Philadelphia Convention, there were many disagreements. Some delegates left the convention. Others refused to sign the Constitution. The Framers feared that Congress and the state legislatures would not ratify the Constitution. They believed that if they went directly to the people, the people would ratify the Constitution. This was the same method for establishing a government that was advocated by the natural rights philosophy and the Declaration of Independence. It was based on the idea of a social contract.

2. What process did the Framers select for ratifying the Constitution? How did the Preamble to the Constitution help them decide on this method?

    The Framers agreed to ask voters to ratify the Constitution in special conventions held in each state. Delegates to the conventions would be elected by popular vote. The Preamble to the Constitution states, "We the People… do ordain and establish this Constitution." The idea contained in the Preamble—that the people consented to the creation of the Constitution and would obey its decisions—inspired the Framers to use the ratification method for gaining the people's approval of the Constitution.

3. What arguments did the Anti-Federalists make against ratifying the Constitution?

    The Anti-Federalists argued that a republican government could only work in small communities where people know each other, have similar incomes, and share similar values. They believed that the new nation would be too large and diverse for the type of government envisioned by the Constitution to succeed. The Anti-Federalists were afraid that the distance between the states and the federal government would make it impossible for people to actively participate in government. This would cause government to rule through military force, which would result in tyranny. The Anti-Federalists argued that the national government would have too much power at the expense of the state governments and that the supremacy clause would eventually destroy state governments. They believed that the necessary and proper clause was too general and that the executive branch had too much power. They argued that a bill of rights was needed to protect the people against the power of the national government. (The proposed Constitution lacked a bill of rights.)

4. How did the Federalists respond to the criticisms of the Constitution made by the Anti-Federalists?

The Federalists responded that a large republic where powers are divided between national and state governments is better than the original concept of a republic. They argued that a government with a carefully designed system of checks and balances would counter the domination of any one branch. The Federalists believed that state governments would be protected from the national government by reserving specific powers for the states. They argued that both the necessary and proper and general welfare clauses were needed to allow government to function. They believed that a strong executive branch was necessary to ensure that government fulfills its responsibilities. The checks and balances provided by the Constitution, they argued, would prevent any person or group from taking complete control of government. The Federalists believed that a bill of rights was not needed because the Constitution is the ultimate protector of people's rights, and does not give government the ability to deprive people of their rights. They argued that a bill of rights would limit the rights of the people to only those specifically listed.

5. The Anti-Federalists lost their battle to prevent adoption of the Constitution. Their struggle, however, permanently shaped the new Constitution. Explain how the ideas and concerns of the Anti-Federalists accomplished this. Why was this struggle important? Why is it relevant today?

The debates over ratification of the Constitution resulted in an agreement to draft a bill of rights. The Bill of Rights helps to protect the basic rights of the American people. Accept any reasonable responses addressing its contemporary relevance.

6. Explain how the ratification process provided a widespread public debate about an important political decision.

The disagreement between the Federalists and Anti-Federalists over ratification of the Constitution resulted in ten months of public debate about the issue. Supporters of the Constitution wrote a series of newspaper articles published in a book called The Federalist. *Anti-Federalist leaders such as Mercy Otis Warren wrote pamphlets against ratification. Both sides of the debate argued passionately to support their points of view.*

LESSON REVIEW

❶ Why did the Framers oppose submitting the Constitution to the existing Congress or state governments for ratification?

❷ What process did the Framers select for ratifying the Constitution? How did the Preamble to the Constitution help them decide on this method?

❸ What arguments did the Anti-Federalists make against ratifying the Constitution?

❹ How did the Federalists respond to the criticisms of the Constitution made by the Anti-Federalists?

❺ The Anti-Federalists lost their battle to prevent adoption of the Constitution. Their struggle, however, permanently shaped the new Constitution. Explain how the ideas and concerns of the Anti-Federalists accomplished this. Why was this struggle important? Why is it relevant today?

❻ Explain how the ratification process provided a widespread public debate about an important political decision.

ACTIVITIES

❶ Learn more about *The Federalist*. Find information in your library or on the Internet. Write your own Federalist paper. Read it to your class.

❷ Imagine that you are an Anti-Federalist. Make a collage that illustrates your point of view about the Constitution. Include references to actual Anti-Federalist writings. Be prepared to defend your design before the class.

❸ Imagine that people in 1787 drove cars like ours. Create a bumper sticker that reflects either a Federalist or Anti-Federalist point of view about the new constitution.

❹ Conduct research to find information about African American Federalist or Anti-Federalist writers, such as Brutus and Federal Farmer.

How did Congress organize the new government?

19

LESSON PURPOSE

The U.S. Constitution is a plan for government. Once the Constitution was ratified, it was the job of the first Congress to use this plan to organize the new government. In this lesson you will read about some of the decisions made by the first Congress. You will learn how Congress organized the executive branch. You will also learn how Congress established a system of federal courts below the U.S. Supreme Court. Finally, you will learn how the Bill of Rights was added to the Constitution.

When you finish this lesson, you should be able to explain how the first Congress organized the executive and judicial branches of government. You should also be able to explain how the Bill of Rights was added to the Constitution.

OVERVIEW

In this lesson, students will learn about the many decisions the first Congress had to make to organize the new government. The lesson opens by showing students how George Washington allayed the Founders' fears of a strong executive branch by his civic virtue and strong sense of responsibility. Students then learn how Congress and the president organized the executive branch and established the federal court system. Students learn about important accomplishments of the first Congress, such as the passage of the Judiciary Act of 1789 and the drafting of the Bill of Rights, which was ratified in 1791.

OBJECTIVES

At the conclusion of this lesson, students should be able to

- explain how Congress and the president organized the executive and judicial branches of government
- describe the Judiciary Act of 1789
- explain how the Bill of Rights was added to the Constitution

TEACHING PROCEDURES

INTRODUCTORY ACTIVITY

Have students read the Lesson Purpose and consider the objectives of the lesson. Write the Terms to Understand on the board or use a vocabulary-building activity of your choice. Have students look up the words in the Glossary at the back of the text. Ask them to look for these words as they read the lesson.

READING AND DISCUSSION

Who was elected the first president?

Ask students to share the most important facts they know about George Washington. Write those facts on chart paper or on the board. Then have students read this section and add any new facts to the list they generated previously. Bring students' attention to the Ideas for Discussion section of Lesson 3, which discussed Cincinnatus as an example of a leader who possessed civic virtue. Ask students why Washington was often compared to Cincinnatus and sometimes portrayed by artists in Roman clothing. Help them to understand that Washington was considered by many to be a model of civic virtue and that like Cincinnatus, he retired to his home and his agricultural pursuits after leading a victorious army.

TERMS TO UNDERSTAND

appellate courts
cabinet
federal district courts
Judiciary Act of 1789
Ninth Amendment
Tenth Amendment

Who was elected the first president?

When the votes in the electoral college were counted, Washington, as expected, was elected president unanimously. John Adams of Massachusetts was elected vice president. Washington took the oath of office on April 30, 1789.

Washington did not really want to be president. He would have preferred to remain at Mount Vernon, his home, and take care of his plantation. But Washington had a strong sense of civic responsibility and felt that it was his duty to serve his country. He wrote, "when I had judged... that it was my duty to embark again on the tempestuous and uncertain Ocean of public life, I gave up all expectations of private happiness in this world." Washington knew that the Founders who were against the Constitution were afraid that it gave too much power to the president. He knew he should not do anything that added to their fears. Yet, he also knew that he had to be a strong leader.

By May of 1789 members of the new Congress of the national government were at work in New York City, the nation's temporary capital. Many people in Congress

George Washington taking the oath of office as the first president of the United States. Why was accepting the presidency so difficult for him?

were worried about how Washington would use his power. They even disagreed on what they should call the president. Some people said he should be called "His Highness, the President of the United States of America." Congress decided that because America was not a monarchy, Washington should simply be addressed as "the President of the United States."

166

How did Congress and the president
organize the executive branch?

Have students read this section. They should understand the origins of the cabinet and the executive departments. These departments were not directly provided for in the Constitution, but were established by Congress. You may wish to have students work with a partner and search through newspapers to find references to the president's cabinet. The groups can then present what they have found in the articles and indicate how the roles of the cabinet positions were described.

This is a view of Federal Hall in New York City, which is where Congress first met. How did Congress help the executive branch of government deal with its responsibilities?

How did Congress and the president organize the executive branch?

The Constitution gives Congress the power to organize the executive branch. Washington could not run the executive branch alone. To help Washington fulfill his responsibilities, Congress created three departments.

- **Department of State**. Thomas Jefferson was selected to serve as Secretary of State to be responsible for the foreign relations of the nation.

- **Department of the Treasury**. Alexander Hamilton, as Secretary of the Treasury, guided the new government in money matters.

- **Department of War**. Henry Knox, as the Secretary of War, handled military affairs and defense.

In addition, Congress created the office of attorney general, whose job was to give the president legal advice. Washington appointed Edmund Randolph to this position.

Washington used these officials as advisers to help him make decisions. These officials became known as the president's **cabinet**. Today, the cabinet positions have grown from the original four to the present number of fifteen. In fact, the executive branch of the federal government has grown far beyond the expectations of the Framers.

How did Congress organize the judicial branch?

Assign this section for students to read, and review with them the information provided on the court system. Help them to understand how the federal court system is organized and how a case can be appealed to the U.S. Supreme Court.

How did Congress add the Bill of Rights to the Constitution?

Have students read this section. Discuss the section with students and ensure that they understand the arguments of the Federalists and the Anti-Federalists and how the compromise on the Bill of Rights was reached. Introduce the rights and freedoms of the Bill of Rights listed in the section to students. These will be discussed in greater detail in later lessons.

How did Congress organize the judicial branch?

Congress set up the judicial branch of government under Article III of the Constitution. Article III provided for a U.S. Supreme Court and said that Congress could establish lower courts as needed.

In 1789, Congress passed a law that organized the court system for the new nation. This law was the **Judiciary Act of 1789**. It stated that the U.S. Supreme Court was to have a chief justice and five associate justices. Over time, Congress has increased the size of the Court to nine justices.

The lower courts that were authorized by the Judiciary Act include two kinds of courts—**federal district courts**, which hear cases involving the Constitution and federal laws, and appellate courts. **Appellate courts** handle those cases that have been tried first in district court and have been appealed. The appellate court is a higher court than a district court. But the U.S. Supreme Court is the highest court of appeals in the nation. In addition to the federal courts, each state has its own courts to rule on state laws.

How did Congress add the Bill of Rights to the Constitution?

When the Constitution was sent to the states for ratification, the Anti-Federalists opposed it. They felt that the Constitution should include a bill of rights. The Federalists claimed that

Why do you think Congress created three levels of federal courts?

What are some of the protections guaranteed by the Bill of Rights?

a bill of rights was not necessary. They said that the Constitution organized government in such a way that it would be impossible to violate people's rights. They also argued that listing individual rights might make people think that these were the only rights guaranteed by government.

Finally, a compromise was reached. The Federalists agreed that when the first Congress met, they would draft a bill of rights to add to the Constitution.

The Bill of Rights was passed by the first Congress. It contains ten amendments. The first eight amendments list basic protections already guaranteed in most state constitutions. These include:

- freedom of religion
- freedom of the press
- freedom of speech
- the rights of assembly and petition
- the right to a speedy, public trial by jury

The **Ninth Amendment** to the Constitution says that the listing of certain rights does not mean that these are the only rights the people have. Finally, the **Tenth Amendment** says that the powers not delegated to the federal government nor forbidden to the states belong to the states or to the people.

Congress proposed the Bill of Rights in 1789. It was ratified by the necessary eleven states on December 15, 1791. The Bill of Rights has proved to be very important to the protection of the basic rights of the American people. You will learn more about the Bill of Rights in the next unit.

---

 see next student page

LESSON REVIEW

The questions in the student book are intended to assess learning and to reinforce knowledge through discussion. The questions are directly related to the lesson objectives. You may wish to include additional questions developed by yourself or by your students.

1. The Constitution describes the organization of the executive and judicial branches only in general terms. Explain how the first Congress and the president organized the executive branch.

   Because Washington could not run the executive branch alone, Congress created three departments to help Washington fulfill his responsibilities. These departments were the Department of State, the Department of the Treasury, and the Department of War. In addition, Congress created the Office of Attorney General to assist Washington with legal advice.

2. How did the first Congress organize the judicial branch?

   Congress passed the Judiciary Act of 1789, which organized the federal court system. This law established a U.S. Supreme Court as the highest court of appeals, which would have a chief justice and five associate justices. It also established two kinds of courts—federal district courts and appellate courts.

3. What is the president's cabinet and what does it do?

   The president's cabinet is composed of advisers who represent the departments of the executive branch. Cabinet officials help the president make decisions.

4. What was the purpose of the Bill of Rights? Why was it included in our Constitution?

   The purpose of the Bill of Rights is to keep the government from violating people's rights. The Bill of Rights was added to our Constitution as a compromise between the Federalists and Anti-Federalists. The Anti-Federalists agreed to support the Constitution if Congress would add a bill of rights to the Constitution when it met for the first time.

(continued next page)

5. What rights are guaranteed in the Ninth and Tenth Amendments? How do these Amendments differ from the other amendments in the Bill of Rights?

The Ninth Amendment states that the rights listed in the Constitution are not the only rights guaranteed to the people. The Tenth Amendment makes it clear that all powers not delegated to the national government, nor forbidden to the states, belong to the states or to the people.

These two Amendments differ from the other eight in that they address protections not already guaranteed in most state constitutions, as well as allocation of power not previously stated elsewhere.

ACTIVITIES

The suggested activities are intended to extend and apply learning outside the classroom. You may wish to have students complete one or more of the activities. Have them share their results with the class..

LESSON REVIEW

❶ The Constitution describes the organization of the executive and judicial branches only in general terms. Explain how the first Congress and the president organized the executive branch.

❷ How did the first Congress organize the judicial branch?

❸ What is the president's cabinet and what does it do?

❹ What was the purpose of the Bill of Rights? Why was it included in our Constitution?

❺ What rights are guaranteed in the Ninth and Tenth Amendments? How do these amendments differ from the other amendments in the Bill of Rights?

ACTIVITIES

❶ Find out the process for amending the U.S. Constitution.

❷ The idea of having one person serve as president was developed when our nation had fewer than four million people. Today we have more than 300 million people. Do you think it is still a good idea to have only one person head the executive branch? Why or why not? What alternatives can you suggest? Make a chart showing how your ideas might improve our government.

❸ Visit the website of the executive branch of our national government, www.whitehouse.gov. Find a list of the fifteen cabinet positions and the functions of each. Which is the newest cabinet position? Why was it created? Write an essay explaining what you learn.

How did political parties develop?

20

LESSON PURPOSE

The new nation faced a number of problems. Differing ideas about how these problems should be resolved led to the rise of political parties. In this lesson you will learn what political parties are and how they began in American politics.

When you finish the lesson, you should be able to describe the two original political parties, their leaders, and the issues that divided them.

OVERVIEW

In this lesson, students learn how political parties were established in the United States. Students first learn why the Framers were opposed to political parties, which they believed were factions who were more concerned about their own selfish interests than the common welfare. Students examine the disagreements that arose between the Federalists, who supported the views of Alexander Hamilton, and the Republicans, who supported the views of Thomas Jefferson. Students learn that the disagreements related to the power of the national government were about how the necessary and proper and general welfare clauses of the Constitution should be interpreted. There were also disagreements about foreign policy. Students learn that political parties were established in the United States as a result of these disagreements. The lesson concludes with a section on how political parties function today.

OBJECTIVES

At the conclusion of this lesson, students should be able to

- explain why the Framers opposed the development of political parties
- describe the two original political parties, their leaders, and the issues that divided them
- describe the role and purpose of political parties today

TEACHING PROCEDURES

INTRODUCTORY ACTIVITY

Have students read the Lesson Purpose and consider the objectives of the lesson. Ask students to speculate on what issues they think might have caused differences of opinion great enough to result in the formation of political parties. Ask students to recall some of the disagreements that arose during the ratification of the Constitution.

Write the Terms to Understand on the board or use a vocabulary-building activity of your choice. Have students look up the words in the Glossary at the back of the text. Ask them to look for these words as they read the lesson.

READING AND DISCUSSION

Why were the Framers of the Constitution against political parties?

Have students read this section. Discuss with them the possibility of a candidate today receiving all the electoral votes in a presidential election. As you discuss this section with students, make sure that they understand the reasons for the Framers' resistance to political parties.

TERMS TO UNDERSTAND

Alien and Sedition Acts
currency
Federalist Party
political parties
Republican Party

Why were the Framers of the Constitution against political parties?

When George Washington was elected as the first president, he received every electoral vote. One reason for this was the great respect people had for him. Another reason was that there were no political parties to run candidates against him.

The Framers were opposed to the idea of political parties. **Political parties** are groups of people who join together because they have similar views about government. The Constitution does not include rules for forming or regulating political parties.

The Framers believed that political parties were factions. As you learned in Lessons 3 and 10, a faction is usually a dissatisfied group formed within a larger group. The Framers thought that factions might fight to promote the interests of their own members. The Framers feared that the strongest faction would then control government. In such a case, government would not protect equally the rights and interests of all the people. Instead, government would promote the interests of the party in power.

What role for the federal government did Alexander Hamilton favor?

When Washington took office, the new nation faced many problems. The country was in debt and needed to create good relations with other nations. People had different ideas about how to solve these problems. As President Washington and his advisers tried to deal with the issues, disagreements arose. These disagreements eventually led to the rise of political parties.

Do you recognize these animals as symbols for contemporary political parties? Why do you suppose they adopted these symbols?

Why was the disagreement about the meaning of the words in the Constitution important?

President Washington chose Alexander Hamilton and Thomas Jefferson to be his advisers. Hamilton was the Secretary of the Treasury. Jefferson was the Secretary of State. The views of Hamilton and Jefferson about the powers of the federal government were often in conflict.

Hamilton wanted a strong federal government. He favored taking a broad view of the meaning of the words in the Constitution. The Constitution does not always use clear terms to describe the power of the federal government. Take, for example, the necessary and proper clause. What does necessary mean? Hamilton believed that necessary meant that which is needful or useful to solve a problem. He argued that the Constitution created government to solve national problems. As long as a problem was national, the federal government could and should deal with it.

On the other hand, Thomas Jefferson believed in small, local government. He favored taking a narrow view of the meaning of the words in the Constitution. To Jefferson, necessary meant "absolutely necessary." The federal government could not do whatever it wanted. Government could not exercise power just because it was convenient to do so. If government were free to define its own powers, it would threaten the liberty of the people.

The conflict about the meaning of the words in the Constitution was an important one. Hamilton would give more power to the federal government. Jefferson would limit it strictly to its enumerated powers.

The people who supported the views of Hamilton eventually became the **Federalist Party**. The people who supported Jefferson became the **Republican Party**. This is not the same Republican Party of today.

Why was the disagreement about the meaning of the words in the Constitution important?

Have students create a chart with two columns. Ask them to write "Hamilton" as the heading of one column and "Jefferson" as the heading of the other column. As students read this section, have them list information related to Hamilton's and Jefferson's points of view regarding the power of government and interpretation of the necessary and proper clause. Students should then write the name of the political party that represents those views at the bottom of each column. Instruct students to keep the chart available because they will be adding information as they read the rest of this lesson. You may choose to have students work with partners or in small groups to complete this activity.

IDEAS FOR DISCUSSION

How well do you understand Jefferson's concern?

To help students understand the ambiguity of the necessary and proper and general welfare clauses, engage them in a discussion about why the Framers included these clauses in the Constitution and about the problems raised by the two clauses. Then have students work in pairs to answer the three questions. Have the groups share and discuss their responses with the class. The following are possible responses:

1. Who would be in a position to decide what was necessary and proper?

   The school principal or vice-principal would be in the position to determine what was necessary and proper. A committee of teachers, students, staff, and parents could also be a part of this decision.

2. Who would decide what the general welfare was?

   The student government should hear from the student body, staff, and parents to decide what the general welfare would be. Input from everyone would be very important.

3. What limitations would there be on the student government's powers?

   Student government would use its own judgment to decide what was necessary and proper. Limits should be imposed to protect all students' rights. The student government would not be allowed to favor one group of students over any other group, and student government would not be allowed to interfere with the basic rights of students.

IDEAS FOR DISCUSSION

How well do you understand Jefferson's concern?

Suppose the members of your student government had the power to make whatever rules for your school they thought were "necessary and proper" for your "general welfare." What rules do you think they should make? Discuss your choices with a partner. Use the questions that follow for guidelines.

❶ Who would be in a position to decide what was necessary and proper?

❷ Who would decide what the general welfare was?

❸ What limitations would there be on the student government's powers?

Who should decide what rules are necessary and proper for the general welfare of your class?

Why was the disagreement about the nation's economy important?

As Secretary of the Treasury, Alexander Hamilton wanted to strengthen the nation's economy. To do this, he wanted to create a strong currency. **Currency** is the form of money that a country uses.

He also wanted to encourage people to manufacture goods on a large scale. At that time, most Americans were farmers. The factories that did exist were small, family-owned businesses.

Hamilton also wanted to solve the problem of the national and state debts. Most of the debt was the result of borrowing to pay for the Revolutionary War. The federal government owed $54 million and the state governments owed about $25 million. Hamilton believed that solving the problem of the debt would strengthen the economy and would establish the public credit of the United States.

To achieve his goals, Hamilton came up with a plan to create a government bank. The bank, Hamilton said, was needed to help collect taxes, make loans to private citizens, and issue paper money. Gold and silver coins were in short supply. Paper money would increase the amount of currency available.

The problem was that the people did not trust paper money. They believed that it would not hold its value. The value of coins was based on the amount of gold or silver in the coin. Thus, the federal government would need to guarantee the value of paper money.

Hamilton advised President Washington that the necessary and proper clause gave government the power to create a bank. He argued that a bank was necessary to allow government to carry out its enumerated powers to collect taxes and regulate trade.

Why was Hamilton worried about national and state debt? Do you think the national and state debt is still something that government officials should worry about? Why or why not?

Why was the disagreement about the nation's economy important?

Have students read this and the next section, adding information to their charts as it relates to the two headings. Based on the information included in their charts, discuss with students the disagreement about the government creating a bank and about the war between France and Great Britain. Have students write at the bottom of their charts the decisions President Washington made to resolve the disagreements.

Why was the disagreement about foreign affairs important?

When students complete their readings, have them add information to their charts as it relates to the two headings. Remind the working groups to write the name of the political party that represents each view at the bottom of the appropriate column.

Thomas Jefferson was against the use of federal power to create a bank. He believed that the necessary and proper clause only allowed government to do those things that were absolutely necessary. Creating a bank did not pass the test.

George Washington listened to the arguments for and against the bank. He then signed the bill from Congress creating the Bank of the United States. The effect of the new law was to increase the power of the federal government. People began to take sides on whether the federal government had acted in accord with the Constitution.

Why was the disagreement about foreign affairs important?

In 1793 war broke out between France and Great Britain. This event raised the level of tension between the Federalists and the Republicans.

Thomas Jefferson wanted a close relationship with France. Many Americans had strong feelings for France. After all, the French had supported the colonies during the Revolutionary War.

During this time the British were seizing American ships on the high seas.

This building in Philadelphia was the site of the First Bank of the United States from 1795 to 1811. What were Jefferson's and Hamilton's opinions on establishing the bank?

John Jay was quoted as saying that he could travel from Boston to Philadelphia by the light of his burning effigies. Why was his treaty with the British unpopular?

Why did the war between France and Great Britain raise the level of tension between the Federalists and the Republicans?

They were searching for weapons going to France. The British also refused to leave the forts they still occupied on land that now belonged to the United States. The Republicans wanted the United States to take strong measures against the British.

Alexander Hamilton wanted a close relationship with Great Britain. Most of the colonists had come from Britain and still had links with people in that nation. In addition, the United States carried on more trade with Great Britain than it did with France. The Federalists wanted the United States to side with the British.

President Washington had sent United States Chief Justice John Jay on a mission to Great Britain. He negotiated a treaty that confirmed that the British would leave the forts they still held in the United States. They agreed to increase trade with the Americans. They did not agree to stop searching American ships for goods going to the enemy, France. The treaty was unpopular and the Republicans were greatly angered.

Washington did not want to take sides in the war between Great Britain and France. To do so, he thought, would be harmful to the United States. He declared that the American government would be neutral. When Washington left the presidency, he cautioned the new nation against entering into any permanent agreements with foreign governments.

Activity handout d 4

What were the Alien and Sedition Acts?

Assign this section to students. Discuss with them how the Alien and Sedition Acts created greater tension between the Federalist and Republican political parties. Ask them whether they believe the Alien and Sedition Acts were fair.

Reading, discussion, and research

Why was the presidential election of 1800 important?

Have students read this section. Discuss with them the differences between the presidential campaign of 1800 and modern presidential campaigns. Help them to appreciate that the election of 1800 was accomplished according to the procedure outlined in the Constitution. Even though a different political party took control of the executive branch of government, the transfer was completed in a democratic manner. Have students research how many times this type of transfer of control has occurred in world history. Have students complete Handout D 4 as a check for understanding of the lesson up to this point.

Answers: 1. **R**; 2. **R**; 3. **F**; 4. **R**; 5. **R**; 6. **F**; 7. **R**; 8. **F**; 9. **F**

What were the Alien and Sedition Acts?

George Washington served two terms as president. When he left office he warned the Americans about the harmful effect of political parties.

By the election of 1796, there was serious hostility between the Federalists and the Republicans. Each party wanted one of its own people to win the presidential election. John Adams, a Federalist, was elected president. Thomas Jefferson, a Republican, was elected vice president.

Jefferson and the Republicans were very critical of the way Adams ran the government. The Republicans organized their opposition. They used the newspapers to build public support for their views.

The Alien and Sedition Acts prevented the press from speaking out against the government. What limits, if any, should be placed on the people's right to criticize the government?

Adams and the Federalists in Congress were able to pass two laws called the Alien and Sedition Acts. The **Alien Act** gave the president broad powers over aliens entering the country. The **Sedition Act** made it a crime for newspaper editors, writers, or speakers to criticize the government.

The Alien and Sedition Acts outraged the Republicans. They knew that the laws were intended to silence them. Several newspaper editors and a member of Congress were fined and put in jail for writing and speaking against the government.

Why was the presidential election of 1800 important?

The election of 1800 was the first time that political parties backed candidates for president. The Federalists worked to re-elect John Adams. The Republicans supported Thomas Jefferson.

Adams and Jefferson did not campaign, the way it is done in modern elections. Instead, the parties ran the campaign, and it was a bitter one. Both parties accused each other of wishing to destroy the Constitution. The Republicans cited the Alien and Sedition Acts as proof that the Federalists were not fit to govern.

The election of 1800 was very important. Even though it had been a bitter campaign, the parties accepted the result.

Thomas Jefferson and Aaron Burr, also a Republican, tied for votes in the electoral college. So, according to the Constitution, the House of Representatives was obliged to select the winning candidate. After thirty-six ballots Jefferson was chosen.

For the first time in modern history, control of a government was transferred

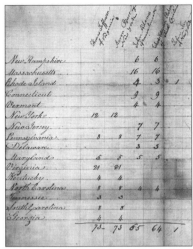

This is the tally of electoral votes from the election of 1800. How was the president selected when Thomas Jefferson and Aaron Burr tied for votes in the electoral college?

from one political party to another as the result of a democratic election. Thomas Jefferson later called it the "revolution of 1800."

Over the long term, the Federalist Party could not compete with the Republicans. Other parties arose to take its place. The modern Democratic Party claims its roots lie with the Republican Party of Thomas Jefferson. The modern Republican Party claims its roots lie with the Republican Party of Abraham Lincoln.

What is the role of political parties today?

Political parties are active today at the local, state, and national levels. Despite the fears of the Framers, they are an important part of the political system.

The following list states some ways that political parties may be useful.

- Political parties give people a way to join with others of similar interests to try to influence their government.

- People, working through their parties, can nominate candidates for public office, raise money for their candidates, and encourage people to vote for them.

- Political parties can and do get many people involved in the process of government.

- Political parties give people a choice of candidates and programs.

- The political party that is not in power can debate and criticize the party in power.

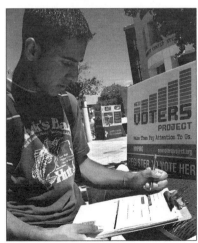

What might be some disadvantages of having only two political parties?

READING AND DISCUSSION

What is the role of political parties today?

Have students read this section, and review with them the ways that political parties are useful to citizens today. You may wish to ask students whether they agree with these listed benefits and whether they can identify any disadvantages of political parties.

 see next student page

LESSON REVIEW

The questions in the student book are intended to assess learning and to reinforce knowledge through discussion. The questions are directly related to the lesson objectives. You may wish to include additional questions developed by yourself or by your students.

1. Why were the Framers of the Constitution against having political parties?

   The Framers were concerned that political parties were factions that would fight to promote their own interests instead of equally protecting the rights and interests of all Americans.

2. What was the disagreement over the meaning of the words in the Constitution?

   The disagreement involved the amount of power and control the federal government should have. Hamilton took a broad view of the meaning of the words of the Constitution and believed that the Constitution created the government to solve national problems. Jefferson, on the other hand, took a narrower view and believed in small, local government. He believed that the national government should not be free to define its own powers because such a government would threaten the liberty of the people.

3. What was the disagreement about the creation of the Bank of the United States?

   Hamilton believed that the best way to solve the problem of the national and state debts was to establish a national bank. Jefferson believed that the

(continued next page)

necessary and proper clause did not give government the power to create such a bank. He believed that the necessary and proper clause allowed the government to do only the things that were absolutely necessary.

4. What was the disagreement about foreign affairs?

The disagreement about foreign affairs centered on the war between France and Great Britain, and whom the United States should support. Jefferson wanted a close relationship with France, whereas Hamilton favored a close relationship with Great Britain. Washington thought that the United States should be neutral. He sent Chief Justice John Jay to Great Britain to negotiate a treaty. Republicans were greatly angered by the treaty.

5. What were the Alien and Sedition Acts? Why were they passed?

Congress passed these two acts with the support of President John Adams and the Federalists. The Alien Act gave the president broad powers over aliens entering the country. The Sedition Act made it a crime for newspaper editors, writers, or speakers to criticize the government. These laws were passed to silence rising Republican opposition to his presidency.

6. Explain how the disagreements about how to solve the new nation's problems led to the rise of political parties.

All these disagreements created and deepened tensions between the two belief systems represented by the Federalist and Republican parties. People found themselves aligning with one of the two political parties. This allowed a way for people to express their opinions by supporting one or the other political party and by electing officials who represented their beliefs.

7. Why was the election of 1800 important?

The election of 1800 was important because for the first time in modern history, control of a government was transferred from one political party to another as a result of a democratic election.

ACTIVITIES

The suggested activities are intended to extend and apply learning outside the classroom. You may wish to have students complete one or more of the activities. Have them share their results with the class.

LESSON REVIEW

❶ Why were the Framers of the Constitution against having political parties?

❷ What was the disagreement over the meaning of the words in the Constitution?

❸ What was the disagreement about the creation of the Bank of the United States?

❹ What was the disagreement about foreign affairs?

❺ What were the Alien and Sedition Acts? Why were they passed?

❻ Explain how the disagreements about how to solve the new nation's problems led to the rise of political parties.

❼ Why was the election of 1800 important?

ACTIVITIES

❶ Draw a cartoon that illustrates the disagreements between the Federalist and Republican parties.

❷ Presidents and vice presidents were elected differently in 1800 than they are today. Make a chart showing what the differences are. Find out which Amendment to the Constitution was passed to correct the problems that occurred in the 1800 presidential election.

❸ Use the Internet to do a research activity. Find current information about the Democratic and Republican parties. Learn what each party believes about how government should be run. Then study a policy issue that interests both parties. Create a chart that illustrates their difference of opinion over the issue.

❹ Find information about the beliefs of third parties, such as the Libertarian Party, the Reform Party, or the Green Party. Write a campaign speech that explains the role of third parties in elections today. Give the speech to your classmates.

How does the U.S. Supreme Court use the power of judicial review?

21

LESSON PURPOSE

Even in our nation's earliest years, people such as Alexander Hamilton and Thomas Jefferson disagreed about exactly what the words in the Constitution mean. Who should decide which reading of the Constitution is correct? This lesson explains how the U.S. Supreme Court established its power to make such decisions. This power of the Court is called the power of judicial review. This power is not mentioned in the Constitution.

When you finish this lesson, you should be able to explain what is meant by judicial review. You should also be able to discuss how the U.S. Supreme Court established its power of judicial review in one of the most important cases in our nation's history.

OVERVIEW

In this lesson, students learn about the ability of the U.S. Supreme Court to exercise judicial review—the power to decide whether a law or action of the government is constitutional. They learn how the U.S. Supreme Court established its power of judicial review through *Marbury v. Madison* (1803), one of the most important U.S. Supreme Court cases in our nation's history. Students learn that throughout history, there have been great differences of opinion about whether the judicial branch should have this power and how it should be used. The controversy raises basic questions about representative government, constitutional government, and the protection of basic rights. Students serve as decision makers in an activity in which they decide whether the U.S. Supreme Court should have the power of judicial review over laws passed by Congress.

OBJECTIVES

At the conclusion of this lesson, students should be able to

- explain what is meant by judicial review
- discuss how the U.S. Supreme Court established its power of judicial review in *Marbury v. Madison*
- explain the arguments for and against the U.S. Supreme Court's power of judicial review

TEACHING PROCEDURES

INTRODUCTORY ACTIVITY

Have students read the Lesson Purpose and consider the objectives of the lesson. Write the Terms to Understand on the board or use a vocabulary-building activity of your choice. Have students look up the words in the Glossary at the back of the text. Ask them to look for these words as they read the lesson.

READING AND DISCUSSION

What is judicial review? How does judicial review apply to laws passed by state governments?

Start the lesson by asking students the following questions before they do the reading:

1. Should the U.S. Supreme Court have the power to declare laws made by a majority vote of representatives in Congress unconstitutional?

   Accept any reasonable responses.

2. Does the ability of the U.S. Supreme Court to declare laws unconstitutional conflict with any of the principles you have studied?

   Students should think about the concepts of republican government and representative democracy from Lesson 3 as possibly being in conflict with the U.S. Supreme Court's power of judicial review.

3. What would be the advantages and disadvantages of giving the U.S. Supreme Court this power?

   Advantages: *The U.S. Supreme Court consists of judges who know the law and have studied the Constitution. The U.S. Supreme Court is not an elected body; therefore, judges do not have to worry about political campaigning. The U.S. Supreme Court's only job is to ensure that the Constitution is not violated.*

   Disadvantages: *Because the U.S. Supreme Court is not elected, the justices may not appear to be accountable for their actions. They alone determine how to interpret the Constitution. U.S. Supreme Court justices may not really represent the best interests of all the people.*

4. Should any other branch of government be given the power to declare laws passed by a majority vote of your representatives in Congress unconstitutional?

   Students should consider the purpose of the principles of separation of power and checks and balances in preventing one branch of government from becoming too powerful and in preventing the abuse of power.

TERMS TO UNDERSTAND

judicial review
Marbury v. Madison
null and void
opinion of the Court

What is judicial review?

Judicial review is the power of the courts to decide whether laws and actions of government are allowed under the Constitution. When a court decides that a law or action is not allowed, it orders that the law or action be considered null and void. A law that is **null and void** may not be enforced. Such a law is considered unconstitutional and not acceptable as a law at all.

How does judicial review apply to laws passed by state governments?

The Framers wanted to be sure that the states obeyed the laws of the federal government. So, in Article VI of the Constitution they said that the U.S. Constitution, federal laws, and treaties are the supreme law of the land. As we discussed in Lessons 16 and 17, this is the supremacy clause. The Constitution, the laws passed by Congress, and treaties are the nation's highest laws and must be obeyed by the states. If state laws conflict with those of the federal government, the U.S. Supreme Court can order that the state laws not be enforced.

What is the power of judicial review? Are decisions of the Supreme Court binding on the states?

The U.S. Supreme Court first used its power of judicial review over state governments in 1796. After the Revolutionary War the United States signed a peace treaty with Great Britain. As part of this treaty, Americans agreed to pay all debts that they owed to British citizens. The state of Virginia passed a law that canceled all debts that its citizens owed to the British. Because this law violated the peace treaty, the Supreme Court ruled that the law could not be enforced. The citizens of Virginia would have to pay their debts.

Does the U.S. Supreme Court have the power of judicial review over acts of the federal government?

The Framers clearly meant that the U.S. Supreme Court should have the power of judicial review over acts of the state governments. The Constitution does not state that the U.S. Supreme Court has the power of judicial review over the legislative and executive branches of the federal government.

How did the U.S. Supreme Court decide the case of *Marbury v. Madison*?

The U.S. Supreme Court established its power of judicial review over the other branches of the federal government in one of the most famous cases in our history. This case, *Marbury v. Madison*, was decided in 1803.

During the last weeks that John Adams was president, he appointed a number of people to office. There had not been enough time to deliver the proper papers to all the appointees before the next president, Thomas Jefferson, took office. Without the proper papers, the appointees could not take the jobs that Adams gave them. When Jefferson did take office, he ordered his secretary of state, James Madison, not to deliver the appointments that were left.

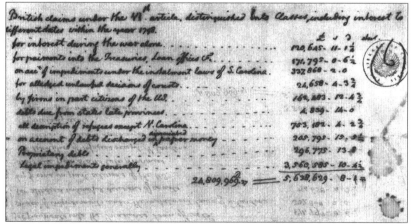

This is a list of debts owed to the British in 1798. It was compiled by Thomas Jefferson. How did the Supreme Court use its power of judicial review to settle the matter of Virginia's British debt? Can you find where the Constitution is mentioned in this note?

5. Does this power appear to conflict with any principle you have studied?

Students should see a conflict between judicial review, separation of powers, and checks and balances.

6. What would be the advantages and disadvantages of not allowing anyone to declare laws made by Congress unconstitutional?

***Advantages:** The people would have a say in their government at all times—laws made by the people's elected representatives could not be overturned by any court. Government would be more representative.*

***Disadvantages:** Elected representatives may not pass laws that are in the best interests of all people. Factions may be able to pass legislation meant to advance their own interests rather than those of society. There would be no check on laws passed by states and the federal government.*

Next, ask students to read the two sections. Ensure that they understand that the supremacy clause made clear the authority of the U.S. Supreme Court to declare the actions of state governments invalid under the Constitution.

Does the U.S. Supreme Court have the power of judicial review over acts of the federal government?

Read this section aloud. Explain to students that although the power of judicial review is not mentioned explicitly in the Constitution, the Framers clearly intended that judicial review would apply to acts of state governments. The Supreme Court's power of judicial review over the executive or legislative branches is not stated in the Constitution but was established in the case of *Marbury v. Madison*, which students will study in detail later in the lesson.

How did the U.S. Supreme Court decide the case of *Marbury v. Madison*?

Have students read this section, which continues on page 185. Explain to them that although the Constitution does not explicitly give the U.S. Supreme Court the power of judicial review, many Framers supported the idea. The case of *Marbury v. Madison* established the Court's power of judicial review over Congress and the executive branch. Lead students through an examination of the case and help them to understand the reasoning the Court used in making its decision.

IDEAS FOR DISCUSSION

Should the U.S. Supreme Court have the power of judicial review over acts of Congress?

Present the Ideas for Discussion to students as indicated. The answers to the Guideline Questions will generate arguments for the position selected by each group. Accept any reasonable responses. As students share their answers, challenge them to defend their opinions with what they have learned in the lesson.

Should the U.S. Supreme Court have the power of judicial review over acts of Congress?

Imagine that you must decide whether the U.S. Supreme Court should have the power of judicial review over laws passed by Congress. Work with a group of three to five students. Read the two opinions below. Consider each position and the possible results of each position. Use the Guideline Questions to help you decide which position your group would support.

OPINION 1

Give the U.S. Supreme Court the power to declare that a law passed by Congress is unconstitutional.

Possible Result Some laws, even though they were passed by a majority of representatives in Congress—people elected by citizens to represent their interests—would not be obeyed or enforced.

OPINION 2

Deny the U.S. Supreme Court the power to declare laws passed by Congress unconstitutional.

Possible Result All laws passed by a majority of representatives in Congress —people elected by citizens to represent their interests—must be obeyed or enforced.

GUIDELINE QUESTIONS

❶ How is each position related to the principles of representative government and majority rule?

❷ Is one position more democratic than the other? Why or why not?

❸ What effect might each position have on the basic rights of the individual?

❹ What effect would each position have on protecting the minority from the whims of the majority?

184

William Marbury. How did the court's ruling limit the powers of Congress?

One person who did not receive his appointment was William Marbury. Marbury believed that he was entitled to have the job. Marbury took his case directly to the U.S. Supreme Court because the Judiciary Act of 1789 stated he had that right.

Chief Justice John Marshall wrote the opinion for the U.S. Supreme Court. The **opinion of the Court** is the Court's decision and the reasoning behind the decision. The Court ruled that Marbury did have a right to his job. But they also said that the part of the Judiciary Act that gave Marbury the right to bring his case directly to the U.S. Supreme Court was unconstitutional.

The Constitution clearly limits the cases that can go directly to the U.S. Supreme Court without being first heard in a lower court. Marbury's case did not fit within these limits. Congress had changed the Constitution when it passed that part of the Judiciary Act. Congress by itself does not have the power to change the Constitution. So, the section of the Judiciary Act that increased the Court's power was ruled unconstitutional.

By declaring part of a law passed by Congress unconstitutional, the U.S. Supreme Court assumed the power of judicial review over the legislative and executive branches. Justice Marshall argued that the people of this nation had adopted the Constitution as the supreme law of the land and consented to be governed by its rules.

These rules include important limits on the powers of Congress. When Congress violates those limitations, it has violated the will of the people.

Marshall said that if the U.S. Supreme Court could not strike down such acts, there would be no effective way to enforce the constitutional limits on the powers of Congress. Its powers would be unlimited, and we would no longer have a constitutional government. Since the decision of *Marbury v. Madison*, the U.S. Supreme Court has exercised the power of judicial review over the federal government.

What was Chief Justice John Marshall's argument for the Supreme Court's power of judicial review?

 see next student page

LESSON REVIEW

The questions in the student book are intended to assess learning and to reinforce knowledge through discussion. The questions are directly related to the lesson objectives. You may wish to include additional questions developed by yourself or by your students.

1. What is judicial review?

   Judicial review is the power of the courts to decide whether laws and actions of government are allowed under the Constitution.

2. How does judicial review apply to the laws passed by state governments?

   The supremacy clause states that the Constitution, federal laws, and treaties are the nation's highest laws. This means that if state laws conflict with those of the federal government, the U.S. Supreme Court can order that the states not enforce those laws.

3. What was the case of *Marbury v. Madison*? How did the U.S. Supreme Court decide this case?

   This case involved presidential appointments made by John Adams during his last weeks in office. The papers for these appointments were not delivered to all the appointees. Thomas Jefferson, the newly elected president, ordered his secretary of state, James Madison, not to deliver the appointments that were left. William Marbury was one of the appointees who had not received his papers. He went to the U.S. Supreme Court directly, believing that the Judiciary Act of 1789 gave him this right. The U.S. Supreme Court ruled that Marbury had the right to his appointment, but that the part of the Judiciary Act of 1789 that allowed him to bring his case directly to the U.S. Supreme Court was unconstitutional.

4. Why was *Marbury v. Madison* such an important case?

   This case was important because it established the U.S. Supreme Court's power of judicial review over the government's executive and legislative branches.

(continued next page)

5. How does judicial review
   protect the rights of the people?

   Judicial review places limits on the laws passed by Congress, the executive branch, and state governments, thus preventing them from violating the will of the people as expressed by the Constitution. If the court could not exercise this power, laws could be passed that would violate the basic rights of the people. Justice Marshall believed that we would no longer have a constitutional government if we did not have the safeguard of judicial review.

6. How might judicial review
   override the will of the majority?

   Citizens might support a law, which Congress then passes, that violates the protections guaranteed in the Constitution. When the law was challenged in the courts, the Supreme Court would have to override the will of the majority.

ACTIVITIES

The suggested activities are intended to extend and apply learning outside the classroom. You may wish to have students complete one or more of the activities. Have them share their results with the class.

LESSON REVIEW

❶ What is judicial review?

❷ How does judicial review apply to the laws passed by state governments?

❸ What was the case of *Marbury v. Madison*? How did the U.S. Supreme Court decide this case?

❹ Why was *Marbury v. Madison* such an important case?

❺ How does judicial review protect the rights of the people?

❻ How might judicial review override the will of the majority?

ACTIVITIES

❶ In the history of our country, there have been several important justices on the U.S. Supreme Court. Learn more about one of the justices listed below. Share what you learned with your class.

   - Oliver Wendell Holmes Jr.
   - John Jay
   - John Marshall
   - Thurgood Marshall
   - Roger B. Taney
   - Earl Warren

❷ Find an article in the newspaper that explains a case or constitutional issue before the U.S. Supreme Court. Be prepared to explain the article to your class.

❸ With your teacher, invite an attorney or a judge to come to your classroom to discuss how our court system works. Prepare questions you want to ask the guest during the visit.

❹ Almost every trial in the United States is open to the public. With your teacher, visit your local courthouse. Talk with one of the judges. Observe a trial. This will allow you to see for yourself how our justice system operates.

How does the U.S. Supreme Court determine the meaning of the words in the Constitution?

22

LESSON PURPOSE

Some parts of the Constitution are clear and easy to understand. Other parts are much more difficult. What is the best way to decide what the Constitution means? In this lesson, you will learn about some of the more common approaches the U.S. Supreme Court has used to decide what the Constitution means.

When you finish this lesson, you should be able to describe these approaches. You should also be able to give the arguments in favor of or against each of these methods.

OVERVIEW

In this lesson, students examine the different approaches used by the U.S. Supreme Court to interpret the meaning of the Constitution. Students are asked to identify arguments in favor of or against the methods presented in the lesson.

OBJECTIVES

At the conclusion of this lesson, students should be able to

- describe the approaches used by the U.S. Supreme Court to decide what the Constitution means
- give arguments in favor of or against these methods

TEACHING PROCEDURES

INTRODUCTORY ACTIVITY

Have students read the Lesson Purpose and consider the objectives of the lesson. Write the Terms to Understand on the board or use a vocabulary-building activity of your choice. Have students look up the words in the Glossary at the back of the text. Ask them to look for these words as they read the lesson.

READING AND DISCUSSION

Why is it difficult to understand the meaning of some parts of the Constitution?

Have students read this section. Review with students the controversy between Jefferson and Hamilton over the interpretation of the necessary and proper clause of the Constitution. Ask students to identify problems that might arise in interpreting the meaning of "unreasonable searches and seizures" or "due process of law." Have students discuss what they think should be used to interpret the meaning of the Constitution and list these ideas on the board or on chart paper.

 see next student page

IDEAS FOR DISCUSSION

What difficulties are there in deciding the meaning of the words in the Constitution?

Have students follow the directions for this section. Ask them to share their opinions with the class. The responses provided are suggestions. Accept any reasonable responses students offer.

1. Would you look up "unreasonable" in a dictionary to find out what it means?

   Advantages: *The definition would be easily accessible and could provide historic variations in the definition of the word.*

   Disadvantages: *Multiple definitions would be listed. Judges would have to decide which definition to use.*

2. Would you try to find out how the Framers might have explained the word "unreasonable"?

   Advantages: *This method would most closely reflect what the Framers were thinking and what they intended when they wrote the Fourth Amendment.*

   Disadvantages: *Because society has changed over time, the Framers' original intention might not be relevant today.*

TERMS TO UNDERSTAND

interpret
Second Amendment

Why is it difficult to understand the meaning of some parts of the Constitution?

Deciding what the Constitution means has been a continuous process throughout our history. Even the justices of the Supreme Court sometimes disagree about the best method of deciding what the Constitution means.

Some parts are easy to understand. For example, Article II says, "The executive Power shall be vested in a President of the United States of America." This is a very specific statement about the head of the executive branch. Not all parts of the Constitution are so clear. For example, the meaning of the following statements in the Constitution is not specific:

- Congress shall have the power to make laws that are "necessary and proper" to carry out its responsibilities.

- Citizens are protected against "unreasonable searches and seizures."

- No state shall "deprive any person of life, liberty, or property without due process of law."

Sandra Day O'Connor, the first woman U.S. Supreme Court Justice. She was appointed in 1988. Who has the power to appoint Supreme Court justices? Why do you think it took so long for a woman to be appointed?

What difficulties are there in deciding the meaning of the words in the Constitution?

Work with a partner. Read the following example of language found in the Constitution.

> **EXAMPLE**
>
> **The Fourth Amendment protects citizens against "unreasonable searches and seizures."**

If you were a member of the U.S. Supreme Court, how would you decide what makes a search or seizure unreasonable?

Read the methods given below. Pick out the advantages and disadvantages of each method presented. Then, determine which method might be best for deciding the meaning of the Constitution. Be prepared to explain your opinion to the class.

1. Would you look up "unreasonable" in a dictionary to find out what it means?

2. Would you try to find out how the Framers might have explained the word "unreasonable"?

3. Would you examine the word "unreasonable" in relation to such basic ideas as natural rights and limited government?

4. Would you examine the word "unreasonable" in relation to the historical, political, and social changes that have occurred since the Constitution was written?

5. Would you rely upon previous Court rulings on "unreasonable" searches and seizures?

3. Would you examine the word "unreasonable" in relation to such basic ideas as natural rights and limited government?

   Advantages: *This method would support and maintain the basic premise of our form of government, which is to protect basic rights and prevent government abuse.*

   Disadvantages: *This method might be influenced by the social values, beliefs, or needs of the time and therefore not be based on a consistent standard.*

4. Would you examine the word "unreasonable" in relation to the historical, political, and social changes that have occurred since the Constitution was written?

   Advantages: *This method would reflect society at particular moments in history. It would also reflect the current trends in society.*

   Disadvantages: *Throughout the course of history, the meaning of the word would always change—there would be no consistent meaning.*

5. Would you rely upon previous Court rulings on "unreasonable" searches and seizures?

   Advantages: *This method might provide a general consensus of how to interpret a particular part of the Constitution. This consensus could be used to consider new cases.*

   Disadvantages: *Previous Court rulings reflect the prejudices and passions of a previous time. Adhering too closely to previous Court rulings may delay social progress.*

READING AND DISCUSSION

How does the U.S. Supreme Court decide what the words in the Constitution mean?

Have students read this section. Then have students compare their responses in the previous activity with the advantages and disadvantages presented here. Ask students to examine how their responses are similar to and different from the explanations offered in the text.

Another way to address this section is to divide the class into four groups, assigning each group to study one of the four methods of interpreting the Constitution. These groups would read and discuss the advantages and disadvantages of their assigned methods. The next step would be to form smaller groups, each consisting of one student from each group. Each student from each larger group would then share their discoveries with the other members of their smaller groups.

see student page 192

IDEAS FOR DISCUSSION

How would you interpret what the words in the Second Amendment mean?

Have students follow the directions for this section. Ask them to share their opinions with the class.

1. In 1791, when the Second Amendment was passed, why did the nation seek to protect liberty by protecting the right to keep and bear arms? What historical background and circumstances led them to this conclusion?

   The former colonists experienced an overbearing and tyrannical government that tried to suppress popular government by force of arms. Possession of arms by ordinary citizens was an essential means of resisting such tyranny during colonial times, which ended only fifteen years before the ratification of the Bill of Rights.

   The colonial Minutemen were able to function only because they had arms that they personally possessed and therefore could readily obtain and use.

The Constitution only grants Congress the authority to establish an army and a navy. What argument can you make that the Constitution also grants Congress the authority to establish an air force?

How does the U.S. Supreme Court decide what the words in the Constitution mean?

When deciding constitutional cases, the justices of the U.S. Supreme Court have to interpret the Constitution. To **interpret** means to decide what the words or phrases actually mean. There are four basic methods that the U.S. Supreme Court has used to interpret the Constitution. Each method has its advantages and disadvantages.

❶ **The plain meaning of the words in the Constitution**
Using this method, the justices consider the literal, or plain, meanings of the words. Sometimes they study what the words meant at the time they were written.

With this method the Court bases its decisions, as closely as possible, on how the Framers meant the Constitution to be interpreted. If the meaning of the words is clear, then this is the best way to know what the Framers meant.

The problem is that at the Philadelphia Convention there was disagreement about the meaning of some words. Another problem is that some questions are not answered at all. For example, the Constitution gives Congress the power to establish an army and a navy. Does this mean that Congress does not have the power to establish an air force?

❷ **The intention of the Framers**
This method is based on the idea that the Constitution by itself does not always have an obvious meaning. Therefore, we should look at the intentions of the people who wrote it. Those who believe in this method say that the justices should base their decisions on how the Framers would have decided. They claim that it is the approach most faithful to the ideas in the Constitution.

The problem is that it is extremely difficult, if not impossible, to figure out what the Framers intended on some issues. There were differences of opinion among the thirty-nine Framers. How can you determine who had the correct view? This method of interpretation also gives no guidelines about types of situations that did not exist when the Constitution was written.

❸ The Constitution is based on some fundamental principles of government

These principles include the natural rights philosophy, constitutionalism, and republican government. As the nation matures so does our understanding of these basic principles. This method says that the justices should make their decisions based on these basic principles and values.

❹ Today's social values and needs

This method says that the justices should use today's social values in interpreting the Constitution. People who hold this view believe that the justices should not ignore the realities of our society today. Justices, they argue, should not hold back social progress by sticking to outmoded interpretations.

People opposed to methods 3 and 4 say that these approaches give the justices too much freedom to decide cases according to their own political ideas and personal beliefs. The justices can simply alter the Constitution as they please.

In deciding a case, U.S. Supreme Court justices are influenced by a number of things. They consider the literal meaning of the words in the Constitution as well as the intention of the Framers. Justices consider the basic principles of the Constitution as well as the previous decisions of the Court. The justices are also aware of the current political, social, and economic situation in the country. Finally, the justices are influenced, as is everyone, by their own personal beliefs.

The U.S. Supreme Court's decisions often raise much controversy—especially when the Court has attempted to define and protect certain basic rights. In the next unit, we will look at some of these controversies.

What are arguments for and against using today's social values and needs to interpret the Constitution?

The American soldiers of the Revolutionary War mainly fought with firearms that they brought with them in joining the army. Without such arms, George Washington's army could never have taken the field.

The new Americans wished to preserve the safeguards that had led them to freedom from oppressive government; keeping and bearing arms was considered a key means to that end.

By the end of the Revolutionary era, possessing and carrying arms was a well-established practice of the newly independent Americans. A government policy of removing the right to keep and bear arms would be universally considered to be the first step in a general suppression of liberty.

2. Do you think the Second Amendment is as important today as it was in the eighteenth century? Explain your answer.

   Yes: *Many people have a sense of being open to the attack of criminals; having firearms readily available is the only way many people are able to feel secure. Police do not necessarily arrive on time, or, at times, at all.*

   No: *When the Bill of Rights was passed, there was no standing army and no organized police force as there is today. The U.S. armed forces are to protect us from external attack, and the police (and, on occasion, the National Guard) from internal dangers. Thus the Second Amendment may still have some importance, but it is not as important today as it was in 1791.*

3. In a 1998 U.S. Supreme Court case, Justice Ruth Bader Ginsburg pointed out that the text of the Second Amendment refers to the right to keep *and bear* arms. Since to *bear* arms means to carry them—not just to possess them—should citizens in every state be allowed to carry firearms on their person? Why or why not?

   Yes: *So long as they are not concealed, this should be permitted: it should be permitted because it is the law of the land. If we do not like it, we must change the law, not ignore or suppress it as we please. We pride ourselves on practicing the rule of law as an essential part of our political and legal systems; we must abide by its premises and rules.*

   No: *Allowing people to carry arms on their persons is an invitation to return to the days of the gun-slinging Old West. We already have tens*

(continued next page)

of thousands of people killed with guns each year. That is quite enough, without inviting the killing and maiming of countless others. Many people would be terrified to walk down a street where many people are seen carrying weapons.

Should they be able to keep them in their vehicles? Why or why not?

Yes: *It is often impractical or unadvisable to carry weapons on one's person. But to be effective, the right to keep and bear arms must allow one the right to have them readily available. Allowing them to be kept in cars is a principal way of making arms readily available.*

No: *Allowing everyone the right to keep guns in vehicles is an open invitation to their widespread abuse. Gang members older than 18 would be allowed guns. Road rage could lead to shootings on our highways. Guns could be stolen from vehicles and used to commit crimes. Where it is necessary for some people to have firearms in their vehicles, they can be issued permits after undergoing background checks.*

4. At present, no one can possess certain kinds of firearms such as fully automatic assault weapons. What limitations, if any, do you think should be placed upon the right to bear arms? How would you justify your position?

None: *The Second Amendment places no such restrictions and therefore no law under the Constitution should. If we want to have limitations, we must change the Second Amendment.*

Limitations are justified: *There is no evidence that the Framers of the Bill of Rights intended that new and terrible weapons be placed in private hands. It is wrong to read such intentions into the Constitution. Therefore, limitations must be allowed.*

Private citizens should not be able to outgun the police. All weapons that do this should be outlawed.

Experience shows that allowing automatic weapons is highly dangerous; automatic weapons are unnecessary in order for citizens to protect themselves.

A general rule should be that weapons that go beyond the simple ability of citizens to protect themselves should not necessarily be allowed. If we do not have such a working rule, people could buy and keep tanks and similar weapons that they claim have a legitimate use for self-defense.

IDEAS FOR DISCUSSION

How would you interpret what the words in the Second Amendment mean?

Senator Orrin Hatch has written: "When our ancestors forged a land 'conceived in liberty,' they did so with musket and rifle...as a nation of armed freemen...[and] they devoted one full amendment out of ten to nothing but the protection of their right to keep and bear arms against governmental interference."

Using library and Internet resources, work in small groups to answer the following questions. Share your answers with the class.

❶ In 1791, when the Second Amendment was passed, why did the nation seek to protect liberty by protecting the right to keep and bear arms? What historical background and circumstances led them to this conclusion?

❷ Do you think the Second Amendment is as important today as it was in the eighteenth century? Explain your answer.

❸ In a 1998 U.S. Supreme Court case, Justice Ruth Bader Ginsburg pointed out that the text of the Second Amendment refers to the right to keep *and bear* arms. Since to *bear* arms means to carry them—not just to possess them—should citizens in every state be allowed to carry firearms on their person? Should they be able to keep them in vehicles? Why or why not?

❹ At present, no one can possess certain kinds of firearms such as fully automatic assault weapons. What limitations, if any, do you think should be placed upon the right to bear arms? How would you justify your position?

 see next student page

LESSON REVIEW

The questions in the student book are intended to assess learning and to reinforce knowledge through discussion. The questions are directly related to the lesson objectives. You may wish to include additional questions developed by yourself or by your students.

1. Why is it sometimes difficult to determine the meaning of the words in the Constitution?

   Some parts of the Constitution are clear and easy to understand, such as, "the executive Power shall be vested in a President of the United States of America," but some parts of the Constitution are not clear, such as the necessary and proper clause.

2. What does it mean "to interpret" the Constitution?

   To interpret the Constitution means to decide what the words or phrases actually mean.

3. What are the four methods that justices might use to interpret the Constitution? What are the advantages and disadvantages of each method?

   a. The plain meaning of the words in the Constitution is one method used to interpret the Constitution.

      Advantages: *If the meanings of the words are clear, then this is a good way to know the Framers' intentions.*

      Disadvantages: *There was disagreement at the Philadelphia Convention about the meaning of some words. Also, some questions were not answered by the specific words of the Constitution. This leaves some issues about the plain meaning of the Constitution unresolved.*

(continued next page)

b. The intention of the Framers is another method of interpreting the Constitution.

Advantages: This approach can be seen as being faithful to the ideas in the Constitution, because it is based on how the Framers themselves would have decided issues of interpretation.

Disadvantages: The difficulty with this method is in determining what exactly the Framers intended. In addition, there were differing opinions among the Framers. Justices would have to decide which opinion to follow.

c. Basic values and principles is another method used to interpret the Constitution.

Advantages: This method is based on the fundamental principles of natural rights, constitutionalism, and republican government. As the nation matures, so will our understanding of these principles.

Disadvantages: This method would rely on justices' understanding and interpretation of these fundamental principles, which might be influenced by their own political ideas and personal beliefs.

d. Today's social values and needs is another method of interpreting the Constitution.

Advantages: This method asks justices to interpret the Constitution using the current values of society. Justices would be able to advance social progress by refusing to stick to the outmoded interpretations of past justices.

Disadvantages: This method also gives justices too much freedom to decide cases according to their own political beliefs and their own interpretations of current social values.

ACTIVITIES

The suggested activities are intended to extend and apply learning outside the classroom. You may wish to have students complete one or more of the activities. Have them share their results with the class.

❶ Why is it sometimes difficult to determine the meaning of the words in the Constitution?

❷ What does it mean "to interpret" the Constitution?

❸ What are the four methods that justices might use to interpret the Constitution? What are the advantages and disadvantages of each method?

❶ Imagine that you are a member of the United States Supreme Court. The Court has agreed to hear a case involving government agencies watching which sites citizens visit on the Internet. This technology did not exist when the Constitution was written. What method for interpreting the Constitution might you use to determine whether the practice is unconstitutional? Explain your reasons.

❷ Examine the following two statements by former justices of the U.S. Supreme Court. What does each statement mean? Do you agree with these statements? Why or why not?

"We are under a Constitution, but the Constitution is what the judges say it is."

Charles Evans Hughes
Chief Justice of the United States, 1930–1941
Associate Justice of the U.S. Supreme Court, 1910–1916

"As a member of this court I am not justified in writing my opinions into the Constitution, no matter how deeply I may cherish them."

Felix Frankfurter
Associate Justice of the U.S. Supreme Court, 1939–1962

unit five

How does the Constitution protect our basic rights?

This unit focuses on five basic rights protected by the Constitution—freedom of expression, freedom of religion, the right to vote, equal protection, and due process. The lessons focus not only on the importance of these rights, but also on how they have been expanded during the past two hundred years. Students begin by examining the rights to freedom of expression and freedom of religion, as well as the reasons the Founders thought these protections were especially important. Students use what they have learned as they make decisions about how these two rights have been applied in U.S. Supreme Court cases.

The unit then describes the history of the right to vote, placing particular emphasis on the expansion of suffrage to groups previously denied this right. Students learn that the expansion of voting rights has been accomplished by amendments to the Constitution, judicial decisions, and legislative enactments at both the state and federal levels, all brought about, in part, by citizen protests, actions, and demands for change.

The last two lessons present the equal protection and due process clauses. Students examine two pivotal U.S. Supreme Court cases—*Plessy v. Ferguson* and *Brown v. Board of Education*—and learn how they affected the lives of African Americans. Students learn that the Fifth and Fourteenth Amendments protect individual liberty against unfair practices by government and that the equal protection clause of the Fourteenth Amendment has been used to prohibit government discrimination against any citizen. Students learn the role played by citizens such as Rosa Parks, Martin Luther King Jr., and the thousands of others who participated in the struggle for equal protection.

The unit concludes with a description of the due process clauses of the Fifth and Fourteenth Amendments and how they differ. Students are asked to evaluate, take, and defend a position on how the U.S. Supreme Court might have dealt with the Gerald Gault case. Finally, students are asked to consider the difficulties faced by the government in balancing the rights of the individual and the rights of the community as the due process clauses are enforced.

UNIT OBJECTIVES

At the conclusion of this unit, students should be able to

- describe freedom of expression, its importance, and why and when it may be necessary to limit this right
- explain why the Founders thought that freedom of religion was important and in what situations the practice of religion may be limited
- describe how the right to vote has been expanded and why this is important
- explain the concept of equal protection of the law and how it has been used to eliminate government discrimination against citizens
- explain due process of law, to whom it applies, and why it is considered so important in a constitutional government

UNIT INTRODUCTION

After you read the introduction with your class, introduce the Key Concepts. The illustrations throughout the unit are excellent teaching tools for reviewing and reinforcing the learning. Use them as you find appropriate.

UNIT PROJECT (OPTIONAL)

Ask your students to write the Key Concepts in their notebooks and write definitions based on their current knowledge. They can change and add to these initial definitions as the unit progresses.

unit five

KEY CONCEPTS

due process of law

equal protection clause

establishment of religion clause

free exercise of religion clause

freedom of expression

freedom of religion

suffrage

You have learned that one of the most important purposes of government is to protect the basic rights of the people. The addition of the Bill of Rights to the Constitution was intended to achieve that purpose.

Adding the Bill of Rights, however, did not automatically guarantee these valued rights to all the people. In this unit, you will learn about five fundamental rights and how they have been extended to many people who were denied them in the past.

How does the Constitution protect freedom of expression?

23

LESSON PURPOSE

In this lesson you will learn about how the Constitution protects freedom of expression. You will also learn why freedom of expression is important to you as an individual and to the preservation and improvement of our constitutional democracy.

When you finish this lesson, you should be able to explain the importance of freedom of expression. You should also be able to describe situations in which it might be reasonable and fair to place limitations on this freedom.

OVERVIEW

In this lesson, students learn what freedom of expression is and how it is protected by the Constitution. Students consider the benefits of freedom of expression and examine whether this right should be limited. Students learn about two important U.S. Supreme Court cases involving freedom of expression in the schools. They learn the guidelines set by the Court for limiting freedom of expression. After discussing *Tinker v. Des Moines School District* (1969), students have an opportunity to apply their knowledge to an examination of *Hazelwood School District v. Kuhlmeier* (1988).

OBJECTIVES

At the conclusion of this lesson, students should be able to

- describe the freedoms included in the First Amendment
- explain the importance of freedom of expression
- describe some situations in which it might be reasonable and fair to place limitations on freedom of expression

TEACHING PROCEDURES

INTRODUCTORY ACTIVITY

Have students read the Lesson Purpose and consider the objectives of the lesson. Write the Terms to Understand on the board or use a vocabulary-building activity of your choice. Have students look up the words in the Glossary at the back of the text. Ask them to look for these words as they read the lesson.

READING AND DISCUSSION

What is freedom of expression?

Have students read this section and discuss with them the excerpt from the First Amendment. Make sure students understand each of the freedoms that compose freedom of expression. They should also understand that the First Amendment protects these freedoms and limits the powers of Congress to take them away. Discuss the following questions:

1. What basic rights are listed in this portion of the First Amendment?

   The basic rights listed in this portion of the First Amendment are freedom of speech, press, assembly, and to petition the government to correct wrongs.

2. Why do you think these particular rights were included?

   These rights were included so that people could express their ideas freely as individuals or within a group of people who hold similar opinions. Having the freedom to say what you believe without fear of punishment encourages citizens to attempt to influence decisions made by government.

3. Why do you think the Framers thought it was important to protect freedom of expression in the Constitution?

   The First Amendment was written because citizens demanded a guarantee of their basic freedoms. The Framers believed that the rights it included were among the most important rights that had to be protected by government.

TERMS TO UNDERSTAND

abridging
assemble
First Amendment
freedom of expression
redress of grievances

What is freedom of expression?

One of the main purposes of government is to protect our freedom. The **First Amendment** to our Constitution protects our freedom of expression. This is what the First Amendment says about freedom of expression:

Congress shall make no law... **abridging** [limiting] the freedom of speech, or of the press; or the right of the people peaceably to **assemble** [get together in one place], and to petition the government for a **redress of grievances** [to correct wrongs].

As you can see, this section of the First Amendment includes several important freedoms. **Freedom of expression** is freedom of speech, of the press, of assembly, and of petition. The right of assembly is the right to meet with others to discuss your beliefs, ideas, or feelings.

It is important to understand that the First Amendment limits the powers of Congress. It prevents Congress from placing unreasonable and unfair limits on freedom of expression. That is why the Amendment begins with the phrase, "Congress shall make no law."

What rights are the people in this photograph exercising?

How does the First Amendment protect the freedom of the press? What are some benefits of this freedom?

What are some benefits of freedom of expression?

The Founders of our nation believed that the right to hold and express one's beliefs was essential if citizens were to participate in the affairs of government. The following arguments highlight the importance of freedom of expression.

❶ Individual development and human dignity
It is important for your growth as a person to have the right to present your ideas and to consider other points of view. Your dignity as a person should be respected by allowing you the freedom to say what you think and to hear what others think.

❷ Advancement of knowledge
It is easier for new discoveries to be made when ideas can be discussed freely. Even if you disagree with someone, that person may say something that helps you test your knowledge and increase your understanding.

❸ The maintenance of representative democracy
Individual citizens participate in running our country by voting their representatives to Congress and other government officials. Citizens can also participate in making decisions about government policies. To make wise choices, you need to have good information. Free expression does not guarantee complete or accurate information, but it increases the chances of getting such information.

What are some benefits of freedom of expression?

Assign this reading. Help students understand the relationship between freedom of expression and political freedom. You may wish to ask students to think of examples in their own lives of times when freedom of expression was important.

Consider dividing the class into groups and having them create cartoons or graphics illustrating one of the benefits of freedom of expression.

IDEAS FOR DISCUSSION

Should schools be allowed to place limits on freedom of expression?

Have students read the summary of facts and findings in the case of *Tinker v. Des Moines School District*, making sure they understand the issues involved. As they share their opinions on the Court's ruling, ask them if they think this kind of issue could happen in a school today.

See Appendix D 5 of this guide for optional activities related to the *Tinker* case. The majority and minority opinions for the *Tinker* decision can be found on many law-related websites.

Should schools be allowed to place limits on freedom of expression?

When should students' freedom of expression be limited? The following is a summary of an important U.S. Supreme Court case that dealt with this question. Read and discuss the summary with a partner. Do you agree or disagree with the decision of the U.S. Supreme Court? Be prepared to share your opinions with the class.

Tinker v. Des Moines School District (1969)

This case involved a few high school students who wore black armbands to school. They were protesting American involvement in the Vietnam War. The school principal told the students to remove their armbands. The students refused and were suspended from school. The suspension was to last until they agreed to come back without the armbands. The parents took the case to court. They argued that the school was depriving the students of their right to freedom of expression.

Do you agree with the Supreme Court's decision in the Tinker case? Why or why not?

The school argued that they were justified in suspending the students. They said the suspension had been necessary to prevent any disturbance that could be caused by wearing the armbands.

The U.S. Supreme Court ruled that the school's action was an unnecessary limitation on freedom of expression. The Court said that a school cannot limit a student's right to freedom of expression unless the student's exercise of that right disrupts the educational process. The Court said there was "no evidence whatever of... interference...with the school's work or... with the rights of other students to be secure and to be let alone."

Justice Abe Fortas wrote the opinion for the Court. He said,

"Any word spoken, in class, in the lunchroom or on the campus, that deviates from the views of another person, may start an argument or cause a disturbance. But our Constitution says we must take this risk... and our history says that it is this sort of hazardous freedom—this kind of openness—that is the basis of our national strength and of the independence...of Americans."

The Court said that students do not give up their "constitutional rights to freedom of speech or expression at the schoolhouse gate." Freedom of expression should be protected unless it clearly violates other important rights and interests.

Should students have the same right to freedom of expression as adults? Why or why not?

Should there be limits to freedom of expression?

Before you have students read this section, ask them to think of situations in which they think freedom of expression might need to be limited, then ask them to explain their opinions. As they read and discuss this section, emphasize that the courts have developed guidelines to help decide when freedom of expression might be limited. Help students understand that a balance must be maintained between protection of freedom of expression and protection of other peoples' rights.

Should people be allowed to demonstrate about any issue that concerns them? Why or why not?

❹ **Peaceful social change**

Freedom of expression allows you to try to influence public opinion by persuasion without feeling you have to resort to violence to make changes. Also, if you have the opportunity to express your opinions freely, you might be more willing to accept government decisions, even decisions you do not agree with.

Should there be limits to freedom of expression?

Many people believe that freedom of expression is necessary for the protection of all our individual freedoms. Does this mean there should be no limits to freedom of expression? Should you have the right to yell "Fire!" in a crowded theater when there is no fire? Such an action may cause bodily harm to others when they run to safety.

Other situations are more complicated. What if you wanted to convince other people that we should change our type of government? Should government be

202

What limits, if any, should there be on freedom of expression? Can you name some situations where freedom of expression might endanger people?

able to keep you from doing so? What if you are part of an unpopular group that wants to have a public demonstration in the streets? Should government be able to stop you because of the possibility of a riot?

Over the years, the courts in our country have developed guidelines to use in limiting freedom of expression. The courts use these guidelines to decide when the right to free expression interferes with other important rights and interests.

Suppose your right to freedom of expression in a particular situation

is dangerous to public safety, national security, or some other important interest. If the danger is great enough, the courts sometimes allow freedom of expression to be limited.

Also, one person's right to freedom of expression may conflict with someone else's rights. The right to a free press might conflict with someone's right to a fair trial in a court of law. For this reason, we accept limitations that are intended to protect everyone's rights.

SOLVE THE PROBLEM

How would you balance the rights and interests in this case?

Conduct the activity as described in the student text.
The following are suggested responses. Accept any reasonable answers.

1. What are the conflicting rights and interests in this case?

    There is a conflict between the rights of students to express themselves in the high school newspaper and the interest of the principal in maintaining a proper learning environment by removing material that he considered inappropriate.

2. In what ways is this case similar to the *Tinker* case? In what ways is it different?

    The principals of both schools interfered with the freedom of expression of students by taking direct action to silence them. The cases were different in that Tinker *involved a situation related only to the expression of those students who chose to be involved, whereas the* Hazelwood *case involved publishing information about others that the principal considered to be inappropriate, personal, and unsuitable for student consumption.*

3. Examine each of the two opinions on the next page. Which opinion would you select to decide this case? Explain your reasoning.

    Accept any reasonable responses.

SOLVE THE PROBLEM

How would you balance the rights and interests in this case?

The following U.S. Supreme Court case involves a situation about the need to balance freedom of expression with other important rights and interests. Work in groups of three to five students to complete this exercise. Each group should read the case and answer the questions that follow it. Then each group should share its answers with the class for further discussion.

Hazelwood School District v. Kuhlmeier (1988)

The journalism class in Hazelwood East High School wrote and published the high school's newspaper. In one issue of the paper, students planned to print an article about teenage pregnancy. The principal of the school thought that the story was not appropriate for younger students.

In the same issue of the paper the students also planned to run a story in which a student wrote about divorce and made negative remarks about her father. The principal said that the newspaper had not given the father a chance to respond to his daughter's remarks. The principal ordered both stories to be removed from the paper before it was printed and distributed.

❶ What are the conflicting rights and interests in this case?

❷ In what ways is this case similar to the *Tinker* case? In what ways is it different?

❸ Examine each of the two opinions on the next page. Which opinion would you select to decide this case? Explain your reasoning.

OPINION 1

A school does not need to tolerate student speech that is inconsistent with its basic mission to educate young people. The public schools are not like the streets, parks, and other public places that are used for purposes of assembly, communicating thoughts between citizens, and discussing public questions. Accordingly, the principal had a right to regulate the contents of the school newspaper in any reasonable manner. It is this standard, rather than the decision in *Tinker*, that governs this case.

OPINION 2

The school principal removed the articles from the newspaper not because the article would interfere with school discipline. He removed the articles because he considered them inappropriate, personal, and unsuitable for student consumption. The principal's action violated the First Amendment's prohibitions against censorship of any student expression that neither disrupts class work nor denies the rights of others.

Explain to the class that the Supreme Court ruled in favor of the principal in the *Hazelwood* case. In a five to three decision, the Court overturned a lower court's decision and upheld the school's right to censor the school newspaper. The newspaper was written and edited by a journalism class as part of the school's curriculum. Therefore, the Court said, it was not to be considered a forum for public expression and school officials may impose reasonable restrictions, such as protecting the privacy of pregnant students. Dissenting justices said that the articles deleted by the principal would neither have disrupted classroom work nor invaded the rights of others, and were, therefore, covered by First Amendment protections of freedom of expression. Ask students whether they think this ruling would be the same today.

This is Robert E. Reynolds, the principal of Hazelwood East High School, with a copy of the student newspaper. Under what conditions, if any, should a principal have the right to limit what can be printed in the school newspaper?

LESSON REVIEW

The questions in the student book are intended to assess learning and to reinforce knowledge through discussion. The questions are directly related to the lesson objectives. You may wish to include additional questions developed by yourself or by your students.

1. How would you define freedom of expression?

   Freedom of expression is freedom of speech, of the press, of assembly, and of petition.

2. What are the benefits of freedom of expression to the individual and to society?

   Freedom of expression promotes individual development and human dignity by allowing you to express your ideas and listen to the ideas of others. The right to express your ideas with others helps advance knowledge, often for the betterment of society. Other important benefits include expressing oneself through voting for representatives and making decisions about government policies. Citizens' freedom of expression provides a forum for peaceful social change.

3. What are some circumstances that might cause government to limit the right to freedom of expression?

   Government might limit expression when it is dangerous to public safety, national security, or other important interests, and when it conflicts with other important rights and interests.

4. What rights and interests are involved when limiting freedom of expression in the public schools?

   The Tinker *decision upheld the right of students to freedom of expression except when the exercise of that right disrupts the educational process. The majority opinion in the* Hazelwood *case held that a school does not have to "tolerate student speech that is inconsistent with its basic educational mission."*

ACTIVITIES

The suggested activities are intended to extend and apply learning outside the classroom. You may wish to have students complete one or more of the activities. Have them share their results with the class.

LESSON REVIEW

❶ How would you define freedom of expression?

❷ What are the benefits of freedom of expression to the individual and to society?

❸ What are some circumstances that might cause government to limit the right to freedom of expression?

❹ What rights and interests are involved when limiting freedom of expression in the public schools?

ACTIVITIES

❶ Learn about the policies in your school district or the rules at your school that regulate how students may exercise freedom of expression. Make a computer presentation so you can share what you learned with your class.

❷ Take photographs that illustrate the four parts of the right to freedom of expression. Make a collage of your photos showing the benefits of freedom of expression.

❸ Suppose that an unpopular group wants to hold a demonstration in a public park in your community. Most people do not agree with the views of this group. People fear that the demonstration might become disorderly and disturb the peace. Work with a partner to create a skit. One of you should be in favor of allowing the group to hold the demonstration. The other should be opposed. Both of you should act out your views in front of the class and let them decide the issue.

❹ Find a newspaper article that discusses someone exercising the right to freedom of expression in your community. Write an editorial based on the article for your school newspaper. In your essay explain the benefits of this right to you and your community.

How does the Constitution protect freedom of religion?

24

LESSON PURPOSE

In this lesson you will learn about freedom of religion. You will learn about the difference between religious beliefs and religious practices. You will learn why there are no limits on beliefs but some limits on religious practices. Finally, the lesson will examine issues about the relationship between religion and public education.

When you finish the lesson, you should be able to explain the importance of freedom of religion. You should be able to describe situations in which religious practices may be limited. You should also be able to explain some of the guidelines the U.S. Supreme Court has used to decide issues related to religion and the public schools.

OVERVIEW

In this lesson, students learn that the very first statement of the First Amendment prohibits Congress from making any law that would establish a religion for citizens, thereby setting the standard for religious freedom in the United States. The lesson begins with an explanation of the establishment and free exercise clauses. The lesson also describes why freedom of religion is important to Americans. Students consider the conflicts between the two clauses of the First Amendment. Students learn that the U.S. Supreme Court has ruled that although people have the right to hold any religious belief or no religious beliefs, their religious practices can be limited when those practices interfere with other public interests. As the lesson continues, students examine the arguments about the involvement of religion in public schools. They learn about current guidelines applied to determine the constitutionality of some laws and actions related to public schools.

OBJECTIVES

At the conclusion of this lesson, students should be able to

- explain the importance of freedom of religion
- explain the establishment and free exercise clauses, and the differences between them
- describe situations in which religious practices may be limited
- explain some guidelines the U.S. Supreme Court has used to decide issues related to religion and public schools

TEACHING PROCEDURES

INTRODUCTORY ACTIVITY

Have students read the Lesson Purpose and consider the objectives of the lesson. Write the Terms to Understand on the board or use a vocabulary-building activity of your choice. Have students look up the words in the Glossary at the back of the text. Ask them to look for these words as they read the lesson.

READING AND DISCUSSION

How does the First Amendment protect freedom of religion?

Read this section with students and help them to understand the meaning of the establishment and free exercise clauses. Ask them to think of examples of what might happen if we did not have these two clauses in the First Amendment.

TERMS TO UNDERSTAND

establishment clause

free exercise clause

How does the First Amendment protect freedom of religion?

The very first part of the First Amendment says that "Congress shall make no law respecting an establishment of religion, or prohibiting the free exercise thereof." The meaning of these words in the First Amendment is explained below.

- **Establishment of religion**
  Congress may not establish, that is institute, an official religion for our country or favor any one religion over others. We call this the **establishment clause**.

- **Free exercise**
  Congress may not stop you from holding any religious beliefs you choose or having no religious beliefs at all. Government may not unfairly or unreasonably limit your right to practice any religious beliefs you wish. We call this the **free exercise clause**.

What does the "free exercise" part of the First Amendment mean?

208

Why did freedom of religion become an important principle in America?

Few of the early English colonies in North America permitted religious freedom. In several colonies, one religious group controlled the whole colony. Everyone living there had to follow the same religious ideas. People who disagreed were often persecuted or forced to leave the colony.

By the end of the colonial period, things had changed. For one thing, there were more religious groups, such as Baptists, Catholics, Jews, Quakers, and others. Most people's attitudes had also changed. More people practiced different religions. People became more accepting of each other's religious differences. Over time, people came to believe strongly that everyone has a right to his or her own religious beliefs.

In addition, men like Thomas Jefferson and James Madison were greatly concerned about the dangers of religious intolerance. They were well aware that throughout history, religious intolerance had often led to conflict and to the violation of individual rights. They thought religious intolerance was a danger to the community and harmful to religion.

The freedom of religion clause in the first part of the First Amendment illustrates the strong belief in America that government should not interfere with religion.

Why did some of the colonists' ideas about religious tolerance change?

Why did freedom of religion become an important principle in America?

Have students read this section and discuss with them the factors that contributed to the growth of religious tolerance among the Founders and other Americans.

Remind students that the Founders had experienced the effects of religious intolerance. This first-hand knowledge convinced them that religious intolerance was a danger to society.

Why do conflicts about freedom of religion exist today?

Assign this section to students, and tell them that they will be learning more about the establishment and free exercise clauses and how they are applied to real-life situations. Explain the differences between these two clauses. Discuss the issue of the courts being continually challenged to decide how the freedom of religion clauses of the First Amendment should be interpreted and applied to various issues.

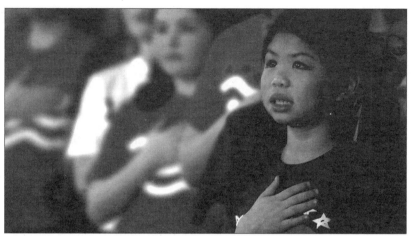

Should your government be able to require students to recite the Pledge of Allegiance if it violates their religious beliefs? Why or why not?

Why do conflicts about freedom of religion exist today?

Americans strongly believe that freedom of religion is an important right. But that does not mean that we have no disagreements about this issue today. Today's conflicts about freedom of religion focus on the following issues:

- **The establishment clause**
  This clause sets forth the idea that government is to be separated from religion.

  The meaning of the establishment clause is a continuing source of conflict among Americans. Does it mean that government may not be involved with religion in any way?

- **The free exercise clause**
  Each person has an absolute right to believe in any religion or in no religion at all. Freedom of belief is an inalienable right that cannot be interfered with by government in any way. The free exercise clause also means that your right to practice your religious beliefs is protected. But does the free exercise clause mean that all religious practices are protected? Can government prohibit a religious practice that endangers public health or safety?

Sometimes there are conflicts between the principles in the establishment and the free exercise clauses. For example, if government pays for prison chaplains, it is supporting religion. On the other hand, to prohibit government from doing this would interfere with the right of prisoners to practice their religion.

Disagreements like these about the relationship between government and religion have caused a number of important cases to be brought before the U.S. Supreme Court. In each case, the Supreme Court has had to decide how the freedom of religion clauses of the First Amendment should be interpreted.

Can government limit your right to practice your religious beliefs?

In certain cases government can limit the way you practice your religious beliefs. The U.S. Supreme Court has ruled that certain religious practices may be forbidden without violating constitutional rights. The Court has said that religious practices may be limited if they are contrary to public morals, endanger health, or harm the common good.

U.S. Supreme Court decisions have said that religious practices involving polygamy—being married to more than one person at the same time—may be forbidden. Government can also require that children be vaccinated against certain contagious diseases before being admitted to public school. They may require vaccination even if it violates a family's religious beliefs.

Under what conditions, if any, should the government be able to control the practice of religious beliefs?

Can government limit your right
to practice your religious beliefs?

Ask students to identify any religious practices that may conflict with the public interest. Then ask them to read the section.

How can we decide issues about
religion in the public schools?

Assign this section. Discuss with students the questions the Supreme Court
has tried to answer regarding religion in the public schools. Ensure that
students understand the impact these issues would have on public education
if allowed or disallowed. Discuss the three guidelines, ensuring students'
understanding of the goals of each factor.

How can we decide issues about religion in the public schools?

At the time the Constitution was written, public schools as we know them did not exist. Children who attended school usually received a great deal of religious training. In fact, their parents expected the schools to give religious instruction.

There has been growing disagreement about whether religious teaching should be supported in public schools. During the past seventy years especially, the U.S. Supreme Court has heard many cases dealing with this subject. Some questions the Court has tried to answer are

- should tax money be used to support religious schools?

- should public schools be allowed to provide periods of time when students can attend special classes to receive religious instruction from their own minister, priest, or rabbi?

- should public schools be allowed to require students to take part in prayers or read the Bible during regular school hours?

The establishment clause requires that government be neutral toward religion. Government cannot support one type of religion over another type, nor can it support religion over nonreligion.

The courts follow guidelines when deciding whether government is complying with the establishment clause. They look at three factors.

❶ The courts examine whether government is actively endorsing religion.

❷ The courts examine whether government is compelling people to participate in religious activities or to accept religious beliefs.

❸ The courts examine whether government is providing special treatment to one type of religion that it is not providing to other types of religion.

If government fails any one of these factors, it is in violation of the establishment clause. In a recent case, for example, the U.S. Supreme Court ruled that a high school could not require its students to participate in a prayer at their graduation ceremony. The Court concluded that the high school, by requiring the prayer, was endorsing religion and compelling the students to participate in the prayer.

*Under what conditions, if any, should a
student be allowed to recite a prayer at
a public school's graduation ceremony?*

How would you decide these issues concerning religion in public schools?

Work in groups of three to five. Read each of the four situations. Use the guidelines discussed in the previous section to decide whether the laws and actions described should be declared unconstitutional. Be prepared to explain your decisions to the class.

❶ Your state passes a law allowing your public school principal to post the Ten Commandments in every classroom.

❷ Your state passes a law that gives parents who send their children to religious schools a tax deduction for tuition, transportation, and educational materials.

❸ Your state allows your public school's algebra teacher to spend part of his class day at a church school, giving instruction to students having difficulty with math.

❹ There is an unused classroom at your public school. The student council requests permission to use it after school hours for voluntary prayer meetings. The principal refuses to make the classroom available.

How do the courts determine whether government is complying with the establishment clause?

SOLVE THE PROBLEM

How would you decide these issues concerning religion in public schools?

Conduct the activity according to the instructions in the student text. You may wish to use Handout D6 of the Appendix. When students have completed this task, share the results of these cases. They are based on the actual U.S. Supreme Court cases and are described in the handout.

 see next student page

LESSON REVIEW

The suggested activities are intended to extend and apply learning outside the classroom. You may wish to have students complete one or more of the activities. Have them share their results with the class.

1. What is the establishment clause?

   This clause prevents Congress from instituting a specific national religion for our country or from favoring one religion over any other.

2. What is the free exercise clause?

   Under the free exercise clause, Congress may not stop you from holding any religious beliefs you choose or from having no religious beliefs at all. The clause also prohibits unreasonable government limitation of your right to practice any religion you choose.

3. Why was freedom of religion an important principle in early America?

   Few early English colonies in North America allowed religious freedom. Many people suffered from religious intolerance in the colonies. As more religious groups came to America, people became more accepting of religious differences and began to believe that everyone had the right to his or her own religious beliefs.

(continued next page)

4. What conflicts exist over the freedom of religion clauses in the First Amendment? Give examples of each.

The conflict over the establishment clause concerns whether government should have any involvement with religion, and if so, how much. Examples include whether government should allow students time to pray while attending school and whether the phrase "under God" should be deleted from the Pledge of Allegiance.

The conflict over the free exercise clause arises when a religious practice endangers public health or safety or is contrary to public morals. Examples include practicing polygamy, handling poisonous snakes, and refusing to vaccinate children against certain contagious diseases prior to entering school.

Sometimes there are conflicts between the two clauses. For example, the government's funding of prison chaplains is considered to be support of religion; however, the government's refusal to provide prison chaplains would interfere with the right of prisoners to practice their religion.

5. Can government limit your right to freedom of belief? Why or why not?

No, government may not limit your freedom to hold any religious beliefs or to hold none at all. This freedom is protected by the free exercise clause of the First Amendment.

6. Can government limit your right to practice your religious beliefs? If so, under what circumstances?

The U.S. Supreme Court has ruled that government may limit religious practices that are contrary to public morals, endanger health, or harm the common good.

7. What conflicts exist between freedom of religion and public education?

Conflicts exist over such issues as whether tax money should be used to support religious schools, whether public schools should be allowed to provide periods of time for students to pray or receive religious instruction, and whether public school students can be required to take part in prayer or read the Bible during school hours.

ACTIVITIES

The suggested activities are intended to extend and apply learning outside the classroom. You may wish to have students complete one or more of the activities. Have them share their results with the class.

LESSON REVIEW

❶ What is the establishment clause?

❷ What is the free exercise clause?

❸ Why was freedom of religion an important principle in early America?

❹ What conflicts exist over the freedom of religion clauses in the First Amendment? Give examples of each.

❺ Can government limit your right to freedom of belief? Why or why not?

❻ Can government limit your right to practice your religious beliefs? If so, under what circumstances?

❼ What conflicts exist between freedom of religion and public education?

ACTIVITIES

❶ Some people have suggested adding an amendment to the Constitution that would allow public schools to set aside time for voluntary prayer. Use the Internet or your school library to find more information about this proposal. Then decide if you would support such an amendment. Write a brief essay explaining why or why not.

❷ Thomas Jefferson and James Madison had strong opinions about the separation of church and state. Write an essay comparing and contrasting your opinions on this issue with those of Jefferson and Madison.

❸ Make an illustration in the style you think might be found in eighteenth-century schoolbooks. In your drawing show your understanding of the establishment clause.

How has the right to vote expanded since the Constitution was adopted?

25

LESSON PURPOSE

The Constitution originally left it up to the state governments to decide who should have the right to vote. In the early years of our nation the states limited the right to vote to white men who owned property. In 1789 white males who did not own property, members of certain religious groups, freedmen, Native Americans, slaves, and women were not allowed to vote.

In this lesson you will learn about how the right to vote has been expanded in the last two hundred years to achieve a basic ideal of our representative democracy—the constitutional right of all adult citizens to vote.

When you finish this lesson you should be able to explain how voting rights were extended by changes in state voting laws, amendments to the Constitution, acts of Congress, and decisions of the U.S. Supreme Court.

OVERVIEW

This lesson focuses on how the right to vote has expanded since the Constitution was adopted. Students learn that the Constitution originally left the decision about who had the right to vote to each state. They study the struggle for the right of suffrage by African Americans, women, Native Americans, and eighteen-year-olds. Students examine the laws passed by some states to prevent African Americans from voting, such as literacy tests, the grandfather clause, and the poll tax, and learn how these restrictions were eliminated as a result of the civil rights movement. Students examine current voting requirements and how the expansion of suffrage has resulted in a truly representative democracy. The lesson concludes by challenging students to reflect on why so few citizens exercise their fundamental right to vote and asks them to consider ways to increase voter participation today.

OBJECTIVES

At the conclusion of this lesson, students should be able to

- list groups who were denied the right to vote in the past
- explain how voting rights were extended by changes to state voting laws, amendments to the Constitution, acts of Congress, and decisions of the U.S. Supreme Court
- suggest some ways to generate greater voter participation in elections

TEACHING PROCEDURES

INTRODUCTORY ACTIVITY

Have students read the Lesson Purpose and consider the objectives of the lesson. Write the Terms to Understand on the board or use a vocabulary-building activity of your choice. Have students look up the words in the Glossary at the back of the text. Ask them to look for these words as they read the lesson.

READING, DISCUSSION, AND ACTIVITY

How was the right of suffrage extended before the Civil War?

Provide the following scenario for consideration and discussion before students read the section:

> All members of the class collected money from their parents for a special event to be held sometime during the last week of school. After the money was collected, the teacher stated that only those students whose parents had contributed $10 or more could take part in deciding when the event would take place and how the money would be spent.

After explaining the scenario, ask students the following questions. Accept any reasonable responses.

- What, if anything, is unfair about this situation?

  Students might suggest that some classmates are being discriminated against because their parents cannot pay as much as others' parents. These students are unfairly denied a voice in the decisions.

- Does the teacher's statement violate any of the rights you have studied?

  As citizens of the class, all students have the same rights unless they have done something that would justify the teacher's limitation of those rights. Students have been denied their right to free expression. The teacher's statement creates a hierarchy that favors students whose parents contributed more money.

After the discussion, help students to connect the restriction imposed by the teacher with the denial of the right to vote.

Next, assign this section to the class to read. During the discussion of the section, ask students the following questions.

- Why do you think requirements such as owning property or belonging to a certain religion were placed on voting rights during the early colonial period?

  There was widespread religious intolerance in the early English colonies.

TERMS TO UNDERSTAND

civil rights movement	Voting Rights Act
Civil War Amendments	Thirteenth Amendment
grandfather clause	Fourteenth Amendment
literacy test	Fifteenth Amendment
poll tax	Nineteenth Amendment
register	Twenty-fourth Amendment
suffrage	Twenty-sixth Amendment

How was the right of suffrage extended before the Civil War?

The colonial limits on who could vote did not change much during the early years of the new nation. Many colonies only allowed white men who owned property and belonged to a particular religious group to vote.

After the Revolution, an increasing number of people objected to these limits on voting rights. States began to do away with property and religious restrictions. In addition, new states joining the Union placed fewer limitations on suffrage. **Suffrage** means the right to vote. In the early 1800s, for example, six new Western states gave the vote to all adult white males.

Although the states took steps before the Civil War to extend suffrage to more people, change was not easy. For example, as late as 1842 in Rhode Island, only men with property were allowed to vote. This situation caused an armed rebellion. The rebellion failed. But the following year Rhode Island adopted a new state constitution that gave voting rights to all male citizens who paid a tax of at least one dollar a year.

What criteria should be used to determine who should be eligible to vote?

Before the Civil War, a large part of the population—including African American men and all women—still could not vote. In the remaining sections of the lesson, you will learn how these groups, Native Americans, and others gained the right to vote.

How did African American men gain the right to vote?

Although many black men fought in the Revolutionary War, the right to vote was not extended to African Americans. In 1860 only six of the thirty-four states allowed freedmen to vote.

After the Civil War, the states approved the Thirteenth, Fourteenth, and Fifteenth Amendments to the Constitution. These amendments are known as the **Civil War Amendments**. The **Thirteenth Amendment** abolished slavery. The **Fourteenth** **Amendment** granted full citizenship to African Americans. The **Fifteenth Amendment** guaranteed the right to vote to men regardless of their "race, color, or previous condition of servitude."

Adding these Civil War Amendments to the Constitution was only the start of an effort to guarantee voting rights to African Americans. Many people in the Southern states did not want black people to vote or hold public office. Some states passed laws that made it impossible for African Americans to vote. Some examples of these laws follow on the next page.

What problems were the Fourteenth and Fifteenth Amendments intended to solve?

People tended to think that only their own beliefs were true and worthy. Property owners were seen as being responsible citizens and therefore capable of voting. Slaves were not allowed to vote and women were considered unable to make political decisions.

- Why do you think more people came to question these voting restrictions after the Revolution?

  Accept any reasonable responses.

- Were these restrictions consistent with the ideals of our form of government? In what ways were they consistent?

  They were not consistent with the ideals of our form of government. In a republican government, all citizens have the right to vote. Furthermore, the Declaration of Independence states that "all men are created equal."

Handout D7 and Handout D8 of this guide are suggested activities for this lesson. If you choose to assign these activities, have students color the maps and answer the accompanying questions in groups of two or three.

READING AND DISCUSSION

How did African American men gain the right to vote?

Have students read this section and help them to understand each of the exclusionary laws that were created to deny blacks the right to vote. Discuss the reasons why the national government had to take steps to enfranchise blacks. It is important that students appreciate that African Americans' struggle to gain the right to vote was long and difficult. This was an arduous battle, despite the ratification of the Fifteenth Amendment in 1870. The Civil Rights Movement is discussed in greater detail in Lesson 26.

- **Literacy tests**

  A **literacy test** requires that a person prove that he or she is able to read and write. Some states required all men to pass these tests before being allowed to vote. Because most African American men had been denied an education they could not pass the test. Often the people who gave the test behaved unfairly. They made it impossible for even educated African American men to pass the test.

- **Grandfather clause**

  Some states had voting laws with wording that we call **grandfather clauses**. A grandfather clause said that a person had the right to vote only if his grandfather had had the right to vote. Few African American men could qualify. Their grandfathers had been slaves and had been denied the right to vote.

- **Poll tax**

  A **poll tax** is a fee that a person must pay in order to vote. Some states charged all people a poll tax. Since most former slaves were very poor, they could not afford to pay the tax and, therefore, could not vote.

  People fought to get these state laws changed, but it took a long time. In 1915, the U.S. Supreme Court said that grandfather clauses were unconstitutional. Some states, however, continued to use literacy tests and poll taxes until the 1960s in order to keep African Americans from voting.

  In the 1950s, more and more people began to demand that the federal government protect the right of African Americans to vote. People of all races worked together to change unfair state laws. People gave speeches and marched in the streets. These actions became known as the **civil rights movement**.

What was unfair about these voting requirements?

What was the poll tax? Why was it used?

As a result of the civil rights movement, the **Twenty-fourth Amendment** was added to the Constitution in 1964. The amendment says that the right to vote in national elections shall not be denied because a person fails to pay a poll tax or any other tax. The U.S. Supreme Court later said that the Twenty-fourth Amendment also applied to state elections.

Congress passed a law called the **Voting Rights Act** in 1965. The law protected the right to vote for all citizens. The law forced the states to obey the Constitution. It made it clear that the right to vote could not be denied because of a person's color.

How did women gain the right to vote?

In 1848, a convention was held at Seneca Falls, New York, that launched a national movement by women to win the right to vote. Although suffrage for women had many supporters among men, the battle was a difficult one. In those days it was common to believe that women should not participate in government. This idea made it harder for women to achieve their goal.

In 1876, Susan B. Anthony led a delegation of women to Philadelphia to celebrate the one-hundred-year anniversary of the

LESSON 25

READING, DISCUSSION, AND ACTIVITY

How did women gain the right to vote?
How did Native Americans gain the right to vote?
How did eighteen-year-olds gain the right to vote?
What are voting requirements today?

Divide the class into four groups. Assign each group one of the sections listed above. Each one of the groups will read its assigned section and prepare to teach the content to the rest of the class. They may choose their method of instruction.

(continued next page)

Some suggestions follow, but students may have other creative ideas.

- Explain the section using appropriate visual support, such as charts, or by writing important events and dates on the board.
- Create a PowerPoint presentation explaining the section.
- Design a timeline that depicts important events and dates.
- Develop a skit or short play that illustrates important events and dates.

When all the lessons are completed, discuss with students the ideas they have learned and whether the activity was effective.

Why do you think women did not gain the vote until 1920?

Declaration of Independence. While there, the women publicly protested their lack of suffrage by reading the Women's Declaration of Rights.

Gaining the right to vote for women was a long, slow process. The earliest gains were made in the western part of the country. The territory of Wyoming granted women the right to vote in 1869. By 1900, Colorado, Utah, and Idaho had followed Wyoming's lead.

It was not until 1912 that the movement to give women the right to vote gained national recognition. Presidential candidate Theodore Roosevelt's Bull Moose Progressive Party supported the movement. In 1913 women were granted the right to vote in the territory of Alaska.

In 1920, the states ratified the **Nineteenth Amendment** to the Constitution, which gave women the vote. One hundred and thirty years after the signing of the Constitution, women had finally gained the right to vote.

How did Native Americans gain the right to vote?

American Indians governed themselves by their own tribal laws, treaties with the United States government, and by special laws passed by Congress. These laws did not recognize American Indians to be citizens of the United States. As a result, they did not have the right to vote.

The first attempt to grant Native Americans citizenship came in 1887 when Congress passed the Dawes Act. The Dawes Act granted a tract of land and citizenship to those who were willing to give up their allegiance to their tribe. The law was strongly resented by most tribes.

Finally, Congress passed a law in 1924 called the Indian Citizenship Act. This law fully recognized Indians as citizens of the United States. The law also gave Indians the right to vote in federal elections.

President Calvin Coolidge with a group of Osage Indians after the signing of the Indian Citizenship Act of 1924. What rights were realized by Native Americans with the passage of this law?

220

How did eighteen-year-olds gain the right to vote?

In the 1960s and 1970s, the government drafted thousands of young men to fight in the Vietnam War. Many of these young men were too young to vote. They did not have a voice in the elections for government officials responsible for deciding America's role in that war. The voting requirement at that time was twenty-one years of age.

Congress passed a law in 1970 lowering the voting age to eighteen. The U.S. Supreme Court then ruled that Congress could only regulate federal elections. At that time, only four states allowed eighteen-

What is the relationship between who is allowed to vote and how democratic a country is?

year-olds to vote. Following the Court's decision, steps were taken to amend the Constitution so that suffrage would be extended to eighteen-year-olds in both state and federal elections.

In 1971, the **Twenty-sixth Amendment** was added to the Constitution. The amendment grants the right to vote to any citizen who is eighteen years of age or older.

What are voting requirements today?

The states, although limited by the Constitution and the federal Voting Rights Act, still make some decisions regarding voting rights. All states have laws saying only citizens have the right to vote, although the Constitution does not require this. Every state requires that persons must live in the state for a period of time before they can vote, and all states except North Dakota require citizens to register

Why should people who are old enough to serve in the armed forces also have the right to vote?

see next student page

IDEAS FOR DISCUSSION

What suggestions do you have for increasing participation in elections today?

Present the activity as outlined in the student text. Discuss with students their opinions and their responses to the questions. Ask them what they might be able to do to stop the decline in voter turnout.

1. Why do you think that older Americans might be more interested in government policies than younger Americans?

   Older Americans have had more time to be involved in government and to form their opinions. The issues dealt with by government are often directly related to older people, such as Social Security, health care, and taxation. Younger people do not see the relevance of many issues dealt with by government and are busy with other parts of their lives, such as school, work, and spending time with friends.

2. What political issues motivate younger citizens to get involved with public life? Give examples.

   Accept any reasonable responses.

3. Some countries increased voter participation by holding elections on Sundays. What other methods can you suggest to increase voter turnout?

   Students might suggest voting online, voting on Saturdays, or voting during two days instead of one. Accept any reasonable responses.

4. In some countries, voter participation is mandatory. What effect might this have on elections? Do you think this is a good way to increase citizen participation in elections?

   Students might suggest that this policy is fair because citizens benefit from the protection and services of government and should therefore have to vote. However, they might think that mandatory voting would result in people voting without taking the time to look at and understand the issues or candidates. It is possible that citizens might not make the best choices if they are forced to vote.

Why do you suppose older Americans vote more frequently than younger Americans?

before voting. To **register** to vote means to have your name added to a list. Voters are required to register to ensure that they are qualified to vote and to keep people from voting more than once.

Throughout our history we have used our Constitution to achieve nearly universal adult suffrage. Today, almost every American of voting age has the right to vote. This has made the United States one of the most democratic nations on earth. Americans can use the power of the ballot box to choose more public officials at more levels of government than can voters in any other democracy.

As the right to vote has expanded, though, the willingness of American citizens to participate has decreased. In recent years there has been a steady decline in voter turnout for elections.

The United States now ranks eleventh among the world's democracies in the percentage of eligible voters who exercise the right to vote.

Many people worry about the unwillingness of so many Americans to use this most fundamental right and duty of citizenship. They fear that not voting may reflect a growing feeling of being disconnected from government. However, if the United States is to be a country that is truly of, by, and for the people, it is essential that the people exercise their right to vote competently and responsibly. Responsible voting is essential to democracy.

see next student page

IDEAS FOR DISCUSSION

What suggestions do you have for increasing participation in elections today?

Generally, better-off and better-educated citizens use their right to vote to a much greater extent than do poor or uneducated citizens. Voter turnout is also related to age. Older Americans are almost twice as likely to vote than are young Americans.

Work in groups of three to five to discuss the following questions. Share your opinions with the class.

❶ Why do you think that older Americans might be more interested in government policies than younger Americans?

❷ What political issues motivate younger citizens to get involved with public life? Give examples.

❸ Some countries increased voter participation by holding elections on Sundays. What other methods can you suggest to increase voter turnout?

❹ In some countries voter participation is mandatory. What effect might this have on elections? Do you think this is a good way to increase citizen participation in elections?

Do you think something should be done to increase voter turnout? Why or why not?

LESSON REVIEW

The questions in the student book are intended to assess learning and to reinforce knowledge through discussion. The questions are directly related to the lesson objectives. You may wish to include additional questions you or your students find useful.

1. What were some of the restrictions on voting rights that kept various groups of people from voting?

   Many colonies allowed only men who owned property and belonged to a particular religion to vote. Such exclusionary laws as literacy tests, the grandfather clause, and poll taxes prevented African Americans from voting. A commonly held belief that women should not participate in politics excluded them from the voting process. Native Americans were not initially recognized as being citizens of the United States and therefore not allowed to vote. They governed themselves according to tribal laws.

2. Explain how each of the following groups of people gained the right to vote.

   African American men—*After the Civil War, the states approved the Fourteenth and Fifteenth Amendments, which granted citizenship to African Americans and guaranteed African American men the right to vote. However, it was not until 1964 that the Twenty-fourth Amendment was added to the Constitution, which rendered powerless the exclusionary laws practiced in some states. The Voting Rights Act of 1965 further enforced the right of African Americans to vote.*

(continued next page)

Eighteen-year-olds—Many young men were drafted to fight in the Vietnam War, even though they were considered too young to have a voice in deciding America's role in that war. In 1971, the Twenty-sixth Amendment lowered the voting age from 21 to 18.

Native Americans—In 1924, Congress passed the Indian Citizenship Act, which fully recognized Native Americans as citizens of the United States and gave them the right to vote in federal elections.

Women—The national movement by women to gain the right to vote began during a convention held in Seneca Falls, New York, in 1848. However, women in most states did not gain the right to vote until 1920, when the Nineteenth Amendment was ratified by the states.

3. What Amendments were added to the Constitution so that more people would have the right to vote?

The Fourteenth, Fifteenth, Nineteenth, Twenty-fourth, and Twenty-sixth Amendments were added to the Constitution to expand voting rights.

4. What laws did Congress pass to protect the constitutional right of citizens to vote?

The Voting Rights Act of 1965 and the Indian Citizenship Act of 1924 were passed to protect the constitutional right of citizens to vote.

5. What actions did citizens take to expand the right to vote to most Americans?

After the Revolution, people began to object to the limits on voting rights and tried to get some of the restrictions removed. In 1848, and again in 1876, women held conventions protesting their lack of suffrage and publicly read the Women's Declaration of Rights. During the Civil Rights Movement that began in the 1950s, many people demanded that the federal government protect the right of African Americans to vote. Their involvement resulted in the Twenty-fourth Amendment and the Voting Rights Act.

ACTIVITIES

The suggested activities are intended to extend and apply learning outside the classroom. You may wish to have students complete one or more of the activities. Have them share their results with the class.

LESSON REVIEW

❶ What were some of the restrictions on voting rights that kept various groups of people from voting?

❷ Explain how each of the following groups of people gained the right to vote.

- African Americans
- eighteen-year-olds
- Native Americans
- women

❸ What amendments were added to the Constitution so that more people would have the right to vote?

❹ What laws did Congress pass to protect the constitutional right of citizens to vote?

❺ What actions did citizens take to expand the right to vote to most Americans?

ACTIVITIES

❶ With help from your teacher, invite someone from the League of Women Voters to come to your class to discuss elections in your state. Prepare questions to ask your guest during the visit.

❷ Use the Internet to find information about the requirements for voting in your state. Obtain a copy of a voter registration form and a sample ballot from a recent election. Your community library, county clerk, or registrar's office should be able to help you. Share the information you find with your class.

❸ Follow a political campaign in your community or state. Learn about the candidates. Keep articles from the newspaper. Keep a journal where you record your impression about the election process.

❹ Write a story that shows how one person's vote can determine the outcome of an election. Share your story with the class.

How does the Constitution safeguard the right to equal protection of the law?

26

LESSON PURPOSE

In this lesson you will be introduced to one of the most important parts of the Fourteenth Amendment to the Constitution—the equal protection clause.

When you finish this lesson, you should be able to explain the purpose of the equal protection clause. You should also be able to describe some of the steps that Congress, the executive branch, the U.S. Supreme Court, and citizens have taken to end unfair discrimination in our nation.

OVERVIEW

This lesson traces the development of equal protection from 1865 to the present. Students are introduced to the Thirteenth and Fourteenth Amendments, which abolished slavery and provided equal protection to African Americans. They learn that the Fourteenth Amendment did not by itself end discrimination, because states continued to pass laws requiring African Americans to attend separate schools and use separate public facilities. In the Ideas for Discussion activity, students are asked to consider the fairness or unfairness of situations related to equal protection. Students then examine the two U.S. Supreme Court cases that dealt with the equal protection clause—*Plessy v. Ferguson* and *Brown v. Board of Education*. The lesson concludes with an account of how the Civil Rights Movement and actions taken by the executive branch ultimately ended unfair discrimination by our government.

OBJECTIVES

At the conclusion of this lesson, students should be able to:

- explain the purpose of the equal protection clause
- explain the purpose of the Fourteenth Amendment, especially as it relates to the equal protection clause
- explain Jim Crow laws
- describe some steps that Congress, the executive branch, the U.S. Supreme Court, and citizens have taken to end unfair discrimination in our nation

TEACHING PROCEDURES

INTRODUCTORY ACTIVITY

Write the Terms to Understand on the board or use a vocabulary-building activity of your choice. Have students look up the words in the Glossary at the back of the text. Ask them to look for these words as they read the lesson.

Have students read the Lesson Purpose and consider the objectives of the lesson. Ask them the following question:

(continued next page)

- The Fourteenth Amendment was passed in 1868 and was supposed to prohibit the states from discriminating against African Americans by guaranteeing equal protection of the law. Why do you suppose that discrimination was still practiced in many states almost 100 years after the ratification of the Fourteenth Amendment?

Encourage students to speculate, then tell them that this lesson will explain why the Fourteenth Amendment was not honored by many states for such a long time.

READING AND DISCUSSION

How did the Constitution end unfair treatment of citizens by government?

Assign this section to students to read. Discuss the Thirteenth and Fourteenth Amendments with them, and help them to understand how states were able to circumvent the Fourteenth Amendment. Tell them that later in the lesson, they will be examining two important U.S. Supreme Court cases—*Plessy v. Ferguson* and *Brown v. Board of Education*—that addressed this issue. An optional activity is to ask students to write descriptions in their notebooks of both Amendments and the rights they protected.

TERMS TO UNDERSTAND

boycott
Civil Rights Act of 1964
equal protection clause
Jim Crow laws
segregation
separate but equal

How did the Constitution end unfair treatment of citizens by government?

Although the Thirteenth Amendment abolished slavery in 1865, it did not end unfair treatment of African Americans by government. Many states in the South passed laws that discriminated against black people. State and local laws required that public facilities such as restrooms, theaters, and parks have separate areas for black people and white people.

Congress adopted the Fourteenth Amendment in 1868. The **equal protection clause** is stated in Section 1 of the amendment. It is the most important constitutional protection that the people have against unfair discrimination by state and local governments. The equal protection clause says that

> no State shall...deny to any person within its jurisdiction the equal protection of the laws.

At the time it was ratified, this clause was intended to prevent discrimination against African Americans and guarantee them the rights that go along with citizenship.

Why did the passage of the Thirteenth Amendment fail to end unfair treatment of African Americans?

Are these situations unfair treatment by government?

With a partner, read each of the following situations.
Explain to the class why each is or is not unfair government treatment.

❶ In your state there is a law that says students belonging to a certain race must go to schools that are separate from those that other students attend.

❷ Your city has a regulation requiring people with particular religious beliefs to live in a special section of town.

❸ Your state has a law that says people must marry within their own race.

❹ Your city fire department will not hire women as firefighters.

❺ You and a friend of the opposite sex work for the state. You both do the same jobs. Yet you are each paid at a different rate.

Under what conditions, if any, would it be fair to pay people at a different rate for doing the same work? Explain your reasoning.

IDEAS FOR DISCUSSION

Are these situations unfair treatment by government?

Follow the activities in the student text. Most students will agree that all these situations are unfair because all people are not receiving equal treatment by government. Some students might suggest that people will get along better if they live with and marry people who are similar to themselves. They might argue that women are not strong enough to use the equipment necessary to put out fires. After students share their ideas, explain to them that through the first half of the twentieth century, this type of unfair treatment by government happened regularly in some states. Ask them whether they think that this type of discrimination still happens even though states can no longer pass such laws.

READING AND DISCUSSION

How did the U.S. Supreme Court interpret the equal protection clause in two separate cases?

Read this section with students, ensuring that they understand that these cases provoked a series of actions and behaviors that greatly affected the lives of African Americans.

The Fourteenth Amendment did not by itself prevent discrimination, however. The states continued to pass laws requiring African Americans to go to separate schools and to use separate public facilities. These laws came to be called **Jim Crow laws**. The states claimed that such laws did not violate the equal protection clause because the separate schools and facilities for blacks were equal to those provided for whites. This is known as the **separate but equal** argument. The U.S. Supreme Court considered this argument in two famous cases: *Plessy v. Ferguson* (1896) and *Brown v. Board of Education* (1954).

How did the U.S. Supreme Court interpret the equal protection clause in two separate cases?

CASE ONE
Plessy v. Ferguson (1896)

The state of Louisiana passed a law requiring railroad companies to provide separate, similar cars for white passengers and black passengers. A group of African American leaders decided to challenge the law.

In what ways did Jim Crow laws violate the equal protection clause?

Homer Plessy bought a railroad ticket and took a seat in a car set aside for whites. Plessy was arrested when he refused to move. The Louisiana state court found him guilty of violating state law. Plessy took his case to the U.S. Supreme Court, arguing that the Louisiana law violated the equal protection clause.

The Supreme Court ruled against Plessy. The Court said that separating the races did not mean that one race was inferior to the other. Because the state law required the facilities to be separate but equal, the Supreme Court said there was no discrimination.

The decision in this case, *Plessy v. Ferguson* (1896), allowed states to practice **segregation**, separation of the races, for almost sixty years. Then, in the case of *Brown v. Board of Education* (1954), the U.S. Supreme Court changed its interpretation of the equal protection clause.

CASE TWO
Brown v. Board of Education (1954)

Linda Brown was a seven-year-old child who lived five blocks from an elementary school. Linda was forced to attend a school for African American children twenty-one blocks away from her home. Linda's parents, along with twelve other parents, brought a lawsuit against the school board of Topeka, Kansas, saying their children had been deprived of equal protection of the law.

One of the lawyers for the parents was Thurgood Marshall, an attorney for the National Association for the Advancement of Colored People. Marshall later became the first African American justice of the U.S. Supreme Court. He argued that segregated schools could not be equal.

This time the Court agreed. It said that placing African American children in schools separate from white children denied them the equal protection of the laws guaranteed by the Fourteenth Amendment. The Court said,

> To separate [children]...solely because of their race generates [causes] a feeling of inferiority... that may affect their hearts and minds in a way unlikely ever to be undone.

These are the lawyers for the Brown family and the other families: George E.C. Hayes, left, Thurgood Marshall, center, and James M. Nabrit Jr. What was their argument before the Supreme Court? How did the Court rule in this case?

READING, DISCUSSION, AND ACTIVITY

How did Congress, the executive branch, and citizens work to end unfair discrimination by government?

Assign this section to students to read. You might wish to have individual students read different parts of the section. Emphasize the dates of these events and the consequences of them. It might be helpful to have students complete Handout D 9. This activity calls for students to list the events in the struggle to end discrimination and provides an equal protection timeline. The List of Events, with missing dates, is reproduced here:

List of Events

- Thirteenth Amendment ratified (1865)
- Fourteenth Amendment ratified (1868)
- Fifteenth Amendment ratified (1870)
- Ex-Confederates regained control of state legislatures in the Southern states (1869–1877)
- Southern states passed segregation laws (1880–1895)
- U.S. Supreme Court upheld "separate but equal" facilities (1896)
- President Roosevelt issued an executive order banning discrimination in hiring by defense contractors (1941)
- President Truman issued an executive order requiring fair employment in federal jobs (1948)
- U.S. Supreme Court struck down segregated schools (1954)
- Black boycott of bus line in Montgomery, Alabama, marked first major attack on segregation of public facilities (1955–1956)
- Civil Rights Acts passed (1954–1964, 1968)
- Voting Rights Act passed (1965)
- Age Discrimination in Employment Act passed (1967)
- Equal Employment Opportunities Act passed (1968)
- Title IX of the Education Act banned discrimination on the basis of sex in educational programs that receive federal aid (1972)
- Education for All Handicapped Children Act passed (1975)
- Proposed equal rights amendment guaranteeing equal rights for women failed to be ratified (1982)

As you conclude this lesson, you might want to talk with students about the limited ability of the law to truly end discrimination. Mention that legislation alone cannot end discrimination—the effort must be shared by individual citizens, schools, churches, and other community groups.

How did Congress, the executive branch, and citizens work to end unfair discrimination by government?

The Court's decision in *Brown v. Board of Education* was the first important step in ending school segregation. Although the *Brown* case was a turning point in the fight against discrimination, it dealt only with segregated schools. The Court decision by itself did not end discrimination. Many states resisted the Court's order to integrate their schools. As late as 1957, the governor of Arkansas tried to stop black students from entering a

What means did leaders of the civil rights movement use to obtain their goals?

white high school in Little Rock. In response, President Dwight Eisenhower ordered federal troops to escort the students and enforce the law.

The civil rights movement started in the 1950s. It was a time when many people of both races worked to end unfair treatment by government. People marched in the streets. They wrote letters to Congress asking for stronger laws. They held boycotts. A **boycott** means that they refused to buy from or deal with stores and companies that practiced racial discrimination.

One of the earliest boycotts began in 1955. Rosa Parks was a working woman who lived in Montgomery, Alabama. She was on her way home one day when the bus she was riding became crowded. Parks refused to give up her seat to a

Who is Rosa Parks? Why did African Americans begin a boycott of buses in Montgomery, Alabama, in 1955?

What democratic ideals were expressed by Martin Luther King Jr. in his "I Have a Dream" speech?

white man. She was arrested for violating a city law. The African American community boycotted the city buses until the city changed the law. The boycott lasted more than a year.

In August of 1963, thousands of Americans marched in Washington, D.C. They wanted to show their support for the civil rights movement. Dr. Martin Luther King Jr. was an important civil rights leader. It was here that Dr. King gave his famous "I Have a Dream" speech. King told the crowd, "I have a dream that my four little children will one day live in a nation where they will not be judged by the color of their skin, but by the content of their character." One day, he hoped, all people would join hands and be "free at last."

In 1964, Congress passed the Civil Rights Act. The **Civil Rights Act of 1964** ended segregation in public places such as restaurants and hotels. The law also said that employers could not discriminate against people because of their race, national origin, religion, or gender.

When African Americans won these civil rights after years of struggle, other groups began to call for equal protection. Women, disabled people, older people, and other groups worked to get laws passed guaranteeing their right to equal protection of the laws. In response to their efforts, Congress and state legislatures have passed laws prohibiting unfair discrimination against these groups.

see next student page

LESSON REVIEW

The questions in the student book are intended to assess learning and to reinforce knowledge through discussion. The questions are directly related to the lesson objectives. You may wish to include additional questions you or your students find useful.

1. What were the purposes of the Thirteenth and Fourteenth Amendments to the Constitution?

   The Thirteenth Amendment (1865) abolished slavery and the Fourteenth Amendment (1868) was designed to prevent state governments from discriminating against African Americans.

2. What is the meaning of the equal protection clause? Why is this clause important?

   The equal protection clause mandates that all states protect their citizens equally in accordance with the law. This clause is important because it guarantees every citizen the right to equal treatment under the law.

3. What did the U.S. Supreme Court decide in the *Plessy v. Ferguson* case? What effects did the decision have on the lives of African Americans?

   The U.S. Supreme Court ruled that separating the races did not mean that one race was inferior to the other. Because state law required that facilities be equal, the Court determined that there was no discrimination. The decision allowed states to practice segregation of the races for almost sixty years after the U.S. Supreme Court's ruling.

(continued next page)

4. What did the U.S. Supreme Court decide
in the *Brown v. Board of Education* case?
Why was this an important decision?

In Brown v. Board of Education, *the U.S. Supreme Court ruled that separating children solely because of their race causes them to feel inferior and denies them the equal protection of the law that is guaranteed by the Fourteenth Amendment. The case is important because it was a turning point in the fight against discrimination and school segregation.*

5. What actions did ordinary citizens take
to help end unfair discrimination?

People marched in the streets and wrote letters to Congress asking for stronger laws. They boycotted stores and companies that practiced racial discrimination. In August of 1963, thousands of Americans marched in Washington, D.C., to show their support for the Civil Rights Movement.

6. What law did Congress pass to
help end unfair discrimination?

Congress passed the Civil Rights Act in 1964, which ended segregation in public places such as restaurants and hotels. It also forbade employers from discriminating against people because of their race, national origin, religion, or gender.

7. What actions did the executive branch
take to help end unfair discrimination?

In 1957, President Eisenhower enforced the U.S. Supreme Court's ruling in Brown v. Board of Education *by ordering the U.S. Army to escort African American students to their school in Arkansas.*

ACTIVITIES

The suggested activities are intended to extend and apply learning outside the classroom. You may wish to have students complete one or more of the activities. Have them share their results with the class.

LESSON REVIEW

❶ What was the purpose of the Thirteenth and Fourteenth Amendments to the Constitution?

❷ What is the meaning of the equal protection clause? Why is this clause important?

❸ What did the U.S. Supreme Court decide in the *Plessy v. Ferguson* case? What effects did the decision have on the lives of African Americans?

❹ What did the U.S. Supreme Court decide in the *Brown v. Board of Education* case? Why was this an important decision?

❺ What actions did ordinary citizens take to help end unfair discrimination?

❻ What laws did Congress pass to help end unfair discrimination?

❼ What actions did the executive branch take to help end unfair discrimination?

ACTIVITIES

❶ Research information about Martin Luther King Jr. Read his *Letter from Birmingham City Jail*. What kinds of inspiration did he have for his ideas about nonviolence? Share what you learned with the class.

❷ "Equal treatment" continues to be an important issue in the United States today. Find information about issues of equality that organized groups are seeking to address today. Explain what these issues are in a report to your class.

❸ Create a timeline of historical events in the struggle to gain equal protection by various groups in America. Each student should research one event to include in a classroom poster commemorating the struggle for equal rights.

How does the Constitution protect the right to due process of law?

27

LESSON PURPOSE

In this lesson we will look at another part of the Constitution that is concerned with fairness. This is the idea of due process of law. The due process clause is intended to guarantee that government will use fair procedures when gathering information and making decisions that affect our rights to life, liberty, or property.

When you finish this lesson you should be able to explain in general terms what due process means. You should also be able to explain how due process applies to the rights of juveniles who are accused of breaking the law.

OVERVIEW

This lesson explains the right of due process as it is expressed in the Fifth and Fourteenth Amendments. Students learn that the Fifth Amendment applies only to federal actions, whereas the Fourteenth Amendment specifically includes state actions. The lesson begins by defining due process and explaining the two ways in which due process is applied. Students apply these definitions to an important U.S. Supreme Court case and decide if the accused was given fair due process. The lesson concludes with a discussion of how government balances the conflict between its responsibility to protect the rights of individuals who are accused of breaking the law and its responsibility to protect everyone else from people who break the law and endanger the lives, liberty, and property of others.

OBJECTIVES

At the conclusion of this lesson, students should be able to

- explain in general terms what due process means
- explain the difference between the Fifth Amendment and the Fourteenth Amendment, and describe why the Fourteenth Amendment was needed
- explain how due process applies to the rights of juveniles who are accused of breaking the law

TEACHING PROCEDURES

INTRODUCTORY ACTIVITY

Write the Terms to Understand on the board or use a vocabulary-building activity of your choice. Have students look up the words in the Glossary at the back of the text. Ask them to look for these words as they read the lesson.

Complete the Prereading Activity on the next page. Then, after the initial discussion in which suggested situations are classified by students, have them read the Lesson Purpose and consider the objectives of the lesson.

PREREADING ACTIVITY

Write the word "fairness" on the board and ask students to provide examples of situations that they think were either fair or unfair. Write their responses on the board.

Explain to students that "fairness" and "justice" mean about the same thing. Then present the three classifications of justice provided below, and guide students in applying these classifications to the situations they suggested. Discuss their responses and ensure that they understand the differences among the three types of justice.

- **Distributive justice.** The fair distribution of the benefits and burdens of society. For example, pay, goods and services, grades (benefits), and the fair distribution of responsibilities and taxes (burdens).

- **Corrective justice.** The fairness of responses to wrongs or injuries. Does the punishment reasonably fit the wrong or injury, or is the punishment excessive—cruel or unusual?

- **Procedural justice.** The fairness of the ways in which information is gathered and decisions are made. Has the accused been allowed to tell his or her side of the story? Has the accused been able to face his or her accuser? Have witnesses been questioned? Have people been tortured or bribed to gain information?

READING AND DISCUSSION

What is due process of law?

Read this section with students. Have students read the Fifth and Fourteenth Amendments to the Constitution in the Reference section of their text. Help them clarify their understanding of the difference between the two applications of due process mentioned in this section. Tell students that the due process clause of the Fourteenth Amendment has been used to make most of the Bill of Rights applicable to state governments.

TERMS TO UNDERSTAND

due process
Fifth Amendment
procedure

What is due process of law?

It is difficult to define due process of law exactly. We may say that **due process** is the right to be treated fairly by government. There are two important ways this meaning is applied.

❶ Due process means that the **procedures**, or methods used to conduct hearings and to apply and enforce the law, must be fair and reasonable. All branches of the federal and state governments must use fair procedures when they are carrying out their responsibilities.

❷ Due process also means that the **content** of laws that legislatures pass must be fair and reasonable. Congress and the state legislatures cannot pass laws that place unfair or unreasonable limitations on people's rights to life, liberty, or property.

The ideas of due process can be found in the body of the Constitution and several amendments. The Fifth and Fourteenth Amendments specifically use the term due process of law.

In what way does due process limit the powers of government?

The Fifth Amendment does not mention state governments. Therefore, this amendment applies only to actions of the federal government.

What rights do you think you should have if you were to be accused of breaking the law?

The **Fifth Amendment** says

No Person shall...be deprived of life, liberty, or property, without due process of law.

The Fourteenth Amendment includes actions by the states. The Fourteenth Amendment says

nor shall any State deprive any person of life, liberty, or property, without due process of law.

In the remainder of this lesson we focus on the first meaning of due process: members of all branches of government must use fair procedures when fulfilling their responsibilities.

We will concentrate on the rights of persons suspected or accused of crimes. We examine the procedures that were followed in a situation that led to a famous U.S. Supreme Court case called *In re Gault* (1967). This case concerns the treatment of a juvenile accused of a crime.

SOLVE THE PROBLEM

What are fair procedures?

Have students complete the exercise as directed in the student text. Below are some possible responses to the problems posed in the exercise.

1. Read the summary of the *Gault* case.

2. Make a list of unfair procedures used by government officials in the case.

   Before the hearing,
   - *The boys were questioned without the presence of a parent or guardian.*
   - *The parents were not notified that Gerald had been taken to a detention home.*

   At the first hearing,
   - *Gerald was not able to confront his accuser.*
   - *No one was asked to swear to tell the truth.*
   - *No representation was provided for Gerald.*
   - *No record of the proceedings was kept, which made it impossible to verify statements made by Officer Flagg and Mrs. Gault.*

   At the second hearing,
   - *The note from the court to Mrs. Gault notifying her of a second hearing was not written on official letterhead.*
   - *The accuser, Mrs. Cook, was not present and therefore could not be questioned.*
   - *No one was asked to swear to tell the truth.*
   - *No record was made of the hearing.*
   - *Gerald did not have a lawyer to represent him.*
   - *Officer Flagg gave the judge a report stating that Gerald had made—not that he was accused of making—insulting phone calls.*
   - *The Gaults had never seen the report.*

What are fair procedures?

Work with a group of three to five students to complete the following exercise.

❶ Read the summary of the *Gault* case.

❷ Make a list of unfair procedures used by government officials in the case.

❸ Read the Fifth, Sixth, and Eighth Amendments to the Constitution. Identify the parts of each Amendment that apply to this case.

❹ Evaluate the facts, then take and defend a position on how the U.S. Supreme Court should have dealt with *In re Gault*.

In re Gault (1967)

Gerald Gault was fifteen years old. On the morning of June 8, 1964, the sheriff of Gila County, Arizona, arrested Gerald and a friend, Ronald Lewis. The sheriff took the boys to the Children's Detention Home.

The boys were accused of telephoning a neighbor, Mrs. Cook, and saying offensive and obscene things to her. Mrs. Cook had then called the sheriff.

While the boys were in detention, Officer Flagg, a deputy probation officer, questioned them. The boys admitted making the calls. Each boy blamed the other.

At the time that Gerald was arrested, his parents were at work. The sheriff who arrested the boys did not tell the parents that Gerald was being taken to a detention home. No one from the sheriff's office called the Gault home.

When Gerald's mother arrived home that evening, she sent her older son to look for Gerald. At the home of Ronald Lewis, he learned that Gerald was being held in the detention home.

Mrs. Gault went to the detention home and Officer Flagg explained why the sheriff had arrested her son. Officer Flagg informed Mrs. Gault that there would be a hearing in juvenile court the next afternoon.

Gerald, his mother, Officer Flagg, and the judge were the only ones at the hearing. Mrs. Cook was not present. During the hearing, no one was asked to swear to tell the truth. No record was made of what was said. No lawyers were present.

At later hearings, the judge, Mrs. Gault, and Officer Flagg agreed on some things that were said at the first hearing but disagreed about others. They agreed that the judge had asked Gerald about the telephone call. They disagreed about what Gerald answered.

His mother remembered that Gerald said he had dialed Mrs. Cook's number and then handed the telephone to Ronald. Officer Flagg said that Gerald had admitted making one insulting remark.

Two or three days later, Officer Flagg drove Gerald home. On that day, Gerald's mother received a note from the court that was written on plain paper. The note said, "Mrs. Gault, Judge McGhee has set Monday, June 15, 1964 at 11 A.M. as the date for further hearings on Gerald's delinquency."

On June 15, the Gaults appeared in court. Mrs. Gault had requested that Mrs. Cook be present but she did not attend. The judge, who had not spoken with Mrs. Cook, said that it was not necessary that Mrs. Cook be in court. Again, no one was asked to swear to tell the truth and no record was made of this hearing.

During the hearing, Officer Flagg handed the judge a report saying that Gerald had made insulting phone calls. The Gaults had never seen the report.

3. Read the Fifth, Sixth, and Eighth Amendments to the Constitution. Identify the parts of each Amendment that should apply to this case.

   Help students to complete this exercise by copying, distributing, and asking students to complete Handout D10 of this guide.

4. Evaluate the facts, then take and defend a position on how the U.S. Supreme Court should have dealt with *In re Gault*.

   Ask students to separate into pairs or groups. Each group should agree on a position regarding the case, and then explain its position to the class. After each group has defended its position, explain to students that the U.S. Supreme Court decided in the Gault *case that juveniles are entitled to many of the same due process rights as adults. These include the right to adequate written notice of the charges, and the right to have an attorney present, to confront hostile witnesses under oath, and to avoid self-incrimination.*

In the end, the judge ruled that Gerald was guilty of violating a state law that said that a person who "in the presence or hearing of any woman or child…uses vulgar, abusive, or obscene language, is guilty of a misdemeanor." The judge sentenced Gerald to the State Industrial School for juvenile delinquents until he reached age 21.

If Gerald had been 18, he would have been tried in a regular criminal court. There, the maximum penalty for making "vulgar, abusive, or obscene" calls would have been a $5 to $50 fine or not more than two months' imprisonment.

The Gaults appealed the case and it eventually reached the U.S. Supreme Court. Gault's lawyers argued that the procedure used in Gerald's case had denied him due process under the Fourteenth Amendment. Attorneys for the state argued that the informal proceedings under the juvenile court system were intended to help juveniles, rather than treat them as regular criminals. They said that this system would be undermined if the Court gave young offenders all the specific guarantees in the Bill of Rights.

What conflicts might arise over protecting the rights of an individual and protecting society?

Protecting the individual from unfair treatment by government is among the most important protections of our constitutional democracy.

We have discussed due process of law as it applies to the rights of someone accused of a crime. It is important to remember that the right to due process means the right to be treated fairly by all the agencies of government, not just the courts and law enforcement.

Due process of law has been called the "primary and indispensable [necessary] foundation of individual freedom" because it protects the individual from government wrongdoing. Due process applies to local school board hearings, to congressional hearings, and to hearings of the administrative agencies of your state and federal governments.

How can the rights of the individual and the rights of society conflict?

Problems of due process involve two government responsibilities. These responsibilities are to

❶ protect the rights of an individual who may have broken the law

❷ protect everyone else from people who break the law and endanger the lives, liberty, or property of others

These responsibilities sometimes conflict. Balancing them is a difficult job. It is the duty of government and the courts to balance these responsibilities.

How might the right to due process of law protect the individual?

Reading and discussion

How can the rights of the individual and the rights of society conflict?

Assign this section to students to read. Ask them to provide some examples of each of the two government responsibilities—protecting the individual accused of a crime and protecting other citizens from those who endanger their lives, liberty, or property. Emphasize that due process is not limited to state or government actions in the courts or law enforcement, but extends to all government agencies. Ask students whether they agree that due process is the "primary and indispensable foundation of individual freedom." Have them share their opinions with the class and explain their reasoning.

LESSON REVIEW

The questions in the student book are intended to assess learning and to reinforce knowledge through discussion. The questions are directly related to the lesson objectives. You may wish to include additional questions you or your students find useful.

1. Where in the Constitution will you find the two due process clauses? In what way are the two clauses different?

   The two due process clauses are found in the Fifth and Fourteenth Amendments. The Fifth Amendment relates to federal action and does not mention state governments; the Fourteenth Amendment incorporates actions taken by state governments.

2. What is the meaning of due process?

   Due process means that the procedures or methods used to conduct hearings or to apply and enforce the law must be fair and that the content of laws passed by legislatures must be fair and reasonable.

3. Why do you think the guarantee of due process is so important?

   Due process is important because it protects the individual from government wrongdoing.

4. Why must all agencies of government protect the individual's right to due process of law?

   All government agencies must adhere to the due process clause because they are part of government, which means that they are subject to the Fifth and Fourteenth Amendments.

ACTIVITIES

The suggested activities are intended to extend and apply learning outside the classroom. You may wish to have students complete one or more of the activities. Have them share their results with the class.

LESSON REVIEW

❶ Where in the Constitution will you find the two due process clauses? In what way are the two clauses different?

❷ What is the meaning of due process?

❸ Why do you think the guarantee of due process is so important?

❹ Why must all agencies of government protect the individual's right to due process of law?

ACTIVITIES

❶ With a partner, videotape an interview with your school principal or a member of your school board. Ask them about the policy in your school district regarding due process rights of students. Show the tape to your class and explain what you learned.

❷ With a partner search the Constitution to see how many references each of you can find to elements related to fair procedures and due process of law. Combine your lists and share them with the class.

❸ Draw a picture or a poster. On one side of your picture illustrate a situation in which a due process right is being violated. On the other side illustrate the same situation but with the due process right being protected.

❹ With your teacher's help, invite a police officer to your class to discuss how the police have to protect due process rights when they suspect that someone has committed a crime. Prepare questions to ask your guest during the visit.

240

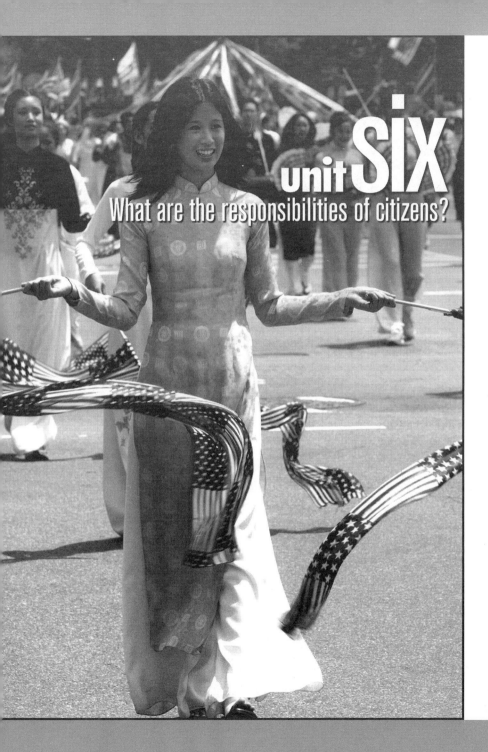

unit SIX

What are the responsibilities of citizens?

UNIT OVERVIEW

This unit emphasizes interdependence and interaction in the global community, and the relationship between the rights and responsibilities of the citizen in the world today. Students are introduced to the various international and nongovernmental organizations that work to promote peaceful interactions among nations. They examine the influence that the Declaration of Independence, the U.S. Constitution, and the Bill of Rights have had on other nations, and review the ways in which ideas about government in other countries have influenced the United States. Students learn the meaning of citizenship and the rights that come with citizenship. Finally, students consider the citizen's responsibility to work for the common good and the citizen's role in political activism.

UNIT OBJECTIVES

At the conclusion of this unit, students should be able to

- explain ways in which nations interact with one another
- identify responsibilities associated with certain basic rights of citizens
- explain the importance of citizen participation
- support their views on the extent to which a citizen should participate

UNIT INTRODUCTION

Read the introduction with your class. Introduce the Key Concepts and tell students that these ideas will be fully explained in the lessons of this unit. The illustrations throughout the unit are teaching tools for reviewing and reinforcing learning. Use them as you find appropriate.

UNIT PROJECT (OPTIONAL)

Ask your students to write the Key Concepts in their notebooks and write definitions based on their current knowledge. They can change and add to these initial definitions as the unit progresses.

unit SIX

KEY CONCEPTS

citizen

international law

nation-state

naturalized citizen

legal permanent resident

You have studied the basic ideas of our constitutional democracy. You have learned about our government's responsibility to protect the basic rights of the people and promote the common welfare. This unit deals with a question of equal or greater importance: what is the role of the citizen?

This book will not answer this question for you. The answer is one you must arrive at yourself. This unit raises some important ideas that you might find useful in deciding what your responsibilities as a citizen are.

What is the relationship of the United States to other nations in the world?

2 8

LESSON PURPOSE

In this lesson you will learn some ways in which countries interact with one another. You will also learn how the ideas about government in the Declaration of Independence and in the U.S. Constitution and Bill of Rights have influenced other countries.

When you finish this lesson, you should be able to explain how countries in the world interact with one another. You should be able to explain how American ideas about freedom and government have influenced people in other countries.

OVERVIEW

In this lesson, students learn about the role of the United States in the international community. They learn about nation-states, international law, and some nongovernmental international organizations that work to promote peaceful interactions among nations. Students review the powers given by the Constitution to our government for the purpose of dealing with other nations, as well as how other countries have influenced our ideas about government.

As the lesson concludes, students reexamine the Declaration of Independence, the Constitution, and the Bill of Rights, and recognize how the democratic ideas expressed in these documents have influenced other nations. Finally, students consider how countries interact and influence one another.

OBJECTIVES

At the conclusion of this lesson, students should be able to

- define nation-states and international law
- explain the ways in which nations interact
- explain how other countries have influenced the United States
- identify ways in which the Declaration of Independence, Constitution, and Bill of Rights have influenced other nations
- describe how countries influence each other

TEACHING PROCEDURES

INTRODUCTORY ACTIVITY

Have students read the Lesson Purpose. Ask them to think of different ways countries might interact with each other. Some examples might include space missions held jointly with other countries, one nation working with another when a disaster hits, or nations conducting trade. Write these ideas on the board or on chart paper. Refer to this list of ideas as students read the lesson, adding any new ideas or insights students have gained as they progress through the lesson. To prepare, you might want to have a collection of newspapers, newsmagazines, or information about specific current events related to topics in this lesson.

Write the Terms to Understand on the board or use a vocabulary-building activity of your choice. Have students look up the words in the Glossary at the back of their text. Ask them to look for these words as they read the lesson.

READING, DISCUSSION, AND RESEARCH

What are nation-states?
Who has authority over nation-states?

Have students read these two sections. Provide the class with newspaper or magazine articles about various nation-states. Have them select examples of ways in which nation-states exercise their sovereignty. Ask if they see any potential problems that might exist between any of the nation-states they have identified from the newspaper or magazine. Explain that although nation-states are sovereign entities with no international authority governing them, this does not mean that they lack rules and methods for cooperation.

TERMS TO UNDERSTAND

humanitarian
international law
nation-state
United Nations

What are nation-states?

There are many countries in the world. A country is also called a **nation-state**. The government of a nation-state claims the authority to govern the people who live within its territory.

The government of a nation-state also makes and carries out agreements with other nation-states. Today there are more than 200 nation-states in the world. Some are tiny countries such as Monaco and Singapore. Others are very large countries such as China and Russia.

Who has authority over nation-states?

At the international level, there is no organization with formal political power comparable to that of the nation-state. There is no international government that has authority over the world's nation-states. That is why each nation-state is said to be sovereign. By sovereign we mean that a country has the right to be free from outside interference within its boundaries.

Nation-states often agree to cooperate with each other. For example, letters

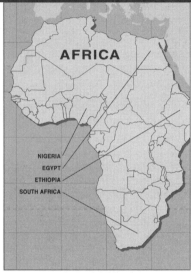

AFRICA

NIGERIA
EGYPT
ETHIOPIA
SOUTH AFRICA

What is government's role in the nation-state?
What are some examples of nation-states?

mailed in one country arrive at their destination in another country. Telephone services function worldwide. Airplanes take off from one country and land in another. Nations trade goods and services daily. These few examples show that countries can live in peace and cooperate in their means of dealing with each other.

In what ways might nation-states agree to cooperate with each other?

What is international law?

One thing that makes interactions among countries possible is a system of international law. **International law** consists of those rules that regulate how countries behave toward one another. International law is usually made by treaties that nation-states make among themselves.

It is up to each nation-state to enforce its treaties. For example, Article VI of the U.S. Constitution says, among other things,

> This Constitution, and the Laws of the United States...and all treaties made under the Authority of the United States, shall be the supreme law of the Land.

This means that all treaties that the United States makes with other nations become part of our national laws, and they have to be enforced by the federal government.

There is no international police organization to enforce international law. This does not mean that it is impossible to make nations live up to their responsibilities to each other. Some nations use economic, political, or military pressure to keep other nations in line.

How do nations of the world interact with each other?

Today, the nations of the world are increasingly dependent on each other. Nations have many ways of interacting. Here are some common examples:

- **Cultural, science, and business exchanges**
  People travel all over the world. People living in different countries share ideas. Doctors, scientists, educators, and business people from many countries meet to share advances in their fields. Students and teachers live with families in

What is international law?

Assign this section to students to read. Then, have them refer to the articles they found in newspapers or magazines in the previous activity. Ask them to locate any references to international law. Generate a class discussion about whether students believe that an international police organization to enforce international law should exist. You can continue this discussion when students read "What international organizations promote interaction among nations?" on the next page.

READING, DISCUSSION, AND ACTIVITY

How do nations of the world interact with each other?

Have students refer to the list that was generated in the Introductory Activity. Write the six categories from the reading on the board and have students place their examples of interaction in the appropriate categories. Ask students to explain each category in their own words. Allow them to add to the list at this time, or have them look for more examples as homework and add them the next day.

READING, DISCUSSION, AND RESEARCH

What international organizations promote interaction among nations?

You might want to have students look for examples of the work of the United Nations (UN) as well as references to the work of the nongovernmental organizations (NGOs) in newspapers, magazines, and on the Internet. Then, have students read this section. Refer them to the question posed in the previous section where they were asked if they believe an international police organization should exist. Discuss with them the role of the UN. Ask students if they believe the role of the UN should be to act as an international police organization. Ask if they think the UN is effective as an organization that promotes peace, cooperation, and respect for human rights. Require that they explain their reasoning.

other countries to learn their language and to learn about their culture. Artists show their work in the museums of other countries.

- **Humanitarian aid**
  The term **humanitarian** means to show concern for the pain and suffering of others. During natural disasters such as floods and earthquakes, countries help the victims in other countries by giving humanitarian aid. Countries send medicine, food, and shelter to suffering people. Individuals and organizations also respond to natural disasters.

- **Trade**
  Countries buy and sell factory goods, farm products, and services to one another.

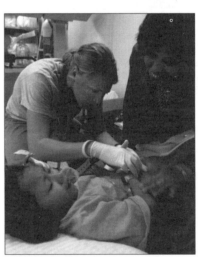

Do you think nations have a responsibility to provide humanitarian aid to the people of other nations? Why or why not?

- **Diplomacy**
  As you learned in Lesson 9, the term diplomacy means the practice of carrying on formal relationships with governments of other countries. The official representatives of countries meet and discuss issues important to their governments. They work together in a peaceful manner to find solutions to common problems.

- **Treaties and agreements**
  Countries make treaties and agreements. They agree to promote trade among themselves. They agree to do certain things to protect the environment. Some agree to help each other in time of war.

- **Military force**
  When two or more countries cannot solve their disagreements peacefully, they sometimes threaten to use military force. Sometimes, the disagreement results in a war.

What international organizations promote interaction among nations?

There is no single organization in the world that has the power to force countries to settle conflicts peacefully. There are some organizations that help countries reach agreements without going to war. The most important worldwide organization is the United Nations. A treaty signed in 1945, after World War II, created the United Nations. The purposes of the **United Nations,** according to its charter, are to maintain international peace and security; develop friendly

What is the United Nations? What does the United Nations do?

relations among nations; cooperate in solving international economic, social, cultural, and humanitarian problems; and promote respect for human rights and fundamental freedoms. Most nations of the world are members of the United Nations.

There are also regional treaty organizations that promote interaction among nations. These organizations deal with regional matters. The Organization of American States (OAS) promotes peace and security among all member nations in the Americas. Other examples of regional organizations are the League of Arab States and the Association of Southeast Asian Nations (ASEAN).

Many international organizations are not under direct government control. These are nongovernmental organizations, often

called NGOs. Some of these organizations provide humanitarian aid, for example, the International Federation of Red Cross and Red Crescent Societies. Others, such as Amnesty International, address human rights concerns.

What powers does the U.S. Constitution give to government to deal with other nations?

Each branch of the U.S. government has certain powers that come from the Constitution. The Constitution gives each branch the following powers to deal with other countries.

What powers does the U.S. Constitution give government to deal with other nations?

Divide the class into partner groups. Have them make a list of examples from current events that illustrate each of the powers mentioned in the text. You may wish to distribute some articles you have selected that illustrate each power, or ask students to find some. Try to acquire articles that depict all three branches of government exercising their powers: Congress, the president, and the U.S. Supreme Court. Examples might include Congress giving the president permission to send troops to an area of the world where conflict is taking place; the president meeting an ambassador from another nation; or the U.S. Supreme Court making a decision about a case that involves another country.

READING AND REVIEW

How have other countries influenced the United States?

This is a review section. Upon completion of the reading, ask students to volunteer examples of how other countries influence the United States. Examples might include food, dress, economics, festivals, medicine, music, quality of life issues, space exploration, sports, or vehicles. Students should give specific examples.

- **Congress**
  Congress has the power to regulate commerce with other countries and with the Indian tribes, declare war, approve treaties, approve ambassadors, raise and support armies, and punish piracies and crimes committed on the high seas.

- **President**
  The president has the power to make treaties and to name ambassadors, with the approval of Congress. The president is also the commander-in-chief of the military forces.

- **U.S. Supreme Court**
  The U.S. Supreme Court has the power to hear all cases affecting ambassadors; cases in which the United States is a party; and cases involving a foreign state, its citizens or subjects.

What do you think citizens of the United States gain from relationships with other countries? What do you think citizens in other countries gain from their relationships with us?

How have other countries influenced the United States?

Many of the ideas about government that you have studied started in other countries. The Founders learned about government from studying the histories of ancient Greece and Rome. From the Greeks and Romans, they learned about republican government, civic virtue, and the common good.

The European philosophers also had a great influence on the Founders. The theories of Baron de Montesquieu of France influenced their thinking about the separation of powers. The writings of John Locke of Great Britain guided their thinking about natural rights.

Colonial Americans also enjoyed the rights of Englishmen. Among these are the right to trial by jury, the right to be secure in one's home, and the right to express one's views about taxes through representatives in government.

How have the Declaration of Independence and the U.S. Constitution and Bill of Rights influenced other countries?

The United States has given many things to the world—advanced medical and industrial technology and the personal computer to name a few. The discoveries

How have democratic ideals from the United States influenced the people of other nations?

and inventions that we as a nation have shared with the world are important, but not as valuable or as lasting as the democratic ideals expressed in the Declaration of Independence and the U.S. Constitution and Bill of Rights. Some of these democratic ideals are listed below.

❶ Power comes from the people and the people are the ultimate source of the authority of their government.

❷ People in government are the servants of the people, not the masters of the people.

❸ All people are political equals. No person's vote counts more than another's.

❹ The people delegate their powers to their government. They consent to be governed only so long as those in power fulfill their responsibilities. They can take back those powers and change their government.

❺ The purpose of government is to protect the people's rights to life, liberty, and property, and to promote the common good.

❻ A nation's constitution should be approved by the people and serve as a higher law that everyone must obey, including the people and those serving in their government.

READING, DISCUSSION, AND ACTIVITY

How have the Declaration of Independence and the U.S. Constitution and Bill of Rights influenced other countries?

After reading this section with students, divide the class into groups of two or three. Write each of the numbered democratic ideals listed in the student book on slips of paper and have each group select one slip. Instruct the groups to draw a graphic that would demonstrate what the idea would look like. Have the groups share their graphics with the class, explaining how the graphic illustrates the democratic ideal. For example, if a group selects number three, the idea that "All people are political equals. No person's vote counts more than another's," the group might draw people walking to a voting booth and placing their votes in a box in one scene. In a second scene, the graphic would show all the votes being counted. The group would then explain that each vote receives the same value and that all votes are counted.

Do you agree with this Chinese student that democracy is worth risking one's life for? Why or why not?

❼ A nation's constitution should include a list of the rights of the people.

During the nineteenth and twentieth centuries, the American ideal of self-government spread around the world. People from many countries read and studied the ideas in the Declaration of Independence and in the U.S. Constitution and Bill of Rights. These documents influenced other countries to adopt similar ideas about government.

The American Revolution gave hope to many people in Europe and Latin America who wanted to promote democratic change in their own countries. The French Constitution of 1791 included many ideas from the United States. The Declaration of Independence and the U.S. Constitution and Bill of Rights also inspired Latin American leaders. In more recent years, when students in the People's Republic of China demonstrated for more freedoms from their government, they carried copies of the Declaration of Independence.

250

IDEAS FOR DISCUSSION

How do countries influence each other?

Work with a partner to discuss the following questions. Be prepared to share your ideas with the class.

❶ What events in the United States today might affect other people or countries of the world? Explain how.

❷ What events in the world today might affect U.S. citizens? Explain how.

❸ What do U.S. citizens gain from our relationships with other countries of the world? What do citizens in other countries gain from their relationships with the United States?

❹ Why is it important that countries be able to have a free exchange of ideas?

IDEAS FOR DISCUSSION

How do countries influence each other?

Introduce the activity as directed in the student text. As students share their ideas, point out similarities and differences. You may wish to write their responses on the board or on chart paper and highlight similarities.

1. What events in the United States today might affect other people or countries of the world? Explain how.

   Examples cited might include the catastrophe of September 11, 2001, the Iraq War, nuclear capacities and threats, environmental issues, human rights issues, trade agreements, or gas prices. Accept any reasonable response.

2. What events in the world today might affect U.S. citizens? Explain how.

   Conflicts between nations, diseases such as AIDS, oil production cuts by OPEC, the value of the U.S. dollar compared to the Euro, or laws passed by other nations that forbid the import of U.S. products. Accept any reasonable response.

3. What do U.S. citizens gain from our relationships with other countries of the world? What do citizens in other countries gain from their relationships with the United States?

   U.S. citizens might benefit from goods, services, or technology developed in other nations. Citizens in other nations might benefit from U.S. medical advances, humanitarian aid, or education in democracy.

4. Why is it important that countries be able to have a free exchange of ideas?

   The free exchange of ideas can promote solutions to cultural, economic, medical, or environmental problems.

LESSON REVIEW

The questions in the student book are intended to assess learning and to reinforce knowledge through discussion. The questions are directly related to the lesson objectives. You may wish to include additional questions developed by yourself or by students.

1. What is a nation-state?

   Countries are also known as nation-states. The government of a nation-state claims the authority to govern the people who live within its territory. The government of a nation-state also makes and carries out agreements with other nation-states.

2. List some ways in which countries interact with each other.

   Countries work together to establish and provide humanitarian aid, become involved in trade, develop and sign treaties and agreements, and provide military support when needed.

3. What powers does the U.S. Constitution give the national government to deal with other countries?

   The Constitution gives Congress the power to declare war, approve treaties, approve ambassadors, raise and support armies, and punish piracies and crimes committed at sea. The president is the commander in chief of the military forces. The U.S. Supreme Court hears all cases affecting ambassadors and all cases in which the U.S. is a party.

4. List some ideas in the Declaration of Independence and the U.S. Constitution and Bill of Rights that have influenced government in other countries.

   Examples include: power comes from the people, all people are political equals, the people consent to be governed, the purpose of government is not to be the master of the people, the purpose of government is to protect the rights of the people, a country's constitution is the highest law and everyone must obey it, and a country's constitution should include a list of the rights of the people.

ACTIVITIES

The suggested activities are intended to extend and apply learning outside the classroom. You may wish to have students complete one or more of the activities. Have them share their results with the class.

LESSON REVIEW

❶ What is a nation-state?

❷ List some ways in which countries interact with each other.

❸ What powers does the U.S. Constitution give the national government to deal with other countries?

❹ List some ideas in the Declaration of Independence and the U.S. Constitution and Bill of Rights that have influenced government in other countries.

ACTIVITIES

❶ Learn more about the United Nations. Why and how was the United Nations established? What does the United Nations do? Share what you learned with your class.

❷ Suppose you make a telephone call to a friend or relative in Mexico or in France. Suppose you send a letter to China using a stamp from the United States. Learn about international agreements that make it possible for your telephone call or letter to reach its destination. Find information about the Universal Postal Union or the International Telecommunications Union.

❸ Choose one of the following countries: China, Colombia, Egypt, France, Indonesia, Israel, Mexico, Nigeria, Panama, Russia, Saudi Arabia, or Vietnam. Learn about the country's relationship with the United States in the past and today. Share what you learned with your class.

❹ Find an article of clothing or other item around your home. Examine the label. Where was the item made? What international agreements exist that regulate how such items are traded on world markets? Identify some items that are manufactured in your state and exported to other countries.

❺ The State Department is the cabinet position in charge of conducting our relations with other nations in the world. Who is the current Secretary of State? Explain some of his or her responsibilities. Write a brief biography of this person.

What are the rights and responsibilities of citizenship?

29

LESSON PURPOSE

In this lesson you will examine the meaning of citizenship and how one becomes a citizen of the United States. You will examine the rights of citizens as well as the responsibilities that accompany our citizenship in this nation. Finally, you will develop positions on what a citizen might do when he or she thinks that a law is unjust.

When you finish this lesson, you should be able to explain the meaning of citizenship and how one becomes a citizen of the United States. You should also be able to explain some of the rights of citizens and the responsibilities that accompany those rights.

OVERVIEW

In this lesson, students will learn what it means to be a citizen of the United States. Students will examine the rights and responsibilities that accompany the right of citizenship. Students will study the dilemma of what to do when a law conflicts with what a citizen thinks is right or just. Finally, students will grapple with what they believe are their own personal responsibilities of citizenship.

OBJECTIVES

At the conclusion of this lesson, students should be able to

- explain the meaning of citizenship and describe how someone becomes a citizen of the United States
- explain the rights of citizens and the basic responsibilities that accompany citizenship in the United States
- explain the procedure that can be used when a citizen thinks a law is unjust
- make and support their decisions using the suggested procedure on a specific issue

TEACHING PROCEDURES

INTRODUCTORY ACTIVITY

Have students brainstorm ideas as to what the term "citizenship" means. Answers might include belonging to a community, our state, and our country. Ask them how someone becomes a citizen. Ask them to think about what rights and responsibilities accompany being a citizen of the United States. They may mention personal rights to religion, association, or travel; political rights to vote, run for office, or due process; and economic rights to ownership of property, choice of work, or operation of a business. Make sure they address responsibilities, which might include getting an education, completing chores at home, doing homework, or obeying laws.

Ask students to read the Lesson Purpose. Explain the objectives of the lesson. Write the Terms to Understand on the board or use a vocabulary-building activity of your choice. You may want students to look up the words in the Glossary at the back of the text.

READING AND DISCUSSION

What does it mean to be a citizen?

Have students read this section. Have them explain in their own words what it means to be a citizen.

How does a person become a citizen of the United States?

Have students read and discuss this section. Write the words "citizen," "legal permanent resident," and "naturalized citizen" on the board. Ask students to define these terms in their own words and write the definitions on the board under the appropriate words. Make sure students are knowledgeable about the rights that citizens have and legal permanent residents do not have.

TERMS TO UNDERSTAND

citizen	personal responsibilities
civic responsibilities	political rights
economic rights	
legal permanent resident	
naturalized citizen	
personal rights	

What does it mean to be a citizen?

A **citizen** is a person who is a legal member of a self-governing community, such as a nation or state. In the United States, there are no degrees or classes of citizenship. In this country, citizenship does not depend on a person's race, gender, or ethnic origin. Every citizen is a full member of the political community.

A citizen is one person among equals. Each citizen possesses equal rights under the law. In addition, our rights as citizens come with certain responsibilities. It is also important to remember that under our federal system, Americans are citizens of both their state and the United States.

How does a person become a citizen of the United States?

Every person born in the United States is a citizen of this country. A person born in another country to parents who are citizens of the United States is also a citizen of this country.

A **legal permanent resident** is someone who is not a citizen of the United States

What is a citizen? Should some citizens have more rights than others? Why or why not?

but who is legally permitted to live here. Legal permanent residents enjoy most of the rights of citizens and like citizens

254

Should a person born in the United States automatically become a citizen? Why or why not?

they must obey the laws and pay their taxes. They have the same rights to due process as citizens.

Legal permanent residents are not full members of the political community because there are some rights that are reserved for citizens. Only citizens may vote in national elections, hold public office, or serve on juries.

In most cases, legal permanent residents can become citizens. An adult permanent resident may apply for citizenship after living in the United States legally for five years. Before becoming a citizen, the person must pass a test to show that he or she understands the history and Constitution of the United States. The person must be of good moral character and demonstrate the ability to communicate in English. A person who gets his or her citizenship in this way is a **naturalized citizen**. The minor child of a naturalized citizen becomes a citizen of the United States when the parents do.

What are the rights of citizens?

There are three categories of rights that are important to democracy and to American citizens. These are personal rights, political rights, and economic rights.

Personal rights are those rights that allow a person to do as he or she wishes so long as those actions are consistent with the public order and do not interfere with the rights of others. The following are some personal rights:

- freedom to associate with whomever one pleases
- freedom of conscience and religion
- freedom of expression for creativity
- freedom to have children
- freedom to live where one chooses
- freedom to have privacy
- freedom to travel

READING, DISCUSSION, AND ACTIVITY

What are the rights of citizens?
What responsibilities accompany
the basic rights of citizens?

Have students work with a partner and read these two sections. Have the partner groups fill out Handout D11 of this guide in their own words as they read these sections.

(continued next page)

After students finish reading and entering the information on the handout, discuss citizens' rights and responsibilities. Ask students if they believe there should be any additional rights or responsibilities added to the handout. If so, have students explain why these rights or responsibilities should be added.

Political rights are those rights that allow citizens to participate in the political process. Without these rights, democracy could not exist. The following are political rights:

- due process of law and fair procedures
- equal protection under the law
- freedom to examine the conduct of public officials
- freedom of expression for political purposes
- freedom of political association and assembly
- freedom to seek and hold public office
- freedom to serve on juries
- freedom to vote in free, fair, and regular elections

Economic rights are those rights needed to earn a living and to acquire and transfer property or to produce goods and services. The following are economic rights:

- freedom to acquire, use, and sell or give away property
- freedom to choose one's work
- freedom to enter into lawful contracts
- freedom to establish and operate a business
- freedom to join professional associations and labor unions

It is important to remember that it is reasonable and fair to place limits on most rights; they are not absolute. Most people argue that the only right that cannot be limited is freedom of belief. All other rights can be limited in certain situations. For example, you learned in an earlier lesson that freedom of expression

can be limited if and when it seriously harms or endangers others.

Some rights may be limited when they conflict with other rights or with other important values and interests. For example, the right to own and use property can conflict with our interest in having a safe and healthy environment.

What responsibilities accompany the basic rights of citizens?

With the rights of citizens of the United States come certain responsibilities. Citizens do not always agree on their responsibilities. Some responsibilities that Americans have agreed upon over the years are listed below.

Personal responsibilities are obligations that each person assumes individually. The following are examples of personal responsibilities:

- accepting the consequences of one's actions

- adhering to moral principles

- behaving in a civil manner

- considering the rights and interests of others

- supporting one's family

- taking care of one's self

Civic responsibilities are obligations that each person has to society. The following are examples of civic responsibilities:

- being informed about public issues

- voting and deciding how to vote

- keeping watch over political

What are some examples of your responsibilities as a citizen of the United States?

leaders and governmental agencies and taking appropriate action if they do not follow constitutional principles

- obeying the laws

- participating in civic groups

- paying taxes

- respecting the rights of others

- serving as a juror

- serving in the armed forces

Citizens must not only be aware of their rights. They must also learn to use their rights responsibly. Fulfilling personal and civic responsibilities is a necessity in a self-governing, free, and just society.

257

READING AND DISCUSSION

Must you obey a law you think is unjust?

Have students read this section. Discuss with them the examples provided in the text, and emphasize the potential consequences for choosing to break a law, but explain that in some extreme situations, it may be a choice some people make. Ask students to provide any additional examples they can think of or have known someone to experience.

Why did Henry David Thoreau (above) and Dr. Martin Luther King Jr. (below) practice civil disobedience? What should a citizen consider before deciding to disobey the law?

Must you obey a law you think is unjust?

When laws or governmental actions conflict with a citizen's views of what is right and wrong, the citizen faces a difficult decision. In our system of government, you have a right to try to have laws changed. There are many ways that you and others can work to change laws that you think are unjust. Until you get them changed, however, you are held responsible for obeying the laws.

Suppose a law requires you to do something you believe is wrong. Must you obey the law? Some people argue that since no government is perfect, a citizen's responsibility to obey the law has limits. In their view, if a law is unjust, the citizen has no responsibility to obey it.

Deciding to disobey a law is a serious step. Disobeying the law has consequences that the citizen must be prepared to accept. Such consequences might include paying fines and even going to jail.

Throughout history, many citizens have accepted the consequences of disobeying the law. In the 1800s the famous American philosopher Henry David Thoreau chose to go to jail rather than pay a tax to support slavery and the Mexican-American War. In the 1950s and 1960s, Dr. Martin Luther King Jr. and others chose to go to jail to protest racial segregation laws. During the Vietnam War, many young men burned their draft cards and refused to serve in the armed forces because they believed the war was unjust.

What responsibilities of citizens are portrayed in this picture?

What are your responsibilities as a citizen?

You have learned a great deal about our nation's government from studying this book. You also have learned about some of the rights and responsibilities of citizenship. You and all citizens will be faced with difficult decisions about your role in a democratic society.

What commitment are you willing to make to the basic principles of our government? How will you decide which of your rights, desires, or interests may have to take second place to your responsibility to the common good? It is your responsibility as a citizen to make these difficult decisions.

What are your responsibilities as a citizen?

Have students read this section and reflect on what they have learned about responsibilities after reading this lesson. Ask them to write their reflections in an essay.

SOLVE THE PROBLEM

What decision would you make?

Divide the class into groups of three to five students. Make sure students understand the decision-making steps that are provided. Allow time for the groups to work through Gail's dilemma using the steps suggested. You may wish to provide poster paper and markers, or use the board, so that the groups can list the alternatives, advantages and disadvantages, and decisions that they will present to the class. Conclude the activity by having the groups discuss their decisions and the rationale they used to reach their decisions. Accept any reasonable responses offered by the groups.

1. What rights do you think Gail has in this situation?

   Gail's rights include freedom of expression, freedom of association, and freedom of political association and assembly.

2. What responsibilities accompany these rights?

   Responsibilities include accepting the consequences of her actions, behaving in a civil manner, and being informed of public issues.

3. What are some alternative actions that Gail might take to solve her problem or reach a decision?

   Alternative 1: Gail could speak with the people who introduced the new policy and ask why they see her actions as a problem.

   Alternative 2: She could arrange a meeting with the officials and representatives from the student group.

   Alternative 3: She could write a letter for the school newspaper questioning the purpose and implementation of the policy.

4. List the advantages and disadvantages of each alternative.

   *Alternative 1: **Advantage:** Everyone would be able to express their ideas and questions could be answered. Perhaps a new policy could be created. **Disadvantage:** Not everyone may have an open mind to listen to what others have to say and may not be willing to change their minds about the new policy.*

What decision would you make?

Work in groups of three to five. Read the story, then work through each of the six steps that follow it. The step-by-step procedure can help you make a good decision. Finally, decide what you think Gail should do. Explain and defend your answer before the class.

A NEW SCHOOL POLICY

Gail was worried. Five of her friends were going to take part in a protest during the last period of school the next day. They were planning to demonstrate against the new school policy prohibiting the wearing of T-shirts with controversial slogans. Like her friends, Gail believed that this situation was unfair to the students. She believed that the T-shirts were legal and not vulgar or offensive. She felt strongly that this policy should be changed.

Gail was worried about what would happen if she joined the picket line. She worried that she might be suspended from school. If this happened it might affect her chances of being accepted by a college. She was also afraid that she might be arrested, especially if the demonstration got out of hand. An arrest on her record could keep her from getting a good job.

On the other hand, she wanted to show her views and help change what she thought was an unjust situation. What should Gail do?

❶ What rights do you think Gail has in this situation?

❷ What responsibilities accompany these rights?

❸ What are some alternative actions that Gail might take to solve her problem or reach a decision?

❹ List the advantages and disadvantages of each alternative.

❺ Decide what you think should be done, considering the advantages and disadvantages of the alternatives.

❻ Be prepared to explain the reasons for your decision and how that decision reflects the basic principles of our government.

After each group has presented its decision, you may wish to discuss the plans presented by the groups and vote to adopt the plan the majority favors. Or, discuss how the procedure above could be used in other situations in which citizens have to make difficult decisions.

Would you protest against a school policy that you thought was unfair, even at the risk of being suspended? Why or why not?

Alternative 2: **Advantage:** *If the officials hear the concerns of the student representatives, they might be willing to revise the new policy.* **Disadvantage:** *A compromise might not be made about the new policy and students would become frustrated.*

Alternative 3: **Advantage:** *Gail's ideas would be expressed and read by a large audience, who in turn could add support to her cause.* **Disadvantage:** *Students and staff might not read her article or people might not feel compelled to support her cause.*

5. Decide what you think should be done, considering the advantages and disadvantages of the alternatives.

   Accept reasonable student responses, making sure that the groups do consider both the advantages and disadvantages for each of their proposed alternatives.

6. Be prepared to explain the reasons for your decision and how that decision reflects the basic principles of our government.

   Make sure that the groups provide reasonable and sound support for their decisions and that the decisions reflect the basic principles of our government.

 see next student page

LESSON REVIEW

The questions in the student book are intended to assess learning and to reinforce knowledge through discussion. The questions are directly related to the lesson objectives. You may wish to include additional questions developed by yourself or by students.

1. What does the term citizen mean?

   A citizen is a person who is a legal member of a self-governing community.

2. Who is a citizen of the United States?

   A person born in the United States or born in another country to parents who are citizens of the United States is a citizen of the United States. People from other countries who have taken a test and an oath to uphold

(continued next page)

the Constitution are naturalized citizens. In addition, minor children of naturalized citizens become citizens when their parents are naturalized.

3. How can noncitizens acquire citizenship in this country?

Noncitizens can acquire citizenship by living in the United States for five years, passing a history and Constitution test, having good moral character, and communicating in English.

4. What are the personal, political, and economic rights of citizens?

Personal rights are those rights that allow a person to do as he or she wishes as long as those actions are consistent with the public order and do not interfere with the rights of others, such as freedom of expression, religion, association, assembly, privacy, etc. Political rights are those that allow citizens to participate in the political process, such as voting, holding office, serving on juries, receiving due process and equal protection of the law, etc. Economic rights are those that allow citizens to earn a living, acquire property, or produce goods and services, such as choosing one's work, establishing a business, and joining professional unions and associations.

5. What responsibilities accompany our basic rights?

Personal responsibilities are the obligations each person assumes individually, such as accepting the consequences for one's actions, behaving in a civil manner, and supporting one's family. Civic responsibilities are the obligations each person has to society, such as being informed about public issues, obeying the laws, paying taxes, serving in the armed forces, etc.

6. What are some consequences to consider when deciding whether to challenge a law that you think is unjust?

When you think a law is unjust and you decide to challenge it, you may have to go to jail or pay a fine. These are considerations that you will have to consider before you decide to take any actions that are not lawful.

ACTIVITIES

The suggested activities are intended to extend and apply learning outside the classroom. You may wish to have students complete one or more of the activities. Have them share their results with the class.

LESSON REVIEW

1. What does the term citizen mean?

2. Who is a citizen of the United States?

3. How can noncitizens acquire citizenship in this country?

4. What are the personal, political, and economic rights of citizens?

5. What responsibilities accompany our basic rights?

6. What are some consequences to consider when deciding whether to challenge a law that you think is unjust?

ACTIVITIES

1. Write a short essay in which you describe the qualities of good citizens in a constitutional democracy. Explain why you think these qualities are necessary.

2. Debate the following questions with groups of three or four students.

   - What should a person do when he or she thinks that a law is unjust? Give examples to support your opinion.

   - Suppose you cannot agree on what is in the common good. Should you pursue your own interests or still try to consider the interests of others? Explain your answer and provide examples.

3. Learn more about resident aliens in the United States. Use the Internet to do some research. In what regions of the country do a majority of resident aliens live? What motivates resident aliens to want to live in the United States?

4. Learn more about individuals who have become naturalized citizens of the United States. Here is a list of people you might want to research in your library or on the Internet.

   - Madeleine Albright
   - Albert Einstein
   - Marcus Garvey
   - Andrew S. Grove
   - Henry Kissinger
   - Chien-Shiung Wu

5. Develop a poster that illustrates the rights of citizens and the responsibilities that those rights carry.

6. Does modern technology make the right to privacy easier or harder to protect? Write a report to share with your class that deals with the issues of privacy today.

How might citizens participate in civic affairs?

30

LESSON PURPOSE

In this lesson you will learn about one of the most important rights of citizenship. This is the right to participate in governing our nation. In this lesson the different ways you might participate in your government and in voluntary organizations outside of government will be discussed. The lesson also suggests things to consider when deciding whether you should participate.

When you finish the lesson, you should be able to support your views on whether, and to what extent, a citizen should participate in government and in voluntary organizations.

OVERVIEW

In this lesson, students learn about civic participation. They will appreciate that the role of monitoring and influencing government is one of the most important responsibilities of citizens. They recall previous learning as they review constitutional principles and consider what actions they might take to fulfill their role as citizens.

Students consider how to participate in civil society—voluntary associations outside of government—in order to achieve their goals. Be sure that students understand that there are often alternative ways to deal with society's problems other than by government intervention. Sometimes government may take the lead, but in other instances, participating in the voluntary associations of civil society is an alternative form of tackling social problems and of civic participation.

Students also examine some criteria to help them decide how they might participate. Students are asked to consider how participating in government relates to the achievement of their personal goals. They learn how to engage in political action to solve a problem and to identify the advantages and disadvantages of participating in political actions. The lesson concludes with a discussion about the importance of citizen participation in a democracy.

OBJECTIVES

At the conclusion of this lesson, students should be able to

- list various ways that citizens can participate in government
- develop and support positions on why and how much a citizen should participate
- explain how participation is related to the purpose of our constitutional government

TEACHING PROCEDURES

INTRODUCTORY ACTIVITY

Have students read the Lesson Purpose. Explain the objectives of the lesson. Write the Terms to Understand on the board or use a vocabulary-building activity of your choice. You may want students to look up the words in the Glossary at the back of the text.

READING, DISCUSSION, AND RESEARCH

What role should citizens have in government?

Ask students to think about and discuss the question posed in the section. Also, ask them to look in newspapers or check the Internet to find out what voluntary organizations citizens can participate in to take part in public affairs. After they have read the section, have students examine their own participation in their most recent school election or any other election process that is relevant. Using a show of hands and a student recorder at the chalkboard, ask the first question. Have the recorder tally the results. Use questions two through seven to guide the discussion.

1. How many members of the class participated in the last election? How many did not?

2. What reasons did individuals have for participating? For not participating?

3. What effect did participation have on those who worked for candidates? On those who voted? On those who did not?

4. Would the outcome have been different if the nonparticipants had voted? Should citizens be forced to vote?

5. Will you participate any differently in the next school election? Why?

6. Do you expect that your role in school elections is similar or different from the role you will take in governmental elections when you turn 18? Explain that citizens aged 18 to 24 are among the least likely to vote.

7. How does low voter turnout affect the political power of young people?

TERMS TO UNDERSTAND

civic life
civic participation
constitutional principle
influence
monitor
political action
social action

What role should citizens have in government?

As you learned in the last lesson, in the United States each citizen is a full and equal member of the political community. Each citizen has certain basic rights and responsibilities. You also learned that government and citizens are both responsible for protecting the rights of individuals. Both are also responsible for promoting the common good.

Citizens have other vital roles in our government. One important role that citizens fulfill is to monitor the decisions and actions of government. To **monitor** means to keep watch over something. Citizens monitor government to be informed about what the government is doing in their name. They also monitor government to ensure that it serves the purposes for which it was created.

Another important role of citizens is to attempt to influence the decisions and actions of government. To **influence** means to have an effect on or to cause changes in something. It is the right of citizens to try to influence the decisions and actions of government that affect our lives.

From where do you get the right to influence your government?

In a sense, citizenship is an office of government. Some people might say that it is the highest office of government because citizens are the source of government's authority. Like any other office, citizenship carries important responsibilities.

Civic participation means taking part in formal political processes and taking part in community activities outside of government. Millions of Americans participate in thousands of voluntary organizations and associations. These organizations seek to improve the life of the community in many different ways. Some benefit the poor, sick, or old people. Other organizations are concerned with the environment, health care, or the needs of children. They deal with many other community problems and issues.

Participating in these organizations gives community members the means to deal with community issues. It also allows them to participate in the way the organizations are run.

Government must deal with some matters such as arresting lawbreakers or establishing rules for building safety. There are other issues where government works with voluntary organizations to solve community problems. In other cases, voluntary organizations act by themselves to address community issues.

How much participation in government should citizens be willing to contribute?

Some citizens do not participate in government. They do not vote or take part in other ways. Some people, however, believe that citizens have a responsibility to participate.

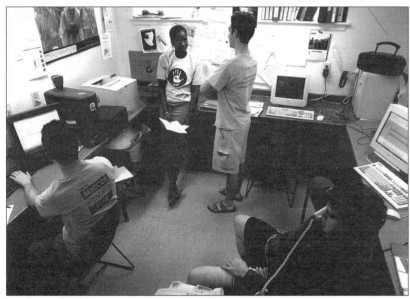

What might be the advantages or disadvantages of joining volunteer organizations to influence government?

How much participation in government should citizens be willing to contribute?

After students read this section, ask them to provide examples of how citizens can monitor and influence government. You might have them look in newspapers for examples of citizens participating in this way. Make a class poster of all the examples students can find.

Make sure students understand the bicycle shop analogy. They will be asked to recall their reasoning later in the lesson.

How would you respond to a poorly fixed bike from the bike shop? Would you respond in a similar way to something the government had done poorly?

Deciding whether to participate in government and how much time to spend is important. To make good decisions, you must think about such things as

❶ the purposes of government

❷ how important your rights are to you

❸ how satisfied you are with the way government is working

An example might help.

If you took your bike in for repairs, you would make sure that the shop repaired bicycles, not cars or toasters. Then when you claimed your bike, you would check it to make sure that they did what you had hired them to do.

If you thought they did a good job but your bike broke the next week, you might bring it back, but you would check or monitor their work more closely.

Suppose the shop wanted to do more repairs than those you requested. You would want to participate in making that decision. If you were denied the right to participate in the decision, you might be very upset, especially when you got the bill.

If the shop did a poor job on the repairs again, you would not go back nor would you recommend them to your friends. You might call various agencies to complain or you might even try to force them out of the bike repair business.

The same is true of government. We should make sure that the people we elect are capable of doing the job we are choosing them for. Once they get the job, we should monitor them to make sure they are doing their job of representing us correctly. If they do a good job, we might not watch them as closely. If they do a bad job, we might check them more closely and might even decide to replace them. Because our officials make decisions that affect us, we are entitled to participate in those decisions.

Of course, not all jobs have to be accomplished by government. Americans are famous for doing many things for themselves. We organize groups to accomplish any number of things. These include building neighborhood swimming pools, discussing foreign policy issues, or improving our communities in hundreds of ways. Participating in these activities is also civic participation.

Some citizens mostly participate in formal governmental processes. Others participate mostly in volunteer groups. Many citizens take part in both forms of civic activity. Americans realize how important civic participation is. When civic participation declines, our democracy declines. It is not just others who are responsible for the civic health of our democracy. We are all responsible.

What are some of the ways citizens can monitor the decisions and actions of government?

How might citizens participate in their government?

Lead students in a discussion that illustrates civic participation. They can participate by being involved in the civic life of their community and by accepting the responsibilities of citizenship. They also might be either leaders or members of nongovernmental organizations that work for the common good.

How might citizens participate in their government?

Civic life is the public life of citizens. Civic life is different, but not necessarily separate, from private or personal life. In our personal life, we concern ourselves with our particular interests, such as getting an education or having a good job. Our civic life, on the other hand, is concerned with our own interests as well as the common affairs and interests of our community and nation.

Civic life includes the things that we do to carry out our responsibilities and roles as citizens. One example of this is monitoring and influencing the decisions of government. Sometimes our actions can be both personal and civic. These include being a decision-maker or being a participant in nongovernmental organizations. For example, we might

- direct the activities or policies of organizations and associations. These could include voting for leaders or holding a leadership position yourself.

- take part in an organization's meetings and community activities such as rallies, fundraising, or writing, or handing out pamphlets and articles.

What are some examples of civic life?

IDEAS FOR DISCUSSION

Should citizens participate in their government?

One way to understand the role of citizens in government is to think about the basic principles of our Constitution. In this case, we are discussing constitutional principles. A **constitutional principle** is an essential idea that we as a nation believe about good government. These are principles that you have learned during your study of this text.

Work with a partner. Read aloud each of the basic principles of government listed below. Then respond to the three questions.

CONSTITUTIONAL PRINCIPLES

- common good
- consent of the governed
- constitutional government
- individual rights
- popular sovereignty
- representative government

❶ What is the meaning of each basic principle of government listed?

❷ What do each of these principles imply about the role of citizens in their government?

❸ What actions might citizens take to fulfill the roles of citizens that you have identified?

IDEAS FOR DISCUSSION

Should citizens participate in their government?

Have students work with a partner to complete this activity. Have students use Handout D12 of this guide to fill in the chart with their responses to the three questions. Have partner groups share their responses.

Possible answers:

Constitutional principle	Meaning of principle	Implications for the role of the citizen	Actions citizens might take
Common good	What is good for all	Citizens do what is good for all people	Join the armed forces, serve on juries
Consent of the governed	People agree on government	People must give their consent	Participate in elections, run for office
Constitutional government	Government with limits	Citizens must obey and follow these limits	Observe the laws set out in the Constitution, pay taxes
Individual rights	Rights that each person has	Individuals have their rights respected by others	The rights of others are neither interfered with nor restricted
Popular sovereignty	The people have the ultimate power in government	The people must monitor the actions of government	The people check what government is doing and how it is exercising its power
Representative government	The people elect officials to exercise power (govern) on their behalf	Elected officials are ultimately responsible to the people who elect them	People choose their representatives by voting. These elected officials can be removed from office if they perform poorly

IDEAS FOR DISCUSSION

How might participating in government help us achieve our personal goals?

Have students recall the analogy of the bicycle repair shop. Then have students work with a partner and read the opening paragraphs in this section. After reading, the partners should then reflect on the personal goals suggested and respond to the four questions. Have students share their responses with the whole class.

Possible answers:

1. Why are these goals important to you?

   Students may indicate that these goals will allow them to live healthy, productive lives. The goals will also provide for the common good of the community and everyone who lives in the community.

2. How might these personal goals be related to the common good? In other words, how might your achievement of these goals help make our country better?

   Students may indicate that a healthy, educated, safe country would be a more productive country. These are common goals that everyone would strive to achieve. They would help to unite the community in working for the same outcome.

3. How might your participation in government help you attain these goals for yourself and for the community?

   Students may indicate that the only way for government to be aware of the personal goals of its citizens would be for people to participate in government and let their ideas be known. The more citizens participate in government, the more government is held accountable to the people.

4. How might your participation in civic life help you attain these goals for yourself and for the community?

   Students might indicate that participating in civic life offers an additional or in some cases an alternative way of acting to attain their goals. Civic organization members can take part in solving community, regional, or national problems.

IDEAS FOR DISCUSSION

How might participating in government help us achieve our personal goals?

As individuals, we have personal goals that we would like to achieve, and that is one reason we participate in government.

Sometimes our personal goals are linked to the common good. A personal goal might be to get a good education. It is also in the common good that communities provide good schools so that everyone in the community can get a good education and be able to contribute to the community. Everyone should have the opportunity to realize that goal.

Suppose that you have four personal goals. They are to

- live in a safe and orderly neighborhood
- get a good education
- live in a healthy environment
- feel that you are a full member of your community and not an outsider

DISCUSS THESE QUESTIONS WITH A PARTNER

❶ Why are these goals important to you?

❷ How might these personal goals be related to the common good? In other words, how might your achievement of these goals help make our country better?

❸ How might your participation in government help you attain these goals for yourself and the community?

❹ How might your participation in civic life help you attain goals for yourself and the community?

How can we determine what serves the common good?

What are the advantages and disadvantages of participation in civic life?

In small groups read the list of ways in which citizens can participate in political and other forms of civic action. Then discuss the three questions at the end. Share your responses with your class.

WAYS CITIZENS CAN PARTICIPATE

- looking for information about government officials and activities in newspapers, magazines, the Internet, and reference materials and judging its accuracy
- voting in local, state, and national elections
- participating in political discussions
- signing a petition
- writing letters to elected representatives
- contributing money to a political party or candidate
- attending meetings to gain information, discuss issues, or lend support
- campaigning for a candidate
- lobbying for laws that are of special interest to you
- taking part in marches, boycotts, sit-ins, or other forms of protest
- serving as a juror
- running for public office

- holding public office
- serving the country through military or other service
- joining independent civic groups and attending meetings
- holding office in and giving financial support to independent civic groups
- taking part in solving public problems by joining voluntary groups, independent of or in cooperation with government
- discussing civic problems and issues informally with friends and neighbors
- becoming informed by reading, watching television programs, or doing Internet research about public problems by yourself or with others

❶ What are the advantages and disadvantages of each form of participation given?

❷ Are all these forms of participation equally important in protecting our basic rights and the common good? Why or why not?

❸ In which of these activities are you most likely to participate?

271

What are the advantages and disadvantages of participation in civic life?

Place students in groups of three to five, and have them examine the ways citizens can participate as listed in the activity. Students should respond to the three questions and share their responses with the class.

Possible student responses:

1. What are the advantages and disadvantages of each form of participation given?

   Instruct the groups to make two columns—one for advantages and one for disadvantages. They should write their ideas in the appropriate column. Accept any reasonable answers.

2. Are all these forms of participation equally important in protecting our basic rights and the common good? Why or why not?

   Students might indicate that the level of importance will depend on the personal goals of each citizen. The conclusion should be that participation is what is important.

   Some students might think that voting is the most important means of participating because this is the way people can have their voices heard and remove people from office who are not representing the common good of the people.

3. In which of these activities are you most likely to participate?

   Students might indicate that being informed of issues is the most important. Citizens need to be aware of the issues and how to correct them, if necessary. The most important responses are those that students support through rational thought.

READING AND DISCUSSION

What is political action and what is social action?

As students read this section, help them understand the two methods available to citizens who wish to address problems in their community—social action and political action. Emphasize that political action can be either informal or formal. Students could then look for examples of political and social action in newspapers or newsmagazines.

What is political action and what is social action?

There are two general ways that citizens can address problems in the community through participation in civic life. They are social action and political action.

Political action comes in two forms: formal and informal.

- Formal political action means voting in elections, petitioning government officials, seeking and holding public office, and similar activities.

- Informal political action means face-to-face meetings with public officials, writing to newspapers stating your opinion on issues, conducting email or telephone campaigns, attending marches and demonstrations, and similar activities.

There is a wide range of political actions that citizens can engage in when attempting to influence the actions of government. These actions are relevant at local, state, and national levels.

To help solve a crime problem you might meet with government officials requesting that they provide more police services to protect your neighborhood. In dealing with poverty, you might create a government program such as a food bank to feed the hungry. Then you might work to get government to adopt and pay for the program.

Social action means that individuals and groups solve community problems without relying on government to do it for them. If you are dealing with crime in your neighborhood, you might form a neighborhood watch group. If you are dealing with poverty, you might work in a food bank organized by a charitable organization.

Why should I participate in the affairs of my community?

Participation in government is in our self-interest. The amount of time spent participating will probably depend on how well we think our elected officials are doing. When everything is going well, we might spend less time. If we are pleased with government, we might vote and do little else. When we are concerned

What are some examples of social action?

that government is not meeting our needs or is violating our rights, we might spend more time. If we are dissatisfied, we might engage in a variety of types of action.

Citizens must actively participate in the civic life of their community and nation if they want their voices heard. Citizenship in a democracy is more than a legal status. Democratic citizenship is a way of life that guides our relationships with other people and with government.

Democracy can exist only if it lives in the minds and hearts of its citizens. Citizens should do more than say they are committed to democracy. They should demonstrate their commitment by their participation. It is up to each citizen to determine the level and nature of her or his participation in the civic life of the community and nation.

At the end of the Constitutional Convention, Mrs. Samuel Powell asked Benjamin Franklin "Well, Doctor, what have we got, a Republic or a Monarchy?" Franklin replied, "A Republic, if you can keep it."
From the notes of James McHenry, delegate from Maryland

Why should I participate in the affairs of my community?

Read this section with your students. Lead a discussion of why it is important to participate in community affairs. Ask students if they can identify any issues or situations in their community or school that they believe are not in the people's best interest.

School issues might be a new tardy policy or dress code; community issues might be new regulations for riding skateboards or scooters on public streets; a state issue might be a new law that raises the age to obtain a driver's license to 18.

LESSON REVIEW

The questions in the student book are intended to assess learning and to reinforce knowledge through discussion. The questions are directly related to the lesson objectives. You may wish to include additional questions developed by yourself or by students.

1. How is political action different from social action?

   Political action relies on government to address a concern in the community. So, citizens need to influence, formally or informally, the actions of government. Social action does not rely on the actions of government, but rather on the concern and goodwill of citizens.

2. Why are both political and social action necessary?

   Political action is necessary for democracy to flourish. Government must be monitored by the people and influenced by the people to solve problems at local, state, and national levels. Social action is necessary so that the people in a community can solve their problems and improve the quality of their lives without depending on government.

3. How is citizen participation in political action related to the purposes of our government?

   The purpose of government is to protect the rights of its citizens. Citizen participation through political action will keep the citizens vigilant as they watch what the government is doing. This will prevent the government from abusing its power and interfering with citizen's rights.

4. Explain why participating in government is in our self-interest.

   When citizens concern themselves with their particular interests, they connect their personal life with their public life. This notion of civic life blends the concerns of our personal interests with the common affairs and interests of our community and nation.

ACTIVITIES

The suggested activities are intended to extend and apply learning outside the classroom. You may wish to have students complete one or more of the activities. Have them share their results with the class.

LESSON REVIEW

❶ How is political action different from social action?

❷ Why are both political and social action necessary?

❸ How is citizen participation in political action related to the purposes of our government?

❹ Explain why participating in government is in our self-interest.

ACTIVITIES

❶ Make a poster that demonstrates the different ways that citizens can participate in government. Take your own photos or use photographs from newspapers and magazines to illustrate each idea on your poster.

❷ Use the Internet to find information about political action groups in your community that work to monitor and influence the decisions and actions of government.

❸ Use the Internet to find information about social action groups in your community that work to address local community problems.

❹ Monitor the newspaper in your community for one week. Look for articles that describe citizens participating in local, state, or national government.

❺ Justice Louis Brandeis of the U.S. Supreme Court wrote, "The only title in our democracy superior to that of President is the title of citizen." Do you think that Justice Brandeis was correct? Write a short essay explaining your opinion.

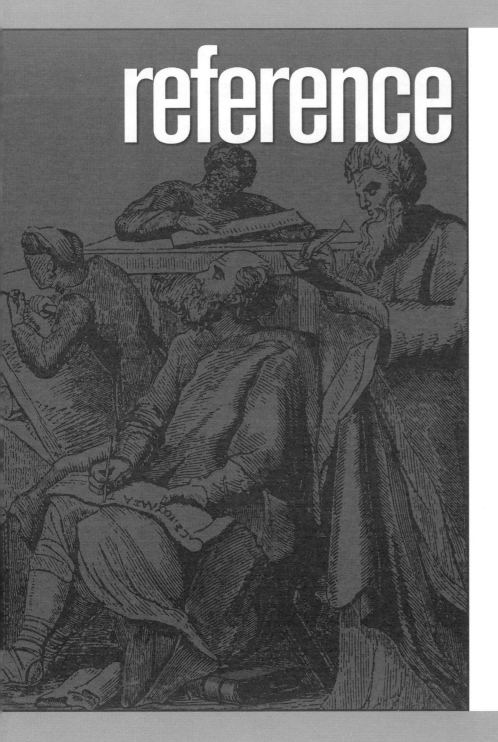

reference

THE DECLARATION OF INDEPENDENCE

**In CONGRESS,
July 4, 1776.
The unanimous
Declaration of the
thirteen united
States of America,**

WHEN in the Course of human Events, it becomes necessary for one People to dissolve the Political Bands which have connected them with another, and to assume among the Powers of the Earth, the separate and equal Station to which the Laws of Nature and of Nature's God entitle them, a decent Respect to the Opinions of Mankind requires that they should declare the causes which impel them to the Separation.

We hold these Truths to be self-evident, that all Men are created equal, that they are endowed by their Creator with certain unalienable Rights, that among these are Life, Liberty, and the Pursuit of Happiness—That to secure these Rights, Governments are instituted among Men, deriving their just Powers from the Consent of the Governed, that whenever any Form of Government becomes destructive of these Ends it is the Right of the People to alter or to abolish it, and to institute new Government, laying its Foundation on such Principles, and organizing its Powers in such Form, as to them shall seem most likely to effect their Safety and Happiness. Prudence, indeed, will dictate that Governments long established should not be changed for light and transient Causes; and accordingly all Experience hath shewn, that Mankind are more disposed to suffer, while Evils are sufferable, than to right themselves by abolishing the Forms to which they are accustomed. But when a long Train of Abuses and Usurpations, pursuing invariably the same Object, evinces a Design to reduce them under absolute Despotism, it is their Right, it is their Duty, to throw off such Government, and to provide new Guards for their future Security. Such has been the patient Sufferance of these Colonies; and such is now the Necessity which constrains them to alter their former Systems of Government. The History of the present King of Great-Britain is a History of repeated Injuries and Usurpations, all having in direct Object the Establishment of an absolute Tyranny over these States. To prove this, let Facts be submitted to a candid World.

He has refused his Assent to Laws, the most wholesome and necessary for the public Good.

He has forbidden his Governors to pass Laws of immediate and pressing Importance, unless suspended in their Operation till his Assent should be obtained; and when so suspended, he has utterly neglected to attend to them.

He has refused to pass other Laws for the Accommodation of large Districts of People, unless those People would relinquish the Right of Representation in the Legislature, a Right inestimable to them, and formidable to Tyrants only.

He has called together Legislative Bodies at Places unusual, uncomfortable, and distant from the Depository of their public Records, for the sole Purpose of fatiguing them into Compliance with his Measures.

He has dissolved Representative Houses repeatedly, for opposing with manly Firmness his Invasions on the Rights of the People.

He has refused for a long Time, after such Dissolutions, to cause others to be elected; whereby the Legislative Powers, incapable of Annihilation, have returned to the People at large for their exercise; the State remaining in the mean time exposed to all the Dangers of Invasions from without, and Convulsions within.

He has endeavored to prevent the Population of these States; for that Purpose obstructing the Laws for Naturalization of Foreigners; refusing to pass others to encourage their Migrations hither, and raising the Conditions of new Appropriations of Lands.

He has obstructed the Administration of Justice, by refusing his Assent to Laws for establishing Judiciary Powers.

He has made Judges dependent on his Will alone, for the Tenure of their Offices, and the Amount and Payment of their Salaries.

He has erected a Multitude of new Offices, and sent hither Swarms of Officers to harass our People and eat out their Substance.

He has kept among us, in Times of Peace, Standing Armies, without the consent of our Legislatures.

He has affected to render the Military independent of and superior to the Civil Power.

He has combined with others to subject us to a Jurisdiction foreign to our Constitution, and unacknowledged by our Laws; giving his Assent to their Acts of pretended Legislation:

For quartering large Bodies of Armed Troops among us:

For protecting them, by a mock Trial, from Punishment for any Murders which they should commit on the Inhabitants of these States:

For cutting off our Trade with all Parts of the World:

For imposing Taxes on us without our Consent:

For depriving us, in many Cases, of the Benefits of Trial by Jury:

For transporting us beyond Seas to be tried for pretended Offenses:

For abolishing the free System of English Laws in a neighbouring Province, establishing therein an Arbitrary Government, and enlarging its Boundaries, so as to render it at once an Example and fit Instrument for introducing the same absolute Rule into these Colonies:

For taking away our Charters, abolishing our most valuable Laws, and altering fundamentally the Forms of our Governments:

For suspending our own Legislatures, and declaring themselves invested with Power to legislate for us in all Cases whatsoever.

He has abdicated Government here, by declaring us out of his Protection and waging War against us.

He has plundered our Seas, ravaged our Coasts, burnt our Towns, and destroyed the Lives of our People.

He is, at this Time, transporting large Armies of foreign Mercenaries to compleat the Works of Death, Desolation, and Tyranny, already begun with circumstances of Cruelty and Perfidy, scarcely paralleled in the most barbarous Ages, and totally unworthy the Head of a civilized Nation.

He has constrained our fellow Citizens taken Captive on the high Seas to bear Arms against their Country, to become the Executioners of their Friends and Brethren, or to fall themselves by their Hands.

He has excited domestic Insurrections amongst us, and has endeavoured to bring on the Inhabitants of our Frontiers, the merciless Indian Savages, whose known Rule of Warfare, is an undistinguished Destruction, of all Ages, Sexes and Conditions.

In every stage of these Oppressions we have Petitioned for Redress in the most humble Terms: Our repeated Petitions have been answered only by repeated Injury. A Prince, whose Character is thus marked by every act which may define a Tyrant, is unfit to be the Ruler of a free People.

Nor have we been wanting in Attentions to our British Brethren. We have warned them from Time to Time of Attempts by their Legislature to extend an unwarrantable Jurisdiction over us. We have reminded them of the Circumstances of our Emigration and Settlement here. We have appealed to their native Justice and Magnanimity, and we have conjured them by the Ties of our common Kindred to disavow these Usurpations, which, would inevitably interrupt our Connections and Correspondence. They too have been deaf to the Voice of Justice and of Consanguinity. We must, therefore, acquiesce in the Necessity, which denounces our Separation, and hold them, as we hold the rest of Mankind, Enemies in War, in Peace, Friends.

We, therefore, the Representatives of the UNITED STATES OF AMERICA, in GENERAL CONGRESS, Assembled, appealing to the Supreme Judge of the World for the Rectitude of our Intentions, do, in the Name, and by Authority of the good People of these Colonies, solemnly Publish and Declare, That these United Colonies are, and of Right ought to be, FREE AND INDEPENDENT STATES; that they are absolved from all Allegiance to the British Crown, and that all political Connection between them and the State of Great Britain, is and ought to be totally dissolved; and that as FREE AND INDEPENDENT STATES, they have full Power to levy War, conclude Peace, contract Alliances, establish Commerce, and to do all other Acts and Things which INDEPENDENT STATES may of right do. And for the support of this Declaration, with a firm Reliance on the Protection of divine Providence, we mutually pledge to each other our Lives, our Fortunes, and our sacred Honor.

Signed by ORDER and
in BEHALF of the CONGRESS,

JOHN HANCOCK, PRESIDENT.

New-Hampshire

Josiah Bartlett,
Wm. Whipple,
Matthew Thornton.

Massachusetts-Bay

Saml. Adams,
John Adams,
Robt. Treat Paine,
Elbridge Gerry.

**Rhode-Island and
Providence, &c.**

Step. Hopkins,
William Ellery.

Connecticut

Roger Sherman,
Saml. Huntington,
Wm. Williams,
Oliver Wolcott.

New-York

Wm. Floyd,
Phil. Livingston,
Frans. Lewis,
Lewis Morris.

New-Jersey

Richd. Stockton,
Jno. Witherspoon,
Fras. Hopkinson,
John Hart,
Abra. Clark.

Pennsylvania

Robt. Morris,
Benjamin Rush,
Benja. Franklin,
John Morton,
Geo. Clymer,
Jas. Smith,
Geo. Taylor,
James Wilson,
Geo. Ross.

Delaware

Casar Rodney,
Geo. Read,
(Tho M:Kean.)

Maryland

Samuel Chase,
Wm. Paca,
Thos. Stone,
Charles Carroll,
of Carrollton.

Virginia

George Wythe,
Richard Henry Lee,
Ths. Jefferson,
Benja. Harrison,
Thos. Nelson, jr.,
Francis Lightfoot Lee,
Carter Braxton.

North-Carolina

Wm. Hooper,
Joseph Hewes,
John Penn.

South-Carolina

Edward Rutledge,
Thos. Heyward, junr.,
Thomas Lynch, junr.,
Arthur Middleton.

Georgia

Button Gwinnett,
Lyman Hall,
Geo. Walton.

THE CONSTITUTION OF THE UNITED STATES

PREAMBLE

We the People of the United States, in Order to form a more perfect Union, establish Justice, insure domestic tranquility, provide for the common defense, promote the general Welfare, and secure the Blessings of Liberty to ourselves and our Posterity, do ordain and establish this Constitution for the United States of America.

ARTICLE I

The Legislative Branch

Section 1

All legislative Powers herein granted shall be vested in a Congress of the United States, which shall consist of a Senate and House of Representatives.

Section 2

House of Representatives: Organization and Power of Impeachment

1. The House of Representatives shall be composed of Members chosen every second Year by the People of the several States, and the Electors in each State shall have the Qualifications requisite for Electors of the most numerous Branch of the State Legislature.

2. No Person shall be a Representative who shall not have attained to the Age of twenty five Years, and been seven Years a Citizen of the United States, and who shall not, when elected, be an Inhabitant of that State in which he shall be chosen.

3. [Representatives and direct Taxes shall be apportioned among the several States which may be included within this Union, according to their respective Numbers, which shall be determined by adding to the whole Number of free Persons, including those bound to Service for a Term of Years, and excluding Indians not taxed, three fifths of all other Persons.]* The actual Enumeration shall be made within three Years after the first Meeting of the Congress of the United States, and within every subsequent Term of ten Years, in such Manner as they shall by Law direct. The number of Representatives shall not exceed one for every thirty Thousand, but each State shall have at Least one Representative; and until such enumeration shall be made, the State of New Hampshire shall be entitled to choose three, Massachusetts eight, Rhode Island and Providence Plantations one, Connecticut five, New York six, New Jersey four, Pennsylvania eight, Delaware one, Maryland six, Virginia ten, North Carolina five, South Carolina five, and Georgia three.

4. When vacancies happen in the Representation from any State, the Executive Authority thereof shall issue Writs of Election to fill such Vacancies.

5. The House of Representatives shall choose their Speaker and other Officers; and shall have the sole Power of Impeachment.

Section 3

The Senate, Organization and Powers to Try Cases of Impeachment

1. The Senate of the United States shall be composed of two Senators from each State, [chosen by the Legislature thereof,]** for six Years; and each Senator shall have one Vote.

2. Immediately after they shall be assembled in Consequence of the first Election, they shall be divided as equally as may be into three Classes. The seats of the Senators of the first Class shall be vacated at the Expiration of the second Year, of the second Class at the Expiration of the fourth Year, and of the third Class at the Expiration of the sixth Year, so that one third may be chosen every second Year; [and if Vacancies happen by Resignation, or otherwise, during the Recess of the Legislature of any State, the Executive thereof may make temporary Appointments until the next Meeting of the Legislature, which shall then fill such Vacancies.]**

3. No Person shall be a Senator who shall not have attained to the Age of thirty Years, and been nine Years a Citizen of the United States, and who shall not, when elected, be an Inhabitant of that State for which he shall be chosen.

4. The Vice President of the United States shall be President of the Senate, but shall have no Vote, unless they be equally divided.

*Changed by Section 2 of the Fourteenth Amendment

**Changed by the Seventeenth Amendment

5. The Senate shall choose their other officers, and also a President pro tempore, in the Absence of the Vice President, or when he shall exercise the Office of President of the United States.

6. The Senate shall have the sole Power to try all Impeachments. When sitting for that Purpose, they shall be on Oath or Affirmation. When the President of the United States is tried, the Chief Justice shall preside; And no person shall be convicted without the Concurrence of two thirds of the Members present.

7. Judgment in Cases of Impeachment shall not extend further than to removal from Office, and disqualification to hold and enjoy any Office of honor, Trust or Profit under the United States; but the Party convicted shall nevertheless be liable and subject to Indictment, Trial, Judgment and Punishment, according to Law.

Section 4

Elections and Meeting of Congress

1. The Times, Places and Manner of holding Elections for Senators and Representatives shall be prescribed in each State by the Legislature thereof; but the Congress may at any time by Law make or alter such Regulations, except as to the Places of choosing Senators.

2. The Congress shall assemble at least once in every Year, and such Meeting shall be [on the first Monday in December,]* unless they shall by Law appoint a different Day.

Section 5

Congress's Rules of Procedure, Powers, Quorum, Journals, Meetings, Adjournments

1. Each House shall be the Judge of the Elections, Returns and Qualifications of its own Members, and a Majority of each shall constitute a Quorum to do Business; but a smaller Number may adjourn from day to day, and may be authorized to compel the Attendance of absent Members, in such Manner, and under such Penalties as each House may provide.

2. Each House may determine the Rules of its Proceedings, punish its members for disorderly Behavior, and, with the Concurrence of two thirds, expel a Member.

3. Each House shall keep a Journal of its Proceedings, and from time to time publish the same, excepting such Parts as may in their Judgement require Secrecy; and the Yeas and Nays of the Members of either House on any question shall, at the Desire of one fifth of those Present, be entered on the Journal.

4. Neither House, during the Session of Congress, shall, without the Consent of the other, adjourn for more than three days, nor to any other Place than that in which the two Houses shall be sitting.

*Changed by Section 2 of the Twentieth Amendment

Section 6

Pay, Privileges, Limitations

1. The Senators and Representatives shall receive a Compensation for their Services, to be ascertained by Law, and paid out of the Treasury of the United States. They shall in all cases, except Treason, Felony and Breach of the Peace, be privileged from Arrest during their Attendance at the Session of their respective Houses, and in going to and returning from the same; and for any Speech or Debate in either House, they shall not be questioned in any other Place.

2. No Senator or Representative shall, during the Time for which he was elected, be appointed to any civil Office under the Authority of the United States, which shall have been created, or the Emoluments whereof shall have been increased during such time; and no Person holding any Office under the United States, shall be a Member of either House during his Continuance in Office.

Section 7

Procedure in Passing Bills, President's Veto Power

1. All Bills for raising Revenue shall originate in the House of Representatives; but the Senate may propose or concur with Amendments as on other Bills.

2. Every Bill which shall have passed the House of Representatives and the Senate, shall, before it becomes a Law, be presented to the President of the United States; if he approves he shall sign it, but if not he shall return it, with his Objections, to that House in which it shall have originated, who shall enter the Objections at large on their Journal, and proceed to reconsider it. If after such Reconsideration two thirds of that House shall agree to pass the Bill, it shall be sent, together with the Objections, to the other House, by which it shall likewise be reconsidered, and if approved by two thirds of that House, it shall become a Law. But in all such Cases the Votes of both Houses shall be determined by Yeas and Nays, and the Names of the Persons voting for and against the Bill shall be entered on the Journal of each House respectively. If any Bill shall not be returned by the President within ten Days (Sundays excepted) after it shall have been presented to him, the Same shall be a Law, in like Manner as if he had signed it, unless the Congress by their Adjournment prevent its Return, in which Case it shall not be a Law.

3. Every Order, Resolution, or Vote to which the Concurrence of the Senate and House of Representatives may be necessary (except on a question of Adjournment) shall be presented to the President of the United States; and before the Same shall take Effect, shall be approved by him, or being disapproved by him, shall be repassed by two thirds of the Senate and House of Representatives, according to the Rules and Limitations prescribed in the Case of a Bill.

Section 8

Powers Delegated to Congress

The Congress shall have Power

1. To lay and collect Taxes, Duties, Imposts and Excises, to pay the Debts and provide for the common Defense and general Welfare of the United States; but all Duties, Imposts and Excises shall be uniform throughout the United States;

2. To borrow Money on the credit of the United States;

3. To regulate Commerce with foreign Nations, and among the several States, and with the Indian Tribes;

4. To establish a uniform Rule of Naturalization, and uniform Laws on the subject of Bankruptcies throughout the United States;

5. To coin Money, regulate the Value thereof, and of foreign Coin, and fix the Standard of Weights and Measures;

6. To provide for the Punishment of counterfeiting the Securities and current Coin of the United States;

7. To establish Post Offices and post Roads;

8. To promote the Progress of Science and useful Arts, by securing for limited Times to Authors and Inventors the exclusive Right to their respective Writings and Discoveries;

9. To constitute Tribunals inferior to the Supreme Court;

10. To define and punish Piracies and Felonies committed on the high Seas, and Offenses against the Law of Nations;

11. To declare War, grant Letters of Marque and Reprisal, and make Rules concerning Captures on Land and Water;

12. To raise and support Armies, but no Appropriation of Money to that Use shall be for a longer Term than two Years;

13. To provide and maintain a Navy;

14. To make Rules for the Government and Regulation of the land and naval Forces;

15. To provide for calling forth the Militia to execute the Laws of the Union, suppress Insurrections and repel Invasions;

16. To provide for organizing, arming, and disciplining the Militia, and for governing such Part of them as may be employed in the Service of the United States, reserving to the States respectively, the Appointment of the Officers, and the Authority of training the Militia according to the discipline prescribed by Congress;

17. To exercise exclusive Legislation in all Cases whatsoever, over such District (not exceeding ten Miles square) as may, by Session of particular States, and the Acceptance of Congress, become the Seat of the Government of the United States, and to exercise like Authority over all Places purchased by the

Consent of the Legislature of the State in which the Same shall be, for the Erection of Forts, Magazines, Arsenals, dock-Yards and other needful Buildings;—and

18. To make all Laws which shall be necessary and proper for carrying into Execution the foregoing Powers, and all other Powers vested by this Constitution in the Government of the United States, or in any Department or Officer thereof.

Section 9

Powers Denied to Congress

1. The Migration or Importation of such Persons as any of the States now existing shall think proper to admit, shall not be prohibited by the Congress prior to the Year one thousand eight hundred and eight, but a Tax or duty may be imposed on such Importation, not exceeding ten dollars for each Person.

2. The Privilege of the Writ of Habeas Corpus shall not be suspended, unless when in Cases of Rebellion or Invasion the public Safety may require it.

3. No Bill of Attainder or ex post facto Law shall be passed.

4. [No Capitation, or other direct, Tax shall be laid, unless in Proportion to the Census or Enumeration herein before directed to be taken.]*

5. No Tax or Duty shall be laid on Articles exported from any State.

*Changed by the Sixteenth Amendment

6. No Preference shall be given by any Regulation of Commerce or Revenue to the Ports of one State over those of another; nor shall Vessels bound to, or from, one State, be obliged to enter, clear, or pay Duties in another.

7. No Money shall be drawn from the Treasury, but in Consequence of Appropriations made by Law; and a regular Statement and Account of the Receipts and Expenditures of all public Money shall be published from time to time.

8. No Title of Nobility shall be granted by the United States: And no Person holding any Office of Profit or Trust under them, shall, without the Consent of the Congress, accept of any present, Emolument, Office, or Title, of any kind whatever, from any King, Prince, or foreign State.

Section 10

Restrictions on States' Powers

1. No State shall enter into any Treaty, Alliance, or Confederation; grant Letters of Marque and Reprisal; coin Money; emit Bills of Credit; make any Thing but gold and silver Coin a Tender in Payment of Debts; pass any Bill of Attainder, ex post facto Law, or Law impairing the Obligation of Contracts, or grant any Title of Nobility.

2. No State shall, without the Consent of the Congress, lay any Imposts or Duties on Imports or Exports, except what may be absolutely necessary for executing its inspection Laws:

and the net Produce of all Duties and Imposts, laid by any State on Imports or Exports, shall be for the Use of the Treasury of the United States; and all such Laws shall be subject to the Revision and Control of the Congress.

3. No State shall, without the Consent of Congress, lay any Duty of Tonnage, keep Troops, or Ships of War in time of Peace, enter into any Agreement or Compact with another State, or with a foreign Power, or engage in War, unless actually invaded, or in such imminent Danger as will not admit of delay.

ARTICLE II

The Executive Branch

Section 1

President and Vice President: Election, Qualifications, and Oath

1. The executive Power shall be vested in a President of the United States of America. He shall hold his Office during the term of four Years, and, together with the Vice President, chosen for the same Term, be elected, as follows.

2. Each State shall appoint, in such Manner as the Legislature thereof may direct, a Number of Electors, equal to the whole Number of Senators and Representatives to which the State may be entitled in the Congress: but no Senator or Representative, or Person holding an Office of Trust or Profit under the United States, shall be appointed an Elector.

3. [The Electors shall meet in their respective states, and vote by Ballot for two Persons, of whom one at least shall not be an Inhabitant of the same State with themselves. And they shall make a List of all the Persons voted for, and of the Number of Votes for each; which List they shall sign and certify, and transmit sealed to the Seat of the Government of the United States, directed to the President of the Senate. The President of the Senate shall, in the Presence of the Senate and House of Representatives, open all the Certificates, and the Votes shall then be counted. The Person having the greatest Number of Votes shall be the President, if such Number be a Majority of the whole Number of Electors appointed; and if there be more than one who have such Majority, and have an equal Number of Votes, then the House of Representatives shall immediately choose by Ballot one of them for President; and if no Person have a Majority, then from the five highest on the List the said House shall in like manner choose the President. But in choosing the President, the Votes shall be taken by States, the Representation from each State having one Vote; A quorum for this Purpose shall consist of a Member or Members from two thirds of the States, and a Majority of all the States shall be necessary to a Choice. In every Case, after the Choice of the President, the Person having the greatest Number of Votes of the Electors shall be the Vice President. But if

there should remain two or more who have equal Votes, the Senate shall choose from them by Ballot the Vice President.]*

4. The Congress may determine the Time of choosing the Electors, and the day on which they shall give their Votes; which Day shall be the same throughout the United States.

5. No Person except a natural born Citizen, or a Citizen of the United States at the time of the Adoption of this Constitution, shall be eligible to the Office of the President; neither shall any person be eligible to that Office who shall not have attained to the Age of thirty five Years, and been fourteen Years a Resident within the United States.

6. [In Case of the Removal of the President from Office, or of his Death, Resignation, or Inability to discharge the Powers and Duties of the said Office, the Same shall devolve on the Vice President, and the Congress may by Law provide for the Case of Removal Death, Resignation or Inability, both of the President and Vice President, declaring what Officer shall then act as President, and such Officer shall act accordingly, until the Disability be removed, or a President shall be elected.]**

7. The President shall, at stated Times, receive for his Services, a Compensation, which shall neither be increased nor diminished during the Period for which he shall have been elected, and he shall not receive within that Period any

other Emolument from the United States, or any of them.

8. Before he enter the Execution of his Office, he shall take the following Oath or Affirmation:—"I do solemnly swear (or affirm) that I will faithfully execute the Office of President of the United States, and will to the best of my Ability, preserve, protect, and defend the Constitution of the United States."

Section 2

Powers of the President

1. The President shall be Commander in Chief of the Army and Navy of the United States, and of the Militia of the several States, when called into the actual Service of the United States; he may require the Opinion, in writing, of the principal Officer in each of the executive Departments, upon any Subject relating to the Duties of their respective Offices, and he shall have Power to grant Reprieves and Pardons for Offenses against the United States, except in Cases of Impeachment.

2. He shall have Power, by and with the Advice and Consent of the Senate, to make Treaties, provided two thirds of the Senators present concur; and he shall nominate, and by and with the Advice and Consent of the Senate, shall appoint Ambassadors, other public Ministers and Consuls, Judges of the supreme Court, and all other Officers of the United States, whose Appointments are not herein otherwise provided for, and which shall be

*Changed by the Twelfth Amendment
**Changed by the Twenty-fifth Amendment

established by Law: but the Congress may by Law vest the Appointment of such inferior Officers, as they think proper, in the President alone, in the Courts of Law, or in the Heads of Departments.

3. The President shall have Power to fill up all Vacancies that may happen during the Recess of the Senate, by granting Commissions which shall expire at the End of their next Session.

Section 3

Duties of the President

He shall from time to time give to the Congress Information of the State of the Union, and recommend to their Consideration such Measures as he shall judge necessary and expedient; he may, on extraordinary Occasions, convene both Houses, or either of them, and in Case of Disagreement between them, with Respect to the Time of Adjournment, he may adjourn them to such Time as he shall think proper; he shall receive Ambassadors and other public Ministers; he shall take Care that the Laws be faithfully executed, and shall Commission all the Officers of the United States.

Section 4

Impeachment and Removal from Office for Crimes

The President, Vice President and all civil Officers of the United States, shall be removed from Office on Impeachment for, and Conviction of, Treason, Bribery, or other high Crimes and Misdemeanors.

ARTICLE III

The Judicial Branch

Section 1

Federal Courts, Tenure of Office

The judicial Power of the United States, shall be vested in one supreme Court, and in such inferior Courts as the Congress may from time to time ordain and establish. The Judges, both of the supreme and inferior Courts, shall hold their Offices during good Behavior, and shall, at stated Times, receive for their Services a Compensation, which shall not be diminished during their Continuance in Office.

Section 2

Jurisdiction of Federal Courts

1. The judicial Power shall extend to all Cases, in Law and Equity, arising under this Constitution, the Laws of the United States, and Treaties made, or which shall be made, under their Authority;—to all Cases affecting Ambassadors, other public Ministers and Consuls; —to all Cases of admiralty and maritime Jurisdiction;—to Controversies to which the United States shall be a Party;— to Controversies between two or more States; [between a State and Citizens of another State;]* between Citizens of different States;— between Citizens of the same State claiming Lands under Grants of different States;—[and between a State, or the Citizens thereof, and foreign States, Citizens or Subjects.]*

*Changed by the Eleventh Amendment

2. In all Cases affecting Ambassadors, other public Ministers and Consuls, and those in which a State shall be Party, the supreme Court shall have original Jurisdiction. In all the other Cases before mentioned, the supreme Court shall have appellate Jurisdiction, both as to Law and Fact, with such Exceptions, and under such Regulations as the Congress shall make.

3. The Trial of all Crimes, except in Cases of Impeachment, shall be by Jury; and such Trial shall be held in the State where said Crimes shall have been committed; but when not committed within any State, the Trial shall be at such Place or Places as the Congress may by Law have directed.

Section 3

Treason: Conviction Of and Punishment For

1. Treason against the United States shall consist only in levying War against them, or in adhering to their Enemies, giving them Aid and Comfort. No Person shall be convicted of Treason unless on the Testimony of two Witnesses to the same overt Act, or on Confession in open Court.

2. The Congress shall have Power to declare the Punishment of Treason, but no Attainder of Treason shall work Corruption of Blood, or Forfeiture except during the Life of the Person attainted.

ARTICLE IV
Relations among the States
Section 1
Full Faith and Credit

Full Faith and Credit shall be given in each State to the public Acts, Records, and judicial Proceedings of every other State; And the Congress may by general Laws prescribe the manner in which such Acts, Records and Proceedings shall be proved, and the Effect thereof.

Section 2

Rights of State Citizens; Right of Extradition

1. The Citizens of each State shall be entitled to all Privileges and Immunities of Citizens in the several States.

2. A Person charged in any State with Treason, Felony, or other Crime, who shall flee from Justice, and be found in another State, shall on Demand of the executive Authority of the State from which he fled, be delivered up, to be removed to the State having Jurisdiction of the Crime.

3. [No person held to Service or Labour in one State, under the Laws thereof, escaping into another, shall, in Consequence of any Law or Regulation therein, be discharged from such Service or Labour, but shall be delivered up on Claim of the Party to whom such Service or Labour may be due.]*

*Changed by the Thirteenth Amendment

Section 3

Admission of New States

1. New States may be admitted by the Congress into this Union; but no new State shall be formed or erected within the Jurisdiction of any other State; nor any State be formed by the Junction of two or more States, or parts of States, without the Consent of the Legislatures of the States concerned as well as of the Congress.

2. The Congress shall have Power to dispose of and make all needful Rules and Regulations respecting the territory or other Property belonging to the United States; and nothing in this Constitution shall be so construed as to Prejudice any Claims of the United States, or of any particular State.

Section 4

Republican Government Guaranteed

The United States shall guarantee to every State in this Union a Republican Form of Government, and shall protect each of them against Invasion; and on Application of the Legislature, or of the Executive (when the Legislature cannot be convened) against domestic Violence.

ARTICLE V

Amendment Procedures

The Congress, whenever two thirds of both Houses shall deem it necessary, shall propose Amendments to this Constitution, or, on the Application of the Legislatures of two thirds of the several States, shall call a Convention for proposing Amendments, which, in either Case, shall be valid to all Intents and Purposes, as Part of this Constitution, when ratified by the Legislatures of three fourths of the several States, or by Conventions in three fourths thereof, as the one or the other Mode of Ratification may be proposed by the Congress; Provided that no Amendment which may be made prior to the Year One thousand eight hundred and eight shall in any Manner affect the first and fourth Clauses in the Ninth Section of the first Article; and that no State, without its Consent, shall be deprived of its equal Suffrage in the Senate.

ARTICLE VI

Supremacy of the Constitution and Federal Laws

1. All debts contracted and Engagements entered into, before the Adoption of this Constitution, shall be as valid against the United States under this Constitution, as under the Confederation.

2. This Constitution, and the Laws of the United States which shall be made in Pursuance thereof; and all Treaties made, or which shall be

made, under the Authority of the United States, shall be the supreme Law of the Land; and the Judges in every State shall be bound thereby, any Thing in the Constitution or Laws of any State to the Contrary notwithstanding.

3. The Senators and Representatives before mentioned, and the Members of the several State Legislatures, and all executive and judicial Officers, both of the United States and of the several States, shall be bound by Oath or Affirmation, to support this Constitution; but no religious Test shall ever be required as a Qualification to any Office or public Trust under the United States.

ARTICLE VII
Ratification

The Ratification of the Conventions of nine States, shall be sufficient for the Establishment of this Constitution between the States so ratifying the Same.

Done in Convention by the unanimous consent of the States present the s e venteenth day of September in the year of our Lord one thousand seven hundred and eighty seven and of the Independence of the United States of America the Twelfth. In witness whereof we have hereunto subscribed our Names,

President and deputy from Virginia

George Washington

New-Hampshire

John Langdon
Nicholas Gilman

Massachusetts

Nathaniel Gorham
Rufus King

Connecticut

William Samuel Johnson
Roger Sherman

New York

Alexander Hamilton

New Jersey

William Livingston
David Brearley
William Paterson
Jonathan Dayton

Pennsylvania

Benjamin Franklin
Thomas Mifflin
Robert Morris
George Clymer
Thomas Fitzsimons
Jared Ingersoll
James Wilson
Gouverneur Morris

THE CONSTITUTION OF THE UNITED STATES

Delaware

George Read
Gunning Bedford, Jr.
John Dickinson
Richard Bassett
Jacob Broom

Maryland

James McHenry
Daniel of St. Tho. Jenifer
Daniel Carroll

Virginia

John Blair
James Madison, Jr.

North Carolina

William Blount
Richard Dobbs Spaight
Hugh Williamson

South Carolina

John Rutledge
Charles Cotesworth Pinckney
Charles Pinckney
Pierce Butler

Georgia

William Few
Abraham Baldwin

Attest:

William Jackson, Secretary

The Constitution was adopted in
Philadelphia on September 17, 1787,
by the Constitutional Convention
and was declared ratified
on July 2, 1788.

AMENDMENTS TO THE THE CONSTITUTION

AMENDMENT I

Congress shall make no law respecting an establishment of religion, or prohibiting the free exercise thereof; or abridging the freedom of speech, or of the press; or the right of the people peaceably to assemble, and to petition the Government for a redress of grievances.

AMENDMENT II

A well regulated Militia, being necessary to the security of a free State, the right of the people to keep and bear Arms, shall not be infringed.

AMENDMENT III

No Soldier shall, in time of peace be quartered in any house, without the consent of the Owner, nor in time of war, but in a manner to be prescribed by law.

AMENDMENT IV

The right of the people to be secure in their persons, houses, papers, and effects, against unreasonable searches and seizures, shall not be violated, and no Warrants shall issue, but upon probable cause, supported by Oath or affirmation, and particularly describing the place to be searched, and the persons or things to be seized.

AMENDMENT V

No person shall be held to answer for a capital, or otherwise infamous crime, unless on a presentment or indictment of a Grand Jury, except in cases arising in the land or naval forces, or in the Militia, when in actual service in time of War or public danger; nor shall any person be subject for the same offence to be twice put in jeopardy of life or limb; nor shall be compelled in any criminal case to be a witness against himself, nor be deprived of life, liberty, or property, without due process of law; nor shall private property be taken for public use, without just compensation.

AMENDMENT VI

In all criminal prosecutions, the accused shall enjoy the right to a speedy and public trial, by an impartial jury of the State and district wherein the crime shall have been committed, which district shall have been previously ascertained by law, and to be informed of the nature and cause of the accusation; to be confronted with the witnesses against him; to have compulsory process for obtaining witnesses in his favor, and to have the Assistance of Counsel for his defence.

AMENDMENT VII

In Suits at common law, where the value in controversy shall exceed twenty dollars, the right of trial by jury shall be preserved, and no fact tried by a jury, shall be otherwise re-examined in any Court of the United States, than according to the rules of the common law.

AMENDMENT VIII

Excessive bail shall not be required, nor excessive fines imposed, nor cruel and unusual punishments inflicted.

AMENDMENT IX

The enumeration in the Constitution, of certain rights, shall not be construed to deny or disparage others retained by the people.

AMENDMENT X

The powers not delegated to the United States by the Constitution, nor prohibited by it to the States, are reserved to the States respectively, or to the people. [The first ten amendments were ratified December 15, 1791.]

AMENDMENT XI

The Judicial power of the United States shall not be construed to extend to any suit in law or equity, commenced or prosecuted against one of the United States by Citizens of another State, or by Citizens or Subjects of any Foreign State. [Ratified February 1795.]

AMENDMENT XII

The Electors shall meet in their respective states and vote by ballot for President and Vice-President, one of whom, at least, shall not be an inhabitant of the same state with themselves; they shall name in their ballots the person voted for as President, and in distinct ballots the person voted for as Vice-President, and they shall make distinct lists of all persons voted for as President, and of all persons voted for as Vice-President, and of the number of votes for each, which lists they shall sign and certify, and transmit sealed to the seat of the government of the United States, directed to the President of the Senate;—the President of the Senate shall, in the presence of the Senate and House of Representatives, open all the certificates and the votes shall then be counted;— The person having the greatest number of votes for President, shall be the President, if such number be a majority of the whole number of Electors appointed; and if no person have such majority, then from the persons having the highest numbers not exceeding three on the list of those voted for as President, the House of Representatives shall choose immediately by ballot, the President. But in choosing the President, the votes shall be taken by states, the representation from each state having one vote; a quorum for this purpose shall consist of a member or members from two-thirds of the states, and a majority of all the states shall be necessary to a choice. [And if the House of Representatives shall not choose a President whenever the right of choice shall devolve upon them, before the fourth day of March next following, then the Vice-President shall act as President, as in the case of the death or other constitutional disability of the President.—]* The person having the greatest number of votes as Vice-President, shall be the Vice-President, if such number be a majority of the whole number of Electors appointed, and if no person have a majority, then from the two highest numbers on the list, the Senate shall choose the Vice-President; a quorum for the purpose shall consist of two-thirds of the whole number of Senators, and a majority of

*Superseded by Section 3 of the Twentieth Amendment

the whole number shall be necessary to a choice. But no person constitutionally ineligible to the office of President shall be eligible to that of Vice-President of the United States. [Ratified June 1804.]

AMENDMENT XIII

Section 1

Neither slavery nor involuntary servitude, except as a punishment for crime whereof the party shall have been duly convicted, shall exist within the United States, or any place subject to their jurisdiction.

Section 2

Congress shall have power to enforce this article by appropriate legislation. [Ratified December 1865.]

AMENDMENT XIV

Section 1

All persons born or naturalized in the United States and subject to the jurisdiction thereof, are citizens of the United States, and of the State wherein they reside. No State shall make or enforce any law which shall abridge the privileges or immunities of citizens of the United States; nor shall any State deprive any person of life, liberty, or property, without due process of law; nor deny to any person within its jurisdiction the equal protection of the laws.

Section 2

Representatives shall be apportioned among the several States according to their respective numbers, counting the whole number of persons in each State, excluding Indians not taxed. But when the right to vote at any election for the choice of electors for President and Vice-President of the United States, Representatives in Congress, the Executive and Judicial officers of a State, or the members of the Legislature thereof, is denied to any of the male inhabitants of such State, being twenty-one years of age,* and citizens of the United States, or in any way abridged, except for participation in rebellion, or other crime, the basis of representation therein shall be reduced in the proportion which the number of such male citizens shall bear to the whole number of male citizens twenty-one years of age in such State.

Section 3

No person shall be a Senator or Representative in Congress, or elector of President and Vice-President, or hold any office, civil or military, under the United States, or under any State, who, having previously taken an oath, as a member of Congress, or as an officer of the United States, or as a member of any State legislature, or as an executive or judicial officer of any State, to support the Constitution of the United States, shall have engaged in insurrection or rebellion against the same, or given aid or comfort to the enemies thereof. But Congress may by a vote of two-thirds of each House, remove such disability.

*Changed by Section 1 of the Twenty-sixth Amendment

Section 4

The validity of the public debt of the United States, authorized by law, including debts incurred for payment of pensions and bounties for services in suppressing insurrection or rebellion, shall not be questioned. But neither the United States nor any State shall assume or pay any debt or obligation incurred in aid of insurrection or rebellion against the United States, or any claim for the loss or emancipation of any slave; but all such debts, obligations and claims shall be held illegal and void.

Section 5

The Congress shall have the power to enforce, by appropriate legislation, the provisions of this article. [Ratified July 1868.]

AMENDMENT XV

Section 1

The right of citizens of the United States to vote shall not be denied or abridged by the United States or by any State on account of race, color, or previous condition of servitude.

Section 2

The Congress shall have the power to enforce this article by appropriate legislation. [Ratified February 1870.]

AMENDMENT XVI

The Congress shall have power to lay and collect taxes on incomes, from whatever source derived, without apportionment among the several States, and without regard to any census or enumeration. [Ratified February 1913.]

AMENDMENT XVII

The Senate of the United States shall be composed of two Senators from each State, elected by the people thereof, for six years; and each Senator shall have one vote. The electors in each State shall have the qualifications requisite for electors of the most numerous branch of the State legislatures. When vacancies happen in the representation of any State in the Senate, the executive authority of such State shall issue writs of election to fill such vacancies: *Provided*, That the legislature of any State may empower the executive thereof to make temporary appointments until the people fill the vacancies by election as the legislature may direct. This amendment shall not be so construed as to affect the election or term of any Senator chosen before it becomes valid as part of the Constitution. [Ratified April 1913.]

AMENDMENT XVIII

Section 1

After one year from the ratification of this article the manufacture, sale, or transportation of intoxicating liquors within, the importation thereof into, or the exportation thereof from the United States and all territory subject to the jurisdiction thereof for beverage purposes is hereby prohibited.

Section 2

The Congress and the several States shall have concurrent power to enforce this article by appropriate legislation.

Section 3

This article shall be inoperative unless it shall have been ratified as an amendment to the Constitution by the legislatures of the several States, as provided in the Constitution, within seven years from the date of the submission hereof to the States by the Congress. [Ratified January 1919.]*

AMENDMENT XIX

The right of citizens of the United States to vote shall not be denied or abridged by the United States or by any State on account of sex. Congress shall have power to enforce this article by appropriate legislation. [Ratified August 1920.]

AMENDMENT XX

Section 1

The terms of the President and the Vice President shall end at noon on the 20th day of January, and the terms of Senators and Representatives at noon on the 3d day of January, of the years in which such terms would have ended if this article had not been ratified; and the terms of their successors shall then begin.

Section 2

The Congress shall assemble at least once in every year, and such meeting shall begin at noon on the 3rd day of January, unless they shall by law appoint a different day.

Section 3

If, at the time fixed for the beginning of the term of the President, the President elect shall have died, the Vice President elect shall become President. If a President shall not have been chosen before the time fixed for the beginning of his term, or if the President elect shall have failed to qualify, then the Vice President elect shall act as President until a President shall have qualified; and the Congress may by law provide for the case wherein neither a President elect nor a Vice President elect shall have qualified, declaring who shall then act as President, or the manner in which one who is to act shall be selected, and such person shall act accordingly until a President or Vice President shall have qualified.

Section 4

The Congress may by law provide for the case of the death of any of the persons for whom the House of Representatives may choose a President whenever the right of choice shall have devolved upon them, and for the case of the death of any of the persons from whom the Senate may choose a Vice President whenever the right of choice shall have devolved upon them.

Section 5

Sections 1 and 2 shall take effect on the 15th day of October following the ratification of this article.

*Repealed by the Twenty-first Amendment

Section 6

This article shall be inoperative unless it shall have been ratified as an amendment to the Constitution by the legislatures of three-fourths of the several States within seven years from the date of its submission. [Ratified January 1933.]

AMENDMENT XXI

Section 1

The eighteenth article of amendment to the Constitution of the United States is hereby repealed.

Section 2

The transportation or importation into any State, Territory, or Possession of the United States for delivery or use therein of intoxicating liquors, in violation of the laws thereof, is hereby prohibited.

Section 3

This article shall be inoperative unless it shall have been ratified as an amendment to the Constitution by conventions in the several States, as provided in the Constitution, within seven years from the date of the submission hereof to the States by the Congress. [Ratified December 1933.]

AMENDMENT XXII

Section 1

No person shall be elected to the office of the President more than twice, and no person who has held the office of President, or acted as President, for more than two years of a term to which some other person was elected President shall be elected to the office of the President more than once. But this Article shall not apply to any person holding the office of President when this Article was proposed by the Congress, and shall not prevent any person who may be holding the office of President, or acting as President, during the term within which this Article becomes operative from holding the office of President or acting as President during the remainder of such term.

Section 2

This article shall be inoperative unless it shall have been ratified as an amendment to the Constitution by the legislatures of three-fourths of the several States within seven years from the date of its submission to the States by the Congress. [Ratified February 1951.]

AMENDMENT XXIII

Section 1

The District constituting the seat of Government of the United States shall appoint in such manner as the Congress may direct: A number of electors of President and Vice President equal to the whole number of Senators and Representatives in Congress to which the District would be entitled if it were a State, but in no event more than the least populous State; they shall be in addition to those appointed by the States, but they shall be considered, for the purposes of the election of President and Vice President, to be electors appointed by a State; and they shall meet in the District and perform such duties as provided by the twelfth article of amendment.

Section 2

The Congress shall have power to enforce this article by appropriate legislation. [Ratified March 1961.]

AMENDMENT XXIV

Section 1

The right of citizens of the United States to vote in any primary or other election for President or Vice President, for electors for President or Vice President, or for Senator or Representative in Congress, shall not be denied or abridged by the United States or any State by reason of failure to pay any poll tax or other tax.

Section 2

The Congress shall have power to enforce this article by appropriate legislation. [Ratified January 1964.]

AMENDMENT XXV

Section 1

In case of the removal of the President from office or of his death or resignation, the Vice President shall become President.

Section 2

Whenever there is a vacancy in the office of the Vice President, the President shall nominate a Vice President who shall take office upon confirmation by a majority vote of both Houses of Congress.

Section 3

Whenever the President transmits to the President pro tempore of the Senate and the Speaker of the House of Representatives his written declaration that he is unable to discharge the powers and duties of his office, and until he transmits to them a written declaration to the contrary, such powers and duties shall be discharged by the Vice President as Acting President.

Section 4

Whenever the Vice President and a majority of either the principal officers of the executive departments or of such other body as Congress may by law provide, transmit to the President pro tempore of the Senate and the Speaker of the House of Representatives their written declaration that the President is unable to discharge the powers and duties of his office, the Vice President shall immediately assume the powers and duties of the office as Acting President.

Thereafter, when the President transmits to the President pro tempore of the Senate and the Speaker of the House of Representatives his written declaration that no inability exists, he shall resume the powers and duties of his office unless the Vice President and a majority of either the principal officers of the executive department or of such other body as Congress may by law provide, transmit within four days to the President pro tempore of the Senate and the Speaker of the House of Representatives their written declaration that the President is unable to discharge the powers and duties of his office. Thereupon Congress shall decide the issue, assembling within forty-eight hours for that purpose if not in session. If the Congress, within twenty-one days after receipt of the latter written declaration, or, if Congress is not in session, within twenty-one days after Congress is required to assemble, determines by two-thirds vote of both Houses that the President is unable to discharge the powers and duties of his office, the Vice President shall continue to discharge the same as Acting President; otherwise, the President shall resume the powers and duties of his office. [Ratified February 1967.]

AMENDMENT XXVI

Section 1

The right of citizens of the United States, who are eighteen years of age or older, to vote shall not be denied or abridged by the United States or by any State on account of age.

Section 2

The Congress shall have power to enforce this article by appropriate legislation. [Ratified July 1971.]

AMENDMENT XXVII

No law, varying the compensation for the services of the Senators or Representatives, shall take effect, until an election of Representatives shall have intervened. [Ratified May 1992.]

GLOSSARY

abolish To formally put an end to.

abridging Limiting or reducing.

advice and consent The right of the U.S. Senate, granted in Article II of the Constitution, to review treaties and major presidential appointments. Two-thirds vote of senators is required for treaties and a simple majority for appointments.

alien A foreign-born resident.

Alien and Sedition Acts Laws passed during President John Adams' administration that made it a crime for editors, writers, or speakers to criticize the government and its Federalist policies.

allegiance (1) Loyalty to a government, ruler, or nation. (2) Loyalty to a person, social group, or cause.

amendment A change in or addition to a legal document.

American Revolution The war fought by the American colonists to gain their independence from Great Britain. It took place from 1775 to 1783.

Amnesty International An international nongovernmental organization that advocates the protection of human rights.

Anti-Federalists People who were against ratification of the Constitution because they thought it gave too much power to the federal government and did not protect the political rights of the people.

appeal The bringing of a court case from a lower court to a higher court in an attempt to have the lower court's decision reversed or for other reasons.

appellate court A judicial body that hears appeals from a lower court.

appellate jurisdiction The legal authority of a court to hear appeals from a lower court.

aristocrats People of the highest class of society who held inherited titles. They were often part of the ruling class in government.

Article I The part of the Constitution that describes the legislative branch of the government and its powers.

Article II The part of the Constitution that describes the executive branch of the government and its powers.

Article III The part of the Constitution that describes the judicial branch of the government and its powers.

Article IV The part of the Constitution that deals with the relationship between the states and the federal government and states' relationships with each other.

Article V The part of the Constitution that describes the process for amending the Constitution.

Article VI The part of the Constitution that deals with debts and contracts that were entered into before adoption of the Constitution; the supremacy of the Constitution; and the requirement of an oath of office for executive, legislative, and judicial officials. It prohibits the institution of a religious test for officeholders.

Article VII The part of the Constitution that describes the requirement for ratification of the Constitution.

Articles of Confederation The first constitution of the United States, created to form a perpetual union and a firm league of friendship among the thirteen original states. It was adopted by the Second Continental Congress on November 10, 1777, and sent to the states for ratification. It came into force on March 1, 1781, and served as the nation's constitution until 1789, when the U.S. Constitution replaced it. The Articles provided for a weak central government.

assembly, right of The right or legal claims that allow a person to meet with others to discuss one's beliefs, ideas, or feelings.

association An organized group of people joined together for a common purpose.

Association of Southeast Asian Nations (ASEAN) "The Association represents the collective will of the ten member nations to work together to secure peace, freedom, and prosperity for their peoples." (ASEAN Declaration 1967)

autocratic government Government in which a single ruler or group has unlimited power.

avarice An excessive desire for money; greed.

bail Money or other security given to obtain a person's release from custody, which is forfeited if the person subsequently fails to appear before the court for trial.

bailiff (1) An officer who carries out legal orders, makes arrests, keeps order in court, or serves as a messenger and doorkeeper. (2) (chiefly British) A local official who has some judicial powers.

balance of power The division of governmental powers among different persons or institutions in such a way that no one individual or group can dominate or control the exercise of power by others.

basic rights Fundamental rights such as life, liberty, and property.

Battle of Saratoga (1777) An important battle of the Revolutionary War that lasted from June to October 1777, when the British surrendered in Saratoga, New York. The American victory prevented the British from splitting the colonies in two, increased American morale, and encouraged the French to sign a treaty with the Americans.

bill A proposed law given to the legislature for approval.

bill of attainder An act of the legislature that inflicts punishment on an individual or group without a judicial trial.

Bill of Rights The first ten amendments to the Constitution. It lists basic rights of the people that the federal government may not interfere with and must protect.

Boston Massacre (1770) On March 5, 1770, a mob of colonists harassed British soldiers guarding the tax collector's office in Boston. The soldiers opened fire, killing five Bostonians.

Boston Tea Party (1773) An act of rebellion against British authority, and in particular in response to the Tea Act, in which a band of colonists boarded ships in Boston Harbor and destroyed thousands of dollars worth of tea by throwing it overboard.

boycott To refuse to buy from or deal with a store or company as an act of protest.

Brown v. Board of Education of Topeka (1954) The U.S. Supreme Court case in which the Court declared that "separate but equal" educational facilities are inherently unequal and therefore a violation of the equal protection of the laws guaranteed by the Fourteenth Amendment.

cabinet The advisors to the president who are the heads of the departments of the executive branch.

charter A written document from a government or ruler that grants certain rights to an individual, group, organization, or to people in general. In colonial times, a charter granted land to a person or a company along with the right to start a colony on that land.

chattel Personal property that can be moved from place to place.

checks and balances The distribution and balancing of power among different branches of government so that no one branch is able to dominate the others.

chief justice The head of a court. The Chief Justice of the United States is the highest ranking judicial official in the nation and is the head of the U.S. Supreme Court.

citizen A person who is a legal member of a nation, country, or other self-governing community.

civic (1) Related to citizens or citizenship. (2) Related to the public affairs of a city or country.

civic life The public life of citizens; that which is concerned with a citizen's own interests and the common affairs and interests of his or her community and nation.

civic participation Taking part in formal political processes and community activities outside of government.

civic virtue The dedication of citizens to the common welfare of their community or country, even at the cost of their individual interests.

civil Related to citizens, particularly the relationship between citizens and government.

civil disobedience The refusal to obey laws one regards as unjust.

civil rights Fundamental rights belonging to every member of a society.

Civil Rights Act of 1964 This law ended segregation in public places including restaurants, movie theaters, and hotels. The law also said that employers could not unfairly discriminate against people because of their race, national origin, religion, or gender.

civil rights movement A social movement in the United States during the 1950s and 1960s, in which people organized to demand equal rights for African Americans and other minorities. People worked together to change unfair laws. They gave speeches, marched in the streets, and participated in boycotts.

Civil War The war between the Northern and Southern states. It took place from 1861 to 1865.

Civil War Amendments The Thirteenth, Fourteenth, and Fifteenth Amendments to the U.S. Constitution ratified after the Civil War. The Thirteenth Amendment abolished slavery. The Fourteenth Amendment granted full citizenship to African Americans. The Fifteenth Amendment guaranteed the right to vote to men regardless of their "race, color, or previous condition of servitude."

commander-in-chief Highest leader of the military forces. According to the Constitution, the president is the commander-in-chief of the nation's armed forces.

commerce The buying and selling of goods, particularly on a large scale.

committees of correspondence Committees that began as voluntary associations and were eventually established by most of the colonial governments. Their mission was to make sure that each colony knew about events and opinions in the other colonies. They helped to unite the people against the British.

common good The good of the community as a whole.

common law The body of unwritten law developed in England from judicial decisions based on custom and earlier judicial decisions, which constitutes the basis of the English legal system and became part of American law.

compromise A way to settle differences by each side giving up some of its claims or demands and agreeing to a common solution.

confederation A form of political organization in which the sovereign states combine for certain specified purposes such as defense. Member states can leave a confederation at any time. The United States was a confederation from 1776 to 1789.

Congress The national legislature of the United States. Congress has two parts, also called houses: the Senate and the House of Representatives.

consent To agree and accept something, approve of something, or allow something to take place.

consent of the governed The expressed agreement by the people to obey the laws and the government they create.

constable A public official with limited police and judicial powers.

constitution A set of customs, traditions, rules, and laws that set forth the way a government is organized and operated.

Constitution, United States The supreme law of the United States that provides the framework for the government. The Constitution outlines the nation's institutions of government and the most important rights of the people. The document was created in 1787 during the Philadelphia Convention. The government created by the Constitution took effect on March 4, 1789.

Constitutional Convention See Philadelphia Convention.

constitutional government A government in which the powers of the ruler or rulers are limited by a constitution.

constitutional principle An essential idea contained in the Constitution. For example, the idea that no branch of government should have a monopoly on power.

contract A binding agreement between two or more persons.

covenant A binding agreement made by two or more persons or parties. The original idea of a covenant was an agreement made in the sight of God. The Mayflower Compact was such a covenant.

cruel and unusual punishment A criminal sanction or penalty that is not in accord with the moral standards of a humane and compassionate society. Such punishments are prohibited by the Eighth Amendment.

currency Any form of money used in a nation.

custom (1) An accepted practice or way of behaving that is followed by tradition. (2) A tax on goods entering a country.

Daughters of Liberty An organization formed by women prior to the American Revolution. They got together to protest treatment of the colonies by their British rulers. They helped make the boycott of British trade effective by making their own materials instead of using British imports.

Dawes Act (1887) An act of Congress that granted American citizenship and small parcels of land to American Indians who would give up allegiance to their tribe, their historical traditions, and ways of life. The law was devastating to Indian cultural traditions and forced many Indians into farming.

Declaration of Independence A proclamation that listed the basic principles of democratic government, stated the colonists' grievances against the king, and gave reasons why the colonists were free from British rule. It was signed by the members of Congress on July 4, 1776.

Declaratory Act (1766) A British law that reaffirmed the right of Parliament to pass laws for the colonies in "all cases whatsoever." The purpose of the law was to remind the colonists that the authority of the king and Parliament was superior to colonial governments.

delegate (1) (noun) A person chosen to act for or represent others. (2) (verb) To entrust someone to represent your interests.

democracy A form of government in which political power is exercised by all citizens, either directly or through their elected representatives.

dictator A head of government who has unlimited power.

dictatorial government A political system in which the ruler or rulers has unlimited power and which denies peoples' fundamental rights.

diplomacy The practice of carrying on formal relationships with governments of other countries.

direct democracy A type of government in which the people themselves meet and make the laws that they decide are needed.

discrimination Unfair treatment of people based on such things as their race, religion, or gender.

district court The court of original jurisdiction for most federal cases. This is the only federal court that holds trials in which juries and witnesses are used. Each state has at least one district court.

diverse (1) Of different kinds, types, or forms. (2) People of many different races, cultures, and ethnic groups.

domestic tranquility As used in the Preamble, this phrase means peaceful conditions within our country.

due process of law A requirement, stated in the Fifth and Fourteenth Amendments, that treatment by state and federal governments that involves life, liberty, or property of individuals be reasonable, fair, and follow known rules and procedures.

duty A tax on goods that are either imported or exported.

economic rights Rights essential to citizens that allow them to earn a living, to acquire and transfer property, and to produce, buy, and sell goods and services in open and free markets.

Eighth Amendment An amendment to the Constitution that bans excessive bail or fines and cruel and unusual punishment.

elector (1) One of the 538 members of the electoral college chosen by the political parties in a state. (2) Any qualified voter.

electoral college The group of presidential electors who cast the official votes for president and vice president after a presidential election. Each state has a number of electors equal to the total of its members in the Senate and House of Representatives.

English Bill of Rights An act passed by Parliament in 1689 that limited the power of the monarch. This document established Parliament as the most powerful branch of the English government.

enumerated powers Those rights and responsibilities of the U.S. government specifically provided for and listed in the Constitution.

equal protection clause Section 1 of the Fourteenth Amendment, which has been used to prevent states from treating individuals unfairly because of their race, national origin, citizenship status, or gender. It prohibits laws that unreasonably and unfairly favor some groups over others; it states that laws may not arbitrarily discriminate against persons.

equal protection of the law See equal protection clause.

equal representation The idea that each state should have the same number of representatives in Congress. The number of representatives in the Senate is based on equal representation.

establishment clause The part of the First Amendment that says the government cannot declare an official religion.

ex post facto law A law that makes an act a crime that was not a crime when the act was committed, that increases the penalty for a crime after it was committed, or that changes the rules of evidence to make conviction easier. Ex post facto laws are forbidden by Article I of the Constitution.

excise A tax on goods produced within a certain country imposed by that country's government.

executive branch The branch of government that carries out the laws made by the legislative branch.

executive power The authority to carry out and enforce the law.

faction (1) A small group within a larger group. (2) According to James Madison, a group that seeks to promote its own special interests at the expense of the common good.

federal courts The courts of the national government that deal with problems between states, with the Constitution, and with laws made by Congress.

federal government Another name for our national government.

federalism or **federal system** A form of government in which power is divided and shared between a central government and state and local governments.

Federalist, The A series of letters to the editor written in 1787–88 by Alexander Hamilton, James Madison, and John Jay, urging the adoption of the Constitution and supporting the need for a strong national government.

Federalists Advocates for ratification of the Constitution and for a strong centralized government; they flourished as a political party in the 1790s under the leadership of Alexander Hamilton. The party disappeared from national politics in 1816.

feudalism A system of social, economic, and political organizations in which a politically weak king or queen shared power with the nobility. The nobility required work and services from the common people in return for allowing them to live on and make use of the noble's land and benefit from the noble's protection.

Fifteenth Amendment An amendment to the Constitution, ratified after the Civil War in 1870, that forbids the denial of voting rights to any person based on race, color, or whether that person was previously a slave.

Fifth Amendment An amendment to the Constitution that states that no person will have their life, liberty, or property taken away by the federal government without due process of law. This amendment protects your right to be treated fairly by the federal government.

First Amendment An amendment to the Constitution that protects freedom of expression and the right of assembly.

First Continental Congress The body of colonial delegates who convened to represent the interests of the colonists and protest British rule. The First Continental Congress met in 1774 and drafted a Declaration of Rights.

Founders The political leaders of the thirteen original colonies. They were key figures in the establishment of the United States of America.

Fourteenth Amendment An amendment to the Constitution that states that no person—including people who are not citizens—will have their life, liberty, or property taken away by state or local governments without due process of law. This amendment protects a citizen's right to be treated fairly by his or her state and local governments. It also defines a citizen as anyone born or naturalized in the United States. It was one of the Civil War amendments.

Fourth Amendment An amendment to the U.S. Constitution that protects citizens from unreasonable searches and seizures and requires that warrants be issued only for "probable cause."

Framers The delegates to the Philadelphia Convention of 1787. They are the group of men who composed the United States Constitution.

free exercise clause The part of the First Amendment that says the government may not stop anyone from holding any religious beliefs they choose and may not unfairly or unreasonably limit anyone's right to practice their religious beliefs.

freedom of assembly The right to meet with others to discuss one's own beliefs, ideas, or feelings.

freedom of belief or conscience The right to freedom from being coerced to believe in something that you do not believe.

freedom of expression The right to make known one's attitudes, emotions, thoughts, feelings, etc., as protected by the First Amendment.

freedom of the press The right to read and write whatever you wish, as well as the right to publish your ideas without government interference.

freedom of religion The right to hold whatever religious beliefs you wish and the right to practice your beliefs without unfair or unreasonable interference from the government.

French Constitution of 1791 A constitution adopted during the French Revolution that established a constitutional monarchy in France. Power was concentrated in the legislative assembly and the power of the king was limited.

fugitive slave clause Article IV, Section 2, Clause 3 of the Constitution, which stated that slaves who escaped must be returned to their owners. It was later abolished by the Thirteenth Amendment.

general welfare What is best for most of the people.

general welfare clause Article I, Section 8, Clause 1 of the Constitution that authorizes Congress to provide for the common defense of the country and for the common good, described as the "general Welfare."

George III King of Great Britain during the American Revolution.

government The people and institutions with authority to make and enforce laws and manage disputes about laws.

grandfather clause A law that stated that a citizen could vote only if his grandfather had been allowed to vote. The law made it impossible for African Americans to vote because their grandfathers had not been allowed to vote.

Great Compromise This was a plan accepted at the Philadelphia Convention that called for Congress to have two houses. In the Senate representation of the states would be equal, with each state having two senators. The House of Representatives would use proportional representation of the states, and therefore, the number of representatives from each state would be determined by its population. Also called the Connecticut Compromise.

habeas corpus See writ of habeas corpus.

Hazelwood School District v. Kuhlmeier (1988) A Supreme Court ruling that students' First Amendment rights were not violated when their principal deleted two articles from the school's newspaper. The Court distinguished between speech that occurs in a public forum and speech that occurs "in school-sponsored expressive activities...related to legitimate pedagogical [teaching] concerns."

hearing A meeting in which citizens give their views to public officials.

higher law As used in describing a legal system, this term refers to the superiority of one set of laws over another. For example, the Constitution is a higher law than any federal or state law. In the natural rights philosophy, it means that natural law and divine law are superior to laws made by human beings.

House of Representatives One part or house of Congress. Often referred to simply as "the House." Each state may send a number of representatives based on its population.

human rights Basic rights and freedoms said to belong to all people everywhere.

humanitarian To have compassion and show concern for the pain and suffering of others.

I Have a Dream **speech** A speech delivered by Martin Luther King Jr. at the Lincoln Memorial in Washington, D.C., on August 28, 1963, during a civil rights march. King spoke against segregation and the unequal treatment of African Americans. Also known as the "March on Washington" speech.

ideal A standard of perfection that serves as a model for imitation.

impeach To bring to trial a public official accused of committing a crime or engaging in misconduct while in office.

impost A tax or customs duty.

In re Gault (1967) A Supreme Court ruling that the due process rights of Gerald Gault, a minor accused of making rude telephone calls, had been violated.

inalienable rights Fundamental rights that every person has that cannot be taken away by government. This phrase was used in the Virginia Declaration of Rights and the Declaration of Independence. Sometimes spelled unalienable rights.

indentured servant A person who voluntarily sold his or her labor for a set period of time in return for the cost of coming to America. The most important source of labor in the colonies in the seventeenth century and for a large part of the eighteenth century.

independence Self-rule; not ruled by another country.

Indian Citizenship Act (1924) An act of Congress that recognized all American Indians as citizens of the United States and granted them the right to vote in federal elections.

individual rights Specific rights that belong to each person, such as those listed in the Bill of Rights, rather than general rights.

international law Rules, usually the result of treaties, that regulate how countries behave toward one another.

International Red Cross and Red Crescent Two international humanitarian organizations that provide assistance to victims of war and natural disasters. There are 181 Red Cross and Red Crescent societies throughout the world. Red Cross societies operate out of countries with majority Christian populations; Red Crescent societies operate out of countries with majority Muslim populations.

International Telecommunications Union An agency of the United Nations dedicated to improving and coordinating international efforts related to telecommunications. Also known as the ITU.

Jim Crow laws Laws common in the South from 1877 until the 1950s that required African Americans to use separate schools and other public facilities and that prevented them from exercising the right to vote.

judicial branch The branch of government that interprets and applies the laws and settles disputes.

judicial review The power of the courts to declare laws and actions of the local, state, or national government invalid if they contradict the Constitution.

Judiciary Act of 1789 A law passed by the first Congress to establish the federal court system. The act determined the organization and jurisdiction of the courts.

jurisdiction The power or authority to hear cases and make decisions.

justice (1) Fair treatment according to law. (2) A member of the Supreme Court.

law A rule established by government or other source of authority to regulate people's conduct or activities. In the United States a bill that is passed by the legislature and is signed by the executive, or which is passed over his or her veto, becomes a law.

law of nature In natural rights philosophy, the law of nature would prevail in the absence of man-made law and contains standards of justice that apply to all people.

legal permanent resident A person who is not a citizen, but who legally lives in the United States. Legal permanent residents enjoy most of the rights of citizens. They have the same right to due process of law as citizens, they must pay taxes, and they may serve in the military.

legislative branch The branch of government that makes the laws.

legislative supremacy A system of government in which the legislative branch has ultimate power.

legislature A group of officials in government who have the authority to make and change laws.

Letter from Birmingham City Jail A letter written to fellow clergymen by Martin Luther King Jr. in Birmingham, Alabama, on April 16, 1963, after his arrest for violating a state court order against participating in protests. In his letter, King explains the reasons for his involvement in the civil rights movement and for his belief in nonviolent methods of protest.

liberty, right to The right to be free. Some examples of liberties are the rights to believe what you wish, to read what you want, to speak freely, and to travel wherever you want to go.

life, right to The right to live without fear of being injured or killed by others or by government.

limited government In natural rights philosophy, a system restricted to protecting natural rights that does not interfere with other aspects of life.

limits Restrictions or boundaries on governmental power.

literacy test A test that requires people to prove that they are able to read and write. Until 1964, these tests were used in various states throughout the country to keep minorities from voting.

lobby To represent a group in trying to influence legislatures.

Loyalists Colonists who opposed American independence and remained loyal to Great Britain during the American Revolution.

magistrate A lower-level judicial officer, usually elected in urban areas, who handles traffic violations, minor criminal offenses, and civil suits involving small amounts of money.

Magna Carta This document, also known as the Great Charter, was agreed to by King John of England in 1215 at the demand of his barons. The Magna Carta granted certain civil rights and liberties to English nobles, such as the right to a jury of one's peers and the guarantee against loss of life, liberty, or property, except in accordance with law. In doing so, it also limited the power of the monarch. The document is a landmark in the history of limited constitutional government.

majority rule A principle of democracy that asserts that the greater number of citizens in any political unit should select officials and determine policies.

Marbury v. Madison **(1803)** A landmark case in which the Supreme Court, for the first time in American history, struck down an act of Congress as unconstitutional, establishing the Court's power of constitutional judicial review.

Massachusetts Body of Liberties (1641) The first American document to describe the rights of individuals.

Massachusetts constitution A state constitution ratified by Massachusetts voters in 1780. It is the oldest written constitution still in use in the world today.

Mayflower Compact An agreement to form a political body signed in 1620 by all adult males aboard the Mayflower before the ship landed in Plymouth, Massachusetts. The signers agreed to submit to "just and equal Laws" put into effect under the compact.

misdemeanor A minor criminal offense that is less serious than a felony, a major offense. The punishment for a misdemeanor is a fine or imprisonment for up to one year.

monarchy A form of government in which political power is held by a single ruler such as a king or queen.

monitor To keep watch over something.

National Association for the Advancement of Colored People An interracial interest group founded in 1909 to advocate the rights of African Americans, primarily through legal and political action. Also called the NAACP.

national government The organization having central political authority in a nation. The representative unit of political organization.

nation-state The modern nation or country as the typical unit of political organization in the world.

natural law A higher, unchanging set of rules that govern human relations believed by the Founders to have come from "Nature and Nature's God" (from the Declaration of Independence).

natural rights A doctrine that human beings have basic rights, such as those to life, liberty, and property in a state of nature and that people create governments to protect those rights.

naturalized citizens People who are born elsewhere but pass a citizenship test on the Constitution and the history of the United States and swear an oath of loyalty to their new country.

necessary and proper clause Article I, Section 8, Clause 18 of the Constitution that gives Congress the power to make all laws that are "necessary and proper" to carry out the powers specifically delegated to it by the Constitution. It is also known as the elastic clause.

New Jersey Plan The plan presented at the Philadelphia Convention that called for a one-house national legislature with each state having equal representation. The New Jersey Plan followed the framework of the Articles of Confederation and favored a weak national government.

Nineteenth Amendment Added to the Constitution in 1920, it gave women the right to vote.

Ninth Amendment This amendment states, in effect, that the Bill of Rights is only a partial listing of the rights of the people.

nongovernmental organization An organization independent of direct governmental control that exists to perform humanitarian or educational services or to affect public policy. Also called an NGO.

Northwest Ordinance (1787) An important law passed by Congress under the Articles of Confederation. The law prohibited slavery in the Northwest Territory and provided for settling the western lands and the admission and organization of new states.

null and void Of no legal or binding force; invalid.

opinion of the Court A written explanation of the Supreme Court's decision in a particular case and its reasoning behind the decision.

ordinance A municipal statute or regulation.

Organization of American States A regional organization composed of North, South, and Central American nations. It was formed in 1948 to promote economic, political, military, and cultural cooperation among its members.

original jurisdiction The legal authority of a court to be the first to hear a case.

override To pass a bill after it has been vetoed. Congress may override the president's veto by a two-thirds vote of both houses.

Parliament The British legislature, which consists of two houses: the House of Lords, representing the nobility, most of whose appointments are no longer hereditary, and the House of Commons, representing the people.

participation Taking part in or sharing in the activities of a group, organization, or system.

Patriots Those Americans who supported the war for independence against Great Britain.

peer A person of equal standing or rank.

persecute To harass or cause suffering to a person or group because of such things as their beliefs or principles.

petition, right to The legal claim that allows a person to ask his or her government to correct things that he or she thinks are wrong or to do things he or she believes are needed.

Petition of Rights (1628) A statute that limited the English monarch's power to tax people without the consent of Parliament and guaranteed certain rights to English subjects.

Philadelphia Convention The meeting held in Philadelphia from May to September 1787 at which the Constitution was written. Also called the Constitutional Convention.

plantation A large farm usually located in the Southern states.

Plessy v. Ferguson **(1896)** The case in which the Supreme Court ruled that "separate but equal" public facilities for blacks and whites were permissible under the Constitution.

political action Any organized attempt to influence the political process, from lobbying legislators to seeking the election or defeat of particular candidates.

political parties Any organization that seeks to achieve political power by electing members to public office so that their political philosophies can be reflected in public policies.

political philosophy A set of ideas about government and politics.

political rights All rights of a citizen in a free society that are clearly expressed and guaranteed by the Constitution and implied by natural laws.

politics A process by which people with different opinions and interests reach decisions without the use of violence.

poll tax A tax that voters in many states were required to pay in order to exercise their right to vote. These barriers were used until 1964 to prevent African Americans from voting.

popular sovereignty The natural rights concept that ultimate political authority rests with the people.

population The number of people living in an area.

Preamble The introduction to the Constitution. It states that the people establish the government and lists the purposes of the government.

press (1) Newspapers, magazines, television, and other news media. (2) The reporters and people who produce them.

principle A general statement of moral or political belief.

privacy, right to The right or legal claim that allows a person to be free from intrusion by government officials into areas of one's life that are of no concern to government.

private domain Areas of a person's life that are not subject to governmental interference.

procedure The methods or steps taken to accomplish something.

Proclamation of 1763 A British law that banned settlement in certain western lands to reduce tensions between the colonists and Native Americans. The law was unpopular among American frontiersmen and traders.

property, right to The right or legal claim that allows a person to own things and to transfer them to others. Your labor or work is also your property.

proportional representation The electoral system in which the number of representatives for a state is based on the number of people who live in that state. Proportional representation is used to determine the number of each state's representatives serving in the House of Representatives.

Quartering Act (1765) Also known as the Mutiny Act, this British law authorized colonial governors to requisition certain buildings for the housing, or "quartering," of British troops.

Quebec Campaign (1775–76) A military expedition that was an attempt by the Americans to protect the American north and persuade the Canadians to join their rebellion against Britain. American forces invaded Canada and captured Montreal in late 1774. The British forced the Americans to retreat in the spring of 1776.

ratification Formal approval of the Constitution by the ratifying conventions held in each state.

ratify To confirm and approve.

ratifying conventions Meetings held in the states to approve the Constitution.

Red Cross See International Red Cross and Red Crescent.

redress of grievances Correction of complaints. The First Amendment protects the right to petition the government to obtain a remedy for a claimed wrong.

regenerate To revive, renew, or give new life to.

register To enroll one's name officially as a requirement for voting.

representative A person elected to act and speak for others.

representative democracy A system of government in which the people elect officials to make and administer laws for their country.

representative government A system for ruling in which elected representatives are chosen by the people to act on their behalf.

republic A nation that has a government in which power is held by the people who elect representatives to manage the government for them for the sake of the common good.

republican government A system for ruling in which power is held by the people who are eligible to elect representatives to run the government for the common good. The term does not refer to a political party.

Republican Party The first political organization formed in opposition to the Federalist Party by the supporters of Thomas Jefferson. It evolved into the Democratic Party in 1828 and has no connection to the present-day Republican Party.

republicanism A form of government in which the supreme political power resides in the people who are qualified to vote; governance is carried out by representatives who are responsible to the people. Republicanism requires the citizenry and public officials to be devoted to the common good.

rights of Englishmen Basic legal claims established over time, that all subjects of the English monarch were understood to have. They included the right not to be kept in prison without a trial and the right to trial by jury.

rule of law The principle that both those who govern and those who are governed must obey the law and are subject to the same laws. This principle is contrasted to the "rule of men," in which those in power make up the rules as they please.

Second Amendment Part of the Bill of Rights added to the Constitution in 1791. The Amendment says "A well-regulated militia, being necessary to the security of a free State, the right of the people to keep and bear Arms, shall not be infringed."

Second Continental Congress The body of delegates representing the colonies that met in 1775 shortly after the start of the Revolutionary War. They organized the Continental Army, called on the colonies to send troops, selected George Washington to lead the army, and appointed a committee to draft the Declaration of Independence.

segregation The separation or isolation of a race, class, or ethnic group from the rest of society.

self-evident Easy for anyone to see; obvious.

self-incrimination, right against The Fifth Amendment guarantees that one cannot be forced to give testimony that could subject oneself to prosecution.

self-interest One's personal concern.

self-sufficient Able to provide for most of one's own needs.

Senate One of the two houses of Congress. Each state is represented by two members in the Senate.

separate but equal The argument, once upheld by the Supreme Court but later reversed, that different public facilities for blacks and whites were constitutional if the facilities were of equal quality.

separation of church and state A basic principle of American government that no one religion should be favored by government over other religions. Nor should government interfere with one's right to practice or not practice religious beliefs. This metaphor was used in 1802 by President Thomas Jefferson to explain his understanding of the protection of religious freedom afforded by the Constitution.

separation of powers The division of powers among the different branches of government. In the United States, powers are divided among the legislative, executive, and judicial branches.

serf In feudal times peasants were also known as serfs. They farmed the land and were not free to leave the area in which they worked.

Shays' Rebellion An armed revolt by Massachusetts farmers in 1786–87 who sought relief from debts and foreclosures of mortgages. Led by Daniel Shays, the group prevented judges from hearing mortgage foreclosure cases and attempted to capture an arsenal.

"The Shot heard 'round the World" A line in a poem by Ralph Waldo Emerson describing the effect of the outbreak of the American Revolution in April 1775. The American Revolution and its principles became extremely influential around the world. It was the first of many rebellions by countries against their colonial rulers.

sit-in Nonviolent demonstration in which persons protesting certain conditions sit down in an appropriate place and refuse to move until their demands are considered or met.

Sixth Amendment An Amendment that guarantees the rights to a "fair and speedy" trial by jury in criminal cases, to be informed of the nature of the charges in the case, to call witnesses, and to have the assistance of a lawyer.

slave A person whose human rights are denied and who is forced to work for another person without compensation.

slave trade The commercial practice of forcibly taking people from their homes in Africa and selling them into slavery in the new world.

social action Attempts by groups or individuals to change society using a variety of means.

social contract An agreement among the people to set up a government and obey its laws. The theory was developed by the natural rights philosopher John Locke to explain the origin of legitimate government.

Sons of Liberty An organization created in 1765 in every colony to express opposition to the Stamp Act. A popular goal of the organization was to force stamp distributors throughout the colonies to resign.

sovereign A person or group having the highest authority or power in a country or state.

speech, freedom of The right to express your beliefs, ideas, or feelings.

Stamp Act (1765) A British law that required the payment of a tax through the purchase of stamps for documents such as newspapers, magazines, and legal and commercial papers of all kinds.

state of nature The basis of natural rights philosophy; a state of nature is the condition of people living in a situation without manmade government, rules, or laws.

subject Someone who owes allegiance to a government or ruler.

suffrage The right to vote.

Sugar Act of 1764 A British law designed to stop smuggling of goods into and out of the colonies. The law gave the British navy greater power to search colonial ships.

supremacy clause Article VI, Section 2 of the Constitution, which states that the Constitution, laws passed by Congress, and treaties of the United States "shall be the supreme Law of the Land" and binding on the states.

tariff A tax on imported or exported goods or a list or system that describes such taxes.

Tea Act (1773) The British law that granted the East India Company a monopoly on the importation of tea into the colonies, thus eliminating the profits of colonial importers and shopkeepers.

Tenth Amendment This Amendment holds that the "powers not delegated to the United States by the Constitution, nor prohibited by it to the States, are reserved to the States respectively, or the people." The Tenth Amendment embodies the principle of federalism, which reserves for the states the residue of powers not granted to the federal government or withheld from the states, and the principle of popular sovereignty, which reserves other rights to the people.

Thirteenth Amendment This Amendment abolished slavery. It was adopted after the Civil War in 1865.

three-fifths clause Article I, Section 2, Clause 3 of the U.S. Constitution, later eliminated by the Fourteenth Amendment. The clause provided that each slave should be counted as three-fifths of a person in determining the number of representatives a state might send to the House of Representatives. It also determined the amount of direct taxes Congress may levy on a state.

***Tinker v. Des Moines School District* (1969)** A Supreme Court case in which the Court ruled that schools cannot limit a student's right to freedom of expression unless the student's exercise of that right disrupts the educational process.

tract An area of land or water.

treason Betrayal of one's country, especially by giving aid to an enemy in wartime or by plotting to overthrow the government. Treason is carefully defined in the Constitution to ensure that government cannot abuse its powers against dissenters.

Treaty of Paris The agreement signed on September 3, 1783, between Great Britain and the United States that ended the Revolutionary War. With the treaty, Great Britain recognized the independence of the United States. Also called the Peace of Paris.

Twenty-fifth Amendment The Amendment that describes who becomes president if the president dies, is removed from office, resigns, or can no longer perform presidential duties. It also describes how the office of vice president is to be filled if a vacancy occurs.

Twenty-fourth Amendment The Amendment adopted in 1964 that forbids the levying of a poll tax or any other tax on eligible voters in elections for federal officials, including the president, vice president, and members of Congress.

Twenty-second Amendment The Amendment that prohibits any person from being elected president more than twice.

Twenty-sixth Amendment The Amendment adopted in 1971 that says a state cannot deny someone the right to vote if they have reached the age of 18 and are otherwise eligible to vote. Although eighteen-year-olds had already been accorded the vote in national elections by the Voting Rights Act of 1970, the Twenty-sixth Amendment assured them the vote in all elections.

tyranny A government in which a single ruler possesses and abuses absolute power.

unalienable rights See inalienable rights.

unconstitutional Not allowed by the Constitution; illegal; contradicts the Constitution.

unitary government A centralized form of government in which states or local governments exercise only those powers delegated to them by the central or national government.

United Nations An international organization created in 1945 to maintain peace through the collective security of its members.

United States Supreme Court The highest court in the United States. See Article III, Section 1 of the Constitution.

GLOSSARY

Universal Postal Union An agency of the United Nations dedicated to improving postal services throughout the world. Also called the UPU.

vassal In feudal times, a person granted the use of land by a feudal lord, in return for which he rendered military or other service.

veto The right of a branch of government to reject a bill that has been passed in an effort to delay or prevent its enactment. Under the U.S. Constitution it is the power of the president to refuse to sign a bill passed by Congress, thereby preventing it from becoming a law. The president's veto may be overridden by a two-thirds vote of both the Senate and House of Representatives.

Virginia Declaration of Rights The first state declaration of rights, which served as a model for other state declarations of rights and the Bill of Rights and influenced the Declaration of Independence. It was adopted on June 12, 1776.

Virginia Plan The plan presented at the Philadelphia Convention that provided for a national government composed of three branches. It proposed a Congress of two houses, both of which would be based on proportional representation. The Virginia Plan favored a strong national government.

Voting Rights Act (1965) The act further protected the right to vote for all U.S. citizens. It forced the states to obey the Constitution. It made it clear that the right to vote could not be denied because of a person's color or race.

writ of habeas corpus A court order directing that a prisoner be brought to court before a judge to determine if the detention of the person is lawful. From the Latin term meaning, "you shall/should have the body."

writs of assistance Documents giving a governmental authority the power to search and seize property without restrictions.

Yorktown Surrender The final military act that ended the Revolutionary War. In October 1781, American and French forces blocked a British escape from the Yorktown Peninsula in Virginia. On October 17–19, 1781, the British forces under Lord Cornwallis surrendered at Yorktown to the American army under George Washington.

INDEX

Lesson Eight

Page 67, *The Rebels of '76*, Prints and Photographs Division, Library of Congress, LC-USZC4-2485; 68, J.L.G. Ferris, *Writing the Declaration of Independence, 1776*, Prints and Photographs Division, Library of Congress, LC-USZC4-9904; 69, Declaration of Independence, National Archives and Records Administration; 70, Pendelton's Lithography, *Thomas Jefferson*, Prints and Photographs Division, Library of Congress, LC-USZ62-117117; 72, Benjamin West, *Reception of the American Loyalists in England*, Picture Collection, The Branch Libraries, The New York Public Library, Astor, Lenox and Tilden Foundations; 73, Colonial boys mocking a Loyalist, The Granger Collection, New York.

Lesson Nine

Page 75, *British Soldiers During a Reenactment of the Battle of Lexington*, © Franklin McMahon/CORBIS; 76, Paul Revere's ride from Boston to Lexington, April 18, 1775, The Granger Collection, New York; 78, Martha Washington visits George Washington at headquarters, Morristown, Picture Collection, The Branch Libraries, The New York Public Library, Astor, Lenox and Tilden Foundations; 79, General George Washington with Lafayette at Valley Forge, 1777, The Granger Collection, New York; 80, Anton Hohenstein, *Franklin's Reception at the Court of France, 1778*, Prints and Photographs Division, Library of Congress, LC-USZC4-623; 81, British surrender at Yorktown, October 19, 1781, after Arthur Burdett Frost, The Granger Collection, New York.

Lesson Ten

Page 83, James B. Marston, *Old State House*, © Burnstein Collection/CORBIS; 84, John Hancock, by unidentified artist after John Singleton Copley, Collection of The New-York Historical Society, accession number 1945.84; 85, E. Percy Moran, *The Concord Stage*, Prints and Photographs Division, Library of Congress, LC-USZC4-4972; 86 (l), North Carolina banknote, 1778, The Granger Collection, New York; 86 (r), South Carolina banknote, 1778, The Granger Collection, New York; 88, Robert Feke, *Portrait of James Bowdoin II*, Bowdoin College Museum of Art, Brunswick, Maine, Bequest of Mrs. Sarah Bowdoin Dearborn; 90, *The Pillory*, The Granger Collection, New York; 91, Liz Roll/FEMA.

Lesson Eleven

Page 93, Articles of Confederation, National Archives and Records Administration; 94, Howard Pyle, Carpenter's Hall, Philadelphia, The Granger Collection, New York; 95, *American Colonies, 1777*, by Mapping Specialists, www.mappingspecialists.com, © 2006 Center for Civic Education; 97, Howard Pyle, A colonial schoolmaster and his pupils, Pennsylvania, The Granger Collection, New York.

Unit Three

Page 103, Henry Hintermeister, *The Foundation of American Government*, detail, Prints and Photographs Division, Library of Congress, LC-USZ62-950.

Lesson Twelve

Page 105, Junius Brutus Stearns, *George Washington as Statesman at the Constitutional Convention*, The Granger Collection, New York; 106, John Vanderlyn, *James Madison*, White House Historical Association (White House Collection); 107, Howard Chandler Christy, *Scene at the Signing of the Constitution of the United States*, U.S. Capitol Historical Society; 108 (l), Photograph by Martin Lenders for the U.S. Census Bureau, Public Information Office (PIO); 108 (cl), Photograph by Lloyd Wolf for the U.S. Census Bureau, Public Information Office (PIO); 108 (cr), Photograph by Lloyd Wolf for the U.S. Census Bureau, Public Information Office (PIO); 108 (r), Photograph by Michael Newell for the U.S. Census Bureau, Public Information Office (PIO); 111, First page of the U.S. Constitution, National Archives and Records Administration.

Lesson Thirteen

Page 113, U.S. Senate, 109th Congress (2006), U.S. Senate Historical Office; 114, © 2006 Jupiterimages Corporation; 115, *Population of American Colonies, 1790*, by Mapping Specialists, www.mappingspecialists.com, © 2006 Center for Civic Education; 118, Department of Defense photo by Master Sgt. Ken Hammond; 119, AP/WORLD WIDE PHOTOS/Joe Marquette.

Lesson Fourteen

Page 121, Currier & Ives, *A Cotton Plantation on the Mississippi*, Prints and Photographs Division, Library of Congress, LC-USZC2-3367; 122, Earle Wilton Richardson, *Employment of Negroes in Agriculture*, detail, Smithsonian American Art Museum, Washington, D.C./Art Resource, NY; 123, Fitz Hugh Lane, *The Fort and Ten Pound Island, Gloucester, 1848*, detail, The Newark Museum/Art Resource, NY; 125, *A Slave-Coffle Passing the Capitol*, Prints and Photographs Division, Library of Congress, LC-USZ62-2574; 126, John Singleton Copley, *Paul Revere*, The Granger Collection, New York; 127, James E. Taylor, *The Primary Causes of War—The Negro and Cotton*, Picture Collection, The Branch Libraries, The New York Public Library, Astor, Lenox and Tilden Foundations.

Lesson Fifteen

Page 129, © CORBIS; 130, AP/WIDE WORLD PHOTOS/Danny Johnston; 132, Photo by Vance Harris, USPS; 133, © Bettmann/CORBIS; 134, Courtesy NASA.

1184; 217, Thomas Kelly, *The Fifteenth Amendment, Celebrated May 19th 1870*, Prints and Photographs Division, Library of Congress, LC-USZC4-2399; 219, Theodor Geisel (Dr. Seuss), *Democracy's Turnstile*, published originally in *PM*, October 12, 1942, courtesy of Mandeville Special Collections Library, University of California, San Diego, copyright holder unknown; 220 (l), Prints & Photographs Division, Library of Congress, LC-USZ62-75334; 220 (r), Prints & Photographs Division, Library of Congress, LC-USZ62-111409; 221 (l) U.S. Air Force photo by Airman Basic Stacey Jeanpaul; 221 (r), AP/WORLD WIDE PHOTOS/Dave Martin; 222, AP/WORLD WIDE PHOTOS/Kuni; 223, AP/WORLD WIDE PHOTOS/Paul Connors.

Lesson Twenty-Six
Page 225, © Bettmann/CORBIS, 226; *Scene in the House on the Passage of the Proposition to Amend the Constitution, January 31, 1865*, Prints & Photographs Division, Library of Congress, LC-USZ62-127599; 227, AP/WORLD WIDE PHOTOS/ Toby Talbot; 228, Ted Streshinsky/CORBIS; 229, AP/WORLD WIDE PHOTOS; 230 (l), AP/WORLD WIDE PHOTOS/Gene Herrick; 230 (r), Prints & Photographs Division, Library of Congress, LC-DIG-ppmsca-03130; 231, AP/WORLD WIDE PHOTOS.

Lesson Twenty-Seven
Pages 233, 234, 235, 239 (l), William Fritsch/Brand X Pictures; 239 (r), © Bettmann/CORBIS.

Unit Six
Page 241, Evan Vucci/epa/Corbis.

Lesson Twenty-Eight
Page 243, AP/WORLD WIDE PHOTOS/J. Scott Applewhite; 244, © 2006 Center for Civic Education; 245, George Bush Presidential Library; 246, Department of Defense photo by Petty Officer 3rd Class Rebecca J. Moat, U.S. Navy; 247, UN photo; 248, U.S. Air Force photo by Tech. Sgt. Brian Davidson; 249, © European Community, 2005; 250, Peter Turnley/CORBIS.

Lesson Twenty-Nine
Page 253, AP/WIDE WORLD PHOTOS/Steven Senne; 254, Photo Courtesy of the Indian Health Service/ U.S. Department of Health and Human Services; 255, Mel Yates/Photodisc Red/Getty Images; 257, James Montgomery Flagg, *I Want You for U.S. Army: Nearest Recruiting Station*, Prints & Photographs Division, Library of Congress, LC-USZC4-3859; 258 (t), Prints & Photographs Division, Library of Congress, LC-USZ61-361; 258 (b), ©Bettmann/CORBIS; 259, AP/WORLD WIDE PHOTOS/ Scott Applewhite; 261, © 2006 Center for Civic Education.

Lesson Thirty
Page 263, CJ GUNTHER/EPA/LANDOV; 264, AP/WORLD WIDE PHOTOS/Steve Cannon; 265, AP/WORLD WIDE PHOTOS/Coke Whitworth; 267, AP/WORLD WIDE PHOTOS/Doug Dreyer; 270, United States Environmental Protection Agency Great Lakes National Program office, photo by David Riecks; 272, Jocelyn Augustino/FEMA.

Reference
Page 275, Scribes in ancient Greece, The Granger Collection, New York; 276, Declaration of Independence, National Archives and Records Administration; 280, U.S. Constitution, National Archives and Records Administration.

QUICKFIND COLOR KEY

UNIT OPENER

TERMS TO UNDERSTAND

LESSON OPENER

IDEAS FOR DISCUSSION

SOLVE THE PROBLEM

PARTICIPATING IN A CLASS ACTIVITY

LESSON REVIEW

ACTIVITIES

THE DECLARATION OF INDEPENDENCE

THE CONSTITUTION OF THE UNITED STATES

AMENDMENTS TO THE THE CONSTITUTION

GLOSSARY

INDEX

PHOTO CREDITS

Adler, David A. *B. Franklin, Printer*. New York: Holiday House, 2001. 128pp. ISBN 0-8234-1675-5. Illustrated with prints and photographs. Chronologies of Franklin and the New World, Source Notes, Web Sites, Bibliography, Index.

Avi. *Night Journeys*. Reissue edition: New York: Avon Books, 2000. 160pp. ISBN 0-3807-3242-4.

Bober, Natalie S. *Countdown to Independence: A Revolution of Ideas in England and Her American Colonies: 1760–1776*. New York: Atheneum Books for Young Readers, 2001. 368pp. ISBN 0-6898-1329-5. Illustrated with prints and photographs. Author's Notes, Bibliography, Index, Reference Notes.

Brady, Sheila, Carolyn Pereira, and Diana Hess. *It's Yours, the Bill of Rights: Lessons on the Bill of Rights for Students of English as a Second Language*. Chicago: Constitutional Rights Foundation, 1991. 111pp. ASIN B0006F1VO8.

Commager, Henry Steele. *The Great Constitution: A Book for Young Americans*. Indianapolis, IN: Bobbs-Merrill, 1961. 128pp. ISBN 0-0272-4200-5.

Crowe, Chris. *Mississippi Trial, 1955*. New York: Phyllis Fogelman Books/Penguin Group USA. 240pp. ISBN 0-8037-2745-3. Historical Note.

Diouf, Sylviane A. *Growing Up in Slavery*. Brookfield, CT: Millbrook Press, 2001. 96pp. ISBN 0-7613-1763-5. Bibliography, Index. Illustrated with prints and photographs.

Faber, Doris, and Harold Faber. *We the People: The Story of the Constitution Since 1787*. New York: Scribner, 1987. 244pp. ISBN 0-6841-8753-1. Bibliography, Index.

Fleming, Candace. *Ben Franklin's Almanac: Being a True Account of the Good Gentleman's Life*. New York: Anne Schwartz Books/Atheneum Books for Young Readers, 2003. 128pp. ISBN 0-689-83549-3. Bibliography, Chronology, Web Resources, Index.

Fradin, Dennis Brindell. *The Signers: The 56 Stories behind the Declaration of Independence*. New York: Walker & Company, 2002. 160pp. ISBN 0-8027-8849-1. Illustrated by Michael McCurdy. Bibliography, Index, Illustrator's Note, Afterword.

Fradin, Dennis Brindell, and Judith Bloom Fradin. *Fight On! Mary Church Terrell's Battle for Integration*. New York: Clarion Books, 2003. 192pp. ISBN 0-618-13349-6. Illustrations, Source Notes, Bibliography, Index.

Freedman, Russell. *Give Me Liberty! The Story of the Declaration of Independence*. New York: Holiday House, 2002. 90pp. ISBN 0-8234-1753-0. Illustrated, Bibliographical References, Index.

Freedman, Russell. *In Defense of Liberty: The Story of America's Bill of Rights*. New York: Holiday House, 2003. 196pp. ISBN 0-8234-1585-6. Illustrated, Notes, Bibliography, Index.

Fritz, Jean. *Shh! We're Writing the Constitution*. New York: Putnam, 1987. 64 pp. ISBN 0-3992-1403-8. Illustrated by Tomie dePaola.

Fritz, Jean. *Why Don't You Get a Horse, Sam Adams?* Original edition: New York: Putnam, 1974. 47pp. ISBN 0-3992-3401-2. Reissue edition: Glenview, Il: Scott Foresman (Pearson K–12), 1996. ISBN 0-6981-1416-7. Illustrated by Trina Schart Hyman.

Fritz, Jean. *Will You Sign Here, John Hancock?* Original edition: New York: Coward McCann, 1976. 47pp. ISBN 0-3992-3306-7. Reprint edition: New York: Putnam, 1997. 48pp. ISBN 0-6981-1440-X.

Gaustad, Edwin S. *Roger Williams: Prophet of Liberty*. New York: Oxford University Press Children's Books, 2001. 144pp. ISBN 0-1951-3000-6. Oxford Portraits. Illustrated with prints and photographs.

Giblin, James. *The Amazing Life of Benjamin Franklin*. New York: Scholastic Press, 2000. 48pp. ISBN 0-5904-8534-2. Important Dates, Selected Listing of Inventions, Sayings from Poor Richard's Almanack, Significant Historical Sites, Bibliography and Source Notes, Artist's Note, Source Notes, and Index.

Gormley, Beatrice. *First Ladies: Women Who Called the White House Home*. New York: Scholastic, 1997. 112pp. ISBN 0-5902-5518-5.

Granfield, Linda. *America Votes: How Our President Is Elected*. New York: Kids Can Press, 2003. 64pp. ISBN 1-5533-7086-4. Illustrated by Steve Björkman.

Greenfeld, Howard. *After the Holocaust*. New York: Greenwillow Books, 2001. 160pp. ISBN 0-6881-7752-2. Illustrated with photographs. Bibliography, Index.

Gündisch, Karin. *How I Became an American*. Chicago: Cricket Books, 2001. 144pp. ISBN 0-8126-4875-7. Translated by James Skofield.

Gutman, Dan. *The Kid Who Ran for President*. New York: Scholastic, 1996. 156pp. ISBN 0-5909-3987-4.

Haskins, James, and Kathleen Benson. *Building a New Land: African Americans in Colonial America*. New York: HarperCollins Juvenile Books, 2001. 44pp. ISBN 0-6881-0266-2. Illustrated by James Ransome. Milestones of the Period, Bibliography, Index.

Hill, Christine M. *John Lewis: From Freedom Rider to Congressman*. Berkeley Heights, NJ: Enslow Publishers, 2002. 128pp. ISBN 0-7660-1768-0. African American biographies. Chronology, Index, Chapter Notes.

Hilton, Suzanne. *We the People: The Way We Were, 1783–1793*. Philadelphia: Westminster Press, 1981. ISBN 0-6643-2685-4.

Irvin, Benjamin H. *Samuel Adams: Son of Liberty, Father of Revolution*. New York: Oxford University Press, 2002. 160pp. ISBN 0-1951-3225-4. Oxford Portraits series. Illustrated with prints and photographs. Chronology, Further Reading, Index.

Kendall, Martha E. *Failure Is Impossible! The History of American Women's Rights*. New York: Lerner Publications Company, 2003. 96pp. ISBN 0-8225-1744-2. Illustrated with prints and photographs. Author's Notes, Bibliography, Index, Timeline, Remarkable Women.

Levy, Elizabeth. *If You Were There When They Signed the Constitution*. Original edition: New York: Scholastic, 1987. Revised edition: 1992. 80pp. ISBN 0-5904-5159-6. Illustrated by Joan Holub and Richard Rosenblum.

Littlefield, Holly. *Children of the Indian Boarding Schools*. Minneapolis: Carolrhoda Books/Lerner, 2001. 48pp. ISBN 1-5750-5467-1. Illustrated with photographs. Index, Glossary.

Maestro, Betsy, and Giulio Maestro. *A More Perfect Union: The Story of Our Constitution*. Original edition: Boston: Lothrop, Lee & Shepard Books, 1987. Reprint edition: Scott Foresman, 1990. 48pp. ISBN 0-6881-0192-5. Illustrated by Giulio Maestro.

Masoff, Joy. *Colonial Times 1600–1700*. New York: Scholastic Reference, 2000. 48pp. ISBN 0-4390-5107-X. Illustrated, includes Bibliography and Index.

McPhillips, Martin. *The Constitutional Convention*. Morristown, NJ: Silver Burdett Press, 1986. 64pp. ISBN 0-3820-6927-0. Turning Points in American History.

Mead, Alice. *Girl of Kosovo*. New York: Farrar, Straus and Giroux, 2001. 128pp. ISBN 0-3743-2620-7.

Meltzer, Milton. *There Comes a Time: The Struggle for Civil Rights*. New York: Random House, 2001. 208pp. ISBN 0-3758-0407-2. Illustrated with photographs. Foreword, Chronology, Bibliography, Index.

Miller, Brandon Marie. *Growing Up in Revolution and the New Nation 1775 to 1800*. Minneapolis: Lerner Publishing Group, 2002. 64pp. ISBN 0-8225-0078-7. Our America series. Illustrated with prints and photographs. Author's Note, Activities, Source Notes, Bibliography, Index.

Morris, Richard. *The Constitution*. Minneapolis: Lerner Publications Company, 1985. 69pp. ISBN 0-8225-1702-7. Revised edition of *The First Book of the Constitution*. New York: Franklin Watts, 1958. Illustrated by Leonard Everett Fisher.

Murray, Stuart. *American Revolution*. New York: DK Publishing, 2002. 64pp. ISBN 0-7894-8556-7. Illustrated with prints and photographs. Index.

Naidoo, Beverley. *The Other Side of Truth*. Original edition: New York: HarperCollins, 2000. 252pp. ISBN 0-0602-9628-3. Reprint edition: New York: HarperTrophy, 2002. 272pp. ISBN 0-0644-1002-1. Winner of Britain's 2000 Carnegie Medal.

Nardo, Don. *The Declaration of Independence: A Model for Individual Rights*. San Diego, CA: Lucent Books, 1999. 96pp. ISBN 1-5600-6368-8.

O'Dell, Scott. *Zia*. Boston: Houghton Mifflin & Co., 1976. Reissue edition: New York: Dell Laurel-Leaf, 1995. 192pp. ISBN 0-4402-1956-6.

Peterson, Helen Stone. *The Making of the United States Constitution*. Champaign, IL: Garrard Publishing Company, 1974. 96pp. ISBN 0-8116-6509-7. Out of print.

Prolman, Marilyn. *The Story of the Constitution*. Chicago: Children's Press, 1995. 36pp. ISBN 0-5160-6692-7.

Robertson, James I., Jr. *Standing Like a Stone Wall: The Life of General Thomas J. Jackson*. New York: Atheneum Books for Young Readers, 2001. 192pp. ISBN 0-6898-2419-X. Illustrated with photographs and prints. Introduction, Epilogue, Notes, Sources, Index.

Sigerman, Harriet. *Elizabeth Cady Stanton: The Right Is Ours*. Oxford: Oxford University Press Children's Books, 2001. 144pp. ISBN 0-1951-1969-X. Oxford Portraits series. Illustrated with prints and photographs. Chronology, Further Reading, Museums and Historic Sites, Biographies of Other Women's Rights Leaders.

St. George, Judith. *John and Abigail Adams: An American Love Story*. New York: Holiday House, 2001. 192pp. ISBN 0-8234-1571-6. Illustrated with prints. Author's Notes, Bibliography, Index, Adams Family Chronology, Websites, Epilogue.

St. George, Judith. *So, You Want to Be President?* New York: Philomel Books, 2000. 52pp. ISBN 0-3992-3407-1. Illustrated by David Small. Winner of the 2001 Caldecott Medal.

Taylor, Mildred D. *Song of the Trees*. Original edition: New York: Bantam Books, 1984. Reissue edition: New York: Bantam Doubleday Dell Books for Young Readers, 1997. 52pp. ISBN 0-4404-1396-6. Illustrated by Jerry Pinkney. Yearling Book Series.

Thomas, Joyce Carol, ed. *Linda Brown, You Are Not Alone: The Brown v. Board of Education Decision*. New York: Jump at the Sun/Hyperion Books for Children, 2003. 128pp. ISBN 0-7868-0821-7. Illustrated by Curtis James.

Turner, Ann Warren. *Nettie's Trip South*. Original edition: New York: Simon & Schuster, 1987. 32pp. Reprint edition: New York: Aladdin Paperbacks, 1995. 32pp. ISBN 0-6898-0117-3. Illustrated by Ronald Himler.

SUGGESTED READING LIST FOR TEACHERS

al-Hibri, Azizah Y., Jean Bethke Elshtain, and Charles C. Haynes. *Religion in American Public Life: Living with Our Deepest Differences*. New York: Norton, 2001. 201pp. ISBN 0-3933-2206-8.

Bahmueller, Charles. *Civitas: A Framework for Civic Education*. Calabasas, CA: Center for Civic Education, 1991. 665pp. ISBN 0-8981-8124-0.

Bahmueller, Charles. *Elements of Democracy*. Calabasas, CA: Center for Civic Education, 2007. 138pp. ISBN 0-89818-201-8.

Baker, Daniel B., ed. *Power Quotes: 4,000 Trenchant Soundbites on Leadership & Liberty, Treason & Triumph, Sacrifice & Scandal, Risk & Rebellion, Weakness & War, and Other Affaires Politiques*. Detroit: Visible Ink Press, 1991. 408pp. ISBN 0-8103-9416-2.

Bernstein, Richard B. *Are We to Be a Nation? The Making of the Constitution*. Cambridge, MA: Harvard University Press, 1987. 342pp. ISBN 0-67404-475-4.

Blaisdell, Thomas C., Jr., et al. *The American Presidency in Political Cartoons, 1776–1976*. Berkeley, CA: University Art Museum, 1976. 278pp. ISBN 0-8790-5027-6.

Bowen, Catherine Drinker. *Miracle at Philadelphia*. Mattituck, NY: Amereon Ltd., 2003. 370pp. ISBN 0-8488-2565-9.

Center for Civic Education. *We the People: The Citizen & the Constitution*, Level I. Calabasas, CA: Center for Civic Education, 2003. 235pp. ISBN 0-89818-171-2.

Center for Civic Education. *We the People: The Citizen & the Constitution*, Level III. Calabasas, CA: Center for Civic Education, 1995. 283pp. ISBN 0-89818-177-1.

Collier, Christopher, and James Lincoln Collier. *Decision in Philadelphia: The Constitutional Convention of 1787*. New York: Ballantine Books, 1987. 448pp. ISBN 0-3453-4652-1.

Constitutional Rights Foundation. *Project History*. Los Angeles: Constitutional Rights Foundation, 2003. 138pp. Catalog number 32030CWB.

Croddy, Marshall, and Coral Suter. *Of Codes and Crowns: The Development of Law*. Los Angeles: Constitutional Rights Foundation, 1992. 96pp. ISBN 0-3180-2222-2.

Degelman, Charles, and Bill Hayes. *Active Citizenship Today Field Guide*. Los Angeles: Constitutional Rights Foundation, 1994. 188pp. ISBN 0-9327-6558-0.

Dunbeck, Kristina. *Leaders of Women's Suffrage*. San Diego, CA: Lucent Books, 2001. 112pp. ISBN 1-5600-6367-X.

Farrand, Max. *The Framing of the Constitution of the United States*. Frederick, MD: Beard Books, 2000. 296pp. ISBN 1-5879-8054-1.

Feelings, Tom. *The Middle Passage: White Ships—Black Cargo*. New York: Dial Books, 1995. 80pp. ISBN 0-8037-1804-7.

Frantzich, Stephen E. *Citizen Democracy: Political Activists in a Cynical Age*. Second edition: Lanham, MD: Rowman & Littlefield, 2004. 246pp. ISBN 0-7425-2953-3.

Hall, Kermit L. *Major Problems in American Constitutional History, Volume I: The Colonial Era through Reconstruction*. Lexington, MA: D.C. Heath, 1992. ISBN 0-6692-1209-1.

Hall, Kermit L. *Major Problems in American Constitutional History, Volume II: From 1870 to the Present*. Lexington, MA: D.C. Heath, 1992. ISBN 0-6692-1210-5.

Hand, Learned. *The Bill of Rights*. Cambridge, MA: Harvard University Press, 1958. ISBN 0-6740-7300-2. Out of print.

Johnson, Johanna. *They Led the Way: 14 American Women*. Reissue edition: New York: Puffin Books, 2004. 126pp. ISBN 0-1424-0057-2. Illustrations by Deanne Hollinger.

Kammen, Michael, ed. *The Origins of the American Constitution: A Documentary History*. New York: Penguin Books, 1986. 407pp. ISBN 0-1400-8744-3.

Kelly, Alfred Hinsey, Herman Belz, and Winifred A. Harbison. *The American Constitution: Its Origins and Development*. Seventh edition: New York: W.W. Norton, 1991. Volume I: 922pp. ISBN 0-3939-6056-0. Volume II: 767pp. ISBN 0-3939-6119-2.

Kerber, Linda K. *Women of the Republic: Intellect and Ideology in Revolutionary America*. Reprint edition: Chapel Hill: University of North Carolina, 1997. 318pp. ISBN 0-8078-4632-5.

Ketcham, Ralph, ed. *The Anti-Federalist Papers and the Constitutional Convention Debates*. Reissue edition: New York: Mentor Books, 1996. 406pp. ISBN 0-4516-2525-0.

McCullough, Julie, ed. *Our Documents: A National Initiative on American History, Civics, and Service Teacher Sourcebook*. Volume III. College Park, MD: National History Day, 2004. 76pp. Available at http://www.ourdocuments.gov/content.php?flash=true&page=sourcebook3.

Morris, Richard B. *Witnesses at the Creation: Hamilton, Madison, Jay, and the Constitution*. Reprint edition: New York: New American Library, 1989. ISBN 0-4516-2686-9.

Murphy, Paul L. *The Constitution in the Twentieth Century*. Washington, D.C.: American Historical Association, 1986. 68pp. ISBN 0-8722-9036-0. Out of print.

National Center for History in the Schools. *Slavery in the 19th Century*. Los Angeles: National Center for History in the Schools, 2000. 68pp. Catalog number NH122-LA4.

Patrick, John J. *The Bill of Rights: A History in Documents*. New York: Oxford University Press, 2003. 208pp. ISBN 0-1951-0354-8. Pages from History series.

Patrick, John J., ed. *The Supreme Court of the United States: A Student Companion*. New York: Oxford University Press, 2002. 400pp. ISBN 0-1951-5008-2. Oxford Student Companions to American Government series.

Pious, Richard M. *The Presidency*. Boston: Longman, 1995. 464pp. ISBN 0-0239-5792-1.

Ravitch, Diane. *The American Reader: Words That Moved a Nation*. Second Revised Edition: New York: Perennial, 2000. 629pp. ISBN 0-0627-3733-3.

Ravitch, Diane, and Abigail Thernstrom. *The Democracy Reader: Classic and Modern Speeches, Essays, Poems, Declarations, and Documents on Freedom and Human Rights Worldwide*. New York: HarperCollins, 1992. 331pp. ISBN 0-0627-0030-8.

Rhodehamel, John H., Stephen F. Rhode, and Paul Von Blum. *Foundations of Freedom*. Los Angeles: Constitutional Rights Foundation, 1991. 111pp. 10450CWB.

Ritchie, Donald. *The Congress of the United States: A Student Companion*. Second edition: New York: Oxford University Press, 2002. 248pp. ISBN 0-1951-5007-4. Oxford Student Companions to American Government series.

Rodell, Fred and Judith Schnell, ed. *55 Men, The Story of the Constitution: Based on the Day-by-Day Notes of James Madison*. Reprint edition: Harrisburg, PA: Stackpole Books: 1986. 281pp. ISBN 0-8117-2171-X. Out of print.

Rossiter, Clinton, ed. *The Federalist Papers: Alexander Hamilton, James Madison, John Jay*. New York: Mentor Books, 1999. 606pp. ISBN 0-4516-2881-0.

Schweizer, Steven L. *Wondering About Politics: Readings in Political Philosophy*. Greatunpublished, 2001. 478pp. ISBN 1-5889-8377-3.

Schulz, Charles. *This Is America, Charlie Brown: The Birth of the Constitution*. Los Angeles: Paramount Studios, 1995. ISBN 6-3034-5165-9. VHS videotape.

Calloway, Colin G. *First Peoples: A Documentary Survey of American Indian History*. Boston: Bedford/St. Martin's, 2004. 587pp. ISBN 0-31239-889-1. Includes documents spanning from pre-1492 through the 1990s, with brief introductions. Timelines, References, and Additional Suggested Readings.

Cronon, William. *Changes in the Land: Indians, Colonists, and the Ecology of New England*. New York: Hill and Wang, 2003. 257pp. ISBN 0-80901-634-6. Environmental history of colonial New England. Compares ecological relationships of precolonial Indians and colonial Europeans, especially conceptions of land ownership.

Debo, Angie. *A History of the Indians of the United States*. Reprint edition: Norman: University of Oklahoma Press, 1984. 450pp. ISBN 0-80611-888-1.

Deloria, Vine, Jr. *American Indian Policy in the Twentieth Century*. Reprint edition: Norman: University of Oklahoma Press, 1992. 272pp. ISBN 0-8061-2424-5.

Deloria, Vine, Jr., and Clifford M. Lytle. *The Nations Within: The Past and Future of American Indian Sovereignty*. Reprint edition: Austin: University of Texas Press, 1998. 296pp. ISBN 0-29271-598-6.

Prucha, Francis Paul. *American Indian Treaties: The History of a Political Anomaly*. Berkeley: University of California Press, 1994. 562pp. ISBN 0-520-20895-1.

Prucha, Francis Paul. *The Great Father: The United States Government and the American Indians*. Two volumes. Lincoln: University of Nebraska Press, 1984. 1355pp. ISBN 0-8032-8734-8. History of United States–American Indian relations from the early republic through the 1970s.

APPENDICES

APPENDIX A

TEST MATERIALS ON THE CONSTITUTION AND THE BILL OF RIGHTS

A 1   Multiple-Choice Test – Teacher's Instructions for Administering

A 2   Multiple-Choice Test – The History and Principles
of the United States Constitution – Teacher's Copy

A 3   Multiple-Choice Test – Answer Guide

A 4   Multiple-Choice Test – Text Correlation

A 5   Multiple-Choice Text – Test Correlation

APPENDIX B

CERTIFICATES

B 1   We the People: The Citizen and the Constitution Certificates

Certificate of Achievement

Certificate of Appreciation

APPENDIX C

APPENDIX D

MULTIPLE-CHOICE TEST — TEACHER'S INSTRUCTIONS FOR ADMINISTERING

1. This test is based on *We the People: The Citizen & the Constitution,* Level II, middle school textbook and is designed as an integral part of the instructional program.

2. Teachers should instruct students to take the test without the aid of notes or their books and to select the best possible answer.

3. A reproducible answer sheet for students is included in the student handout section as Appendix D 14.

4. The teacher's answer guide for the test is in this section as Appendix A 3.

5. Teachers who have not taught the entire curriculum should refer to the test–text correlation, Appendix A 4, to determine which questions pertain to lessons they have covered. They should instruct students to answer only the questions that were covered. In evaluating performance, a student's percentage should be based only on the questions used. Students may retake the test to achieve an acceptable score.

6. Certificates of achievement may be awarded to students at the teacher's discretion. Certificates of appreciation may be awarded to those individuals who contribute to the success of your program. Sample certificates are included as Appendix B. Additional free color certificates may be obtained by calling the Center toll-free at 800-350-4223 or by emailing your request to wethepeople@civiced.org.

Name

Class

Date

Instructions

For each question, select the one best answer.

Mark your answers on a separate answer sheet as instructed by your teacher.

Test on the History and Principles of the United States Constitution

1. **The Founders were the**
   a. people who opposed the Articles of Confederation.
   b. political leaders of the colonies.
   c. British governors of the colonies.
   d. people who supported the king.

2. **The Founders believed that natural rights meant the right to**
   a. education, privacy, and security.
   b. life, liberty, and property.
   c. clothing, food, and shelter.
   d. freedom, work, and protection.

3. **An agreement to create a government and follow its laws is known as a**
   a. natural agreement.
   b. constitution.
   c. social contract.
   d. declaration of intent.

4. **Citizens who put the common good above their own selfish interests demonstrate**
   a. democracy.
   b. separation of powers.
   c. balance of powers.
   d. civic virtue.

5. **A constitutional government always includes**
   a. a strong executive.
   b. a limitation of powers.
   c. a written constitution.
   d. the idea of judicial review.

6. **A constitution is considered a higher law if it**
   a. must be obeyed by those running the government.
   b. can never be changed.
   c. comes from a divine source.
   d. keeps the government above the people.

7. **Dividing the government into different branches is an example of**
   a. federalism.
   b. constitutional government.
   c. separation of powers.
   d. private domain.

8. **The system of checks and balances was established to**
   a. prevent political parties from being created.
   b. provide government officials with unlimited powers.
   c. prevent branches of government from abusing power.
   d. guarantee that people's rights are never limited.

9. **The Magna Carta, an agreement between the nobles and the king of England, required**
   a. the king to govern according to established rules of law.
   b. the king to return taxes unfairly collected.
   c. the king and the nobles to represent the common people.
   d. the king and the nobles to agree on all new laws enacted.

10. **To protect themselves from the abuse of power, the colonists created their colonial governments to include**
    a. a classical republic.
    b. judicial supremacy.
    c. a constitutional monarchy.
    d. representative government.

11. **The colonists argued that laws such as the Stamp Act of 1765**
    a. were consistent with their rights as Englishmen.
    b. were invalid because the colonists were not allowed
       to vote for members of Parliament.
    c. were justified to help pay English debts.
    d. did not raise enough money to help the colonies.

12. **The Declaration of Independence was**
    a. the peace treaty that ended the American Revolution.
    b. an explanation of the colonists' revolt against Britain.
    c. the first U.S. Constitution.
    d. the first ten amendments to the Constitution.

13. **The purpose of government as described in
    the Declaration of Independence is to**
    a. protect the people's natural rights.
    b. prevent attacks by foreign countries.
    c. make agreements with other nations.
    d. serve as a check on special interest groups.

14. **Diplomacy played an important role in the
    American Revolutionary War by ensuring that**
    a. the Quebec campaign would succeed.
    b. Martha Washington could assist the troops with supplies.
    c. France would provide loans and military assistance to the Americans.
    d. Benjamin Franklin could negotiate a treaty with Britain.

15. **Early state constitutions included the principle
    of popular sovereignty, which means that**
    a. the government has supreme power over the people.
    b. the government has the power to make laws.
    c. the government gets its right to govern from the people.
    d. the legislature has absolute supremacy.

16. **The authors of the Articles of Confederation feared a strong national
    government, so they created a single branch of government, the**
    a. legislature.
    b. executive.
    c. judiciary.
    d. monarchy.

17. **An important difference between the Articles of Confederation
    and the Constitution is that the Constitution gives**
    a. Congress the power to act directly on the people.
    b. Congress the right to establish a national school system.
    c. any state the right to leave the Union if it wishes.
    d. smaller states greater power.

18. **The purpose of the Philadelphia Convention was to**
    a. declare independence from Great Britain.
    b. ratify the Articles of Confederation.
    c. secretly take control of the new states.
    d. improve the Articles of Confederation.

19. **Giving states with larger populations a greater
    number of representatives in Congress is called**
    a. equal representation.
    b. adequate representation.
    c. proportional representation.
    d. legislative representation.

20. **The decision to divide Congress into two houses,
    with equal representation in one and proportional
    representation in the other, was called the**
    a. Great Compromise.
    b. Virginia Plan.
    c. New Jersey Plan.
    d. New York Compromise.

21. **The Framers resolved the conflict between the Northern and Southern states by**
    a. exempting the South from certain parts of the Constitution.
    b. prohibiting the expansion of slavery into new territories.
    c. expanding trade with Southern states.
    d. allowing the slave trade to continue.

22. **Powers that are specifically granted to Congress by the Constitution are called**
    a. executive powers.
    b. bureaucratic powers.
    c. judicial powers.
    d. enumerated powers.

23. **The general welfare clause of the Constitution allows Congress to**
    a. override the president's veto by a two-thirds vote of both houses.
    b. provide for the common defense and common good of the United States.
    c. declare a person guilty of violating the law and set the punishment without a court trial.
    d. make all laws that are necessary and proper for carrying out the other powers of Congress.

24. **The Constitution grants the president the power to**
    a. make laws that Congress refuses to make.
    b. veto laws passed by Congress.
    c. declare war.
    d. put people in jail without a trial.

25. **The system the Framers created for choosing the president is known as**
    a. the electoral college.
    b. voter registration.
    c. nomination by convention.
    d. political campaigning.

26. **One way of ensuring the neutrality of the national judiciary was to**
    a. have judges be elected by the people.
    b. have judges be appointed for four-year terms.
    c. allow judges to hold their offices for life with good behavior.
    d. allow judges' salaries to be decided by popular vote.

27. **The Anti-Federalists were people who**
    a. opposed increasing the power of the national government.
    b. opposed the creation of the Articles of Confederation.
    c. were loyal to the British monarch.
    d. supported Shays' Rebellion.

28. **To get enough support for the ratification of the Constitution, the Federalists agreed to**
    a. remove the necessary and proper clause.
    b. amend the three-fifths clause.
    c. outlaw slavery in the territories.
    d. add a bill of rights.

29. **The Constitution was ratified by a vote of**
    a. state legislatures.
    b. special state conventions.
    c. all registered voters.
    d. members of Congress.

30. **A system of government in which power is shared by the national government, the state governments, and the people is called a**
    a. unitary system.
    b. totalitarian system.
    c. federal system.
    d. confederation system.

31. **"This Constitution, and the Laws of the United States… shall be the supreme Law of the Land" means that**
    a. only the laws of the U.S. Constitution must be obeyed.
    b. the Constitution may not be changed.
    c. the laws of the U.S. government may not be changed.
    d. federal law will prevail over state laws if the two conflict.

32. **The first ten amendments to the Constitution are called the**
    a. Statement of Purposes.
    b. Preamble.
    c. Bill of Rights.
    d. Freedom Principle.

33. **Political parties came about as a result of**
    a. a constitutional amendment.
    b. disagreements over the powers of the national government.
    c. conflicts between the Senate and House of Representatives.
    d. an act of Congress.

34. **In the case *Marbury v. Madison*, the Supreme Court established its power of judicial review, which allows the court to**
    a. hear any case it wants to at any time.
    b. dispute the results of presidential elections.
    c. argue that it does not have to follow the Constitution.
    d. declare laws passed by Congress unconstitutional.

35. **The Supreme Court can serve as a check on the power of the legislature by**
    a. impeaching members of Congress.
    b. declaring laws or actions unconstitutional.
    c. approving amendments passed by popular vote.
    d. approving presidential vetoes of congressional laws.

36. **One problem with a Supreme Court justice trying to determine the intention of the Framers when interpreting the Constitution is that**
    a. the Framers answered all Constitutional questions fully and clearly.
    b. the Supreme Court has ruled that interpretation of the Constitution is illegal.
    c. there were many Framers and they did not always agree.
    d. the justice might interpret the Constitution incorrectly and be vetoed by the president.

37. **Individual development and human dignity, the advancement of knowledge, and peaceful social change are some of the benefits of**
    a. a trial by jury.
    b. ex post facto laws.
    c. bills of attainder.
    d. freedom of expression.

38. **The Constitution guarantees, with some limits, each citizen's right to free**
    a. speech, healthcare, shelter, and public welfare.
    b. speech, quality of life, and public education.
    c. speech, press, and practice of a professional trade.
    d. speech, press, assembly, and religious belief.

39. **The establishment clause limits the government's ability to**
    a. support an official state religion.
    b. set up public universities and colleges.
    c. compel students to recite the Pledge of Allegiance.
    d. raise and support standing armies.

40. **The issue of allowing prayer in public schools has faced controversy because of differing interpretations of the**
    a. free speech and due process clauses of the Constitution.
    b. representation and apportionment clauses of the Constitution.
    c. establishment and free exercise clauses of the Constitution.
    d. supremacy and declarative clauses of the Constitution.

41. **The Nineteenth Amendment**
    a. freed the slaves.
    b. formally ended the Revolutionary War.
    c. gave women the right to vote.
    d. ended prohibition.

42. **The Fourteenth Amendment was intended to guarantee the equal protection of the laws to**
    a. African Americans.
    b. women.
    c. Native Americans.
    d. whites who did not own property.

43. **The primary purpose of the civil rights movement was to**
    a. encourage civic participation among immigrants.
    b. oppose the Vietnam War.
    c. obtain equal protection of the laws for African Americans.
    d. ensure that public schools remain segregated.

44. **The right to due process of law means that**
    a. laws will be publicly debated.
    b. important public questions must be settled by direct vote of the people.
    c. proposed laws must be passed by both houses of Congress.
    d. laws and procedures of government must be fair and reasonable.

45. **The guarantee of due process is important because it ensures that**
    a. governmental institutions can enact important policies.
    b. judges have discretion in sentencing.
    c. juveniles do not get the same protections as adults.
    d. government treats individuals fairly.

46. **The United States has given much to the world. Among the democratic ideals other nations have learned from our country is**
    a. consent of the governed.
    b. separation of powers.
    c. legislative supremacy.
    d. necessary and proper laws.

47. **The Constitution gives our government powers to deal with other nations. Among those powers is the authority**
    a. of Congress to approve treaties.
    b. of the Supreme Court to regulate commerce.
    c. of individual states to make treaties.
    d. of the president to address the United Nations.

48. **Citizens have both personal and civic responsibilities that go along with their rights. An example of a civic responsibility is**
    a. supporting one's family.
    b. making charitable donations.
    c. serving as a juror.
    d. contributing money to a political party.

49. **Henry David Thoreau and Dr. Martin Luther King Jr. are examples of people who went to jail because they**
    a. supported the impeachment of the president.
    b. disobeyed laws that they believed were unjust.
    c. refused to serve in the military.
    d. committed violent acts of protest.

50. **Participation in the political life of our nation is consistent with the principle of**
    a. judicial activism.
    b. popular sovereignty.
    c. autocratic government.
    d. the supremacy clause.

1.	b	15.	c	29.	b	43.	c
2.	b	16.	a	30.	c	44.	d
3.	c	17.	a	31.	d	45.	d
4.	d	18.	d	32.	c	46.	a
5.	b	19.	c	33.	b	47.	a
6.	a	20.	a	34.	d	48.	c
7.	c	21.	d	35.	b	49.	b
8.	c	22.	d	36.	c	50.	b
9.	a	23.	b	37.	d		
10.	d	24.	b	38.	d		
11.	b	25.	a	39.	a		
12.	b	26.	c	40.	c		
13.	a	27.	a	41.	c		
14.	c	28.	d	42.	a		

Question 1. **LESSON 1**	Question 15. **LESSON 10**	Question 29. **LESSON 18**	Question 43. **LESSON 25, 26**
Question 2. **LESSON 2**	Question 16. **LESSON 11**	Question 30. **LESSON 17**	Question 44. **LESSON 27**
Question 3. **LESSON 2**	Question 17. **LESSON 11, 15**	Question 31. **LESSON 17**	Question 45. **LESSON 27**
Question 4. **LESSON 3**	Question 18. **LESSON 12, 13**	Question 32. **LESSON 19**	Question 46. **LESSON 28**
Question 5. **LESSON 4**	Question 19. **LESSON 13**	Question 33. **LESSON 20**	Question 47. **LESSON 28**
Question 6. **LESSON 4**	Question 20. **LESSON 13**	Question 34. **LESSON 21**	Question 48. **LESSON 29**
Question 7. **LESSON 5**	Question 21. **LESSON 14**	Question 35. **LESSON 15, 21**	Question 49. **LESSON 29**
Question 8. **LESSON 5**	Question 22. **LESSON 15**	Question 36. **LESSON 22**	Question 50. **LESSON 10, 30**
Question 9. **LESSON 6**	Question 23. **LESSON 15**	Question 37. **LESSON 23**	
Question 10. **LESSON 7**	Question 24. **LESSON 15, 16**	Question 38. **LESSON 19, 23, 24**	
Question 11. **LESSON 7**	Question 25. **LESSON 16**	Question 39. **LESSON 24**	
Question 12. **LESSON 8**	Question 26. **LESSON 16**	Question 40. **LESSON 24**	
Question 13. **LESSON 8**	Question 27. **LESSON 18**	Question 41. **LESSON 25**	
Question 14. **LESSON 9**	Question 28. **LESSON 18**	Question 42. **LESSON 25**	

UNIT 1	LESSON	QUESTION
	1	1
	2	2, 3
	3	4
	4	5, 6
	5	7, 8

UNIT 2		
	6	9
	7	10, 11
	8	12, 13
	9	14
	10	15, 50
	11	16, 17

UNIT 3		
	12	18
	13	18, 19, 20
	14	21
	15	17, 22, 23, 24, 35
	16	24, 25, 26

UNIT 4	LESSON	QUESTION
	17	30, 31
	18	27, 28, 29
	19	32, 38
	20	33
	21	34, 35
	22	36

UNIT 5		
	23	37, 38
	24	38, 39, 40
	25	41, 42, 43
	26	43
	27	44, 45

UNIT 6		
	28	46, 47
	29	48, 49
	30	50

CERTIFICATE OF ACHIEVEMENT

Certificates of achievement may be awarded
to students at the teacher's discretion.
A sample certificate is provided.

CERTIFICATE OF APPRECIATION

Certificates of appreciation may be awarded to those
persons who contribute to the success of your program.
A sample certificate is provided.

FREE COLOR CERTIFICATES

Additional certificates of achievement and
appreciation may be obtained from the Center
by calling 800-350-4223 or by emailing your
request to wethepeople@civiced.org.

WE THE PEOPLE

THE CITIZEN & THE CONSTITUTION

For the study of the
history and principles of
the United States Constitution
and Bill of Rights

PRESENTED TO

_____

PRESENTED BY

_____

Certificate
of
Achievement

Funded by the U.S. Department of Education under the Education for Democracy Act approved by the United States Congress

WE THE PEOPLE

THE CITIZEN & THE CONSTITUTION

For outstanding contributions to civic education

PRESENTED TO

_____

PRESENTED BY

_____

Certificate of Appreciation

Funded by the U.S. Department of Education under the Education for Democracy Act approved by the United States Congress

What is a simulated congressional hearing?

A simulated congressional hearing is the culminating activity for We the People: The Citizen and the Constitution. The simulated hearing is an authentic, performance-based assessment where students demonstrate their understanding of the U.S. Constitution and the Bill of Rights.

During the simulated hearing, students assume the role of constitutional experts. Students present prepared oral statements before a panel of judges, usually adults from the community. Following the formal presentations, students respond to follow-up questions from the panel of judges. The purpose of the follow-up questions is to give students the opportunity to demonstrate the depth of their understanding of the Constitution and Bill of Rights and to allow students time to clarify issues they may have raised in their formal statements.

This teacher's edition provides all the materials you need to prepare your class to participate in a simulated congressional hearing:

- A test on the Constitution and Bill of Rights

- Hearing questions for each of the six units of the student text

- Instructions for how to organize and prepare your students

- Instructions for the panel of judges

- Scoring sheets for the panel of judges

- Suggested follow-up questions for the panel of judges

- Certificates of achievement and appreciation

- A list of suggestions from teachers who have participated in the program

What is a competitive hearing?

Each state has adopted a geographic organizational plan for the simulated congressional hearing. This is known as the congressional-district-level hearing. Every congressional district has a district coordinator for the We the People program. The district coordinator is responsible for the organization of district hearings for elementary, middle, and high school students.

High school classes compete at the congressional district level. The winner of the district competition progresses to the state level, and the winner of the state competition progresses to the prestigious national competition in Washington, D.C. This is not the case at the middle school level. If a middle school class chooses to participate in its congressional-district-level hearings, they are measured against a standard of competence for their own grade level. If all middle school teachers involved choose to participate in an actual middle school competition, they may do so.

District-level competitions are held under the supervision and authority of the district coordinators. They have the final word on all decisions regarding rules and logistics.

To inquire about participation in your congressional district hearing, contact your district coordinator. If you do not know who your coordinator is, contact your state coordinator from the list provided in the We the People brochure, or contact the Center for Civic Education at 800-350-4223.

Should a district coordinator be involved in my class's simulated hearing?

It is your decision whether to involve your district coordinator. You should notify the district coordinator about your hearing. You may want to ask your district coordinator for support, help in finding judges, or even to participate as a judge.

If your class participates in a hearing, please complete the Event Report Form, Appendix C 9. The form is also available on the Center's website at www.civiced.org in the Teacher Resources section.

How do students prepare for participating in a simulated congressional hearing?

Studying the *We the People* text is the best preparation for participating in the simulated congressional hearing. The instructional activities in each lesson require students to analyze, evaluate, take, and defend positions on a variety of constitutional issues. Each lesson is designed to help students acquire the knowledge, critical-thinking, and participation skills necessary to successfully take part in a hearing.

All students in the class must participate in the simulated congressional hearing. All students study the entire text. The teacher then divides the class into six equal groups (if possible) corresponding to the units of the text. Student preparation is based on topical questions. Each group assumes responsibility for preparing and presenting the question related to their unit.

Students may use the text or any other reference materials to prepare a formal response to their question. Students are encouraged to investigate related topics in preparation for the follow-up questions that the panel of judges may ask during the actual hearing.

What criteria will the panel of judges use to evaluate student performance?

The panel of judges will score each group of students on six criteria:

- Understanding of constitutional principles
- Application of constitutional principles
- Reasoning
- Supporting evidence
- Responsiveness to questions from the panel of judges
- Cooperation and participation among the members of the group

At the conclusion of each presentation, the panel of judges provides feedback. Judges generally speak to the strengths of the presentation; they may offer suggestions for improvement. Judges give the teacher or scorekeeper the score sheets.

Who are the participants in a simulated congressional hearing and what should each do?

Students

The class is organized into groups, one group of students for each unit of the text. It is expected that every student in the class will participate in the activity. The number of students in each group should be as equal as possible, but each group should include at least three students.

Students should prepare a four-minute presentation responding to the question for their unit. Responses may be written on note cards and read aloud or memorized and recited. No other materials or references may be used.

Each group of students meets with the teacher to decide how responsibilities will be divided among the members of the group. Each group member should have a speaking role during the opening statement before the panel of judges. Each group member should also participate in the six-minute follow-up questioning period after the formal presentation. Evidence of cooperation and full participation by all members of the group is one criterion that will be evaluated.

After the four-minute opening statement, judges will ask suggested follow-up questions for six minutes (each hearing lasts a total of ten minutes). Follow-up questions are provided for the panel of judges. Students should not be permitted to see the follow-up questions in advance of the hearing. The purpose of the follow-up questions is to probe students' understanding of the material. It is also an opportunity for the judges to engage in discussion with students. Follow-up questions should only encompass the material in the group's unit. Judges may decide to formulate their own questions; they are encouraged to do so.

Judges

Eighteen judges, three for each group of students, is ideal but not always practical. Minimally, three judges are needed to listen to and evaluate the presentations from all six groups.

People who serve as judges usually are recruited from the community. Suggestions for invitations include, but should not be limited to, the following:

- Your district social studies supervisor
- Professors from local colleges or universities
- Members of Congress or staffers from your congressional representative's local office
- Members of state legislatures or staffers
- Members of the city council or mayor's office
- Leaders of community groups or service organizations
- Lawyers
- Judges
- Social studies teachers
- We the People alumni

Once you have selected your panel of judges, provide each member of the panel with the following items:

- *We the People* text
- Appendix C 3, Suggestions from Teachers
- Appendix C 5, Judges' Instructions
- Appendix C 6, Judges' Unit and Follow-up Questions
- Appendix C 7, Judges' Score Sheet

It is best to send the judges these materials a couple of weeks in advance of the event. You should also schedule a pre-event meeting with the judges. During the meeting review the procedures for the hearing and respond to questions that the judges may have. Remember that most of your judges have little or no classroom experience. You may want to share some of the characteristics of your class and tactfully remind the judges of your students' ages and level of education. Also, emphasize the importance of comments to students at the end of each presentation. Judges should have a good experience interacting with your students.

Remind judges that at the conclusion of the hearing they have additional time to tabulate scores. Judges should consult each other but need not agree among themselves before completing their written comments and tabulating final scores. Judges must return their scoring sheets to the teacher before leaving the hearing site.

Timekeeper

Each hearing should have a timekeeper to officially keep and enforce time limits during each presentation. This person should be someone other than one of the judges.

The timekeeper should allot ten minutes for each group's presentation: four minutes for the formal statement and six minutes for follow-up questioning from the judges. Timing should start when students begin their opening statement. In the event that the full four minutes are not used for the opening statement, the remaining time should be allotted to the follow-up period. Judges may allow a student to speak beyond the time limit so that the student may finish a sentence or thought. Be mindful, however, that fairness is always an issue and exceptions to the rule should be applied judiciously.

The timekeeper should give notice when one minute remains for the opening statement. The timer may do this by holding up a card showing that one minute remains. At the end of the four minutes, the timekeeper calls time. Repeat the process during the follow-up questioning period.

Audience

A simulated hearing is an excellent opportunity for your students to demonstrate to the community what they know and what they can do. Having an audience lends formality and excitement to the event. In addition, it helps to publicize the program, both in your school and community.

Suggestions for those you might want to invite to the simulated congressional hearing:

- Parents
- Your *We the People* congressional district, regional, and state coordinators
- District superintendent
- Curriculum coordinators
- Building principal and staff
- Members of Congress or staffers from your congressional representative's local office
- State legislators
- City officials
- Journalists from both the print and electronic media
- Interested community organizations
- Other teachers in your school
- Other classes in your school

It is best to send invitations at least two weeks in advance of the event. The invitation should briefly describe the program and specify time and location. On the day of the hearing, someone should be available to greet guests and direct them to the site where the event will occur.

How can I recognize student achievement in the program?

You will likely want to hold an awards ceremony immediately after the simulated hearing. Certificates of achievement may be given to students, and certificates of appreciation may be given to people who have supported the program in your school or district. You may want to invite a distinguished guest to present the awards or to speak to the assembled group.

Often, a reception for students and guests follows the awards ceremony. The reception need not be elaborate. The important thing is to create an opportunity for your students and the adults to interact.

How can I organize a simulated congressional hearing?

To ensure a successful hearing and a good experience for your students, follow these steps (appropriate modifications should be made to suit individual situations):

Step 1. Prepare students

After students have studied the entire curriculum, administer and score the multiple-choice test.

Divide the class into six groups and assign each group to a unit. Explain to your students the purposes and procedures of a real congressional hearing. Explain the roles students will play and the procedures that will be followed.

Distribute the appropriate hearing question to each group. Students need to prepare a four-minute presentation addressing the issues raised in the question. Answers to the questions are in their *We the People* textbook. Encourage students to phrase answers in their own words and not to recite verbatim from the text. Questions may require students to gather additional information or form their own opinions.

Inform students about the following guidelines for the formal presentations:

- Students may use notes during their prepared presentations
- All students in each group should be prepared to speak during the formal presentation
- Students may not use visual aids such as posters, videos, computer presentations, pictures, or charts

Allow class time for groups to meet and prepare for the hearing. If desired, arrange for one or more outside experts to assist students in preparing their presentations. Subject matter experts, speech or debate specialists, attorneys, and other community representatives can be helpful and stimulating.

Students also should prepare for six minutes of spontaneous follow-up questioning from the judges. Inform students about the guidelines for responding to the follow-up questions:

- Students may not use notes during this period
- All students in the group should participate in responding to the judges' questions
- Students may assist each other during the response period
- Students may politely disagree with the responses of other members of the group

Note: These guidelines are intended to be flexible and may be modified to meet the needs of individual teachers and their classes.

Step 2. Determine the time and location for the hearing

Under the most favorable circumstances, the hearing would be conducted in an auditorium or other facility that can accommodate an audience. If it is not feasible to conduct the hearing in such a space, it may be conducted in a classroom with a smaller audience.

The simulated hearing may be held either during the school day or during evening hours when more parents are able to attend.

You may want to involve a cosponsoring organization to help in planning and running the hearing. Possible cosponsors might include local bar associations, judges' associations, historical societies, or community service groups. Cosponsors may help provide a site for the hearing, help students prepare for the hearing, donate refreshments, etc.

Each congressional district has a coordinator. You should attempt to involve your We the People congressional district coordinator in your program. This person is available to help you organize your simulated hearing. Please call your state coordinator or the Center for Civic Education at 800-350-4223 to identify your district coordinator.

Step 3. Select and invite judges

Step 4. Invite guests

Step 5. Invite a member of Congress to participate

The Center recommends that a member of Congress (or staff representative), in whose district the school is located, be invited to participate by

- signing certificates
- visiting classes
- speaking to students and teachers
- observing or participating in simulated congressional hearings
- presenting certificates or speaking at awards ceremonies

Step 6. Prepare certificates of achievement and certificates of appreciation

Each student earns a certificate of achievement by passing the test on the principles and history of the Constitution and participating in the simulated congressional hearing. The Center for Civic Education will provide free certificates of achievement for each class set of materials used. The Center will provide certificates of appreciation for those who assist with the program.

You may order your certificates by calling the Center at 800-350-4223 or by sending an email request to wethepeople@civiced.org. You may also download certificates from the Center's website. Another choice may be to make photocopies of the sample certificate that is included with this set of materials.

Your member of the House of Representatives or someone on her or his staff should sign the certificates. An official of your school district also may sign the certificates.

Step 7. Organize your awards ceremony and reception

Step 8. Arrange the hearing room

If the hearing is held in a school auditorium or other large meeting room, arrange tables and chairs in a "V" shape at the front of the room. The open end of the "V" should face the audience. The panel of judges sits along one arm of the "V." Each group of students should be seated along the other arm when it is their turn to present their unit. If needed, provide microphones for both the panel of judges and students.

Arrange an area of the room with seating for students waiting their turn to present.

If the hearing is to be held in a classroom, arrange the space so that a set of chairs faces the judges, in a "V" shape if possible. These chairs are for students who will be presenting to the judges; other students will remain at their desks.

Arrange seating for the timekeeper in a location where he or she can be seen by both students and the judges.

Step 9. Meet with the judges

Instruct the judges that student groups will have prepared statements to present. Each group of students will be prepared to respond to a hearing question for their assigned unit. During the follow-up question period, panel members may ask students to explain or expand upon their prepared statement. Follow-up questions should not raise topics with which students are not familiar. Rather, they should help students demonstrate their knowledge and understanding of the basic constitutional principles they have studied.

Judges may ask follow-up questions that allow students to apply historical or contemporary events to their unit topic. Judges should address the entire group when asking a specific question.

Review the procedures for conducting the simulated hearing with the panels of judges. Be prepared to respond to the judges' questions and concerns.

Step 10. Conduct the hearing

What procedures should be followed during the simulated hearing?

1. Start the session by giving a brief overview of the We the People curriculum and a rationale for studying the Constitution and Bill of Rights. You may want to share some examples of student work and offer some anecdotes related to what students did during their study of the curriculum.

2. Introduce any dignitaries who are present in the audience. If you have cosponsoring organizations, people from those groups should also be introduced.

3. Introduce the judges. The initial introduction should identify the simulated congressional committee members by their actual professions. After the introductions, however, students may address the judges as "congressman" or "congresswoman." The moderator of the panel may be addressed as the chair of the committee.

4. You may call upon designated judges to make some brief opening remarks.

5. Call the first student group forward. Students sit in the chairs facing the judges.

6. The chairperson on the panel of judges should ask students to introduce themselves. Name cards for students and the judges are helpful.

7. The chairperson should read aloud the unit question in its entirety.

8. Students then present their prepared statement in response to the designated question for their unit. Timekeeping begins at this moment.

9. At the conclusion of the prepared statement, the judges begin their follow-up questions.

10. After each group's presentation and the follow-up period, each judge on the panel should offer brief feedback to students on their performance. The judges may use their scoring sheet as a guide. This evaluation period is not timed.

11. At the conclusion of the evaluation feedback, students return to the audience and you may call the next group forward.

SIMULATED CONGRESSIONAL HEARING — SUGGESTIONS FROM TEACHERS

Introducing the simulated congressional hearing

Talk to students about the simulated hearing at the beginning of their study. This will generate excitement for the project. This discussion will also allow students to focus on planning their presentations.

Show a video of a class participating in a simulated congressional hearing; videos are available from your district coordinator.

Involve parents in the process as early as possible

Send home a letter explaining the program; talk about the program at "Back to School Night"; have students write discussion reviews from their classes for the parent newsletter.

As homework, suggest that students discuss a related issue with their parents and older siblings. Require a signed note from parents saying the discussion took place. The more you stimulate discussion at home, the more your students will experience reinforcement of the concepts being studied.

Invite parents to come to the class and join in the discussions and activities.

Four to five weeks preceding the simulated congressional hearing

Divide the class into unit groups.

Present the simulated congressional hearing questions to each group. It is helpful to get an adult volunteer for each unit. Consider parents, community members, librarians, high school or college students, local attorneys, and alumni.

Gather reference materials for the classroom from the library or other sources. Make the materials available to all students.

After organized readings of related materials, help students begin a web or concept map of their responses to the questions. They can then easily see which concepts need more information. The webs may be used later for paragraph development.

Review and make suggestions to students about their presentations. Check accuracy of information and clarity of expression. Confer with the writers to discuss needed revisions. Students should do all the writing themselves. You and other adults are free to give suggestions, but it is the students' choice whether to heed your advice. Please do not deny students the valuable experience of writing and revising thoughts by making changes for them. This could and should be a rather lengthy process, and it will force students to think through their responses again and again. This is where real learning occurs. Students must make the final decisions about their essays.

Listen to students' ideas and testimony and do not be judgmental. Give positive suggestions.

Be sure that each presentation stays within the prearranged time limits: ten minutes for the presentation and follow-up questions. Division of the time between prepared and spontaneous questions has some flexibility for elementary students.

If you are holding a classroom hearing, you should then determine date, time, and place of the event. Obtain a commitment from community resource people to judge the hearings. Consider asking attorneys, local judges, law enforcement personnel, university professors, members of the clergy, administrators, city politicians, or similar resource people. Aim for high-profile people to act as judges. Students will take themselves and the program more seriously if judges are widely respected in the community.

Two weeks preceding the simulated congressional hearing

If you can make arrangements for local attorneys or qualified community members to work directly with students, begin regular study sessions with them. A good arrangement is for each unit to have a community or attorney partner. Ask the partner to work with the oral delivery of the presentations and to practice possible follow-up questions. If you cannot secure enough partners, you might use parents or other adults or share partners among units. In addition to preparation, this is the time to invite parents, school officials, community members, and other interested parties to attend your classroom hearing.

Students will be more willing and attentive to detail if they feel that the guests and hearing judges for the evening are important people. Take risks with invitations. Many people in the community will be supportive of a program like this. Of course, include invitations to parents, grandparents, other classes, and school staff as well. Consider having students prepare the invitations.

Consider contacting local media or have a parent make the contact with information about the program and your hearing date and time.

Parents will be excited about the program and eager to see the classroom hearing. You might ask some of them to provide refreshments for the event. Food creates a feeling of celebration, and students will be ready to celebrate the enormous amount of work they put into their program. A classroom hearing with refreshments can be a great send-off to classes that are preparing for district-sponsored hearings.

One week preceding the simulated hearing

Practice, practice, practice.

This is the time to polish public speaking skills. Urge students to speak audibly, slowly, and with an interesting expression. Work on eye contact, posture, and minimizing movement (e.g., swinging feet, happy fingers, etc.).

All prepared presentation material must be on note cards. Students may not use notes or prepared statements during the follow-up questioning.

Practice will make students more comfortable with the material they have prepared and with the spontaneous thinking needed for follow-up questions. Classmates may ask follow-up questions to each unit. Often, this questioning is the more challenging part of the hearing.

Consider assigning the practice of presentations as homework every evening this week. Have a parent sign the note cards verifying that the student practiced his or her speech.

Determine the appropriate attire for your students at the hearing. Most students will want to dress professionally. Discuss the dress standards as a class.

If you are using programs for the classroom hearing, they should be prepared during this time.

Consult your district coordinator for help throughout the We the People program and especially for your simulated congressional hearing.

INSTRUCTIONS

As you know from studying your *We the People: The Citizen & the Constitution* textbook, members of Congress make laws. These laws should protect our rights and promote our welfare. To make good decisions about which laws they want to pass, members of Congress need to gather information. This information will help them understand how to address our nation's problems and pass good laws.

One way that members of Congress get the information they need is by holding congressional hearings. At these hearings, they ask experts to answer questions about important issues that affect proposed laws.

For this activity, you will play the role of an expert who has been asked to speak at a congressional hearing. Each unit group will act as a team of experts on one of the six units of your text.

You will need a good understanding of your unit. You will also have to prepare answers to the questions assigned to your unit. At the hearing, committee members might ask you other questions about the information you have presented.

Your unit group should meet before the congressional hearing to prepare answers to your assigned questions. Most of the information you need for preparing good answers is in your text. In some cases, you might want to ask parents, teachers, and friends for their ideas about government in the United States today. Each member of your group should contribute to the presentation and speak at the hearing.

UNIT 1

WHAT WERE THE FOUNDERS' BASIC IDEAS ABOUT GOVERNMENT?

Congress has formed a congressional committee. This committee will examine the U.S. Constitution and the purposes of government. The members of your group are expert witnesses who will appear before the committee. You will be asked to testify on the following questions.

1. John Locke was an English philosopher who thought about why it was necessary to have a government.

   ● What did Locke think would happen without government?

   ● What did Locke believe to be the purpose of government?

   ● Do you think government might have purposes that Locke did not mention? Explain your answer.

UNIT 1 | WHAT WERE THE FOUNDERS' BASIC IDEAS ABOUT GOVERNMENT?

Congress has formed a congressional committee. This committee will examine the U.S. Constitution and the purposes of government. The members of your group are expert witnesses who will appear before the committee. You will be asked to testify on the following questions.

2. The Founders were concerned with how to preserve a republican form of government.

- According to the Founders, what was republican government?

- What weaknesses did the Founders think would lead to the failure of republican government?

- How did the Founders think these weaknesses could be prevented? Do you think the Founders' solutions were correct? Why or why not?

UNIT 1

WHAT WERE THE FOUNDERS' BASIC IDEAS ABOUT GOVERNMENT?

Congress has formed a congressional committee. This committee will examine the U.S. Constitution and the purposes of government. The members of your group are expert witnesses who will appear before the committee. You will be asked to testify on the following questions.

3. Most nations have a constitution, but they do not all have constitutional governments.

- How might people organize a constitutional government to prevent the abuse of power?

- Give an example of a nation in today's world that you think is not a constitutional government. Give reasons for your choice.

UNIT 2

WHAT SHAPED THE FOUNDERS' THINKING ABOUT GOVERNMENT?

Congress has formed a congressional committee. This committee will examine the U.S. Constitution and the purposes of government. The members of your group are expert witnesses who will appear before the committee. You will be asked to testify on the following questions.

1. The Declaration of Independence told the world why the Americans wanted to free themselves from British rule. The Declaration stated the Founders' beliefs about government.

   ● Using the Declaration as your source, in your own words describe the principles of good government.

   ● Where did the Founders get these ideas?

   ● Do you think these principles are valid today? Why or why not?

UNIT 2

WHAT SHAPED THE FOUNDERS' THINKING ABOUT GOVERNMENT?

Congress has formed a congressional committee. This committee will examine the U.S. Constitution and the purposes of government. The members of your group are expert witnesses who will appear before the committee. You will be asked to testify on the following questions.

2. Great Britain had colonies in North America for more than one hundred and fifty years. During that time the colonists had considerable experience governing themselves.

    ● Why did American colonists have the rights of Englishmen?

    ● What ideas did colonists in America use when they formed their own governments?

    ● How did the British government tighten control over the colonies?

UNIT 2

WHAT SHAPED THE FOUNDERS' THINKING ABOUT GOVERNMENT?

Congress has formed a congressional committee. This committee will examine the U.S. Constitution and the purposes of government. The members of your group are expert witnesses who will appear before the committee. You will be asked to testify on the following questions.

3. By the late 1780s, many Founders believed that the Articles of Confederation were not working well.

   ● What were some achievements of the Congress under the Articles of Confederation?

   ● What shortcomings did many Founders see in the Articles?

   ● What arguments could you have made in support of the Articles?

UNIT 3

WHAT HAPPENED AT THE PHILADELPHIA CONVENTION?

Congress has formed a congressional committee. This committee will examine the U.S. Constitution and the purposes of government. The members of your group are expert witnesses who will appear before the committee. You will be asked to testify on the following questions.

1. Because of different economic systems, Northern and Southern states had different interests. These conflicting interests led to disagreements at the Philadelphia Convention.

   - Describe at least two disagreements between Northern and Southern states at the convention.

   - What parts of the Constitution are the result of compromises that settled disagreements between the Northern and Southern states?

   - Do you think the Framers should have made these compromises? Why or why not?

UNIT 3

WHAT HAPPENED AT THE PHILADELPHIA CONVENTION?

Congress has formed a congressional committee. This committee will examine the U.S. Constitution and the purposes of government. The members of your group are expert witnesses who will appear before the committee. You will be asked to testify on the following questions.

2. Articles I, II, and III of the Constitution list the powers of the Congress, president, and the legislative, executive, and judicial branches of the national government.

   ● Describe some of the powers the Constitution gives to the Congress. In what ways does the Constitution limit the power of Congress?

   ● Describe some of the powers of the president. In what ways does the Constitution limit the power of the president?

   ● Describe some of the powers of the judiciary. In what ways does the Constitution limit the power of the U.S. Supreme Court?

UNIT 3 | WHAT HAPPENED AT THE PHILADELPHIA CONVENTION?

Congress has formed a congressional committee. This committee will examine the U.S. Constitution and the purposes of government. The members of your group are expert witnesses who will appear before the committee. You will be asked to testify on the following questions.

3. The Framers put forth various plans to solve the problem of representation in Congress.

   ● What were the advantages and disadvantages of the Virginia Plan?

   ● What were the advantages and disadvantages of the New Jersey Plan?

   ● Do you think the Great Compromise was a good solution to the problem of representation? Why or why not?

UNIT 4

HOW WAS THE CONSTITUTION USED TO ESTABLISH OUR GOVERNMENT?

Congress has formed a congressional committee. This committee will examine the U.S. Constitution and the purposes of government. The members of your group are expert witnesses who will appear before the committee. You will be asked to testify on the following questions.

1. One of the enduring contributions of the Framers was the creation of the federal system of government.

   ● What is a federal system of government? Compare it with a unitary or a confederational system of government.

   ● How are powers distributed between the states and the national government under our federal system? Give examples.

   ● What are the advantages and disadvantages of the federal system? Give some current examples.

UNIT 4

HOW WAS THE CONSTITUTION USED TO ESTABLISH OUR GOVERNMENT?

Congress has formed a congressional committee. This committee will examine the U.S. Constitution and the purposes of government. The members of your group are expert witnesses who will appear before the committee. You will be asked to testify on the following questions.

2. Judicial review is an important part of our constitutional system of government.

- How did the Supreme Court acquire the power of judicial review?

- Do you think the Supreme Court should have the power to declare an act of Congress unconstitutional? Why or why not?

- How should justices determine the meaning of the words of the Constitution?

UNIT 4

HOW WAS THE CONSTITUTION USED TO ESTABLISH OUR GOVERNMENT?

Congress has formed a congressional committee. This committee will examine the U.S. Constitution and the purposes of government. The members of your group are expert witnesses who will appear before the committee. You will be asked to testify on the following questions.

3. Political parties are an important part of our political system today, yet they are not mentioned in the Constitution.

- Why did the Framers fear political parties?

- Why and how did political parties develop?

- Do political parties play a useful role today? Why or why not?

UNIT 5

HOW DOES THE CONSTITUTION PROTECT OUR BASIC RIGHTS?

Congress has formed a congressional committee. This committee will examine the U.S. Constitution and the purposes of government. The members of your group are expert witnesses who will appear before the committee. You will be asked to testify on the following questions.

1. The very first amendment, added to the Constitution in 1791, contains guarantees of freedom of religion.

    ●   Why did the Founders think freedom of religion was so important?

    ●   Explain the difference between the establishment and free exercise clauses.

    ●   Do you think limitations should ever be imposed on the free exercise of one's religious beliefs? Explain your answers.

UNIT 5

HOW DOES THE CONSTITUTION PROTECT OUR BASIC RIGHTS?

Congress has formed a congressional committee. This committee will examine the U.S. Constitution and the purposes of government. The members of your group are expert witnesses who will appear before the committee. You will be asked to testify on the following questions.

2. Due process of law has been called the "primary and indispensable foundation of individual freedom" because it protects the individual from government wrongdoing.

- What is the right to due process? Where in the Constitution is due process protected and how is the meaning of due process applied?

- How does the equal protection clause of the Fourteenth Amendment prevent state governments from practicing unfair discrimination?

- Should young people under the age of eighteen have the same due process rights as adults? Why or why not?

UNIT 5

HOW DOES THE CONSTITUTION PROTECT OUR BASIC RIGHTS?

Congress has formed a congressional committee. This committee will examine the U.S. Constitution and the purposes of government. The members of your group are expert witnesses who will appear before the committee. You will be asked to testify on the following questions.

3. The First Amendment states that laws shall not be passed that abridge freedom of speech.

● Why did the Founders think freedom of speech was so important?

● Do you believe there are times when freedom of expression should be limited? Explain your response.

● Should a public speaker who calls for violent action be protected by the First Amendment whereas an audience member who performs the action can be sent to prison? Why or why not?

UNIT 6

WHAT ARE THE RESPONSIBILITIES OF CITIZENS?

Congress has formed a congressional committee. This committee will examine the U.S. Constitution and the purposes of government. The members of your group are expert witnesses who will appear before the committee. You will be asked to testify on the following questions.

1. Many people believe that an informed citizenry is essential if democracy is to work.

   ● Should people be required to pass periodic citizenship tests to maintain their citizenship? Why or why not?

   ● Would you favor requiring literacy tests, fairly administered, before allowing citizens to vote? Why or why not?

UNIT 6

WHAT ARE THE RESPONSIBILITIES OF CITIZENS?

Congress has formed a congressional committee. This committee will examine the U.S. Constitution and the purposes of government. The members of your group are expert witnesses who will appear before the committee. You will be asked to testify on the following questions.

2. Voting is one way a citizen may participate in politics. Many other activities are available.

- What activities besides voting are available to citizens?

- Which of these activities, if any, do you think is most useful? Explain your answer.

- How should a citizen decide which of these various activities to participate in?

UNIT 6

WHAT ARE THE RESPONSIBILITIES OF CITIZENS?

Congress has formed a congressional committee. This committee will examine the U.S. Constitution and the purposes of government. The members of your group are expert witnesses who will appear before the committee. You will be asked to testify on the following questions.

3. Today, the nations of the world are increasingly dependent on each other.

- How have the U.S. Constitution and Bill of Rights influenced other countries?

- How have other countries influenced the United States?

- How do nations of the world interact with each other?

Structure of the Hearings

During simulated congressional hearings on the U.S. Constitution and Bill of Rights, students appear before a panel of judges role-playing a congressional committee. The panels are composed of three knowledgeable people from the community. The panel of judges questions students who are representing constitutional experts called on to answer questions about the U.S. Constitution and Bill of Rights. The panel listens to oral presentations from small groups of students on selected constitutional issues chosen from one unit of the *We the People: The Citizen & the Constitution* text. Students should be treated as experts who have been asked to testify before the congressional committee on their particular topic.

The panel selects one member to act as chair. The chair begins the proceedings. On entering the hearing room, the chair introduces the judges and asks students to introduce themselves. One judge reads the entire question. Students have four minutes to respond. A group should not be penalized for using less than their allotted time during prepared statements. Any excess time will be added to the six-minute follow-up period.

The classes are divided into groups, one group for each of the six units in the text. Each group has been given questions in advance to prepare for questioning on its topic.

Students will respond to their group's question with a four-minute prepared presentation. They may use notes during this presentation. Then they respond for six minutes to follow-up questions by the judges. During the follow-up questioning period, they cannot use notes. Each of the six groups will thus appear before the judges for a total of ten minutes.

The judges listen to each group's presentation, question the group on its topic, and score the group. The class's total score consists of the combined scores received by its six groups.

Students might be nervous. Therefore, it is the task of the judges to encourage them to feel at ease so that they may demonstrate their knowledge. The simulated hearing serves as the culmination of their classroom learning.

Hearing Questions

After hearing a group's prepared presentation, there is a six-minute follow-up question-and-answer period. The follow-up questioning constitutes the judges' most challenging task. The Center for Civic Education provides suggested follow-up questions. Judges are encouraged to use these questions whenever appropriate. Follow-up questions should be addressed to the entire group; singling out a particular student to answer should be avoided. Judges should focus much of their questioning on what students said in their six-minute prepared presentations. Therefore, judges may want to formulate their own questions.

Judges should phrase follow-up questions concisely. It is best not to ask multipart follow-up questions. During the final minute—indicated by a signal from the official timer—questions should be either brief summary questions or requests for concluding remarks.

Timing

For each hearing, there will be an official timekeeper. The timekeeper keeps strictly to the framework of ten minutes per group: four minutes for the initial oral presentation and six minutes for the follow-up questioning. Timekeepers will silently notify groups by holding up a card when they have one minute left in their initial oral presentation time and will silently notify judges when there is one minute left in the follow-up question period. When time expires, the timekeeper stops all participants by holding up a printed card with the word *Time!*

Every effort should be made to observe time limits. At the discretion of judges, however, extra time may be allowed to compensate a group for any situation that significantly reduces their allowed response time. For example, if a judge has taken inordinate time to phrase a question, extra time may be granted to allow students to adequately respond.

Use of Notes or Materials

Students may use written aids on note cards or on paper not larger than 8½ x 11 inches during their six-minute presentation period. No other materials or references may be used. Neither notes nor any other materials may be used during the follow-up questioning period.

Judging Criteria

Judges score each student group on six criteria: understanding, constitutional application, reasoning, supporting evidence, responsiveness, and participation. These criteria are fully explained on the Judges' Score Sheet (Appendix C 7). Throughout their assessment of student performance, judges should be careful to base their scores on the six established criteria, not on their agreement or disagreement with students' positions.

For each criterion listed, each judge scores the group on a scale of 1 to 10, with 10 being the highest score. Judges must use a separate form for each group. Before beginning a hearing, judges should ascertain that they have the appropriate score sheet (correct teacher name, school name, and unit number). The scorekeeper will total class scores on a separate summary form.

Special care must be taken in judging a group on participation. Groups in which most members speak should be rated higher than those in which one or two students dominate the entire ten minutes. Because it is recognized that certain students have an especially difficult time with speaking in public, it is the policy of the We the People program that a group not be penalized if one or two students do not participate because of shyness, language problems, handicaps, etc. In rating participation, judges should evaluate the extent to which most students respond.

Judges may keep score sheets for all groups seen during one session. Score sheets may be revised during that session. For example, if after judging two or three groups, the judges think they were too harsh or too easy on the first group, they may adjust their scores. Once scores have been turned in, it is no longer possible to make revisions. Judges may consult with one another about scoring; however, they do not need to agree on their scores.

Feedback

Although students should be given some oral feedback, they should not be told how their presentations were scored. Feedback should include comments on the groups' strengths and suggestions for improvement. Time constraints require that feedback be brief.

UNIT 1

WHAT WERE THE FOUNDERS' BASIC IDEAS ABOUT GOVERNMENT?

1. John Locke was an English philosopher who thought about why it was necessary to have a government.

- What did Locke think would happen without government?

- What did Locke believe to be the purpose of government?

- Do you think government might have purposes that Locke did not mention? Explain your answer.

Suggested follow-up questions

a. How did Locke influence the Founders and Framers? Explain your answer.

b. How is the purpose of school similar to or different from the purpose of government? Explain your answer.

c. Do we as a nation emphasize rights to the detriment of responsibilities? Explain your answer.

d. How does our nation protect the common welfare while protecting natural rights? Should more importance be placed upon one or the other? Explain your answer.

e. Do you believe that the rights of some American citizens are not sufficiently protected today? Support your viewpoint. If greater protection is needed, how should citizens respond?

f. Does the U.S. government and its leaders follow the principles established by Locke? Explain your answer.

g. How would Locke view attempts by government to place warnings on music, movies, and video games? Explain your answer.

h. What mechanisms are in place to ensure that government does not violate our natural rights? Have these mechanisms worked? Why or why not?

UNIT 1

WHAT WERE THE FOUNDERS' BASIC IDEAS ABOUT GOVERNMENT?

2. The Founders were concerned with how to preserve a republican form of government.

   - According to the Founders, what was republican government?

   - What weaknesses did the Founders think would lead to the failure of republican government?

   - How did the Founders think these weaknesses could be prevented? Do you think the Founders' solutions were correct? Why or why not?

Suggested follow-up questions

a. How is the common welfare promoted in a republican form of government? Are these methods successful today? Why or why not?

b. Would you favor a direct democracy over representative democracy? Why or why not?

c. Does an independent judiciary support or conflict with republicanism? Explain your answer.

d. Does a republican form of government mean that all those eligible must vote in order that government be effective? Why or why not?

e. In a republican form of government, should representatives vote their consciences or the will of those they represent? Should they ever compromise? Why or why not?

f. What led the Framers to establish a republican form of government? Explain your answer.

g. Who does the federal government represent today? Does our current government follow the principles of our Founders and Framers? Explain your answer.

UNIT 1   WHAT WERE THE FOUNDERS' BASIC IDEAS ABOUT GOVERNMENT?

3. Most nations have a constitution, but they do not all have constitutional governments.

• How might people organize a constitutional government to prevent the abuse of power?

• Give an example of a nation in today's world that you think is not a constitutional government. Give reasons for your choice.

Suggested follow-up questions

a. Is it appropriate for the government to pass laws limiting our First Amendment rights?

b. What responsibilities does a citizen have in a constitutional government? Explain your answer.

c. What limitations does the U.S. Constitution place on majority rule?

d. Explain a time in our history when the federal government went beyond the limitations placed upon it. How was the situation handled? Explain your answer.

e. Does a written constitution ensure that government works for the good of the people? Why or why not?

UNIT 2

WHAT SHAPED THE FOUNDERS' THINKING ABOUT GOVERNMENT?

1. The Declaration of Independence told the world why the Americans wanted to free themselves from British rule. The Declaration stated the Founders' beliefs about government.

   • Using the Declaration as your source, in your own words describe the principles of good government.

   • Where did the Founders get these ideas?

   • Do you think these principles are valid today? Why or why not?

Suggested follow-up questions

a. Thomas Jefferson stated that laws should expire after a generation or that every generation should have a revolution. Do you think the right of the people to revolt is relevant today? Why or why not?

b. Did the Declaration reflect the opinions of all the colonists at the time? Why or why not?

c. What mechanisms are in place that would allow us to revolt against our government? Explain your answer.

d. What basic rights would you add to the Declaration? Explain your answer.

e. What ideas of the Declaration are reflected in the Constitution and Bill of Rights? Explain your answer.

f. Do you think the diversity of Americans increases their acceptance of people with different beliefs and lifestyles? Why or why not?

g. Should a portion of our nation or a state that wishes to remove itself from the United States be allowed to do so? Why or why not?

UNIT 2

WHAT SHAPED THE FOUNDERS' THINKING ABOUT GOVERNMENT?

2. Great Britain had colonies in North America for more than one hundred and fifty years. During that time the colonists had considerable experience governing themselves.

● Why did American colonists have the rights of Englishmen?

● What ideas did colonists in America use when they formed their own governments?

● How did the British government tighten control over the colonies?

Suggested follow-up questions

a. Did colonists expect more rights than English commoners? Why or why not?

b. To what extent did the early state governments stay true to or move away from the principles of the Declaration of Independence? Support your answer.

c. What was the English Bill of Rights?

d. Why is the Magna Carta an important document?

e. Why did the British believe the tax and trade laws were fair?

f. What were Americans like in the 1780s? How did these lifestyles influence the governments they created? Explain your answer.

UNIT 2

WHAT SHAPED THE FOUNDERS' THINKING ABOUT GOVERNMENT?

3. By the late 1780s, many Founders believed that the Articles of Confederation were not working well.

- What were some achievements of the Congress under the Articles of Confederation?

- What shortcomings did many Founders see in the Articles?

- What arguments could you have made in support of the Articles?

Suggested follow-up questions

a. The Northwest Ordinance forbade slavery, yet it was allowed in the thirteen states. How do you explain this contradiction?

b. Were individual rights more secure under the Articles than they were under British rule? Why or why not?

c. Do you think the Framers were justified in creating a new constitution? Would it have been possible to amend the Articles to fix their shortcomings? Explain your answer.

d. Compared to the Articles, what shortcomings do we have with the U.S. Constitution today? How would you suggest fixing them? Explain your answer.

e. What was Shays' Rebellion and why did it frighten many Americans? What effects did the rebellion have on the Articles of Confederation? Explain your answer.

f. What would our nation be like if the Articles of Confederation had remained? Give examples to support your view.

UNIT 3 | WHAT HAPPENED AT THE PHILADELPHIA CONVENTION?

1. Because of different economic systems, Northern and Southern states had different interests. These conflicting interests led to disagreements at the Philadelphia Convention.

   - Describe at least two disagreements between Northern and Southern states at the convention.

   - What parts of the Constitution are the result of compromises that settled disagreements between the Northern and Southern states?

   - Do you think the Framers should have made these compromises? Why or why not?

Suggested follow-up questions

a. Were all Americans represented at the Philadelphia Convention? Why or why not?

b. Why did the Framers disregard their original purpose for meeting in Philadelphia? Why were the meetings kept secret from the American people? Do you agree with these decisions? Why or why not?

c. Does compromise support or conflict with the fundamental principle of representative government? Explain your answer.

d. Do you think the Framers erred in compromising on slavery? Were there any other solutions available to them? Explain your answer.

e. The whole Constitution is sometimes described as a compromise. How should leaders decide when to compromise and when to hold firm? Support your opinion.

f. What was the result of the Great Compromise? What were its effects on the North and on the South?

g. If a new constitutional convention were to be called, what groups would you include? Explain your answer.

h. What changes do you think should be made to the Constitution? Support your answer.

UNIT 3

WHAT HAPPENED AT THE PHILADELPHIA CONVENTION?

2. Articles I, II, and III of the Constitution list the powers of the Congress, president, and the legislative, executive, and judicial branches of the national government.

- Describe some of the powers the Constitution gives to the Congress. In what ways does the Constitution limit the power of Congress?

- Describe some of the powers of the president. In what ways does the Constitution limit the power of the president?

- Describe some of the powers of the judiciary. In what ways does the Constitution limit the power of the U.S. Supreme Court?

Suggested follow-up questions

a. What checks are placed on the president? Can you cite any examples of these checks in action? Are they enough or would you place further checks on the president? Why or why not?

b. Should the president be subject to civil trials while in office? Why or why not?

c. Should the president be required to come before Congress to explain his or her actions? Why or why not?

d. What impact did the Framers' knowledge and experiences have on the creation of the executive branch? Explain your answer.

e. What role did George Washington play in the formation of the executive branch?

f. Does the office of the president reflect a principle of republicanism (representative government)? Why or why not?

g. What examples can you cite of a current or recent president using Article II powers?

h. Why was the electoral college created? Is it needed today? Why or why not?

UNIT 3

WHAT HAPPENED AT THE PHILADELPHIA CONVENTION?

3. The Framers put forth various plans to solve the problem of representation in Congress.

- What were the advantages and disadvantages of the Virginia Plan?

- What were the advantages and disadvantages of the New Jersey Plan?

- Do you think the Great Compromise was a good solution to the problem of representation? Why or why not?

Suggested follow-up questions

a. What are the advantages and disadvantages of equal representation?

b. What are the advantages and disadvantages of proportional representation?

c. Do you think that small or large states benefited the most from the Great Compromise? Explain your answer.

d. Why did small states want equal representation?

e. Why did large states want proportional representation?

SIMULATED CONGRESSIONAL HEARING — JUDGES' UNIT & FOLLOW-UP QUESTIONS

UNIT 4 | HOW WAS THE CONSTITUTION USED TO ESTABLISH OUR GOVERNMENT?

1. One of the enduring contributions of the Framers was the creation of the federal system of government.

   ● What is a federal system of government? Compare it with a unitary or a confederational system of government.

   ● How are powers distributed between the states and the national government under our federal system? Give examples.

   ● What are the advantages and disadvantages of the federal system? Give some current examples.

Suggested follow-up questions

   a. What happens when state constitutions and the U.S. Constitution conflict? Support your position.

   b. What is the difference between a national government and a federal system?

   c. How are the principles of popular sovereignty and republicanism (representative government) reflected in a federal system? Explain your answer.

   d. Given the size of our nation as compared to the landmass and population in 1787, should we add regional governments? Why or why not?

   e. What issues should fall under the federal government's domain and which should remain with the states? What criteria would you establish for any given issue? Explain your answer.

   f. Given the great mobility of our populace and current technology, is it still necessary to have separate national, state, and local governments and/or separate powers?

   g. Which level of government has the greatest impact on your quality of life? Support your answer.

UNIT 4

HOW WAS THE CONSTITUTION USED TO ESTABLISH OUR GOVERNMENT?

2. Judicial review is an important part of our constitutional system of government.

- How did the Supreme Court acquire the power of judicial review?

- Do you think the Supreme Court should have the power to declare an act of Congress unconstitutional? Why or why not?

- How should justices determine the meaning of the words of the Constitution?

Suggested follow-up questions

a. Is the power of judicial review essential to a constitutional government? Why or why not?

b. Do you believe that an independent judiciary is essential to good government?

c. Describe one method of interpreting the Constitution. What are the strengths and weaknesses of this method?

d. What checks are there on judicial review? Are they effective? Explain your position.

e. Is judicial review consistent with democracy, republicanism (representative government), and popular sovereignty? Why or why not?

f. If the Supreme Court did not act as the ultimate guardian of our political system as defined in our Constitution, what or who would serve that purpose? Explain your answer.

g. If the Supreme Court has the power to declare laws null and void, should this power be clearly stated in the Constitution rather than implied? Why or why not?

UNIT 4 | HOW WAS THE CONSTITUTION USED TO ESTABLISH OUR GOVERNMENT?

3. Political parties are an important part of our political system today, yet they are not mentioned in the Constitution.

- Why did the Framers fear political parties?

- Why and how did political parties develop?

- Do political parties play a useful role today? Why or why not?

Suggested follow-up questions

a. Would you favor a constitutional amendment that banned political parties? Why or why not?

b. Have political parties helped or hindered the democratic process? Explain your answer.

c. Have political parties helped or hindered the legislative process? Explain your answer.

d. If we were a nation of only one political party, would that be a problem? Why or why not?

e. What does the growing number of independent parties say about our system? Explain your answer.

f. What principles do the modern Republican and Democratic parties stand for? Which party more closely represents the ideals of the Federalists and which represents the ideals of the Republicans of Jefferson's time? Explain your answer.

g. If James Madison were writing his Federalist 10 today, speaking out against factions, what examples would he use? Explain your answer.

h. Do factions have a right to participate in the political process? Would you regulate the political influence of special interests? Explain your answer.

UNIT 5 | HOW DOES THE CONSTITUTION PROTECT OUR BASIC RIGHTS?

1. The very first amendment, added to the Constitution in 1791, contains guarantees of freedom of religion.

● Why did the Founders think freedom of religion was so important?

● Explain the difference between the establishment and free exercise clauses.

● Do you think limitations should ever be imposed on the free exercise of one's religious beliefs? Explain your answers.

Suggested follow-up questions

a. Would you favor or oppose an amendment to allow the Ten Commandments to be posted in schools? Why or why not? Explain your answer.

b. If freedom of religion was so important, why did the Framers not include it in the body of the Constitution?

c. What are some benefits of freedom of religion? Explain your answer.

d. Under what conditions do you think public schools should have the right to limit a student's free exercise of religion? Explain your answer.

e. Congress and various state legislatures allow a prayer to be recited at the opening of each legislative session. Is this practice a violation of the establishment of religion clause? Why or why not?

f. Do you think that the establishment clause and the free exercise clause support contradictory principles? If you believe they are contradictory, how should the conflict be resolved? Support your answer with examples.

UNIT 5 HOW DOES THE CONSTITUTION PROTECT OUR BASIC RIGHTS?

2. Due process of law has been called the "primary and indispensable foundation of individual freedom" because it protects the individual from government wrongdoing.

- What is the right to due process? Where in the Constitution is due process protected and how is the meaning of due process applied?

- How does the equal protection clause of the Fourteenth Amendment prevent state governments from practicing unfair discrimination?

- Should young people under the age of eighteen have the same due process rights as adults? Why or why not?

Suggested follow-up questions

a. What is the most important due process right? Explain your answer.

b. Is there a difference in due process rights for citizens and illegal immigrants? Should there be? Why or why not?

c. Why is it important to assure procedural due process for people accused of serious crimes? How does protecting the rights of the accused also protect the rights of law-abiding citizens? Explain your answer.

d. How does due process help to ensure that public officials will not abuse their power? Explain your answer.

e. What processes do you believe are required under the Fifth and Fourteenth Amendments? What is the difference between the two amendments? Explain your answer.

f. Is it appropriate to limit the Fourteenth Amendment's protection against unreasonable search and seizure in school settings? Why or why not?

g. In times of crisis, such as war or mayhem, should due process be limited? Why or why not?

UNIT 5 | HOW DOES THE CONSTITUTION PROTECT OUR BASIC RIGHTS?

3. The First Amendment states that laws shall not be passed that abridge freedom of speech.

* Why did the Founders think freedom of speech was so important?

* Do you believe there are times when freedom of expression should be limited? Explain your response.

* Should a public speaker who calls for violent action be protected by the First Amendment whereas an audience member who performs the action can be sent to prison? Why or why not?

Suggested follow-up questions

a. In the case of *Tinker v. Des Moines*, the court said that although students do not give up their rights at the schoolhouse gate, expression that interferes with the school's mission can be limited. Does the *Tinker* decision give school officials too much authority to limit free speech? Explain your position.

b. The French philosopher Voltaire said he might not agree with what you are saying but he would defend to the death your right to say it. What is your opinion of this idea? Explain your answer.

c. Should it be lawful to put information on the Internet about how to make a bomb? Why or why not?

d. Should expression that is offensive to some students be restricted by "speech codes"? Should speech codes be subject to the limitations of the First Amendment or should schools and colleges be allowed to limit expression as they see fit? Why or why not?

e. Is it appropriate to allow government greater flexibility to regulate commercial speech, such as advertising, than political speech? Why or why not?

f. In your opinion, do time, place, and manner restrictions violate the right to free expression? Why or why not?

SIMULATED CONGRESSIONAL HEARING — JUDGES' UNIT & FOLLOW-UP QUESTIONS

UNIT 6

WHAT ARE THE RESPONSIBILITIES OF CITIZENS?

1. Many people believe that an informed citizenry is essential if democracy is to work.

   ● Should people be required to pass periodic citizenship tests to maintain their citizenship? Why or why not?

   ● Would you favor requiring literacy tests, fairly administered, before allowing citizens to vote? Why or why not?

Suggested follow-up questions

a. Should people be required to have the ability to read and write before they can vote? Why or why not?

b. Is possessing civic virtue the definition of a good citizen? Why or why not?

c. Should a high school diploma be required of all citizens? Why or why not?

d. What are the expectations of a citizen? How are these expectations different from those of a visitor to our country? Explain your answer.

e. How do Americans and recent immigrants learn what is expected of citizens? Give examples.

f. In some countries, a person must serve in the military before becoming a citizen or gaining the right to vote. Do you think this requirement is reasonable? Why or why not?

g. What is the most important responsibility of a citizen today? Explain your answer.

UNIT 6 | WHAT ARE THE RESPONSIBILITIES OF CITIZENS?

2. Voting is one way a citizen may participate in politics. Many other activities are available.

● What activities besides voting are available to citizens?

● Which of these activities, if any, do you think is most useful? Explain your answer.

● How should a citizen decide which of these various activities to participate in?

Suggested follow-up questions

a. How can students your age participate in government? Explain your answer.

b. How would you encourage more people to participate in government? Explain your answer.

c. If people vote and engage in civic participation, does that mean they are good citizens? Why or why not?

d. Should the government give rewards for civic participation and penalties for not participating? Why or why not?

e. What is government's role in improving civic participation? Is government at fault for the lack of civic participation? Explain your answer.

f. What are the advantages of U.S. citizenship, if any? Should there be a required renewal of citizenship? Should people who violate the law lose their citizenship? Explain your answer.

UNIT 6

WHAT ARE THE RESPONSIBILITIES OF CITIZENS?

3. Today, the nations of the world are increasingly dependent on each other.

- How have the U.S. Constitution and Bill of Rights influenced other countries?

- How have other countries influenced the United States?

- How do nations of the world interact with each other?

Suggested follow-up questions

a. What does it mean to be a sovereign nation?

b. How do nation-states enforce international law?

c. What power does the U.S. Constitution give the president to deal with other nations?

d. What power does the U.S. Constitution give the Congress to deal with other nations?

e. Who has authority over nation-states?

SIMULATED CONGRESSIONAL HEARING – JUDGES' SCORE SHEET   UNIT ____

Teacher _____

School _____

Congressional District _____

State _____

Date _____

For each criterion listed, score the group on a scale of 1 to 10, with 10 being the best score.
Use a separate form for each group.

1-2 = Poor   3-4 = Fair   5-6 = Average   7-8 = Above Average   9-10 = Excellent

		SCORE	NOTES
1	**UNDERSTANDING** To what extent did participants demonstrate a clear understanding of the basic issues involved in the question?		
2	**CONSTITUTIONAL APPLICATION** To what extent did participants appropriately apply knowledge of constitutional history and principles?		
3	**REASONING** To what extent did participants support positions with sound reasoning?		
4	**SUPPORTING EVIDENCE** To what extent did participants support positions with historical or contemporary evidence, examples, and/or illustrations?		
5	**RESPONSIVENESS** To what extent did participants' answers address the question asked?		
6	**PARTICIPATION** To what extent did most group members contribute to the group's presentation?		
	GROUP TOTAL		

JUDGE	TIEBREAKER*

*Tiebreaker Designate a score of any number between 0 and 100 that reflects this group's OVERALL performance. (This score will be used only in the event of a tie.) Use the following scale:

Outstanding	**90 to 100**	points
Very Good	**80 to 89**	points
Above Average	**70 to 79**	points
Average	**50 to 69**	points
Below Average	**30 to 49**	points
Poor	**0 to 29**	points

C 8

SCOREKEEPER'S SUMMARY SCORE SHEET

Teacher _____

School _____

Congressional District _____

State _____

Date _____

For each group, record the totals from the Simulated Congressional Hearing—Judges' Score Sheets (one per judge) in the spaces provided.

Then, add the group totals to determine the Combined Group Total. For example, if group one received scores of 48, 46, and 51 from three judges, you would record a 145 for unit one's group.

Add all Combined Group Totals to obtain the Class Grand Total.

Unit Group Number	JUDGE 1		JUDGE 2		JUDGE 3		Combined Group Total
UNIT 1		+		+		=	
UNIT 2		+		+		=	
UNIT 3		+		+		=	
UNIT 4		+		+		=	
UNIT 5		+		+		=	
UNIT 6		+		+		=	

CLASS GRAND TOTAL = _____

Scorekeeper

Make sure that you retain all Simulated Congressional Hearing — Judges' Score Sheets to use in case of ties. When two or more classes have the same grand totals, the tiebreaker points from all the judges should be added together to determine the winner.

C 9
EVENT REPORT FORM

Center for Civic Education • 5145 Douglas Fir Road • Calabasas, CA 91302 • (800) 350-4223

Please print with ballpoint pen

Date of event _____ - _____ - _____

Organizer _____

State/District Coordinator? ☐ yes ☐ no

Location of event _____

Address _____

City _____ State _____ Zip _____ Country _____ Language of event _____

☐ We the People: The Citizen and the Constitution
(circle one) elementary   middle   high school

Level ☐ state   ☐ school
☐ region   ☐ class
☐ congressional district   ☐ youth organization
☐ other

☐ We the People: Project Citizen
(circle one) portfolio   hearing   both

☐ School Violence Prevention Demonstration Program

☐ Foundations of Democracy

Winning class/youth organization _____

Number of volunteers (judges, trainers, timers, facilitators, and others) _____

Funding source (International program only) _____

Type of event   ☐ competitive   ☐ noncompetitive/showcase

Participating Teachers or Youth Organization Leaders   Use multiple forms if necessary

Teacher/Leader Mr. / Mrs. / Ms. _____

School/Organization Name _____

☐ Public ☐ Private ☐ Parochial ☐ Youth Org. ☐ Other _____

School/Organization Address _____

Phone (   ) _____   Fax (   ) _____

Email _____

Grade level _____ Course _____

Number of classes participating _____   Number of students per class/organization _____

Teacher/Leader Mr. / Mrs. / Ms. _____

School/Organization Name _____

☐ Public ☐ Private ☐ Parochial ☐ Youth Org. ☐ Other _____

School/Organization Address _____

Phone (   ) _____   Fax (   ) _____

Email _____

Grade level _____ Course _____

Number of classes participating _____   Number of students per class/organization _____

Teacher/Leader Mr. / Mrs. / Ms. _____

School/Organization Name _____

☐ Public ☐ Private ☐ Parochial ☐ Youth Org. ☐ Other _____

School/Organization Address _____

Phone (   ) _____   Fax (   ) _____

Email _____

Grade level _____ Course _____

Number of classes participating _____   Number of students per class/organization _____

Teacher/Leader Mr. / Mrs. / Ms. _____

School/Organization Name _____

☐ Public ☐ Private ☐ Parochial ☐ Youth Org. ☐ Other _____

School/Organization Address _____

Phone (   ) _____   Fax (   ) _____

Email _____

Grade level _____ Course _____

Number of classes participating _____   Number of students per class/organization _____

STUDENT HANDOUT FOR LESSON 10

Name _____

Class _____

Date _____

BASIC IDEAS ABOUT GOVERNMENT FOUND IN STATE CONSTITUTIONS

Basic idea	Meaning in your own words
Natural rights and higher law	
Social contract	
Popular sovereignty	
Representation	
Separation of powers	
Checks and balances	
Legislative supremacy	

D 2

STUDENT HANDOUT FOR LESSON 13

Name

Class

Date

HOW MANY REPRESENTATIVES SHOULD A STATE HAVE?

SMALL STATES

Step 1 List the small states	Step 2 List the population	Step 3 List one representative for each state	Step 4 List the number of representatives by population (30,000 people = 1 representative)
1.			
2.			
3.			
4.			
5.			
6.			
7.			
Step 5 TOTALS			

LARGE STATES

Step 1 List the large states	Step 2 List the population	Step 3 List one representative for each state	Step 4 List the number of representatives by population (30,000 people = 1 representative)
1.			
2.			
3.			
4.			
5.			
6.			
Step 5 TOTALS			

STUDENT HANDOUT FOR LESSON 17

Name _____

Class _____

Date _____

Action	National government	State governments	Both	Neither
1. You want a law to help control what people can put on the Internet for children to see and read.				
2. You want to increase the age at which people may buy tobacco to twenty-five.				
3. You want a law that helps to control who may or may not buy and sell guns.				
4. You want a law to limit driving privileges for people over eighty-five years of age.				
5. You think that we no longer need a one-cent coin. You want a law to end the minting of pennies.				
6. You want a law to stop the sale of sport shoes made by children who work long hours for little pay in some other countries.				
7. You want a law to make it more difficult for parents of very young children to get a divorce.				
8. You think that the leader of a neighboring country is not able to run the government of that country. You want a law to punish anyone who supports this leader.				
9. You want a treaty that requires all nations to pass laws to clean up the air and water.				
10. You want a law to raise the minimum age requirement for children to remain in school.				

Name

Class

Date

FEDERALIST OR REPUBLICAN?

Instructions: Put an **F** in front of each statement that describes the Federalists.
Put an **R** in front of each statement that describes the Republicans.

_____ 1. Believed in strong local governments, as opposed to a strong national government

_____ 2. Led by Thomas Jefferson

_____ 3. Favored supporting the English in the war against France

_____ 4. Wanted to limit the powers of Congress through a strict interpretation of the necessary and proper clause

_____ 5. Was against using federal power to create a bank

_____ 6. Believed that the necessary and proper clause could be used to create a national bank

_____ 7. Believed that the United States should recognize its debt to the French and support them in their war against England

_____ 8. Believed that America should develop as a manufacturing and trading nation

_____ 9. Led by Alexander Hamilton

1. Have students read the account of the *Tinker v. Des Moines School District* (1969) case in the Ideas for Discussion section and discuss with them the case's relevance. Focus the discussion on some of the reasons why freedom of expression is important and the difference that it might make in their lives.

2. Interested students might research cases that occurred after the *Tinker* case that dealt with symbolic speech—the wearing of headgear or insignia, the use of the American flag on clothing, or the right to free assembly (e.g., creating and operating student clubs on campus).

3. Tell students that they are about to take part in an activity that will demonstrate what life might be like in a country without First Amendment rights. Choose one of the following activities to use with the entire class or divide the class into groups and assign each group one of the activities.

Activity A – Control the Press

a. Appoint a "censorship board" of three class members. They are governed by only one rule: any information allowed to leave the classroom must make the teacher and her or his decisions look good. Failure to follow this rule will result in a call home and a trip to the principal's office. (Suggest that the new rule is in response to a new school-wide policy designed to help students do better in school.)

b. Appoint four "members of the Free World Press"; have them wait in another classroom for a few minutes.

c. Announce to the class the following three new rules:

- Anyone talking without permission will get 30 minutes detention

- Anyone arguing with the teacher will get 30 minutes detention

- Anyone leaving his or her seat for any reason during the class period will get 30 minutes detention

Explain that these new rules are designed to keep better order in the classroom. Have pairs of students acting as reporters write headlines and brief articles summarizing the new rules governing their classroom for the outside world (i.e., the rest of the school).

d. Announce that the censorship board will impose punishments for negative articles. If the censorship board is unwilling to establish meaningful punishments, they will have to accept the consequences mentioned above. The censorship board should then choose the article that shows the teacher and the new rules in the best light as the official version of events. It should also impose penalties on those groups that reported unfavorably on the teacher or the new rules.

e. Members of the Free World Press should then reenter the room and be given the officially accepted version of events. They should write a brief account of the new rules as they have been permitted to see them.

f. Discuss the situation by asking the following questions:

- How would you compare the censored version of events with the actual events?

- What did you think of the new rules?

- What would you want to include in an article you were writing about the event?

- Did the fear of punishment keep you from saying what you wanted to in your article?

- How do you think fear of punishment affects the press in countries that do not have a free press?

- Do you think that a censorship board is even needed, or would fear keep people from writing what they want?

Activity B – Divide and Conquer

a. Put up a poster with the following three new rules:

- Anyone talking without permission will get 30 minutes detention

- Anyone arguing with the teacher will get 30 minutes detention

- Anyone leaving his or her seat for any reason during the class period will get 30 minutes detention

b. Allow students to create informal gatherings to discuss the fairness of the new rules.

c. Tell them that if they can develop a class-wide alternative to the rules given, they might be able to convince the teacher to change the rules.

d. Immediately change your mind about allowing the "assemblies" to take place, citing a need for better order, which was the reason for the rules in the first place.

e. Solicit individual written suggestions for change. Suggest that there will be serious steps taken to deal with anyone who suggests something too radical or whose suggestion contains critical overtones.

f. Discuss the fears and frustrations of working alone to confront repressive authority as compared to working with a group.

g. Discuss the activity using the following questions:

- How did you feel when you were told you could not work together?

- Did the fear of punishment keep you from arguing about the restriction on group activity?

- What were the benefits and costs of working alone?

- What would be the benefits and costs of working with a group?

Activity C—Suppress Discussion and Thought

a. Announce the three new class rules noted in Activity B. Do not allow discussion.

b. Assign a short group assignment of your choosing. Reading the student text for this lesson would be appropriate.

c. Tell students that they may discuss the assignment but they are not to discuss the new rules. ("It's just something that was necessary for a more orderly and efficient classroom!") Also warn them that there are students throughout the room who have been asked to report instances of unauthorized discussion to you in secret at a later time. There will be an unnamed consequence, depending on the severity of the offense, for those who are reported.

d. After providing a few minutes to complete the group work, move on to a discussion.

e. Discuss the activity using the following questions:

● Was it hard to refrain from discussing the new rules?

● Did you discuss them anyway? If not, why not? If you did, were you worried about being reported?

● Are there countries where adults face the same problems in discussing and criticizing their government that you just faced with the new rules? Can you name some?

● How can people express their opinions in those countries and avoid being punished by the government? Were there really any "spies" in our class? Does this tell us that sometimes the fear of being caught acts to keep people from speaking freely?

Name _____

Class _____

Date _____

DECIDING ISSUES USING CONSTITUTIONAL GUIDELINES

After reading the situations in your book, answer these four questions.

What is the law or action?	
Does it have an educational purpose?	
What will happen if this law or action is implemented?	
How would this law or action affect the involvement of government?	

In deciding whether government is complying with the establishment clause, the courts look at three guidelines. Explain whether you think the laws and actions described in your book meet each of the requirements below.

Guidelines	Meets requirement
1. The courts examine whether government is actively endorsing religion.	
2. The courts examine whether government is compelling people to participate in religious activities or to accept religious beliefs.	
3. The courts examine whether government is providing special treatment to one type of religion that it is not providing to other types of religion.	
What is your decision? Is the issue constitutional or unconstitutional? Why or why not?	

CASE 1 The Ten Commandments

Citation *Stone v. Graham*, 101 S.Ct. 192 (1980) 66 L.Ed.2d. 199

Issue Does the posting of a copy of the Ten Commandments in public school classrooms violate the establishment clause of the Constitution?

Facts The state of Kentucky passed a law requiring all classrooms to post a copy of the Ten Commandments. The state argued that "secular application of the Ten Commandments is clearly seen in its adoption as the fundamental legal code of Western Civilization and the Common Law of the United States." The copies would be financed through voluntary contributions.

The state law was sustained by a state trial court and was affirmed by a tie vote of the state supreme court.

Decision In a 5–4 decision, the state law was overturned, with Justices Brennan, White, Marshall, Powell, and Stevens constituting the majority. The Court said, "The Ten Commandments are undeniably a sacred text in the Jewish and Christian faiths, and no legislative recitation of a supposedly secular purpose can blind us to that fact."

CASE 2 Tax Deductions

Citation *Mueller v. Allen*, 103 S.Ct. 3062 (1983) 77 L.Ed.2d. 721

Issue Is the establishment clause of the First Amendment violated if a state provides state income tax deductions for educational expenses to parochial schools?

Facts The Minnesota state legislature passed a law granting a tax deduction to parents for school expenses in the areas of tuition, transportation, and educational materials at public, private, and parochial schools. A cap of $500 for K–6 expenses and $700 for 7–12 expenses was written into the law. In Minnesota, 91,000 of the state's 820,000 students were enrolled in private schools, and 95% of that 91,000 attended parochial schools.

Decision In a 5–4 decision, Justice Rehnquist noted in the majority opinion that Minnesota law provided a wide variety of tax deductions and that this particular deduction did not give special treatment to parochial school parents but was open to all parents of school-age children. He also argued that the effect of the tax deductions was a well-educated citizenry, which was constitutionally permitted.

CASE 3 Public School Teachers in Parochial Schools

Citation *Aguilar v. Felton*, 105 S.Ct. 3248 (1985) 87 L.Ed.2d. 290

Issue Can public schools provide instruction in a parochial school setting?

Facts New York City schools had regularly used Title I funds to send their teachers into parochial schools to provide remedial math, reading, and English instruction during the school day. Grand Rapids schools provided a similar program that offered a wider range of subjects and included paying rent to the parochial schools for the use of their classrooms during the instructional period.

The concept of "shared time" was used in the arguments before the Court. These students were said to be enrolled part-time in the public school and part-time in the parochial school. In both cases, these parochial school classrooms were designated as being public school classrooms and all religious symbols had been draped or removed.

Decision In a 5–4 decision, Justice Brennan found that the program would cause "excessive entanglement" of the church and state, since teachers would have to be supervised to make sure that no religious instruction was being provided.

CASE 4 Equal Access to School Facilities

Citations *Widmer v. Vincent*, 102 S.Ct. 269 (1981)
Brandon v. Board of Education, 635 F.2d 971 (1980)
Bender v. Williamsport Area School District, 106 S.Ct. 1326 (1986)
Lubbock Independent School Board v. Lubbock ACLU, 669 F.2d. 1038 (1982)

Issue Can schools allow student religious groups the use of school facilities on the same basis as any other student groups on campus?

Facts In the *Widmer* case, a student religious group at the University of Kansas City had been able to use the campus facilities from 1973–77, although the university had a 1972 regulation that banned the use of campus facilities for the purpose of religious worship or religious teaching. Starting in 1978, the school officials decided to enforce this rule, and no longer allowed the group to use campus facilities. The college students filed a lawsuit claiming violation of their constitutional rights under the First Amendment.

In the *Brandon* case, several students asked the principal for permission to conduct voluntary prayers prior to the start of school each day. The principal, the superintendent, and the school board rejected the request. Students filed a lawsuit claiming that their rights to free exercise of religion, free speech, and free assembly were being violated.

In the *Bender* case, a student religious group asked to meet during the school's activity period to discuss religion as well as to conduct voluntary prayers. School officials rejected their request and students filed a lawsuit claiming that their constitutional rights to freely exercise their religion, to free speech, and to freely assemble had been violated.

In the *Lubbock* case, the school board had allowed school prayers and Bible readings over school public address systems. In addition, Bibles had been distributed to elementary students. The school board was ordered by a U.S. court of appeals to stop these practices. As a result, the school board adopted a policy that allowed student groups (including religious ones) to use school facilities for meetings as long as attendance at such meetings was voluntary.

Decisions In the *Widmer* case, the U.S. Supreme Court ruled 8–1 that the college students' rights were being violated because religious and nonreligious speech are protected.

In the *Brandon* case, the district court dismissed the case and the court of appeals affirmed that dismissal. The appellate court noted that public schools do not have the tradition of being public forums, unlike colleges and universities, and that students still could freely exercise their religion, although not in a school setting. The U.S. Supreme Court refused to hear the case.

In the *Bender* case, students won in district court but lost in the court of appeals. The U.S. Supreme Court ruled that Bender had no standing because he was no longer on the school board nor a parent of one of the affected students. The case was sent back to the district court.

In the *Lubbock* case, the court of appeals found that the new policy was a violation of the establishment clause and stated that no use of public school facilities for meetings of student religious groups before or after school hours was constitutionally permissible. The U.S. Supreme Court refused to hear the case.

THE PEOPLE ★★★★★ THE CONSTITUTION ★★★★★ THE CITIZEN & THE CON

D 7

STUDENT HANDOUT FOR LESSON 25

Name _____

Class _____

Date _____

Part A: The Growth of Democracy: Maps and Activities

Student Instructions

Use the information sheet, Part B, to color code three copies of this map.

Each map represents a different census year—1820, 1830, and 1840.

Map Key

RED	Property, tax, or other qualification
GREEN	Adult white males
BLUE	All adult males

VOTING QUALIFICATIONS BY STATE IN 1820, 1830, AND 1840

State	1820	1830	1840
Alabama	Adult white males	Adult white males	Adult white males
Arkansas			Adult white males
Connecticut	Property, tax, or other	Adult white males	Adult white males
Delaware	Property, tax, or other	Property, tax, or other	Property, tax, or other
Georgia	Property, tax, or other	Property, tax, or other	Property, tax, or other
Illinois	Adult white males	Adult white males	Adult white males
Indiana	Adult white males	Adult white males	Adult white males
Kentucky	Adult white males	Adult white males	Adult white males
Louisiana	Property, tax, or other	Adult white males	Adult white males
Maine	Property, tax, or other	All adult males	All adult males
Maryland	Adult white males	Adult white males	Adult white males
Massachusetts	Property, tax, or other	Property, tax, or other	Property, tax, or other
Michigan			Adult white males
Mississippi	Property, tax, or other	Property, tax, or other	Adult white males
Missouri		Adult white males	Adult white males
New Hampshire	Property, tax, or other	Property, tax, or other	Property, tax, or other
New Jersey	Property, tax, or other	Property, tax, or other	Property, tax, or other
New York	Property, tax, or other	Adult white males	Adult white males
North Carolina	Property, tax, or other	Property, tax, or other	Property, tax, or other
Ohio	Property, tax, or other	Property, tax, or other	Property, tax, or other
Pennsylvania	Property, tax, or other	Property, tax, or other	Property, tax, or other
Rhode Island	Property, tax, or other	Property, tax, or other	Property, tax, or other
South Carolina	Property, tax, or other	Property, tax, or other	Property, tax, or other
Tennessee	Property, tax, or other	Property, tax, or other	Adult white males
Vermont	All adult males	All adult males	All adult males
Virginia	Property, tax, or other	Property, tax, or other	Property, tax or other

Part C: Map Questions

Complete the maps and answer the questions below. The data provided on Part B: Information Sheet can be entered into an Excel spreadsheet or copied and used for reference. Answer the following questions based on the maps you have completed.

1. How many states had property, tax, or other voting qualifications

   in 1820? _____ in 1830? _____ in 1840? _____

2. How many states allowed all adult white males to vote

   in 1820? _____ in 1830? _____ in 1840? _____

3. How many states allowed all adult males to vote

   in 1820? _____ in 1830? _____ in 1840? _____

4. Which part of the country had the fewest voting restrictions?

   _____

5. How many new states were added to the United States between 1820 and 1840? What were the voting qualifications in these new states?

   _____

6. After completing the maps on the growth of democracy in the United States, what did you learn about voting rights between 1820 and 1840?

   _____

   _____

   _____

   _____

   _____

   _____

   _____

   _____

Part D: Map Questions

Research the answers to these questions.

1. Between 1820 and 1840, how were average people able to be involved in government?

2. Find evidence to support the following statement: "More than any other person, [Andrew] Jackson stood for the growing power of the people in government."

The Growth of Democracy: Generalizations

Teacher Instructions

Distribute Handout D 8—The Growth of Democracy: Generalizations (see next page). Have students assess the generalizations listed based on the maps they completed in Handout D 7.

Generalizations 1, 3, 4, 5, 6, 7, 10, 11, 13, and 15 should be marked with a plus sign; generalizations 2, 8, 9, and 14 should be marked with a minus sign. Generalization 12 is accurate, but the data provided is not sufficient to reach this conclusion.

The Growth of Democracy: Generalizations

Use the maps you colored to evaluate the following generalizations. Put a plus sign (+) in the blank for generalizations that are accurate. Put a minus sign (−) by those statements that are contradicted by the maps. Put a question mark (?) in the blank if there is not enough information on the maps to make a judgment.

_____ 1. In 1820, most states required a person to own property, pay taxes, or meet some similar qualification in order to vote.

_____ 2. More states had less restrictive qualifications for voting in 1840 than in 1830.

_____ 3. In 1830, the states that had the fewest restrictions on voting were in the Northeast.

_____ 4. By 1840, the more Western states were more democratic than the Eastern states.

_____ 5. In 1830, the more Northern states were more democratic than the Southern states.

_____ 6. The new states admitted to the United States between 1820 and 1840 had fewer voting restrictions than the older states.

_____ 7. In 1820, Tennessee required a person to own property in order to vote.

_____ 8. Pennsylvania changed its voting requirements between 1820 and 1840.

_____ 9. Alabama allowed all adult males to vote in all three census years.

_____ 10. Maine changed its voting requirements between 1820 and 1830.

11. In 1840, Mississippi allowed all adult white males to vote.

12. Michigan was admitted to the United States between 1830 and 1840.

13. Only white men were allowed to vote in most states in 1840.

14. In 1840, voting qualifications were more limiting than they were in 1820.

15. In 1840, a larger percentage of the population of Western states was eligible to vote than in the Eastern states.

D 9
STUDENT HANDOUT FOR LESSON 26

Name _____

Class _____

Date _____

Ending Discrimination

1. Below are some important events in our nation's struggle to end discrimination. The dates for some events are missing. Find these dates in your text and add them to your list.

2. Put the events listed on the timeline on the next page.

3. Study your timeline carefully. Does it provide any insight into the struggle for the right to equal protection?

List of Events

● Thirteenth Amendment ratified (1865)

● Fourteenth Amendment ratified (1868)

● Fifteenth Amendment ratified (1870)

● Ex-Confederates regained control of state legislatures in the Southern states (1869–1877)

● Southern states passed segregation laws (1880–1895)

● U.S. Supreme Court upheld "separate but equal" facilities (1896)

● President Roosevelt issued an executive order banning discrimination in hiring by defense contractors (1941)

● President Truman issued an executive order requiring fair employment in federal jobs (1948)

● U.S. Supreme Court struck down segregated schools (1954)

● Black boycott of bus line in Montgomery, Alabama, marked first major attack on segregation of public facilities (1955–1956)

● Civil Rights Acts passed (1954–1964, 1968)

● Voting Rights Act passed (1965)

● Age Discrimination in Employment Act passed (1967)

● Equal Employment Opportunities Act passed (1968)

● Title IX of the Education Act banned discrimination on the basis of sex in educational programs that receive federal aid (1972)

● Education for All Handicapped Children Act passed (1975)

● Proposed equal rights amendment guaranteeing equal rights for women failed to be ratified (1982)

D 9

STUDENT HANDOUT FOR LESSON 26

Name ______________________________

Class ______________________________

Date ______________________________

Equal Protection Timeline

1860 ______________________________

1870 ______________________________

1880 ______________________________

1890 ______________________________

1900 ______________________________

1910 ______________________________

1920 ______________________________

1930 ______________________________

1940 ______________________________

1950 ______________________________

1960 ______________________________

1970 ______________________________

1980 ______________________________

Name

Class

Date

Due Process in the Constitution

Use the Constitution and the Bill of Rights to complete the chart below.

Due process rights	Where guaranteed in the Constitution
Protection against unreasonable searches and seizures	
Right to remain silent	
Right to an attorney	
Right to know the charges against oneself	
Right to reasonable bail	
Right to a trial by jury	
Right to a public trial	
Right to a speedy trial	
Right to call witnesses in one's favor	
Right to cross-examine witnesses against oneself	
Right against oneself	
Protection against cruel and unusual punishments	
Protection against double jeopardy	

STUDENT HANDOUT FOR LESSON 29

Name ______________________________

Class ______________________________

Date ______________________________

Rights and Responsibilities

Complete this handout as you read about the rights of citizens and the basic responsibilities that accompany those rights. Provide as many examples of each as you can.

Rights and responsibilities	Examples
Personal rights	
Political rights	
Economic rights	
Personal responsibilities	
Civic responsibilities	

Name _____

Class _____

Date _____

Ideas for Discussion: Should Citizens Participate in Their Government?

Complete the handout by placing your information in the appropriate columns.

Constitutional principle	Meaning of principle	Implications for the role of the citizen	Actions citizens might take
Common good			
Consent of the governed			
Constitutional government			
Individual rights			
Popular sovereignty			
Representative government			

Name _____

Class _____

Date _____

REFLECTING ON YOUR EXPERIENCE

It is always a good idea to think about or reflect on experiences you have had or projects you have completed. That is one way to learn, to avoid mistakes in the future, and to improve your performance.

Now that your class has completed this study, you have an opportunity to reflect on or evaluate what and how you and your classmates learned. You also have an opportunity to think about what you might do differently if you were to study other topics similar to this.

Use the following questions to help you reflect upon and evaluate your experience:

1. What did I personally learn about issues we studied from working with my classmates?

_____
_____
_____

2. What did we, as a class, learn about the issues from the reading, the class discussions, and critical thinking exercises?

_____
_____

3. What skills did I learn or improve on as a result of this experience?

_____
_____

4. What skills did the class learn or improve on as a result of this experience?

_____
_____

5. What are the disadvantages of working with study partners and in small groups?

6. What are the advantages of working with study partners and in small groups?

7. What did I do well?

8. What would I want to do differently the next time I study a topic similar to this?

9. What did we, as a class, do well?

10. What would we want to do differently the next time we study a topic similar to this?

STUDENT ANSWER SHEET

WE THE PEOPLE ★★★★★★ THE CITIZEN & THE CONSTITUTION ★★★★★★

Name _____

Class _____

Date _____

Instructions

For each question, select the one best answer. Mark your answers on this answer sheet as instructed by your teacher.

Cross off the correct answer with an X.

1. a b c d
2. a b c d
3. a b c d
4. a b c d
5. a b c d
6. a b c d
7. a b c d
8. a b c d
9. a b c d
10. a b c d
11. a b c d
12. a b c d
13. a b c d

14. a b c d
15. a b c d
16. a b c d
17. a b c d
18. a b c d
19. a b c d
20. a b c d
21. a b c d
22. a b c d
23. a b c d
24. a b c d
25. a b c d
26. a b c d

27. a b c d
28. a b c d
29. a b c d
30. a b c d
31. a b c d
32. a b c d
33. a b c d
34. a b c d
35. a b c d
36. a b c d
37. a b c d
38. a b c d
39. a b c d

40. a b c d
41. a b c d
42. a b c d
43. a b c d
44. a b c d
45. a b c d
46. a b c d
47. a b c d
48. a b c d
49. a b c d
50. a b c d

D 15
STUDENT MULTIPLE-CHOICE TEST

Name _____

Class _____

Date _____

TEST ON THE HISTORY AND PRINCIPLES OF THE UNITED STATES CONSTITUTION

Instructions

For each question, select the one best answer. Mark your answers on a separate answer sheet as instructed by your teacher.

1. The Founders were the
   a. people who opposed the Articles of Confederation.
   b. political leaders of the colonies.
   c. British governors of the colonies.
   d. people who supported the king.

2. The Founders believed that natural rights meant the right to
   a. education, privacy, and security.
   b. life, liberty, and propery.
   c. clothing, food, and shelter.
   d. freedom, work, and protection.

3. An agreement to create a government and follow its laws is known as a
   a. natural agreement.
   b. constitution.
   c. social contract.
   d. declaration of intent.

4. Citizens who put the common good above their own selfish interests demonstrate
   a. democracy.
   b. separation of powers.
   c. balance of powers.
   d. civic virtue.

5. A constitutional government always includes
   a. a strong executive.
   b. a limitation of powers.
   c. a written constitution.
   d. the idea of judicial review.

6. A constitution is considered a higher law if it
   a. must be obeyed by those running the government.
   b. can never be changed.
   c. comes from a divine source.
   d. keeps the government above the people.

7. Dividing the government into different branches is an example of
   a. federalism.
   b. constitutional government.
   c. separation of powers.
   d. private domain.

8. The system of checks and balances was established to
   a. prevent political parties from being created.
   b. provide government officials with unlimited powers.
   c. prevent branches of government from abusing power.
   d. guarantee that people's rights are never limited.

9. The Magna Carta, an agreement between the nobles and the king of England, required
   a. the king to govern according to established rules of law.
   b. the king to return taxes unfairly collected.
   c. the king and the nobles to represent the common people.
   d. the king and the nobles to agree on all new laws enacted.

10. To protect themselves from the abuse of power, the colonists created their colonial governments to include
    a. a classical republic.
    b. judicial supremacy.
    c. a constitutional monarchy.
    d. representative government.

11. The colonists argued that laws such as the Stamp Act of 1765
    a. were consistent with their rights as Englishmen.
    b. were invalid because the colonists were not allowed to vote for Parliament.
    c. were justified to help pay English debts.
    d. did not raise enough money to help the colonies.

12. The Declaration of Independence was
    a. the peace treaty that ended the American Revolution.
    b. an explanation of the colonists' revolt against Britain.
    c. the first U.S. Constitution.
    d. the first ten amendments to the Constitution.

13. The purpose of government as described in the Declaration of Independence is to
    a. protect the people's natural rights.
    b. prevent attacks by foreign countries.
    c. make agreements with other nations.
    d. serve as a check on special interest groups.

14. Diplomacy played an important role in the American Revolutionary War by ensuring that
    a. the Quebec campaign would succeed.
    b. Martha Washington could assist the troops with supplies.
    c. France would provide loans and military assistance to the Americans.
    d. Benjamin Franklin could negotiate a treaty with Britain.

15. Early state constitutions included the principle of popular sovereignty, which means that
    a. the government has supreme power over the people.
    b. the government has the power to make laws.
    c. the government gets its right to govern from the people.
    d. the legislature has absolute supremacy.

16. The authors of the Articles of Confederation feared a strong national government, so they created a single branch of government, the
    a. legislature.
    b. executive.
    c. judiciary.
    d. monarchy.

17. An important difference between the Articles of Confederation and the Constitution is that the Constitution gives
    a. Congress the power to act directly on the people.
    b. Congress the right to establish a national school system.
    c. any state the right to leave the Union if it wishes.
    d. smaller states greater power.

18. The purpose of the Philadelphia Convention was to
   a. declare independence from Great Britain.
   b. ratify the Articles of Confederation.
   c. secretly take control of the new states.
   d. improve the Articles of Confederation.

19. Giving states with larger populations a greater number of representatives in Congress is called
   a. equal representation.
   b. adequate representation.
   c. proportional representation.
   d. legislative representation.

20. The decision to divide Congress into two houses, with equal representation in one and proportional representation in the other, was called the
   a. Great Compromise.
   b. Virginia Plan.
   c. New Jersey Plan.
   d. New York Compromise.

21. The Framers resolved the conflict between the Northern and Southern states by
   a. exempting the South from certain parts of the Constitution.
   b. prohibiting the expansion of slavery into new territories.
   c. expanding trade with Southern states.
   d. allowing the slave trade to continue.

22. Powers that are specifically granted to Congress by the Constitution are called
   a. executive powers.
   b. bureaucratic powers.
   c. judicial powers.
   d. enumerated powers.

23. The general welfare clause of the Constitution allows Congress to
   a. override the president's veto by a two-thirds vote of both houses.
   b. provide for the common defense and common good of the United States.
   c. declare a person guilty of violating the law and set the punishment without a court trial.
   d. make all laws that are necessary and proper for carrying out the other powers of Congress.

24. The Constitution grants the president the power to
    a. make laws that Congress refuses to make.
    b. veto laws passed by Congress.
    c. declare war.
    d. put people in jail without a trial.

25. The system the Framers created for choosing the president is known as
    a. the electoral college.
    b. voter registration.
    c. nomination by convention.
    d. political campaigning.

26. One way of ensuring the neutrality of the national judiciary was to
    a. have judges be elected by the people.
    b. have judges be appointed for four-year terms.
    c. allow judges to hold their offices for life with good behavior.
    d. allow judges' salaries to be decided by popular vote.

27. The Anti-Federalists were people who
    a. opposed increasing the power of the national government.
    b. opposed the creation of the Articles of Confederation.
    c. were loyal to the British monarch.
    d. supported Shays' Rebellion.

28. To get enough support for the ratification of the Constitution, the Federalists agreed to
    a. remove the necessary and proper clause.
    b. amend the three-fifths clause.
    c. outlaw slavery in the territories.
    d. add a bill of rights.

29. The Constitution was ratified by a vote of
    a. state legislatures.
    b. special state conventions.
    c. all registered voters.
    d. members of Congress.

30. A system of government in which power is shared by the national government, the state governments, and the people is called a

    a. unitary system.
    b. totalitarian system.
    c. federal system.
    d. confederation system.

31. "This Constitution, and the Laws of the United States… shall be the supreme Law of the Land" means that

    a. only the laws of the U.S. Constitution must be obeyed.
    b. the Constitution may not be changed.
    c. the laws of the U.S. government may not be changed.
    d. federal law will prevail over state laws if the two conflict.

32. The first ten amendments to the Constitution are called the

    a. Statement of Purposes.
    b. Preamble.
    c. Bill of Rights.
    d. Freedom Principle.

33. Political parties came about as a result of

    a. a constitutional amendment.
    b. disagreements over the powers of the national government.
    c. conflicts between the Senate and House of Representatives.
    d. an act of Congress.

34. In the case *Marbury v. Madison*, the Supreme Court established its power of judicial review, which allows the court to

    a. hear any case it wants to at any time.
    b. dispute the results of presidential elections.
    c. argue that it does not have to follow the Constitution.
    d. declare laws passed by Congress unconstitutional.

35. The Supreme Court can serve as a check on the power of the legislature by

    a. impeaching members of Congress.
    b. declaring laws or actions unconstitutional.
    c. approving amendments passed by popular vote.
    d. approving presidential vetoes of congressional laws.

36. One problem with a Supreme Court justice trying to determine the intention of the Framers when interpreting the Constitution is that

   a. the Framers answered all Constitutional questions fully and clearly.

   b. the Supreme Court has ruled that interpretation of the Constitution is illegal.

   c. there were many Framers and they did not always agree.

   d. the justice might interpret the Constitution incorrectly and be vetoed by the president.

37. Individual development and human dignity, the advancement of knowledge, and peaceful social change are some of the benefits of

   a. a trial by jury.

   b. ex post facto laws.

   c. bills of attainder.

   d. freedom of expression.

38. The Constitution guarantees, with some limits, each citizen's right to free

   a. speech, healthcare, shelter, and public welfare.

   b. speech, quality of life, and public education.

   c. speech, press, and practice of a professional trade.

   d. speech, press, assembly, and religious belief.

39. The establishment clause limits the government's ability to

   a. support an official state religion.

   b. set up public universities and colleges.

   c. compel students to recite the Pledge of Allegiance.

   d. raise and support standing armies.

40. The issue of allowing prayer in public schools has faced controversy because of differing interpretations of the

   a. free speech and due process clauses of the Constitution.

   b. representation and apportionment clauses of the Constitution.

   c. establishment and free exercise clauses of the Constitution.

   d. supremacy and declarative clauses of the Constitution.

41. The Nineteenth Amendment
    a. freed the slaves.
    b. formally ended the Revolutionary War.
    c. gave women the right to vote.
    d. ended prohibition.

42. The Fourteenth Amendment was intended
    to guarantee the equal protection of the laws to
    a. African Americans.
    b. women.
    c. Native Americans.
    d. whites who did not own property.

43. The primary purpose of the civil rights movement was to
    a. encourage civic participation among immigrants.
    b. oppose the Vietnam War.
    c. obtain equal protection of the laws for African Americans.
    d. ensure that public schools remain segregated.

44. The right to due process of law means that
    a. laws will be publicly debated.
    b. important public questions must be settled by direct
       vote of the people.
    c. proposed laws must be passed by both houses of Congress.
    d. laws and procedures of government must be fair and reasonable.

45. The guarantee of due process is important because it ensures that
    a. governmental institutions can enact important policies.
    b. judges have discretion in sentencing.
    c. juveniles do not get the same protections as adults.
    d. government treats individuals fairly.

46. The United States has given much to the world. Among the democratic
    ideals other nations have learned from our country is
    a. consent of the governed.
    b. separation of powers.
    c. legislative supremacy.
    d. necessary and proper laws.

47. The Constitution gives our government powers to deal with other nations. Among those powers is the authority
   a. of Congress to approve treaties.
   b. of the Supreme Court to regulate commerce.
   c. of individual states to make treaties.
   d. of the president to address the United Nations.

48. Citizens have both personal and civic responsibilities that go along with their rights. An example of a civic responsibility is
   a. supporting one's family.
   b. making charitable donations.
   c. serving as a juror.
   d. contributing money to a political party.

49. Henry David Thoreau and Dr. Martin Luther King Jr. are examples of people who went to jail because they
   a. supported the impeachment of the president.
   b. disobeyed laws that they believed were unjust.
   c. refused to serve in the military.
   d. committed violent acts of protest.

50. Participation in the political life of our nation is consistent with the principle of
   a. judicial activism.
   b. popular sovereignty.
   c. autocratic government.
   d. the supremacy clause.

We the People: Project Citizen

Project Citizen is a curricular program for middle, high, and postsecondary school students and youth groups that promotes competent and responsible participation in local, state, and federal government. The program is designed to help students learn how to monitor and influence public policy. In the process, they develop support for democratic values and principles, tolerance, and feelings of political efficacy.

Entire classes of students or members of youth organizations work cooperatively to identify a public policy problem in their community. They then research the problem, evaluate alternative solutions, develop their own solution, and create a political action plan to enlist local or state authorities to adopt their proposed policy. Participants develop a portfolio of their work, and present their project to a panel of civic-minded community members.

Project Citizen is administered with the assistance of a national network of coordinators in every state in the nation and conducted with the assistance of the National Conference of State Legislatures.

We the People: Project Citizen is funded by the U.S. Department of Education under the Education for Democracy Act approved by the United States Congress. Additional funding at the state level is also provided by an increasing number of state legislatures.

To contact your state coordinator or to request free instructional materials, visit the Center for Civic Education's website at www.civiced.org/project_citizen.php. Order the *Project Citizen* text from the Center for Civic Education's online store at http://civiced-store.stores.yahoo.net/index.html or e-mail our sales department at sales@civiced.org.

Representative Democracy in America: Voices of the People

This six-part video series introduces citizens, particularly young people, to the representatives, institutions, and processes that realize the goal of a government of, by, and for the people. Developed with the involvement of students, teachers, scholars, and other educational leaders, the videos help students understand the essential elements of representative democracy and encourage their commitment to becoming responsible participants. The video series is accompanied by an instructional package.

The programs are best integrated at the high school level. They are designed to be used as a complete series, but may also be used independently. The six programs, each approximately 15 minutes in length, address the following topics:

- The roots of representative democracy
- Federalism and the separation of powers
- The roles of representatives, executives, and justices in our democracy
- Our representatives and how they are chosen
- The role of the citizen in a representative democracy

Representative Democracy in America: Voices of the People is a five-year national project to reinvigorate and educate Americans on the critical relationship between government and the people it serves. The Center for Civic Education, the Center on Congress at Indiana University, and the Trust for Representative Democracy/National Conference of State Legislatures are implementing the project.

Representative Democracy in America: Voices of the People was funded by the U.S. Department of Education under the Education Act approved by the U.S. Congress. To order *Representative Democracy in America: Voices of the People*, e-mail our sales department at sales@civiced.org.

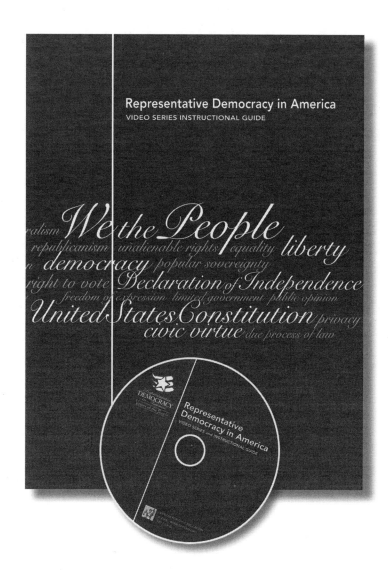

Foundations of Democracy

Foundations of Democracy is a K–12 curricular program based on concepts fundamental to an understanding of politics and government, such as Authority, Privacy, Responsibility, and Justice. This multi-disciplinary program draws upon such fields as political philosophy, political science, law, history, literature, and environmental studies.

The Foundations curricular materials are designed to progress sequentially in scope and complexity through four levels: Grades K–2, 3–5, 6–9, and 10–12. The primary goal of the Foundations of Democracy program is to promote civic competence and responsibility among the nation's elementary and secondary students.

In this course of study, students are challenged to discuss and debate situations involving such topics as the use of authority, the protection of privacy, and the choices that need to be made between competing values and interests. Students are asked to decide how responsibilities should be fulfilled and how justice could be achieved in a number of situations. The methodology employed helps students develop their own positions, and support their positions with reasons.

Foundations of Democracy curricular materials are developed and disseminated with support from the Office of Juvenile Justice and Delinquency Prevention (OJJDP) of the U.S. Department of Justice and the U.S. Department of Education.

To order books from our Foundations of Democracy Series, visit the Center for Civic Education's online store at http://civiced-store.stores.yahoo.net/index.html or e-mail our sales department at sales@civiced.org. The Center also offers sample lessons online at www.civiced.org/lessons_index.php.

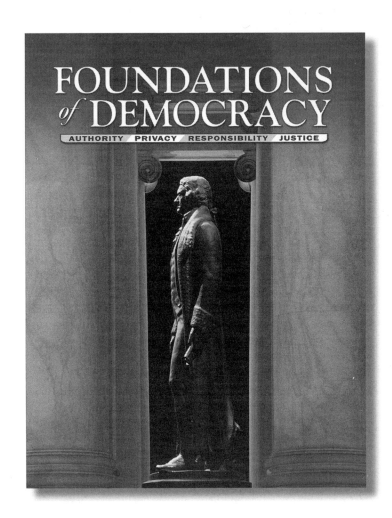

Elements of Democracy

Elements of Democracy is intended to bring a sense of clarity to the meanings of fundamental terminology surrounding the theory and practice of democracy. In this attempt to facilitate the understanding of the complex terms required to comprehend and discuss democracy, the authors expect and encourage the readers to inquire further into their significance and the controversies that underlie these terms.

The ideas that surround the practice of democracy are among the most consequential of the modern world, and destined only to become more so. *Elements of Democracy* is an attempt to explore the range of ideas that make up the vocabulary of democracy. For example, the section titled "Concepts and Fundamental Principles of Democracy" encompasses such subjects as Democracy and Equality, the Common Good, and the Role of Law in Democracy; other sections include "The Political Processes of Democracy" and "Democracy and Citizen." An excellent resource for high school, college level, and adult audiences.

Elements of Democracy was developed by the Center for Civic Education and funded by the U.S. Department of Education under the Education for Democracy Act approved by the United States Congress. *Elements of Democracy* is a project of the Alliance for Representative Democracy, a consortium of the Center for Civic Education, the Trust for Representative Democracy/National Conference of State Legislatures, and the Center for Congress at Indiana University.

To order *Elements of Democracy*, visit the Center for Civic Education's online store at http://civicedstore.stores.yahoo.net/index.html or e-mail our sales department at sales@civiced.org. The Center also offers sample lessons online at www.civiced.org/lessons_index.php.

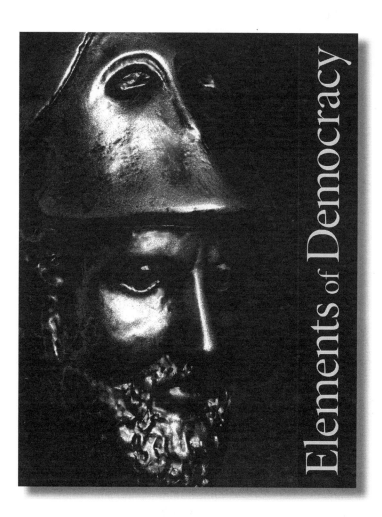

445

American Legacy

American Legacy: The United States Constitution and Other Essential Documents of American Democracy is an 80-page, pocket-sized (3.5 x 6.5") booklet that includes the U.S. Constitution and the Declaration of Independence together with passages from 27 other documents that encompass essential ideas of American democracy. The documents are arranged chronologically, beginning with the Mayflower Compact.

Included are excerpts from documents such as: *The Federalist*, Chief Justice John Marshall's decision in *Marbury v. Madison*, George Washington's "Farewell Address," Thomas Jefferson's first inaugural address, Sojourner Truth's "Ain't I a Woman?", Abraham Lincoln's first inaugural address, the Gettysburg Address, the Emancipation Proclamation, Learned Hand's "The Spirit of Liberty," Martin Luther King Jr.'s "I Have a Dream," and the Civil Rights Act of 1964.

The booklet has an extensive index to the Constitution. It also contains the Oath of Allegiance for New Citizens and the Pledge of Allegiance.

To order *American Legacy*, visit the Center for Civic Education's online store at http://civiced-store.stores.yahoo.net/index.html or e-mail our sales department at sales@civiced.org.

American Legacy was produced with the assistance of the U.S. Department of Education under the Education for Democracy Act approved by the United States Congress.

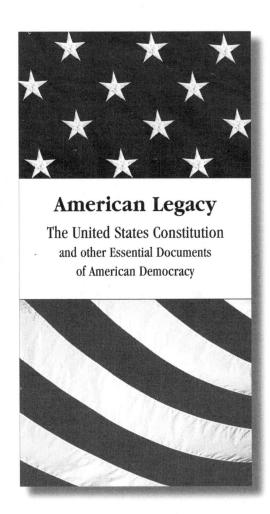

American Legacy
The United States Constitution
and other Essential Documents
of American Democracy